GENESIS, EMPLOYMENT, AFTERMATH: FIRST WORLD WAR TANKS AND THE NEW WARFARE, 1900-1945

Modern Military History

Series Editors

ALARIC SEARLE, Reader in Military History, University of Salford, UK

DONALD J. STOKER, Jr., Professor of Strategy and Policy, US Naval War College, Naval Postgraduate School, Monterey, CA, USA

This series is dedicated to making available, at a reasonable price, quality academic military history, based on innovative and thorough scholarly research. While the main emphasis is on the publication of single-authored monographs, there will be scope for edited collections which focus primarily on new perspectives and evidence, as well as occasional translations of important foreign-language studies. *Modern Military History* will be framed in an 'inclusive' fashion, so that it encompasses armies, navies and air forces. While the traditional core concerns of military history – such as tactics, combat experience, technology, strategy and officer education – remain important fields of consideration, the encouragement of new angles and original approaches, whether methodologically, geographically or thematically, form a significant part of the editors' agenda.

Titles

No 1   *Genesis, Employment, Aftermath: First World War Tanks and the New Warfare, 1900-1945* edited by Alaric Searle (ISBN 978-1-909982-22-2)

Genesis, Employment, Aftermath

First World War Tanks and the New Warfare, 1900-1945

Modern Military History No.1

Edited by
Alaric Searle

Helion & Company Limited

Helion & Company Limited
26 Willow Road
Solihull
West Midlands
B91 1UE
England
Tel. 0121 705 3393
Fax 0121 711 4075
Email: info@helion.co.uk
Website: www.helion.co.uk
Twitter: @helionbooks
Visit our blog http://blog.helion.co.uk/

Published by Helion & Company 2015

Designed and typeset by Bookcraft Ltd, Stroud, Gloucestershire
Cover designed by Paul Hewitt, Battlefield Design (www.battlefield-design.co.uk)
Printed by Gutenberg Press Limited, Tarxien, Malta

Text © individual contributors 2015
Illustrations open source save for that on page 9, which appears courtesy of the Salford Local History Library, Salford City Art Gallery and Museum, Salford.
Maps © Helion & Company Limited 2015. Maps designed by George Anderson

Cover: An American tank unit equipped with French-manufactured Renault FT-17s.

ISBN 978 1 909982 22 2

British Library Cataloguing-in-Publication Data.
A catalogue record for this book is available from the British Library.

All rights reserved. No part of this publication may be reproduced, stored in a retrieval system, or transmitted, in any form, or by any means, electronic, mechanical, photocopying, recording or otherwise, without the express written consent of Helion & Company Limited.

For details of other military history titles published by Helion & Company Limited contact the above address, or visit our website: http://www.helion.co.uk.

We always welcome receiving book proposals from prospective authors.

Contents

List of Photographs	vii
List of Maps and Diagrams	viii
Acknowledgements	ix
About the Contributors	x
Introduction: Genesis, Employment, Aftermath *Alaric Searle*	1

Genesis
1 Images of War, Armament and Mechanization in Imperial Germany, 1880-1914 — 13
Markus Pöhlmann

Britain
2 Practical Considerations in British Tank Operations on the Western Front, 1916-1918 — 31
Bryn Hammond

France
3 The Development of French Tank Warfare on the Western Front, 1916-1918 — 57
Olivier Lahaie

Germany
4 From the *Bremerwagen* to the A7V: German Tank Production and Armoured Warfare, 1916-1918 — 80
Ralf Raths

Intelligence
5 Scouting for Brigands: British Tank Corps Reconnaissance and Intelligence, 1916-1918 — 108
Jim Beach

	Communications	
6	The Development of Tank Communications in the British Expeditionary Force, 1916-1918 *Brian N. Hall*	136
	Other Theatres	
7	Beyond the Western Front: Tanks in Palestine and Russia, 1916-1921 *Steven J. Main & Alaric Searle*	163
	Mass Production	
8	'A Charming Toy': The Surprisingly Long Life of the Renault Light Tank, 1917-1940 *Tim Gale*	191
	Aftermath	
9	The Battle of Cambrai: Reactions, Commemoration and Symbolism, 1917-1942 *Alaric Searle*	210

Select Bibliography	238
Index	240

List of Photographs

1	The Salford Presentation Tank '214', 1919	9
2	Mock-up of the Burstyn Motorgeschütz, Vienna	27
3	J.F.C. Fuller (1878-1966)	38
4	St Chamond Tank	69
5	A7V, 1918	88
6	Tank column, Amiens, August 1918	123
7	Pigeon about to be released from tank sponson	142
8	Derelict Mark I, Gaza, 1917	165
9	Renault tanks, 1918	199
10	'With Mr Punch's jubilant compliments to Sir Douglas HAIG and his Tanks'	213

List of Maps and Diagrams

Maps

1	Tanks at Flers-Courcelette, 15 September 1916	47
2	Amiens Offensive, August 1918	51
3	Villers Bretonneux	99
4	Second Gaza, April 1917	167
5	Third Gaza, November 1917	170
6	Russia, 1919	172
7	Russia, 1919	177
8	Cambrai, 20-21 November 1917	214

Diagrams

1	Tank Company and Infantry Battalion forming up for the attack	146
2	Tactical formation adopted by 6th, 20th and 12th Divisions for operations with tanks, 20 November 1917	147

Acknowledgements

The idea for this volume grew out of a one-day conference, held at the University of Salford in 2008, which examined British and German experiences of tank warfare in the First World War. Some of the original papers given at the conference, which was supported finacially by the *Arbeitskreis Militärgeschichte* (AKM) and the European Studies Research Institute (ESRI) at the University of Salford, have now evolved into some of the chapters in this book. The support of the AKM and ESRI should be recorded once again, since the conference acted as an important catalyst for this book.

The editor would also like to acknowledge the following: Chapter One is a revised and reworked version of Markus Pöhlmann, *Before the Tank: Armament and Mechanisation in Imperial Germany, 1880-1914*, Centre for European Security, Working Papers in Military and International History No. 1 (Salford, 2010); Chapter Two is a revised version of Bryn Hammond, *Practical Considerations in British Tank Operations on the Western Front, 1916-1918*, Centre for European Security, Working Papers in Military and International History No. 2 (Salford, 2011); Chapter Four is an amended version of an article which previously appeared as Ralf Raths, 'German Tank Production and Armoured Warfare, 1916-1918', *War & Society*, 30 (March 2011), pp. 24-47, and appears here with kind permission of the editors and publishers of the journal.

For permission to quote from material for which they hold the copyright, the editor and authors would like to thank: the Clough Williams-Ellis Foundation for permission to quote from a letter to F.E. Hotblack in the Hotblack Papers, Tank Museum Archive, Bovington (Chapter 5); the Trustees of the Liddell Hart Centre for Military Archives, King's College London (Chapter 6); the Salford Local History Library, Salford City Art Gallery and Museum, Salford, for permission to reproduce the photograph of the Salford presentation tank (Introduction).

About the Contributors

JIM BEACH is Senior Lecturer in Twentieth Century History at the University of Northampton and was previously Lecturer in Military History at the University of Salford. He is the author of *Haig's Intelligence: GHQ and the German Army, 1916-1918* (Cambridge UP, 2013), as well as numerous articles in scholarly journals. He is the Honorary Secretary of the Army Records Society. He was awarded his PhD in History by University College London.

TIM GALE is the author of *The French Army's Tank Force and Armoured Warfare in the Great War: The Artillerie Spéciale* (Ashgate, 2013). He is Treasurer of the British Commission for Military History. He was awarded his PhD in French military history by King's College London.

BRIAN N. HALL is Lecturer in Contemporary Military History at the University of Salford. He has published articles in journals such as *War & Society*, *War in History* and the *Journal of Military History*, and is currently completing a book which examines the role and contribution of communications to British military operations on the Western Front during the First World War. He was awarded his PhD in military history by the University of Salford.

BRYN HAMMOND Head of Collections and Curatorial Development at the Imperial War Museums, London. He is the author of *Cambrai 1917: The Myth of the First Great Tank Battle* (Weidenfeld & Nicolson, 2008) and *El Alamein: The Battle that Turned the Tide of the Second World War* (Osprey, 2012). He was awarded his PhD by the University of Birmingham, where he is also an Honorary Research Fellow of the Centre for War Studies.

OLIVIER LAHAIE is a Lieutenant-Colonel in the French Army. He is a former tank platoon leader and he served with the UN and SFOR in Bosnia. His current posting is at the Castle of Vincennes (Defence Historical Service). He publishes regularly in French historical and military journals and is author of *La Bataille d'Angleterre (1940)*, published in 2010. He was awarded his PhD for a thesis on French intelligence during the Great War by the Sorbonne in Paris.

About the Contributors

STEVEN J. MAIN is Director of the Russian Military Studies Office, a private think tank, based in Scotland, offering research expertise on the Russian military, both past and present. For over seventeen years, he served as an analyst working for the UK Ministry of Defence. He has published extensively on Soviet and Russian military affairs, particularly in the *Journal of Slavic Military Studies* and *Europe-Asia*. He was awarded his PhD in Soviet military history by the University of Edinburgh.

MARKUS PÖHLMANN is a staff member at the *Zentrum für Militärgeschichte und Sozialwissenschaften*, Potsdam, the German armed forces' Research Centre for Military History and Social Sciences. He is the author of *Kriegsgeschichte und Geschichtspolitik: Der Erste Weltkrieg* (Schöningh, 2002), a consideration of the evolution and impact of the German official history of the First World War, as well as numerous articles in journals and edited collections. He also serves as a member of the Executive Committee of the *Arbeitskreis Militärgeschichte*. He was awarded his PhD by the Universität Bern.

RALF RATHS is Director of the German Tank Museum, Munster, where he was previously Scientific Director. He holds a degree in history from the Universität Hannover and, in addition to other publications, he is author of the book *Vom Massensturm zur Stoßtrupptaktik: Die deutsche Landkriegtaktik im Spiegel vom Dienstvorschriften und Publizistik 1906 bis 1918* (Rombach, 2009), which examines the evolution of German ground warfare doctrine until the end of the First World War.

ALARIC SEARLE is Reader in Military History, and Associate Director, Politics and Contemporary History, at the University of Salford. As well as articles in scholarly journals, he is the author of *Wehrmacht Generals, West German Society, and the Debate on Rearmament, 1949-1959* (Praeger, 2003). He is a member of the Executive Committee of the *Arbeitskreis Militärgeschichte*, as well as holding the position of *Privatdozent* at the University of Munich. He was awarded his PhD by the Free University Berlin.

Introduction:
Genesis, Employment, Aftermath

Alaric Searle

As we enter a period when historians are taking the opportunity to reflect once again on the Great War, the historical debate over new technology, and whether it was fully exploited by senior military officers, is likely to be revisited once more. As far as military history in Great Britain is concerned, this debate is, though, rather a tired one. More recently, the trend among the more serious works of scholarship has been towards comparative perspectives and attempting to use archival material from different countries.[1] In line with this trend, the aim of this volume is to reconsider a number of aspects of the history of First World War tanks, as well as identifying new areas, but examining the subject within an international context, with contributions on Britain, France, Germany and Russia.

Many books have been written on the history of British tanks in the First World War, commencing with the memoirs of Tank Corps officers and those involved in the technical and industrial development of the new 'engines of war'. Over the last two decades a number of scholarly works have considered the production, employment and impact of tanks on the British Army's conduct of the war. But rather less is known about the development of French tanks and the German tank programme.[2] This collection seeks to bring together leading military historians from Britain, France and Germany. At the same time, the intention is also to consider a range of themes which are not restricted to the war in France and Belgium, while paying attention to

---

1   For instance: Alexander Watson, *Enduring the Great War: Combat Morale and Collapse in the German and British Armies, 1914-1918* (Cambridge, 2008); Jonathan Boff, *Winning and Losing on the Western Front: The British Third Army and the Defeat of Germany in 1918* (Cambridge, 2012); and, Robert T. Foley, 'Dumb Donkeys or Cunning Foxes? Learning in the British and German Armies during the Great War', *International Affairs*, 90/2 (2014), pp. 279-98.
2   References to recent secondary studies will be kept to a minimum in this introduction as all the chapters in the volume cite the most recent literature extensively. In addition, there is a select bibliography available at the end of this book.

overlooked aspects of the employment of tanks, such as intelligence and communications. And, we cannot forget either the impact of the tank on the popular imagination – it is as much a part of the story as the first tank battles.

Moreover, the appearance of tanks in other theatres, Palestine and Russia in particular, suggests that the history of First World War tanks should be reconsidered within the context of the war as a 'global conflict'.[3] In fact, the 'continued life' of tanks beyond the armistice on 11 November 1918 in the West raises an interesting question about the duration of the First World War. Can it really be considered as the Great War, 1914-1918? Or, was it the Great War, 1914-1919, as many war memorials in Britain proclaim? Could we even start to think about a different era, the Great War, 1914-1921, in order that events surrounding the Russian Revolution and Civil War be seen as part of the conflict?[4] The collapse of Empires, the global nature of the conflict, and the after-shocks which the war caused, of which the Russian Revolution was one of the key but not the only instance of the continuation of violence, all point towards the 'extension' of the conflict beyond November 1918.

As such, then, the focus in this introduction is to reflect upon the three words which form the main title of this work – genesis, employment, aftermath – in essence, the concern is to think about First World War tanks beyond the confines of the period 1914-1918. While it may be thought there is little left to write about the first tanks, this volume aims to suggest new paths for reconsidering some of the key dimensions of the emergence of a new form of warfare, as well as to place the tank within an international, comparative framework. So, it is useful at this point to refer to some of the historical controversies which took place soon after the Great War, and others which occurred later among historians, as well as identifying new areas of research which could be usefully pursued in more detail in the future.

Genesis

The story of the 'invention' of the tank, not to mention its various precursors, has been recounted on numerous occasions – frequently, it has to be said, from the perspective of the British experience. What is most noteworthy here is the way in which the accounts provided in the early histories have to some extent continued to condition perceptions of the subject.[5] The views of the British pioneers have led, most

---

3 For discussions of the war as a global conflict, see: Daniel Marc Segesser, *Der Erste Weltkrieg in globaler Perspektive* (Wiesbaden, 2010); and, Hew Strachan, 'The First World War as a Global War', *First World War Studies*, 1 (March 2010), pp. 3-14.
4 In fact, it is worth noting that the National Socialist world view considered the aftermath of the conflict as part of a history of heroic struggle and humiliation, running from 1914-1923. On this, see Patrick Alberts, 'Memory, Entertainment, Propaganda: The Great War and German Popular Cinema, 1933-1945', PhD thesis, University of Salford, 2013.
5 See, in particular: Clough & A[mabel] Williams-Ellis, *The Tank Corps* (London, 1919); Albert Stern, *Tanks 1914-1918: Log-Book of a Pioneer* (London, 1919); and, J.F.C. Fuller,

notably, to the notion that the British 'invented' the tank but that the army in the field was resistant to new technology. The opposing view produced by later 'revisionist historians', especially defenders of the British Commander-in-Chief in France, Field-Marshal Sir Douglas Haig, have tended to the other extreme, that of claiming that the British Army adapted quickly to new technology and used it as best they could. The argument made by both sides is, though, rather problematic, as every army is made up of many constituent parts; a tendency to innovation in one, does not guarantee a willingness to innovate in another. An international, comparative perspective does raise, however, three significant areas which are worthy of further thought, best summarized under the simple headings of invention, innovation and collaboration.

The argument over who 'invented' the tank still appears unresolved, or, put another way, continues to create distorted perspectives. As the two chapters on French tanks in this volume make plain, just as in the case of gas warfare, Britain and France were working on similar solutions to trench warfare at around the same time. The only difference was that the British tank appeared on the battlefield before the first French machine did. Yet, after the war the British pioneers were more or less adamant that Britain had 'invented' the tank. According to one of Britain's tank pioneers, Major-General Ernest Swinton, '[t]he tank was the one complete British innovation in the war and a great one.'[6] In the same way, while it can be stated that Britain was the first nation to employ tanks on the battlefield, it would be difficult to argue convincingly that the 'first tank' was 'invented' in Britain. An Imperial Austrian officer, Gunther Burstyn, had patented his *Motorgeschütz* in 1912, while the Australian Mr. L.E. de Mole had presented a design to the War Office in London in the same year.[7] These were just two examples of designs developed before the Mark I was used in the first tank attack in history on 15 September 1916.

Still, the individual and national claims of paternity should not distract us from another equally important issue: what caused some nations to innovate successfully and others not? As Markus Pöhlmann's chapter demonstrates, the hesitancy over the need for an armoured fighting vehicle in Germany was, in many ways, a rational response to the dangers of pursing new and untried technology and, during the war, a reasonable reaction given the shortage of raw materials in the country, not to mention the large quantities of fuel which would have been required to have powered a large fleet of tanks. Yet, the debate over military innovation and the tank has tended to

---

Tanks in the Great War, 1914-1918 (London, 1920). The extent of the influence of Fuller's book can be seen in the treatment of precursors of the tank to be found in Major-General Ernest D. Swinton, 'Tanks', in *The Encyclopaedia Britannica: The New Volumes*, iii (London & New York, 12th edn, 1922), pp. 677-98, here 678-81.

6   Swinton, 'Tanks', p. 696.
7   Richard L. DiNardo & Austin Bay, 'The First Modern Tank: Gunther Burstyn and his *Motorgeschütz*', *Military Affairs*, 50 (January 1986), pp. 12-15; and, E. Dwyer Gray, 'Story of the Tanks: De Mole's Travelling Caterpillar Fort', *The Argus* [Melbourne, Austr.], 9 August 1924.

focus on the interwar period, even though questions relating to the causes of innovation, or the failure to innovate, can just as easily be applied to the early development of the tank.[8] At the same time, there were specific design challenges which all the early pioneers faced, but according to Major Walter G. Wilson the British solution led to 'the only successful heavy machine'. He also held the view that the British design which placed the tracks all around the vehicles had proved a better concept than the French St Chamond and Schneider tanks, and the German A7V, all three of which were essentially 'an armoured box supported on caterpillars'.[9]

The cases of both Germany and France, as explained in the chapters by Olivier Lahaie and Ralf Raths, demonstrate the difficulties caused in technological innovation by arguments between departments, competing designs, as well as personal jealousies and bureaucratic turf wars. It is certainly instructive that Britain differed from the other nations because not only was the material necessary for building and arming tanks easier to obtain due to the involvement of Winston Churchill, the First Lord of the Admiralty, the Royal Naval Air Service also played a part in the development of the new weapon.[10] In other words, two arms of service were involved in the development of Britain's tank, which may well have contributed to a type of innovation not possible in the French and German armies. Moreover, the 'culture' and 'corporate identity' of the Tank Corps, and its precursor organizations, was clearly both influenced and facilitated by the army's tolerance of unconventional approaches, as well as the high proportion of civilians in its ranks.[11]

Beyond the usual notion of 'genesis', which is assumed to relate to mechanical precursors of the tank and its 'final invention', the question of international collaboration in both production and design requires mention, too. Like the issue of the dynamics of innovation, international collaboration has either been forgotten or is assumed to be a phenomenon of later eras. But there were thoughts of collaboration between Britain

---

8   Important for the scholarly debate on military innovation is the study, W. Murray & A.R. Millett (eds.), *Military Innovation in the Interwar Period* (Cambridge, 1996), esp. Chap. 1, pp. 6-49, on tank warfare.
9   Flintshire County Record Office, Hawarden, D/B/262, typewritten notes by Walter G. Wilson (1920), attached to copy of Stern's *Log-Book of a Pioneer*, and presented to Maj. H. Buddison; comments made with reference to pp. 113, 233, of the book, illustrations of French and German tanks. Wilson is credited with the idea of the wrap-around tracks on the Mark I. See A.A. Miller, 'Wilson, Walter Gordon (1874-1957)', *Oxford Dictionary of National Biography* (online ed.), http://www.oxforddnb.com/view/article/36970>.
10 For more on this, see Eric Grove, 'Air Force, Fleet Air Arm – or Armoured Corps? The Royal Naval Air Service at War', in Tim Benbow (ed.), *British Naval Aviation: The First 100 Years* (Farnham, 2011), pp. 27-56. It is worth noting here that Major Walter Wilson rejoined the navy on the outbreak of war, serving with the naval armoured car division, only transferring to the army in 1916, thus bringing a different perspective to the development of the early tank prototypes to that of an officer from the army.
11 According to Major-General Sir Hugh Elles, of the 20,000 men that composed the Corps only 2-3% were professional soldiers. H. Elles, 'Introduction', in C. & A. Williams-Ellis, *The Tank Corps*, p. x.

and France, with a first meeting in June 1916 between Ernest Swinton and the father of the French tank force, J.B.E. Estienne, which was the culmination of the recognition by the two allies that they ought to keep each other informed of their respective progress. There was an obvious logic to cooperation, had the two countries been able to agree on a division of labour, such as the British concentrating on the production of heavy tanks, the French on light tanks. But, by the end of 1917, the two nations were no closer to any agreement on either the production or employment of tanks, despite the establishment of an Inter-Allied Tank Committee. To make matters worse, the construction of an Allied tank factory at Neuvy Pailloux dissolved into chaos.[12]

Nonetheless, while it would be very easy to dismiss all attempts at inter-Allied cooperation as a total failure, there were many causes of this. American attempts to produce Renault tanks and British heavy tanks in the United States ran into many difficulties, although the main problem was that they simply did not have enough time to get production moving before the war ended. By December 1918, ten American-built Renault tanks had been delivered to France; during 1919, one hundred American Mark VIII 'Liberty' tanks were produced, machines based on the basic British Mark V tank design (although it was essentially a different machine) with an American Liberty engine installed. Still, it should be remembered that American soldiers fought in British and French machines in France, there was an awareness of the need for the three allies to 'internationalize' their training and tactics, while the Battle of Moreuil on 23 July 1918 saw a joint action between the British 9th Tank Battalion and the French 3rd Division. While the various attempts at cooperation seem to have consisted of 'missed opportunities', the whole issue of inter-Allied collaboration – whether in tank production or tactics and planning – is as much part of the genesis of tank warfare as the invention of the first machines.[13]

Employment

Turning to the actual employment of Great War tanks in battle, there are a number of controversies which require some comment. The oldest of these was started soon after the war by Major-General Swinton, who claimed that the first employment of British tanks on 15 September 1916

> was contrary to the views of those who had originated the Arm, who were responsible for its production and had most studied its action. They held that the utmost value should be obtained from the new weapon and that the secret of its existence should not be given away until a surprise attack could be carried out

---

12　Elizabeth Greenhalgh, 'Technology Development in Coalition: The Case of the First World War Tank', *International History Review*, 22 (2000), pp, 803-36.
13　Dale E. Wilson, *Treat 'Em Rough! The Birth of American Armor, 1917-20* (Novato, CA, 1990), pp. 73-85; and, Greenhalgh, 'Technology Development in Coalition', passim.

on a sufficiently extensive scale to give a chance of achieving a decisive success. In this sense the launching of the tanks was a repetition of the error made by the Germans when they released gas on a small section alone on April 22 1915.[14]

He was not the only tank pioneer who disagreed violently with the decision. Churchill added his voice to the criticism of the decision to employ them on the Somme. In his history-cum-memoir of the war, he wrote of the 'most improvident disclosure of the caterpillar vehicles', going on to say that he had been 'so shocked at the proposal to expose this tremendous secret to the enemy upon such a petty scale… that I sought an interview with Mr. Asquith'. He concluded that the premature employment of British tanks meant their existence had been 'recklessly revealed to the enemy'.[15]

Needless to say, this view has become largely discredited. It became very clear, and fairly quickly, that any successful tank offensive required the numerous technical, tactical and organizational difficulties to be not simply ironed out, but refined, reconsidered and intensive training regimes introduced. It took over a year after the first, modest, tank action, before a mass tank attack could be conducted successfully at Cambrai on 20 November 1917. Even the formalization of training took over a year, not least of all as schools for the Six-Pounder gun, driving and maintenance, anti-gas and wireless signalling had to be established.[16] None other than the chief General Staff Officer of the Tank Corps, J.F.C. Fuller, argued in 1920 that 'the only true test of efficiency *is* war', so that 'the final test a machine or weapon should get is its first battle', and without this test 'no deductions can be made as to its future improvement'.[17]

Among the other historical claims and assertions over the employment of tanks, there is less unity among historians. The first of these surrounds the first mass tank attack which launched the Battle of Cambrai on 20 November 1917. There is little doubt about the place of this battle in the history of the war: but the question of who was responsible for the failure to anticipate the German counter-attack is one which historians of the war argued over for years. In the immediate aftermath of the German counter-attack, however, the outrage over the 'squandering' of the initial victory was fuelled in Britain by public affection for the new weapon of war, as explained in Searle's chapter. The remarkable fascination which the tank aroused in Britain can

---

14 Swinton, 'Tanks', p. 682.
15 Winston S. Churchill, *The World Crisis 1911-1918* (London, abridged & rev. edn, 1931), pp. 651-3.
16 See here the manual, *Instructions for the Training of the Tank Corps in France*, Issued by HQ, Tank Corps (1 December 1917). The first official publication on tank warfare, *SS. 164. Notes on the Use of Tanks*, was issued by the General Staff in May 1917. See Jim Beach, 'Issued by the General Staff: Doctrine Writing at British GHQ, 1917-1918', *War in History*, 19 (2012), p. 472.
17 Fuller, *Tanks in the Great War*, p. 59.

be tracked in cartoons which appeared in newspapers and weeklies during the war, as well as the use of the image of the tank in advertisements.[18]

The controversy which has dominated the historiography of the last twenty years relates, though, to whether British tanks could have been, or in fact were, a 'war winner' in 1918. The argument put forward by Tim Travers has been that misperception, and a failure to understand the nature of the new weapon, left British tanks under-used when they had the potential to make a more decisive contribution to the Allied victory during the Hundred Days.[19] The debate among mainly English-speaking historians over this has, however, been extremely one-sided. It has often not taken account of the complexities of tank warfare: not simply the constraints on tank operations, explained in the chapter by Bryn Hammond, but also other crucial aspects of Tank Corps activities, especially intelligence (covered in the chapter by Jim Beach) and communications (detailed by Brian Hall in his chapter). But it has likewise failed to acknowledge the role played by the French armoured force, especially the two-man Renault FT-17 tank, which began to appear on the battlefield in increasing numbers in 1918.[20] This machine was not only used by the French Army, the American Tank Corps also participated in battles in which Renault tanks were employed. The question thus requires rephrasing: did *Allied* tanks make a major contribution to the defeat of the Imperial German Army in the West in 1918?

Another interesting dimension to the employment of tanks can be found in the differing historical treatment of the first tank-versus-tank battle in history at Villers-Bretonneux on 24 April 1918. According to two later accounts by Fuller, the Germans had employed four of their A7V tanks and knocked out two Mark IV 'female' tanks (those only carrying machine-guns), although one of the German tanks was put out of action. But the 'male' Mark IV which had engaged the German tanks was then hit by a field-gun and put out of action.[21] But, a later German account from 1928 differs significantly in both its description and in the basic facts. A former Great War tank officer described the great victory and success of the German tanks employed at Villers-Bretonneux in clearing British infantry from the village; and, he noted

---

18 See the cartoon in the *Daily Mirror*, 5 December 1917, with two children in a living-room in a soap-box style armoured car and tank. For the use of the tank image in advertising, see the advertisement for 'Wright's Coal Tar Soap', with a tank shaped like a bar of soap, and the request to 'Include a supply in the next parcel to your Soldier Friend', in *The Army and Navy Gazette*, 58 (26 May 1917), p. iv of the advertising section.
19 Tim Travers, 'Could the Tanks of 1918 Have Been War-Winners for the British Expeditionary Force?' *Journal of Contemporary History*, 27 (1992), pp. 389-405.
20 On French armour in the First World War, see the important new study by Tim Gale, *The French Army's Tank Force and Armoured Warfare in the Great War: The Artillerie Spéciale* (Farnham, 2013).
21 Fuller, *Tanks in the Great War*, p. 201; idem, *Memoirs of an Unconventional Soldier* (London, 1936), pp. 265-6. According to the earliest history of the Tank Corps, there were three German machines which knocked out the two Mark IV females tanks. C. & A. Williams-Ellis, *The Tank Corps*, pp. 172-3.

that two German tanks had entered combat against five enemy machines, leading to the destruction of three of them.[22] The first historical example of a tank-versus-tank engagement had ended ultimately with two completely different versions of the action.

A final claim made in relation to the employment of tanks does not concern the war in the West, rather it is the assertion made by Fuller in his memoirs that 'a small British tank force, supported by a Division or two of infantry for line of communication and police work in its rear, could in a few weeks have turned the Bolsheviks out of Moscow'.[23] Just how serious is such a claim? On the one hand, it could be dismissed out of hand as completely unrealistic. The Red Army enjoyed solid support in certain regions of the country, while years of deprivation could be ascribed to the corruption of the Tsarist regime and the British could be portrayed as 'imperialist invaders'. On the other hand, the reaction to the employment of tanks by the British on the part of the Red Army and Bolshevik leaders suggests they were extremely alarmed by the possible impact of such weapons on their troops and on the civilian population. Certainly, the distances which an armoured force would have had to have covered to make a decisive difference would have been great, but determined action might have just held the possibility of tipping Russian opinion against the Red Army.

Aftermath

If we turn, finally, to the aftermath of the Great War, one of the most overlooked aspects is the way in which the tank took on a range of connotations and associations in different countries. In Britain and France, 'the tank' became very quickly a symbol of victory. What is particularly interesting is that in the case of France this symbolism coalesced around the Renault FT-17 tank, rather than the flawed St Chamond and Schneider tanks. In fact, this symbolic meaning of the Renault light tank could be found in Britain as well in August 1918. A cartoon published in *Punch* shows two German soldiers puffing and panting as they run as part of a group of fellow soldiers from a Renault, with charging French soldiers with fixed bayonets in hot pursuit. One is saying to the other: 'Himmel! The All-Highest has the truth spoken – the worst *is* behind us.'[24]

One notable aspect of the post-war history of British wartime tanks was the commemoration of the role of the machine in the war which found expression in a scheme which saw 'presentation tanks' being delivered to cities and towns. Some 265 machines in total were presented to towns with a population of over 10,000 who

---

22　Oberleutnant [Ernst] Volckheim, ' "Vor zehn Jahre". Angriffsschlacht deutscher Kampfwagen bei Villers-Bretonneux am 24. April 1918', *Deutsche Wehr*, Nr. 15, 18 April 1928, pp. 304-5. The German account does appear suspect, not least of all as the author uses it for a call to keep the tank spirit alive, since the German Army had been 'robbed' of tanks through the 'Versailler Diktat'.
23　Fuller, *Memoirs*, pp. 375-6.
24　Untitled cartoon, *Punch*, 155 (21 August 1918), p. 123.

Photo 1: The Salford Presentation Tank '214', 1919

could claim 'conspicuous achievements' in the buying of war bonds and certificates. The tanks had been signed over to the National War Savings Committee by the Army Council, but it was the Committee which took charge of the ceremonial presentation of the relics of the war. There was a certain awareness that the tank had become associated in the public's mind with the savings movement in Britain, but at the same time there was a tension between the transition to peace and displaying machines which had either dealt out death to the enemy or, in some cases, had been turned into flaming infernos for the crews.[25]

To illustrate the curious case of the presentation tanks, it is useful to look at just one example, namely, that of the tank presented to the City of Salford, next to Manchester in northern England. On 17 May 1919, the *Salford City Reporter* informed its readers that 'Salford's War Tank' was to be formally presented to the Mayor in a few days' time; the tank itself had already arrived at Liverpool Street Station. A procession was to be formed to accompany the tank to the ground at the junction of Chapel Street and Oldfield Road where it was to be displayed, with a military escort to be provided

---

25 Patrick Wright, *Tank: The Progress of a Monstrous War Machine* (London, 2000), pp. 90-4, 122-4.

by a detachment from the 7th and 8th Lancashire Fusiliers. The presentation was to inaugurate a special campaign for war bonds and savings certificates which was to last a week.[26]

The report the following week described the presence of the tank next to the Lancashire Fusiliers Memorial on Chapel Street as 'sentinel-like'. On its short journey to its new resting place, the tank had 'behaved itself admirably' and it now stood as 'a permanent reminder of its daring exploits in France'. Although it was considered by some as the ugliest object in Salford, it was a 'symbol of the engineering ingenuity, which… helped Britain and the Allies to win the war'. At the short ceremony, Sir Charles Mandelberg, Chairman of the local War Savings Association, invited a local MP to hand over the tank to the people of Salford.[27] The tank then spent almost eight years looking across the road at Salford Royal Hospital before the City Council voted unanimously in early May 1927 that it should be broken up and two guns placed near it be removed.[28]

In addition to the tank as a 'symbol of engineering ingenuity', its positive association as a symbol of victory was not the only meaning with which the tank became invested in Britain. For some members of the working-class, tanks became representative of the state and its fear of Bolshevism and workers' uprisings. Six tanks were sent to control crowds on the streets of Glasgow in early 1919, after demonstrations caused the government to fear that this was the beginning of a Bolshevik revolution in Britain.[29] This new investiture of political meaning which images of the tank could transmit can also be seen in the employment of captured British machines against the Spartacus uprising in Berlin in 1919, where, along with heavy artillery and mortars, government troops and *Freikorps* units suppressed the attempted revolution. Until then, tanks had been portrayed in Germany as a symbol of the material advantage which the country's enemies had enjoyed, almost as a form of 'unfair means' used against the heroic defenders of the Fatherland. The employment of tanks by government troops against revolutionaries turned the existing political symbolism on its head.[30]

---

26 'Salford's War Tank. Formal Presentation to the Mayor on Monday. Inauguration of a Week's Savings Campaign', *Salford City Reporter*, 17 May 1919.
27 'Tank "214". The Latest Gift to Salford. Its Arrival in the Borough', *Salford City Reporter*, 24 May 1919.
28 'Tank to be Broken Up. Guns to be Removed from Present Site', *Salford City Reporter*, 7 May 1927.
29 According to Fuller, they were 'found to be exceedingly useful as armoured police taxis'. Fuller, *Memoirs*, p. 396. See <http://www.theglasgowstory.com/imageview.php?inum=TGSE00437> for a photograph of a tank in the centre of Glasgow in 1919.
30 Paul Fox, '"A New and Commanding Breed": German Warriors, Tanks and the Will to Battle', *War & Society*, 30 (March 2011), pp. 1-23. It should be noted that at least one A7V took part in suppressing the uprising. One photograph shows an A7V with the words 'Panzer-Kraftwagen-Abteilung / Regierungs-treue-Truppen' [Tank Unit, Government-

In other words, only a few months after the war, the tank was able to be invested with new meaning (either as a symbol of menace and oppression against civilians, or as a saviour against chaos). This transformation was communicated through the experience of crowds, via newspaper reports, but also through the power of the news photograph. There was, of course, another dimension to the employment of tanks on the streets of cities to make an impression on civilians. The British Army of the Rhine made use of Mark V tanks during occupation duties in northern Germany in the aftermath of the war.[31] In his memoirs, Fuller quotes from a letter sent by the commander in April 1920, requesting more tanks because: 'The prestige of the British troops is still high in the eyes of the Germans, and there is abundant evidence that this is largely due to the enormous effect of tanks on the civilian population.'[32] As with so many other aspects in the history of the tank, Great War machines provide the first examples of tanks being used for occupation duties after a conflict.

In the aftermath of the war, a further element in the history of Great War tanks was their continued use in combat. During the Russian Civil War, first a handful of French Renault FT-17 tanks fell into the hands of the Red Army, followed several months later by British Mark V and Whippet tanks, a subject explored in more detail in the chapter by Main and Searle. There was, in fact, nothing new in the use of captured tanks: the First World War saw the Germans make use of both French and British tanks which they had captured.[33] The history of these *Beutepanzer* became the first examples in the history of the tank of what could be described as an early, unintended form of 'technology transfer', which saw a copy of the Renault FT-17 manufactured by the Bolsheviks.

Even more significant was the continued employment of the Renault FT-17 in several armies and a variety of conflicts, from the Spanish Civil War (1936-39) to the Winter War between the Soviet Union and Finland (1939-40), covered in Tim Gale's chapter. The long life of the Renault FT-17 beyond the armistice was due to two things: first, the tank could mount at 37 mm gun, which made an extremely useful weapon in destroying bunkers and smaller defensive points; and, second, the sheer numbers available made it almost inevitable that it would be sold throughout the world – at the end of the war there were well in excess of 2,000 Renaults in French service.[34] Thus, following the destruction and capture of a number of Renault FT-17s by the German Army during their conquest of France in 1940 and in Yugoslavia in 1941 surviving

---

loyal Troops] painted crudely on the front. See the photo at <http://en.valka.cz/viewtopic.php/t/89604/start/-1>.
31   For a photograph of two Mark Vs in the centre of Cologne (1919/20), see David Fletcher, *Mark V Tank* (Oxford, 2011), p. 33.
32   Fuller, *Memoirs*, p. 396.
33   On this subject, Fred Koch, *Beutepanzer im Ersten Weltkrieg: britische, französische und russische Kampf- und Panzerwagen im deutschen Heer* (Wölfersheim-Berstadt, 1994).
34   Robert Doughty, *Phyrric Victory: French Strategy and Operations in the Great War* (Cambridge, Mass., 2008), p. 514, gives the erroneous figure of 3,187.

machines were pressed into service for airfield security and other lighter duties, under the new designation, PzKpfw 18R 730(f).

Epilogue: The Long History of Great War Tanks

In conclusion, one of the most peculiar visual images of First World War tanks are a series of photographs which show two British Mark V tanks, apparently knocked out in the *Lustgarten* in the centre of Berlin, probably in May 1945. Further photographs indicate that they were left there for some time, but the ones taken closest in time to their final 'employment in action' show that close to them a field gun appears to have been destroyed. It has proved impossible to establish with any accuracy how the tanks came to be there, or if indeed an attempt was made to send them into action against the Russians in the last days of the war.[35] One possibility is that they were taken from the military museum, the *Zeughaus*, either to be employed in combat, or to remove them to a place of safety.

One intriguing aspect of this 'last stand' of Great War tanks in 1945 is the question of the origin of the two machines. The *Beutepanzer* which Germany held in her possession at the end of the Great War, tanks captured by the Imperial German Army from the British and French, were later broken up for scrap as a result of the terms of the Versailles Treaty. Hence, presuming the *Reichswehr* did not conceal any tanks, it is likely that some British tanks captured by the Russians during the Civil War, and turned into war memorials, were transported back to Germany for public display by the *Wehrmacht* after the invasion of the USSR in 1941. However, rather than display them in a museum, it may be that these two tanks were put on public display outside in the centre of Berlin. If this is the explanation for their presence in the ruins of the city in mid-1945, their 'redeployment' as a *German* war memorial suggests the intention may have been to communicate a National Socialist message about correcting the result of the First World War.[36]

This brief survey of the history of First World War tanks finds, then, a final punctuation mark in the ruins and chaos of Berlin in May 1945. Whatever the truth relating to a series of intriguing photographs, it demonstrates that the history of the first tanks cannot be restricted to the period September 1916 to November 1918.

---

35 A series of photos can be viewed at <http://beutepanzer.ru/Beutepanzer/uk/MK_V/Mk_V.htm>
36 The positioning of the two tanks, which is clearer in some photographs, does suggest they may have been 'outdoor exhibition pieces'. The damage to one tank could quite easily have been incurred during artillery battles or in infantry combat in the last days of the war. The tanks may have even been used as cover for some infantry during the fighting.

1

Images of War, Armament and Mechanization in Imperial Germany, 1880-1914

Markus Pöhlmann

It must have been a strange spectacle for the observers of Germany's 1889 Imperial manoeuvres. On 21 September that year, unknown vehicles moved into the fortified position of the defending corps, carriages with an armoured, cylindrical body with a cupola on top. They were armed with quick-firing guns which opened fire as soon as they had been manoeuvred into their fire bases. The reception of this new weapon remained rather cool, however, which can be explained by considering the rest of this episode. The *Fahrpanzer* (armoured carriages), manufactured by the *Krupp-Grusonsche Werke* in Magdeburg, had opened fire as ordered. But the subsequent order of 'cease fire' had been missed by the crews, who – blinded and deafened by the smoke and blast of the firing guns – were stoically working away in their turns. Finally, the umpire had to dispatch a messenger who approached the fire base informing the crews of the end of the exercise.[1]

It did not take long until the soldiers found a nickname for the new weapon: *Tiene*. Its double meaning referred, firstly, to the female first name, and, secondly, to the fire brigades' mobile water chariots, which were a common sight in Germany's cities before the installation of fire hydrants. For the historian facing the question why the tank was invented by the British and not the German Army, the anecdote leaves a final argument that, if the Germans cannot claim paternity for the 'technological artefact', it can at least do so for the term 'tank'.[2]

---

1   Anon., 'Das fahrbare gepanzerte Schnellfeuergeschütz: 1. Teil', *Militär-Wochenblatt*, 23 November 1889, col. 2145-2148, and Generalmajor z.D. Schröder, *Schumann und die Panzer-Fortifikation* (Berlin, 1890), pp. 110-11.
2   For the origins of the term 'tank' as a camouflage designation, see Patrick Wright, *Tank: The Progress of a Monstrous War Machine* (Harmondsworth, 2000), p. 30.

Of course, the question, why the tank was a British and not a German invention, is not about national prestige. In fact, it is more interesting and more complex than it might first appear. It touches on questions of armament, military cultures and images of war. Furthermore, it holds an obvious political dimension: in the light of the German defeat of 1918, inter-war commentators reflecting on the potential of the new weapon repeatedly blamed the military administration, namely the Prussian Ministry of War, for not having promoted the research and development of tanks both before and during the war. Had the tank actually won the war? Ernst Kabisch, a retired general and author of several popular war books called the lack of German tanks during the 1918 spring offensive the 'jag' in Ludendorff's 'sword of Michael'. Could not 200 German light tanks have achieved what the British Army had managed shortly before in August, Kabisch asked?[3] And General Herman von Kuhl, probably the most influential military writer in the interwar years, came to the conclusion that 'ultimate pressure' could have been built up during the spring offensive if '600 tanks had cleared the way for our infantry'. With the support of tanks, 17th Army would have 'probably managed a breakthrough through the strong enemy positions around Arras'.[4] As late as 1969, General Walther Nehring, one of the founding fathers of the *Wehrmacht*'s *Panzer* arm, complained that from the perspective of hindsight all this was 'hard to understand'. Had the Russo-Japanese War of 1904/05 not proved the strength of a defence that applied the massive firepower of well-positioned machine guns?[5] Even the authors of the German Official History – generally known as strong supporters of the Supreme Command of Paul von Hindenburg and Erich Ludendorff – criticized the tank as an 'obvious gap' in the army's armament scheme.[6]

This chapter seeks to illustrate the conditions of technological innovation in the Imperial German Army prior to 1914 using military mechanization as an example. The term 'mechanization' needs to be differentiated from 'motorization': whereas the latter describes the application of the motor for the purposes of military transportation into battle, the former describes its application as an armoured weapon platform. Consequently, mechanization is a phenomenon which goes beyond the most obvious example of the main battle tank. Self-propelled mobility, armour, and firepower

---

3   Ernst Kabisch, *Michael: Die Große Schlacht in Frankreich im Lenz 1918* (Berlin, 1935), pp. 181-2.
4   Albrecht Philipps (ed.), *Die Ursachen des Deutschen Zusammenbruchs im Jahre 1918: 4. Reihe. Die Ursachen des Deutschen Zusammenbruches im Jahre 1918: 1. Abteilung. Der militärische und außenpolitische Zusammenbruch. lm Auftrage des Vierten Unterausschusses […]*, 19 vols., vol. 3 (Berlin, 1928), p. 81.
5   General [Walther] Nehring, *Die Geschichte der deutschen Panzerwaffe 1916 bis 1945* (Berlin, 1969), p. 18. For a similar tone, see also Walther Albrecht, *Gunther Burstyn (1879-1945) und die Entwicklung der Panzerwaffe* (Osnabrück, 1973), p. 191.
6   Bundesarchiv-Militärarchiv, Freiburg i. Br. (hereafter, BA-MA), W-10/50421, part 1, Lt.-Col. (rtd) Wilhelm Müller-Loebnitz, 'Deutsche Rüstung 1918', unpublished study, October 1939, p. 17.

are the constructive preconditions and the military parameters of mechanization.[7] The discussion here will illustrate the specific attitude of the armament bureaucracy towards innovation; this will then be followed by an appraisal of Wilhelmine military culture with regard to technology. A representation of the contemporary image of a future war will enables us to discuss the role that the tank – had it been invented before 1914 – could have played in such a scenario. Finally, a number of projects in mechanization will be described which amount to a 'pre-history of the tank'. The question, therefore, will be why such a technological artefact had *not* been invented by the outbreak of the Great War and this although – at least from the vantage point of General Nehring's 'hindsight' – the need had been so apparent. The basis for such an attempt in terms of primary sources is, compared to the French or British case, rather disappointing and, perhaps for this reason, the topic has received little scholarly attention.[8]

It will be argued that there is a much more convincing rationale which can help explain the 'non-invention' of the tank in Germany than that claimed by the current historical orthodoxy. The attitude towards mechanization, as displayed by the officer corps and the military administration, was less motivated by ignorance, romantic technophobia or domestic concerns than by a rather pragmatic estimation of the technical possibilities for mechanization. Before 1914 the general conditions for the invention of the tank were on the whole favourable. Before the war, the German Empire possessed one of the most powerful industrial bases in the world. Nowhere else in Europe were the production figures for steel higher.[9] To this day, the brand name *Krupp* stands as

---

7   The history of the tank provides ample evidence of terminological lags. The appearance of new technological artifacts often predates its terminology. The German soldiers, when confronted with British tanks from 1916 onwards, used a number of official and unofficial terms for the 'thing', among them the foreign word 'tank'. See the comprehensive PhD dissertation by Alexander Fasse, 'Im Zeichen des "Tankdrachen": Die Kriegführung an der Westfront 1916-1918 im Spannungsverhältnis zwischen Einsatz eines neuartigen Kriegsmittels der Alliierten und deutschen Bemühungen um seine Bekämpfung', Humboldt-Universität Berlin (2007), available as an online-publication at <http://www.edoc.hu-berlin.de/docviews/abstract.php?lang=ger&id=28331> [accessed 21 January 2013]. A similar terminological lag can be identified for the concept of mechanization. See Genmaj. a.D. L. Müller, 'Mechanisierung und Motorisierung', *Militär-Wochenblatt*, 4 January 1933, col. 834.
8   Recent studies on German tank production and operations during the Great War are: Heinrich Kaufhold-Roll, *Der deutsche Panzerbau im Ersten Weltkrieg* (Osnabrück, 1995); Wolfram Funk, Karl-Theodor Schleicher & Rolf Wirtgen (eds.), *Sturmpanzerwagen A7V: Vom Urpanzer zum Kampfpanzer Leopard 2. Ein Beitrag zur Militär- und Technikgeschichte* (Bonn, 2003); and, finally, Ralf Raths' chapter in this book.
9   Paul Kennedy, *The Rise and Fall of the Great Powers: Economic Change and Military Conflict 1500-2000* (New York, 1987), pp. 194-256 (for the general industrial trend), 256 (for steel production).

a symbol for the era's heavy industry and for its military potential.[10] Moreover, in the emerging motor industry, Germany was, together with France, a world leader. With Karl Benz, Gottlieb Daimler and Rudolf Diesel, the country had produced a number of prominent engineers and civilian innovators in this field.[11]

But military innovation also requires technologically-minded personnel in the armed forces themselves. At this point, we could stick to the hypothesis that the sheer size of the second biggest army in the world guaranteed a sufficient pool of innovative officers. Any serious international comparison must come to the conclusion that the German Army of 1914 was a well-equipped and well-trained fighting force.[12] But if this is so, and if the general economic and military conditions had been so favourable, then the question still remains: Why did the Germans not invent the tank?

Technological Innovation and Armament before 1914

Social systems in competitive situations – and, war is surely one of the most competitive situations in human life – secure their future existence through innovation. This might happen by means of a single weapon, through a clearly definable technological push or through a less spectacular process of transformation.[13] Innovation can be achieved either through invention or through imitation. It can be interpreted as an end result or as a process. The latter is influenced by a number of factors. First of all, innovation needs initial support from individuals who – either by virtue of their prominent position or their charismatic commitment – function as gate-keepers and opinion leaders. But even if individuals do play a role, sustainable innovation will only be brought forward by formal and informal groups. This starts with the invention itself, which, since industrialization, has only rarely been the product of one single person's efforts and ideas. Networks play a crucial role in the military discourse on an innovation and in relations to its political dimensions. Not surprisingly, the introduction of a new piece of technology was and still is a process in which diverging ideas

---

10 For an introduction see Michael Epkenhans, 'Military-Industrial Relations in Imperial Germany, 1870-1914', *War in History*, 10/1 (2003), pp. 1-26.
11 For the German motor industry, which, from 1900 onwards, lost ground its French competitor, see Karl H. Metz, *Ursprünge der Zukunft: Die Geschichte der Technik in der westlichen Welt* (Paderborn, 2006), pp. 252-5.
12 See Dieter Storz, *Kriegsbild und Rüstung vor 1914: Europäische Landstreitkräfte vor dem Ersten Weltkrieg* (Herford, 1992); and, Antulio J. Echevarria II, *After Clausewitz: German Military Thinking before the Great War* (Lawrence, KS, 2000).
13 See Stephen Peter Rosen, *Winning the Next War: Innovation and the Modern Military* (Ithaca, NY, 1991); furthermore, Dennis E. Showalter, 'Army and Society in Imperial Germany: The Pains of Modernization', *Journal of Contemporary History* 18 (1983), pp. 583-618; and, Carl-Axel Gemzell, *Organisation, Conflict, and Innovation: A Study of German Naval Strategic Planning, 1888-1940* (Stockholm, 1973).

and interests may collide.[14] Military staffs and technical commissions are important for identifying innovation being carried out by a potential enemy.[15] They are also decisive in the research and development process (R&D) and responsible for the smooth implementation of the innovation into the military machinery.

Finally, we have to consider the specific binary framework of peace and war in which armed forces function.[16] Times of peace offer fairly organized R&D processes; on the other hand, peacetime bears the danger of routine and of not thinking ahead. The actual need for innovation is harder to define, the character of future war and its timing are obsured by the 'fog of peace'.[17] In times of war, on the other hand, the demands are very specific. R&D tends to be more improvised. Despite this difficult general situation, the state of emergency minimizes legal restrictions and safety provisions. It creates a situation of extreme learning pressure for the armed forces and it allows the release of enormous scientific and economic resources for the purpose of war.[18] It is hard to judge if the general conditions for military innovation are more favourable during times of peace or times of war. It depends to a great degree on the specific character of the armed forces, their ability and willingness to learn under stress and at all levels. But it also depends on the war's character and – a crucial factor – on its duration.[19] The longer the duration of a war, the better are the chances for a restructuring of the R&D processes. The war's own dynamic, in turn, retroacts on R&D, it retroacts on armament as a whole, and on a specific society's ability and willingness to allocate resources for the invention or production of specific weapons.[20] This theoretical framework has to be applied to the historical case study of military mechanization in Imperial Germany.

The armaments of this country – like most European military powers between 1880 and 1914 – were distinguished by rapid technological innovation, improved industrial capacities, changes in the relationship between military administration and

---

14 A particular pre-1914 pattern for the acceptance of military technology – one that might easily be applied to the German experience as well – is described in Tim Travers, *The Killing Ground: The British Army, the Western Front and the Emergence of Modern Warfare 1900-1918* (Barnsley, 2003; 1st edn, 1987), p. 76.
15 See: Ernest R. May (ed.), *Knowing One's Enemies: Intelligence Assessment Before the Two World Wars* (Princeton, NJ, 1984); Markus Pöhlmann, 'German Intelligence at War, 1914-1918', *Journal of Intelligence History* 5 (Winter 2005), pp. 25-54; Matthew S. Seligmann, *Spies in Uniform: British Military and Naval Intelligence on the Eve of the First World War* (Oxford, 2006); and, Jim Beach, 'British Intelligence and German Tanks, 1916-1918', *War in History*, 14/4 (2007), pp. 454-75.
16 Rosen, *Winning the Next War*, pp. 8-38.
17 The term is borrowed from Talbot C. Imlay & Monica Duffy Toft (eds.), *The Fog of Peace and War Planning: Military and Strategic Planning under Uncertainty* (London & New York, 2006); see also Echevarria, *Clausewitz*, p. 223.
18 Metz, *Ursprünge*, p. 412.
19 See Rosen, *Winning the Next War*, p. 38.
20 This is why armament, first of all, remains a contested political process. See Michael Geyer, *Deutsche Rüstungspolitik 1860-1980* (Frankfurt/Main, 1984).

private industry, budgetary restrictions and competing armament interests between the branches. Furthermore, from 1900 onwards, a sequence of international crises also began to influence military procurement.[21] The international arms race, triggered by these crises, was not limited to quantities alone. In fact, quality did matter too: it is intriguing to see that, on the German side, a number of armament schemes were primarily initiated by external pressure. As early as 1886, the French Army had introduced a new rifle (*Fusil Lebel Modèle 1886*), and by doing so had triggered hectic R&D activities in Germany. The result – the *Gewehr 88* – was an interim solution that did not meet expectations. Hasty activism had thus brought about a rather improvised product. But the opposite approach could also carry the seeds of disaster. This became apparent when, in 1897, the French Army introduced the world's first field cannon with an effective hydro-pneumatic recoil buffer (*Materiel de 75 mm Modèle 1897*). The Prussian War Ministry had been familiar with the principle for a long time, but disappointing shooting tests and a negative judgement by the oligopolistic Krupp factory (which was trying to sell a competing device) had convinced the military procurement bureaucracy that the recoil mechanism was unreliable. It did not take long until it became clear that the new French field gun now outclassed the opposing German guns and created a real asymmetry in artillery warfare. The following R&D race to catch up with the French field artillery from 1897 to 1905 became no less than a traumatic experience for the armament bureaucracy.[22]

A third example can be given. The idea that pre-1914 military establishments had remained ignorant of the machine guns deadly potential belongs to the more persistent legends of modern historiography.[23] In fact, its performance during the wars in South Africa and Manchuria had been observed very closely. The introduction of the new weapon proceeded cautiously yet steadily.[24] The problem was not so much in identifying the potential, but in understanding what Tim Travers has called the machine's 'internal logic' once it had been officially accepted. The machine gun remained a 'weapon of opportunity' with particular combat value in fortified positions – i.e., in

---

21 For two very valuable overviews, see: David Stevenson, *Armaments and the Coming of War: Europe 1904-1914* (Oxford, 1996); and, David G. Herrmann, *The Arming of Europe and the Making of the First World War* (Princeton, NJ, 1996). Herrmann focusses on the crucial period of 1905-1914.
22 See Volker Mollin, *Auf dem Weg zur "Materialschlacht": Vorgeschichte und Funktionieren des Artillerie-Industrie-Komplexes im Deutschen Kaiserreich* (Pfaffenweiler, 1986), pp. 244-90.
23 See John Ellis, *The Social History of the Machine Gun* (London, 1976).
24 See: Anon., 'Ueber Maschinengewehre in der englischen Armee', *Militär-Wochenblatt*, 4 May 1905, col. 1285-90 (on British experiences and the machine gun's character as a 'weapon of opportunity'); M. [Friedrich von Merkatz?], 'Ueber Organisation und Verwendung der Maschinengewehre', *Militär-Wochenblatt*, 11 October 1910, col. 2945-6 (on lessons from 1904/5 and organisational questions); and, finally, Helm, 'Hinweise für die taktische Verwendung der Maschinengewehre beim Kampf um Festungen', *Militär-Wochenblatt*, 27 July 1911, col. 2159-65 (on fire power in defensive positions).

the defence.[25] As the German Army tried to avoid positional warfare at all costs and aimed at keeping the operations mobile, it is not surprising that the machine gun did not receive top priority in the army's procurement and training.[26] On the other hand, it was exactly this urge for offensive, mobile operations that fostered the swift introduction of howitzers and mortars from 1906 onwards. The weapons that surprised the military experts in the summer of 1914 had not been designed for the stalemate to come but for the purpose of crushing the Belgian and French border fortresses and, thus, preparing the way for the main body of the invading army.[27]

These examples show, firstly, that the stimuli for armament projects can be very distinct. They show, secondly, that a hasty as well as an inert attitude could yield negative consequences. But the main problem in the era in question was not to be found in a single innovation. The problem was the sheer mass of ideas and demands that resulted in a form of innovation-overload: smokeless powder, an artillery piece with a recoil buffer, the machine gun, a new rifle, radio, telephone, the motor-car, the airship, the aeroplane – these innovations challenged the army's intellectual and bureaucratic intake capacities. Or, as the German historian Dieter Storz, once laconically stated: 'The problem with these new weapons was that they all turned up at the same time.'[28]

Both private industry and individual inventors had to deal with a bureaucracy that was in a process of rapid, organizational adoption of new weaponry.[29] It is worth mentioning that it was not the lack of external suggestions with regard to military innovations but the abundance of them which caused the problems. In May 1908, the Prussian War Ministry laid out its procedures regarding the offers of private inventors in an article in the semi-official journal, *Militär-Wochenblatt*.[30] According to this article, the bulk of the inventors were 'people who do not hold down a proper job and do not aspire to one, like veterans or pensioners. Even members of the fair sex

---

25 Travers, *Killing Ground*, pp. 65-6. The machine gun's early introduction in the cavalry does not serve as proof of the army's understanding of the new weapon's offensive value. It rather demonstrates the described doctrinal uneasiness, as a weapon of dubious quality had been attached to a branch whose combat value in modern battle had been called into question by a substantial proportion of the officer corps and contemporary military commentators.
26 Dennis E. Showalter remarks that 'defence was not the German army's overriding concern'. Showalter, 'Army and Society in Imperial Germany', p. 591.
27 For the development of heavy artillery prior to 1914, see Georg Ortenburg, *Waffen der Millionenheere: 1871-1914* (Bonn, 1992), pp. 83-119, 157-66.
28 Storz, *Kriegsbild*, p. 371.
29 See Stevenson, *Armaments*, pp. 41-7. The most recent analysis of Germany's armament bureaucracy is Oliver Stein, *Die deutsche Heeresrüstungspolitik 1890-1914: Das Militär und der Primat der Politik* (Paderborn, 2007).
30 The Prussian War Ministry held the responsibility for the weapon procurement of all national contingents of the army – i.e. the Bavarian, Saxon and Württemberg armies as well.

are among them.' The problem was that these people were 'rock-solidly convinced' about proposals that were actually 'at least in 99 percent [of cases] absolutely useless'. The sheer mass of submissions meant both a bureaucratic burden and an intellectual nuisance. As to the ministry's 'rules of engagement' for private offers, the same article stated: 'As long as an external proposal does not coincide with an ongoing R&D project, the ministry pays no attention to inventions until they have stood the test of a wider [i.e. civilian] public'.[31]

What we see is a particular practice with regard to technology for which the oft-repeated allegation 'technophobia' is inadequate as an explanation. Nor was the technological state of the Prussian-German Army of 1914 the mere consequence of 'backward-looking prejudices that had accumulated over 4 decades of peacetime'.[32]

The ministry's procurement agencies – namely the commissions for infantry, artillery, military engineering and transportation – as well as the General Staff did, in fact, observe the trends in technological progress with interest. But they were reluctant to adopt what today's marketing experts call an 'early adopter attitude'. They promoted or initiated innovations only when the military need was imminent or until another military power had come forward with a particular innovation. The primary argument in the contemporary discourse was *Kriegsbrauchbarkeit*, sustainable usability for the purposes of warfare – be it the recoil buffer, the bicycle, the machine gun or the tank.[33]

With regard to the tank, the military bureaucracy's attitude towards such an innovation can only be explained by a combination of attitudes and circumstances: the ministry and the procurement agencies found themselves in an era of enormous technological change resulting in a characteristic form of 'institutional stress'. This situation challenged the traditional R&D process, in particular the assumption that military innovation should come from within the military itself. Combined with a more general 'late adopters attitude', this meant that the idea for a hitherto unknown motorized and armoured weapon platform with cross-country mobility did not probably fill the bureaucracy with enthusiasm.

---

31 Anon., 'Ueber militärtechnische Erfindungen', *Militär-Wochenblatt*, 30 May 1908, col. 1589-95, here 1589-90.
32 Eric Dorn Brose, *The Kaiser's Army: The Politics of Military Technology in Germany during the Machine Age, 1870-1918* (Oxford, 2001), p. 240.
33 See the reiterating demands in: Anon., 'Ein neues Feldgeschütz', *Militär-Wochenblatt*, 20 February 1895, col. 426-31; Anon., 'Ueber die Kriegsbrauchbarkeit der Fahrräder: Teil 1', *Militär-Wochenblatt*, 18 December 1897, col. 2911-16; E. Hartmann, 'Die Maschinengewehre und ihre Kriegsbrauchbarkeit', *Kriegstechnische Zeitschrift*, 10 (1907), 1-14; and, Anon., 'Heeres-Rundschau: England – Neue Tanks', *Kriegstechnische Zeitschrift*, 20 (1917), pp. 1161-2.

Military Culture and Mechanization

In the wake of the onward march of industrialization, technology confronted the Prussian-German officer corps as a predominant cultural activity. Their own military culture has to be understood as a tool to interpret situations and to make choices from an otherwise 'bewildering range of alternatives'.[34] These alternatives could both be intellectual or material. Among the more material alternatives were new weapons and the idea of the tank. Therefore, the soldiers did not stand idle when it came to commenting on the experience of the machine age. Machines were entering their professional life and they enforced standardization and regulation of long-established processes – particularly with regard to command, control and communications, to the production and employment of weapons, and military transportation. Central categories and role models of nineteenth century military cultures had to be reconsidered. The Age of Enlightenment had shattered the idealistic concept of war as a 'sphere of clashing wills, rising emotions, uncertainty, and confusion', as Azar Gat has put it, and industrialization prompted a further 'scientization' of warfare. Hence, it is not surprising that war itself found its popular metaphor as the 'war machine'.[35] The officer corps' reaction had not been as downright reactionary as the orthodox historiography of the 1960s, 1970s and 1980s sometimes suggested.[36] Rejecting the Enlightenment and, at the same time, embracing modern technology might seem paradoxical only at first glance. The case of the Prussian-German Army proves that this was common practice for the fin-de-siècle officer.[37] The Wilhelmine man has been characterized as a hopeless epigone. This might be true but he was also a refreshing eclectic.[38] It was

---

34   For its definition of military culture, this discussion makes use of Peter H. Wilson, 'Defining Military Culture', *Journal of Military History*, 72 (2008), pp. 11-41, here 14. For the cultural background, see Siegfried Giedion, *Mechanization Takes Command* (Oxford, 1948), although this classic study displays astonishingly little interest in the military dimensions of the topic.
35   A classic interpretation of this topos can be found in J.F.C. Fuller, *Armament and History: A Study of the Influence of Armament on History from the Dawn of Classical Warfare to the Second World War* (London, 1946), pp. x-xi. See also Azar Gat, *The Development of Military Thought: The Nineteenth Century* (Oxford, 1992), p. 47 (for quote), and Daniel Pick, *War Machine: The Rationalisation of Slaughter in the Modern Age* (New Haven & London, 1993), pp. 165-6, for contemporary images of the 'war machine'.
36   A poignant criticism of this school of thought and an early plea for a more balanced interpretation can be found in Showalter, 'Army and Society in Imperial Germany', passim.
37   For a useful critical review of the paradox of the 'reactionary modernism', as introduced by Jeffrey Herf, see Thomas Rohkrämer, 'Antimodernism, Reactionary Modernism and National Socialism: Technocratic Tendencies in Germany, 1890-1945', *Contemporary European History*, 8 (1999), pp. 29-50, here 32, 49.
38   The epigonal mentality is treated in Martin Doerry, *Übergangsmenschen: Die Mentalität der Wilhelminer und die Krise des Kaiserreichs*, 2 vols. (Weinheim & Munich, 1986).

not the Enlightenment which was challenged by the professional soldiers but rather some of its unquestionably crucial socio-political consequences.

Officers perceived technology as an intellectual and military challenge, sometimes as an opportunity, sometimes as a threat. The diving lines ran right through the corps – a corps that was undergoing a process of rapid professional diversification. A hussar officer surely had an understanding of his trade and of technology that differed considerably from the understanding of a howitzer company's captain, the commandant of an airship or a military railways dispatcher in the Great General Staff.[39] But the problem with the German Army went deeper, as – when necessary – it expected the hussar to familiarize himself with the job of the train dispatcher and vice versa. By the mid-1890s, the army lived through a permanent process of technological transformation in which diverging ideas and interests were not the exception but the rule.[40]

Given these contested conditions of military thinking and professional practice, it may suffice to argue that the officer corps tended to accept technology more openly, wherever it consolidated existing leadership principles and the orthodox image of a future war, and wherever technology served to optimise existing doctrines. But wherever military innovation challenged leadership principles or doctrines, it was met with scepticism. In the German Army, initiative in leadership and the pursuit of mobility lay at the basis of command. It is, therefore, quite revealing to observe how the much-praised German approach to the conduct of war reacted ambiguously to the idea of armour as a concept. 'Armour' was regarded as the polar opposite to 'mobility'. Judging from this military outlook, which was governed by a characteristic blend of pragmatism and a belief in the capacity of will-power to solve problems, the tank was at first regarded as an uncontrollable, an immobile and an uncreative piece of machinery.

Images of Future War

However, it is obvious that the decision makers' attitude towards weapons and doctrines did not depend on their cultural outlook alone but on the future war scenarios that they had developed as well.[41] And here, for the era in question, one dictum by J.F.C. Fuller seems to be of particular importance: when 'a soldier sets out to propose the type of army required for the next war, rightly he considers the opening phase of that war'.[42] This, in turn, meant that the choice of weapons depended heavily on the

---

39 This fragmentation is (over-) stated in Brose, *The Kaiser's Army*, pp. 5-6.
40 See Storz, *Kriegsbild*, pp. 295, 305.
41 For the recent debate over German strategic and operational planning, see: Terence Zuber, *Inventing the Schlieffen Plan: German War Planning 1871-1914* (New York, 2002); Robert T. Foley, *German Strategy and the Path to Verdun: Erich von Falkenhayn and the Development of Attrition, 1870-1916* (Cambridge, 2005); and, Gerhard P. Groß, 'There was a Schlieffen Plan: New Sources on the History of German Military Planning', *War in History* 15 (2008), pp. 389-431.
42 Fuller, *Armament*, p. 35.

decision, not how the war should be fought in general, but how the initial operations should be fought in particular.

Even if one concedes the possibility that the German Army's operational planning had been more flexible than the orthodox interpretation of the one gigantic battle of annihilation à la Schlieffen maintains, the big picture remains the same: war was expected to materialize in a Western- and Central-European theatre, with the German Army aiming at carrying the war to the opponents' territories by offensive operations. The conflict would take on the character of mass war. It was also common knowledge that firepower would be required on an unprecedented scale. This insight modified the interrelation of attack and defence in favour of the latter. The German Army did not meet this challenge by adopting a defensive dislocation, trusting in modern firepower, extending the border fortifications and initiating extensive logistic and economic preparations for the long war. Quite the contrary happened. The danger of an exhausting two-front war was to be checked through rapid operations, conducted by a tactically superior German force.[43] What would have been the role of the tank in such a scenario?

Terrain and infrastructure in Western Europe was fairly suitable for the use of tanks before 1914. In Central Europe, on the other hand, insufficient roads and long distances had clearly limited the tanks' radius to the border regions. The advantage of 'armour' had surely provided some opportunities against firepower in defensive positions close to the border, such as fortified positions on the Upper Rhine or in Russian Poland. The topographic preconditions might have been advantageous, but the tactical ones were not. The vehicles had never been able to keep pace during the rapid, initial flanking operations which were at the core of the German war plan. Given this stress on mobile operations, the priority for tanks was low; and, thus neither a strategic failure in the pre-war armament policy nor military technophobia were the reasons why the tank had remained only a vision prior to 1914.[44]

The decade before the outbreak of war also saw a particularly broad spectrum of popular future war scenarios in which military analyses, political perspectives and commercial interests all influenced the plots.[45] This (pulp-) fictional dimension to military literature is relevant in so far as it could work as a medium in which professional military ideas could be transmitted to a wider public. It is also relevant because the visionary ideas, often brought forward by military amateurs, could add up to the particular 'institutional stress' mentioned earlier. In the political and the media arena of early twentieth century Germany, military bureaucracies could find themselves in

---

43 See Gerhard P. Groß, *Mythos und Wirklichkeit: Die Geschichte des operativen Denkens im deutschen Heer von Moltke d. Ä. bis Heusinger* (Paderborn, 2012), pp. 102-3.
44 See Storz, *Kriegsbild*, p. 371.
45 See: Ignatius F. Clarke, *Voices Prophesying War: 1763-1984* (London, 1966); and, Henning Franke, *Der politisch-militärische Zukunftsroman in Deutschland 1904-1914: Ein populäres Genre in seinem literarischen Umfeld* (Frankfurt/Main, 1985).

a situation where they had to adjust themselves to the presumably strange ideas of gas clouds, zeppelin attacks, intercontinental rocket assaults – or gigantic 'land ironclads'.

The military and literary quality of this genre was more or less heterogeneous. Among the more serious contributions one can count *Ein neues Wörth*, by Julius Hoppenstedt, which features a historical setting from 1870, fought out with the mass armies and the weapons arsenals of 1909.[46] And, in an anonymous refutation of a pamphlet by the French colonel Arthur Boucher (*L'Offensive contre l'Allemagne*), an air fleet of 1,000 planes sows 'death and destruction', while the German emperor survives a French air raid in his armoured command-tent.[47] As the authors clung to the existing arsenal, weapon projects like the tank did not appear.

Interestingly, H.G. Wells' vision of future war in the short story 'The Land Ironclads' (1903), probably the first story of tank warfare, remained practically unknown in Germany. The text was not reviewed in German military journals which are usually a reliable indicator of the level of awareness of foreign military publications. A German translation does not exist to this day, although Wells was certainly read in Germany before the 1914. His *Anticipations of the Reaction of Mechanical and Scientific Progress Upon Human Life and Thought* appeared in a first translation in 1905. His military visions *The War of the Worlds* and *The War in the Air* found a publisher in 1901 and 1909, respectively. It seems as if the reason for this relative ignorance was neither the author nor the content, but rather the medium: the story initially appeared serialized in a popular, illustrated, monthly periodical, the *Strand Magazine*, something which might have impeded the international circulation of the text.[48] Victory through machines had been a prominent motif in this future war genre. Yet, it was not fictional wonder weapons but existing machines that remained the war-winning tools: British dreadnoughts, German torpedo boats and the *Zeppelins*.[49] This is why no popular future war story in Germany featured a Teutonic version of the 'Land Ironclads'. In the end, neither the operational realities of a major war in Europe, nor the popular fictional images of war, demanded a military artefact like the tank prior to 1914.

---

46 Major [Julius] Hoppenstedt, *Ein neues Wörth: Ein Schlachtenbild der Zukunft* (Berlin, 1909).
47 Von einem aktiven deutschen General [Anon.], *Und dann...?! Fortsetzung der Schlacht auf dem Birkenfelde in Westfalen 191...! Errettung des deutschen Reiches vom Untergang!* (Leipzig, 2nd edn, 1912), pp. 15, 56.
48 For Wells, see also T.H.E. Travers, 'Future Warfare: H.G. Wells and British Military Theory, 1895-1916', in Brian Bond & Ian Roy (eds.), *War and Society. A Yearbook of Military History* (London, 1975), pp. 67-87.
49 Antulio Echevarria II, *Imagining Future War: The West's Technological Revolution and Visions of Wars to Come* (Westport, Conn. & London, 2007), pp. 58-63.

Pre-war Projects

Even without the tank's actual appearance as a weapons platform, a number of pre-war projects in armour and mechanization can be identified. The first which needs to be mentioned is the proto-mechanization of the artillery which started in 1905 with the introduction of the shielded field gun, a decision which triggered a complete range of technical and tactical changes. The concept of armouring guns and, at the same time, making them mobile also becomes evident in the test of a tractor-drawn armoured road train loaded with artillery, an experiment motivated by British experiences with armoured trains in the South African War.[50]

But the weapon that actually came closest to what we would identify as a tank was the 1889 *Krupp-Grusonsche Fahrpanzer* described in the introduction. Its designer, Maximilian Schumann, was a gifted military engineer, but apparently he had some difficulties in lobbying for his plans and products in publications. Besides, Schumann lacked a clear tactical vision for his weapon. The *Fahrpanzer* was an armoured carriage with a 5.3 cm quick-firing gun. He had designed it as a mobile support weapon for fortresses or fortified positions. The step from a horse-drawn or tractor-drawn carriage to a self-propelled carriage detached from its original assignment in positional warfare was not taken, not least of all because automotive engineering was still in its infancy during the 1890's and, likewise, because the expertise of his employer, the Krupp-Grusonwerke in Magdeburg, was in steel and fortifications, not in vehicle manufacturing. The *Fahrpanzer* was sold to a number of countries, including Switzerland and Romania, who included it in their defensive systems. But it seems that it remained rather a slow seller.[51] There is a final element of irony in the fact that the gun's last deployment was that of an improvised, dug-in, *anti*-tank weapon on the Western Front in 1918.[52]

With regard to armoured vehicles there had been a number of projects, among them one of a private inventor, the 1909 weapon carrier, *Meteor*. It was an open car, armed with a machine gun, which could go into reverse and was supposed to have amphibian qualities. All in all, the military value of the *Meteor* did probably not go beyond that of a soap box derby car and a certain degree of sympathy can be felt for the War Ministry's reluctance to engage actively with private inventors.[53] Among the more serious projects were the 1905 *Austro-Daimler* armoured car and the 1906 *Erhardt* anti-balloon-gun. The *Daimler* armoured car was presented in 1905. It had a rather weak 30-hp engine and could be equipped alternatively with a machine gun or a 3.7 cm gun. Its true innovation was the all-round armour and the pivoted turret.

---

50 Otfried Layriz, *Der mechanische Zug mittels Straßenlokomotiven: Seine Verwendbarkeit für die Armee im Kriege und Frieden* (Berlin, 1906).
51 For Maximilian Schumann and his work, see Schröder, *Schumann*, passim.
52 See Fritz Heigl, *Taschenbuch der Tanks* (Munich, 1926), p. 345.
53 Anon., 'Das Automobilmaschinengewehr Schlayer', *Kriegstechnische Zeitschrift* 12 (1909), pp. 472-4.

The military journals discussed its assignment in reconnaissance missions and as an armoured personnel carrier.[54] Nevertheless, in the light of the car's technical parameters, the critics remained sceptical. 'It appears as if the time for armoured cars has not come yet', read the judgement in a March 1910 article in the *Militär-Wochenblatt*.[55]

The *Erhardtwagen*, on the other hand, was 60-hp strong. With its four-wheel-drive, a pivoted turret and a 5.3 cm quick-firing gun, it looked the more promising technical solution.[56] But unlike the Austro-Daimler, it was not constructed for a combat support role but as a mobile anti-aircraft platform. Both types were tested, but technical problems and the limited cross-country-performance made the army shy away from the introduction of armoured cars in 1910. Consequently, there was no direct evolutionary path from the armoured car to the tank.[57]

Even though these projects had already contained a number of the important features of a tank, one crucial missing link remained – the caterpillar track.[58] A survey of the historical records of the German Patent and Trade Mark Office indicates that the focus of civilian R&D were pedrail systems. While it was possible to identify at least sixteen patent applications for pedrails in the period 1913-1918, none was found for track systems.[59] Yet, the ministry's transportation commission and military writers

---

54   See Anon., 'Das Panzerautomobil', *Kriegstechnische Zeitschrift* 9 (1906), pp. 81-7. The best history of German armoured cars is Heinrich Kaufhold-Roll, *Die deutschen Radpanzer im Ersten Weltkrieg: Technische Entwicklung und Einsätze* (Osnabrück, 1996), see pp. 15-17 for the *Austro-Daimler*. The archival situation on the Austro-Daimler is very sketchy. See Mercedes Benz Classic, Archive, Stuttgart, DMG, Bd. 54, Korrespondenz Paul Daimler 12 (1919), Anon., Der Daimler-Panzerwagen mit Vierräderantrieb und doppelter Lenkung, memorandum, 10 May 1919.

55   Rbg. [Otto Romberg], 'Militärtechnische Umschau: Gestaltung des Kraftfahrzeugwesens', *Militär-Wochenblatt*, 19 March 1910, col. 825-30, here 828-9.

56   See Kaufhold-Roll, *Radpanzer*, pp. 18-19. The archive of the Rheinische Metallwaren- und Maschinenfabrik Erhardt, today part of Rheinmetall Inc., contains no material on the armoured cars or tank projects.

57   The army harked back to armoured cars as early as autumn 1914. Following a request by the High Command, the companies Erhardt, Damiler and Büssing developed prototypes and these cars were soon integrated into an experimental unit. Although Western Front trench warfare offered no opportunities for armoured cars, the unit operated with some success on the Balkans in 1916 and on the Italian Front in the following year. The total number of German armoured cars during the war, including captured Italian and Russian vehicles, amounted to 33 to 45 vehicles in total. For an early description of armoured cars during the First World War see Anon., 'Der Panzerkraftwagen: Seine geschichtliche und technische Entwicklung', *Kriegstechnische Zeitschrift*, 20 (1917), pp. 1-12. See also G.P. von Zezschwitz (ed.), *Heigl's Taschenbuch der Tanks: Teil III: Der Panzerkampf* (Munich, 1938), pp. 252-3, 290-2, and Kaufhold-Roll, *Radpanzer*, pp. 11-12.

58   This failing was acknowledged by the Prussian Ministry of War as early as October 1918. See the memorandum at BA-MA, W-10/50770, 'Reichstagsmaterial. T. D. Betr. Kampfwagen (Tanks)' [copy], 23 October 1918.

59   Deutsches Patent- und Markenamt, Munich, Catalogue, Deutsche Gruppenmappe 63c, p. 31.

Photo 2: Mock-up of the Burstyn Motorgeschütz, Vienna

theoretically knew about the caterpillar system, as the British Hornsby model was presented in a 1912 article in the journal, *Kriegstechnische Zeitschrift*. The judgement of an anonymous author is further proof for what was described earlier as a classic late-adopters attitude: 'A highly interesting machine, indeed. But time will show if it has practical usability and if the machine will not be extremely pricey and difficult to manufacture.'[60] The two remaining years were not enough to provide further opportunity for tests with the new tractor. So, when the British tanks appeared in September 1916, the Germans had to turn for help to their Austrian allies, since they had imported a number of American caterpillar tractors before the war.[61]

In at least two cases the War Ministry had to deal with more ambitious proto-tank projects. The first proposal stemmed from a civilian engineer named Friedrich Goebel who apparently held some money in reserve and certain contacts within the military.

---

60   Anon., 'Der "Raupen"-Zieher, eine Lastenzugmaschine', *Kriegstechnische Zeitschrift*, 15 (1912), pp. 25-9, quote, 29.
61   Albrecht, *Burstyn*, pp. 17, 50. More than a month after the arrival of the British tanks, the *Militär-Wochenblatt* published a first, yet still speculative notice on the new weapon. See Anon., 'Amtliche Mitteilungen des Großen Hauptquartieres', *Militär-Wochenblatt*, 24 October 1916, col. 1775-82.

For several years, Goebel badgered the ministry with a number of projects. His first project envisioned a cross-country vehicle with pedrails – similar to the device in H.G. Wells' 'Land Ironclads'. When the experts were finally fed up with watching Goebel's vehicles falling from platforms, or getting stuck in the mud during his public shows, the ministry cancelled the co-operation.[62]

A better-known, and technically much more sophisticated project, was the 1912 *Motorgeschütz* (motor gun) developed by an Austrian first-lieutenant, Gunther Burstyn. At the basis of Burstyn's project lay the idea of armoured artillery, hence the designation *Motorgeschütz*. He envisioned – by the standards of the First World War – a very light tank with a turret and three to four man crew. The tracks were constructed with wire-woven chains, as the engineer was ignorant of the Holt-system when he submitted his proposal. A peculiar construction was the two pairs of booms which were intended to enhance the vehicle's climbing power.[63] The project of this active and technically adept officer was rejected first by the transportation commission of the Austrian Ministry of War and, subsequently, by both the artillery and the transportation commissions of the Prussian War Ministry. Without doubt, the *Motorgeschütz* had not fully resolved a number of flaws in its construction – for example, through ignorance of the Holt-system, the weak engine and the poorly designed booms. But Burstyn's fate was sealed perhaps more by the fact that his motor gun fell between the stools of motor and artillery procurement. Burstyn himself could not profit from any sustainable sponsorship from influential soldiers or politicians. Here, the case of the British tank pioneer Colonel Ernest D. Swinton invites comparison, as his success was to a certain extend founded in his excellent links to the political and military establishments.[64] Furthermore, Burstyn's proposal suffered from bad timing, as he approached the Ministry of War in the middle of its biggest armament scheme ever. Understandably, the focus was on the implementation of existing projects and not on the invention of new vehicles.[65] But considering the construction capacities of a major European armaments factory at this time, there can be no doubt that the Burstyn project could have been transformed into a serviceable tank within several months.

Conclusion

To sum up this brief account of the pre-history of the tank, and the potential of military mechanization in Germany prior to 1914, it might be helpful to consider, finally,

---

62 Bayerisches Hauptstaatsarchiv, Abteilung Kriegsarchiv, Munich, MKr 1570, memorandum entitled 'Kampfwagen', Prussian Ministry of War to Bavarian Military Pleniponentiary, 14 October 1918. See also Fr. Hassler, 'Aus der Geschichte der Kampfwagen', *Technikgeschichte*, 23 (1934), pp. 99-112, here 103.
63 See Albrecht, *Burstyn*, pp. 74-81.
64 J.P. Harris, *Men, Ideas and Tanks: British Military Thought and Armoured Forces, 1903-1939* (Manchester & New York, 1995), pp. 14-18.
65 See Stein, *Heeresrüstungspolitik*, pp. 296-368.

three of the weapons projects discussed earlier: Schumann's *Fahrpanzer*, the Erhardt armoured car and Burstyn's motor gun. Each one contained innovative tactical or construction ideas. The initiatives for each of these projects had stemmed from very different directions. The idea behind Schumann's *Fahrpanzer* had been to equip fortifications with mobile, armoured, quick-firing guns in order to counter the challenge of modern artillery in the offensive. Erhardt's armoured car had, originally, been designed as an anti-balloon-gun put on wheels – and, as such, was a response to the expansion of modern war into the third dimension. Burstyn's motor gun came closest to what military history today would define as an armoured weapon platform in land warfare. These three examples demonstrate that the remaining gap between the idea and the construction of a tank had indeed been small. Perhaps, it had been smaller in Germany than in many other European armies. So, was the tank notion 'in the air', as Major Bertram Clough Williams-Ellis suggested when looking back in 1919 on the pre-war era and the first months of the war?[66]

The answer is both 'yes' and 'no'. What was available technologically were the three prerequisites for mechanization: firepower, mobility and armoured protection. But the weapon system which finally materialized in the summer of 1916 was more than just the sum of these three elements. This discussion has put forward a number of reasons why the tank was not developed in Imperial Germany. First, military mechanization as an integral concept in land warfare remained of secondary importance for a procurement bureaucracy that found itself under intense pressure in dealing with rapid technological changes. Evolution rather than revolution was the motto of the day. Furthermore, the dominant future war image – offensive, mobile warfare – provided no place for the slow and technically unreliable tank. This German case study in the tank's 'non-invention' shows, therefore, that early twentieth century armament as a contested politico-military process followed a rationale which was orientated rather on assumed military probabilities than on the technological attractiveness of an individual weapon.

With regard to military culture, the approaches of the German officer corps towards machinery were many and varied, and they were in very many ways ambivalent as well. Technical specialists were working side by side with more traditionally-oriented soldiers; and, sometimes, they worked against each other. The response to technological advances in the military world was not the military elite's ideological adherence to the 'traditional'. It was a pragmatic, considered decision in favour of what was seen as 'reliable'. And the nature of this doctrinal or technological reliability was the subject of permanent, both intellectual and bureaucratic, negotiations within the officer corps. A good example is the combustion engine, one of the central components of a tank. The motor had not yet passed the test as a war-winner, but the frequently lauded human will, in combination with massed rifle fire *and* modern artillery, appeared to have done so. At least it had in France in 1870/71, as well as in Manchuria in 1904/05.

---

66 Maj. Clough Williams-Ellis & A. Williams-Ellis, *The Tank Corps* (London, 1919), p. 8.

The fact that no military power had developed the tank prior to 1914 shows that national approaches to technology, or indeed the great powers' military cultures, had not been fundamentally different, even though the contemporary rhetoric sometimes suggested it was. The question why the German Army had not invented the tank before 1914 is thus easy to answer. It was a complicated piece of technology to construct, not least of all because the soldiers saw no place for it in their future war scenarios – and, because Germany's potential enemies had not developed the weapon either.

2

Practical Considerations in British Tank Operations on the Western Front, 1916-1918

Bryn Hammond

Any examination of the British Army's use of a wholly new invention – the tank – in combat in the First World War must inform an understanding of how that force 'learned the lessons of the fighting'[1] and how, with increasing success, it sought to achieve 'the most thorough co-operation between the various elements of the British Army'[2] in 1918. Without a previous model for its use and under the pressure of events, the British Expeditionary Force (BEF) on the Western Front developed effective tactics for the tank Marks available and integrated them into what might, with caution, be termed a 'true weapons system'.[3] Whilst it cannot be denied that the BEF was by no means tactically infallible, its proven ability to adapt to the changing environment in which it fought indicates a flexibility that, given the circumstances in which it went to war, and its performance in the first two years of the war, might be considered surprising.

In the historiography of the British Army in the First World War, the concept of a 'learning curve' was first expounded by a group of military historians, including

---

1   This theme is explored in Christopher Brynley Hammond, 'The Theory and Practice of Tank Co-Operation with Other Arms on the Western Front during the First World War', unpublished PhD thesis, Birmingham University (2005), which examines the development of British tactical doctrine for armour in the First World War.
2   Robin Prior & Trevor Wilson, *Command on the Western Front: The Military Career of Sir Henry Rawlinson, 1914-1918* (Oxford, 1992), p. 309. See J. P. Harris & Niall Barr, *Amiens to the Armistice: The BEF in the Hundred Days' Campaign, 8 August–11 November 1918* (London, 1998), pp. 297-8, for a discussion of the fallibility of the British Army's weapons system in 1918.
3   Prior & Wilson, *Command on the Western Front*, p. 309.

Gary Sheffield, Simon Robbins, Peter Simkins and Brian Bond,[4] to describe this process. However, under critical scrutiny and with further consideration, the smooth conceptual 'curve' first morphed to assume a more jagged or erratic form and has now largely been abandoned altogether, with its proponents favouring reference to the 'learning process' as a more accurate locution.[5] William Philpott, whose interests lie across both British and French conduct of the war, has been especially critical stating that 'as with other models of military change, the "learning curve" has now had its day, being too amorphous a concept, and too Anglo-centric a debate, to do justice to the fundamental rethinking of warfare that occurred between 1914 and 1918.'[6]

In connection with the *practical* application of tactical theory, historians have given consideration to the extent to which there was a structured and published *doctrine* the BEF developed or, as some suggest, an *ethos*, or commonly-understood way of approaching a task, that guided its operational planning and execution. This concept of an ethos has considerable merit in connection with the present work since it is underpinned less by theory and more by practicalities.[7] More recently still, Stephen Badsey has considered whether a hybrid approach existed with the development of a 'practical military doctrine' (in this case for cavalry).[8]

Learning through after-action analysis – which was a methodology applied to a greater or lesser extent by all the major combatants in the war – was pursued assiduously within the BEF. In the case of the tank, there is clear evidence that the General Headquarters (GHQ) of the BEF took ownership of the process of codifying and disseminating tactical guidance for military operations involving tanks before their first use in operations. This guidance, which was grounded in the commonly-understood principles of the army's *Field Service Regulations Part I (Operations)* (FSR),[9] was developed and refined through the various Stationery Service ('S.S.') training

---

4   For the 'learning curve' see, for example: Gary Sheffield, *Forgotten Victory – The First World War: Myths and Realities* (London: Headline, 2001); Gary Sheffield, *The Somme* (London, 2003); and, Simon Robbins, *British Generalship on the Western Front, 1914-18: Defeat into Victory* (London, 2005).
5   See Gary Sheffield, *The Chief: Douglas Haig and the British Army* (London, 2011), which focuses now on the 'learning process' for both Haig and the wider BEF.
6   William Philpott, 'Beyond the "Learning Curve": The British Army's Military Transformation in the First World War', RUSI Analysis, 10 Nov 2009 [<http://www.rusi.org/analysis/commentary/ref:C4AF97CF94AC8B/#.Ul-8NHLh5Yg> accessed 17 October 2013]; *Field Service Regulations (1909) Part I. (Operations)*, reprinted with Amendments, 1914 (London, 1914).
7   See A. Palazzo, *Seeking Victory on the Western Front: The British Army and Chemical Warfare in World War 1* (London, 2000), and Simon Robbins, *British Generalship on the Western Front in the First World War, 1914-1918* (London, 2001).
8   Stephen Badsey, *Doctrine and Reform in the British Cavalry, 1880-1918*, Birmingham Studies in First World War History (Aldershot, 2008).
9   *Field Service Regulations (1909) Part I. (Operations)*.

pamphlets produced as the war progressed, but remained utterly consistent, specifically incorporating experience based on operational analysis.[10]

It remains vitally important that in reviewing the development of theories for tank use in combat and the implementation of these theories on the battlefield, historical analysis must be founded on an understanding and acceptance of the practicalities associated with tank employment. Whilst much has been written on the invention and development of the tank, much less has been produced by way of detailed analysis of the tank's combat use during the Great War and on the practical considerations which affected that use.[11] This chapter emphasizes the relevance of such functional questions to a discussion of how successful, or otherwise, the British military were in their use of tanks on the Western Front between 1916 and 1918. It makes use of artefacts, archival material and personal experience accounts in the Imperial War Museums' (IWM) collection to provide an important sense of the practicalities governing tank operations and an essential reminder of the conditions in which tank crews served.

The use of such resources requires further comment on the difficulties they can raise. Museum collections connect between the theoretical and the practical. But museum objects and artefacts remain an under-used resource in this regard for military historians. Whilst oral history may be considered a less reliable source by some historians in connection with the detail of military operations and critical decisions made in those operations, it has much value for the front-line soldier's combat experience, giving real insights into the weaponry and equipment used and the conditions under which men fought. Careful utilization of these sources, in combination with other forms of personal experience narratives like published autobiographies and unpublished memoirs, and when supported by a robust and detailed examination of the primary material such as war diaries, operational orders and after-action reports, enhances any purely academic examination of combat and military operations.

Tanks: The Perceived Need

In approaching the subject, David Fletcher's definition of the tank is a useful guide to the weapon that was ultimately produced and a description of what we would understand the tank to be today:

---

10 Hammond, 'Theory and Practice of Tank Co-Operation', p. 401.
11 David J. Childs, *A Peripheral Weapon?: The Production and Employment of British Tanks in the First World War* (Westport, Conn., 1999), and John Glanfield, *The Devil's Chariots: The Birth and Secret Battles of the First Tanks* (Stroud, 2001), are the most recent, detailed accounts. But J.P. Harris, *Men, Ideas and Tanks: British Military Thought and Armoured Forces, 1903-1939* (Manchester, 1995) covers the subject concisely and well, as does David Fletcher, *Landships: British Tanks in the First World War* (London, 1984) and *The British Tanks, 1915-19* (Marlborough, 2001).

> Put simply the tank is a device which transports men and guns, behind the relative safety of armour plate, to a point on the battlefield where they can do most good, or harm. Since the component parts – the guns, armour, power unit and tracks – are integral, then the whole thing becomes a weapon in itself, rather than a means of transport for a weapon.[12]

However, this definition does not adequately connect with the ideas of those who first perceived the need for an armoured fighting vehicle and what they believed they sought.

On the outbreak of war in 1914 there was no apparent need for such a weapon. The war was generally expected to be a relatively short one of manoeuvre. However, by the beginning of 1915, when this expectation had not been realized, the political and military climate in states engaged in the war became more conducive to the encouragement of ideas for the use of new technology. The arrival of trench warfare and the military's inability to break the stalemate was a profoundly disillusioning experience. But it also provided a more favourable environment for the conception and development of new and radical technological means to break the incipient deadlock and for their promotion and support by otherwise relatively conservative governments and institutions.

From the British point of view, there is widespread agreement in the memoirs of key commanders that, almost as soon as the armies of both sides commenced digging trenches, individuals began to look for new ways to break the Western Front stalemate. Ideas for a form of mobile strong-point to operate with the infantry in the attack, from which the tank concept developed, were probably widely prevalent amongst officers and men of the BEF soon after the first experiences of attacking strongly entrenched positions on the Aisne in September 1914.[13]

The ideas may have been vague but, in general, the perceived need was obvious and the first proposals were for armoured and machine-gun armed vehicles with caterpillar tracks or similar means to cross broken ground. The need to get the infantry through barbed wire was also understood and appreciated from the outset. It can also be added that the same Colonel Ernest Swinton, a man whose drive and energy did much to ensure that the 'tank idea' became a reality, and whose early guidance on the tactical employment of the new weapon contained much that was valuable, saw the principal need as being for what he termed 'Machine Gun Destroyers'.[14] In very broad

---

12 Fletcher, *Landships*, p. 1.
13 See Brig.-Gen. J. Charteris, *At GHQ* (London, 1931), p. 165[n].
14 See memorandum by Swinton to GHQ, at Tank Museum Archive & Reference Library, Bovington, Dorset (hereafter, TMARL), Ernest Swinton Papers, 'A', 'The Necessity for Machine Gun Destroyers', 1 June 1915. In his post-war memoirs Swinton described how, in October 1914, he had vaguely pictured 'some form of armoured vehicle immune against bullets, which should be capable of destroying machine guns and of ploughing a way through wire'. Maj.-Gen. Ernest Swinton, *Eyewitness* (London, 1932), p. 64.

terms, we can see that the solution it was hoped that the tank might offer to certain elements of the tactical conundrum were those aspects on which, ultimately, for the British Expeditionary Force at least, they delivered – namely, as a means to overcome the combination of artillery, barbed wire and machine-guns that characterized the defensive systems of their opponents.

It must be stressed, of course, that for the British a readiness to embrace new technological means with which to fight did not just extend to the invention and development of the tank. A confluence of simultaneous changes was already taking place in the British Army on the Western Front. Whilst the mortar, hand-grenade, automatic rifle and rifle grenade, in the form of the 3-inch Stokes light trench Mortar,[15] the time-fused 'Mills Bomb',[16] the Lewis Gun[17] and the rifle grenade,[18] all represented examples of new weapons technology adopted by the BEF in 1915, the need to embrace technological solutions to the complex problems offered by modern, industrial warfare also manifested itself in areas as diverse as communications, aerial photography and reconnaissance, the location of enemy artillery, medical care and supply and logistics. The technology was not necessarily required to be sophisticated in its design. It was in its use that its value lay. A good example was the Tucker microphone which, from 1916, proved a boon to the successful location of German artillery from sound waves.[19] The use of several such microphones in combination at various locations close behind the front line permitted a sound-ranging section to locate accurately the position of an enemy artillery battery. This simple device became a vital part of British counter-battery techniques.[20]

---

15 For example, Imperial War Museums (hereafter, IWM), ORD 27, 3-inch Stokes light trench Mortar, <http://www.iwm.org.uk/collections/item/object/30025461> accessed 17 October 2013].
16 For example, IWM MUN 1362, Grenade, Hand, No. 5, <http://www.iwm.org.uk/collections/item/object/30020035>: accessed 17 October 2013].
17 For example, IWM FIR 9341, Gun, Lewis, .303 inch, <http://www.iwm.org.uk/collections/item/object/30033289> accessed 17 October 2013].
18 Examples are IWM MUN 3205, Grenade, Rifle No 3 Mk 1 Hales, <http://www.iwm.org.uk/collections/item/object/30023645> and IWM MUN 1380, Grenade, rifle and hand, No 23 Mk II <http://www.iwm.org.uk/collections/item/object/30022776> accessed 17 October 2013].
19 This was the invention of Corporal William Sansome Tucker, formerly a lecturer at Imperial College London. By the use of an electrically-heated thin wire stretched over a hole in an ammunition box, it was possible to distinguish between the low boom of a gun firing and the loud, high-pitched crack of a high velocity shell travelling faster than sound. The change in pressure caused by a gun report produced a jet of air which cooled this wire, lessening its electrical resistance, and a galvanometer could record the effect.
20 For more on the development of sound-ranging and British counter-battery techniques, see: Peter Chasseaud, *Artillery's Astrologers: A History of British Survey & Mapping on the Western Front 1914-1918* (Lewes, 1999); John R. Innes, *Flash Spotters and Sound Rangers: How They Lived, Worked and Fought in the Great War* (London, 1935); Sir Lawrence Bragg, Maj.-Gen. A.H. Dowson & Lt.-Col. H.H. Hemming, *Artillery Survey in the First World*

It is only necessary to point to the rapid expansion in the use and development of aircraft and associated paraphernalia for a particular task, namely aerial reconnaissance, to see how quickly all powers (not just the British) were prepared to adopt technological solutions to the problems raised by trench warfare. The Royal Flying Corps was very much part of the army until April 1918, and its successor the Royal Air Force remained a servant to the land forces until the war's end. The need for fighter or 'scout' aircraft and the consequent development of aerial combat weaponry, and the rise of the fighter ace, principally came from the need to protect other aircraft engaged in the fundamentally important tasks of photographic reconnaissance, artillery observation, contact patrols, and so on. Whilst reconnaissance aircraft had already proved useful in the period of mobile warfare in August and September 1914, the air dimension suggested definite possibilities in overcoming some of the key operational difficulties encountered as the front stagnated. As soon as these possibilities were realized, military commanders proved more than ready to employ the technology and turn it to their advantage.[21]

The introduction of the tank, when it came about, was therefore into a force already adjusting to and, crucially, accepting necessary change in its methods of making war. Innovation was being embraced by the BEF, not with suspicion and reluctance, but readily as an essential precondition for winning the war. Furthermore, the flow of ideas in this supposedly stagnant environment began at a very early date.[22] The tank was a wholly new weapon developed in an uncoordinated and fragmentary fashion, at a time of intense crisis, initially at least without a clearly defined specification to be met. It is a matter of no surprise, therefore, that theories for such a weapon's employment were consequently diverse. Indeed, just as ideas concerning the design and construction of what became the tank were initially vague, so too for some time there was no single, clearly defined concept of its purpose.

Operational Analysis not Operational Theory

Understanding why and how military commanders used tanks in the Great War requires us to shed the baggage of interpretations based on the inter-war drive for mechanization in military forces and our knowledge of the tank in the shape and form

---

War (London, 1971); and, Roy Macleod, 'Sight and Sound: Surveyors, Scientists and the Battlefield Laboratory, 1915-16', *War & Society*, 18 (2000), pp. 23-46.

21 See David Jordan, 'The Army Co-operation Missions of the Royal Flying Corps/Royal Air Force, 1914-18' (unpublished PhD thesis, Birmingham University, 1997), for a detailed analysis of the link between the RFC and RAF and the BEF's operations on the Western Front. See also Nigel Steel and Peter Hart, *Tumult in the Clouds: The British Experience of War in the Air, 1914-1918* (London, 1997).

22 The contrary view, that amongst the high commands of most armies in 1914 and 1915 there was a prevailing mindset deeply suspicious of innovation, can be found in Glanfield, *The Devil's Chariots*, p. 17.

it manifested itself during the Second World War and subsequent conflicts. With perhaps one exception, the tanks designed and used by all powers in the Great War were very different animals to those used later. This important point is considered in more detail below.

Perhaps more controversial, but equally important, is the need to divorce a consideration of the *actual* employment of tanks in the war from the *theoretical*. A considerable distortion of the issues related to tank operations in the First World War has resulted from considerations of these operations as a background to later theory and practice for the employment of armour. This is especially true regarding the paper produced in May 1918 by John Frederick Charles Fuller (the Tank Corps' chief staff officer for much, but not all, of the war), entitled 'The Tactics of the Attack as Affected by the Speed and Circuit of the Medium D Tank' (more familiarly known as 'Plan 1919').[23]

This is not to denigrate those who theorized about armoured warfare in the last year of the war (for, as David Childs has stressed, Fuller was only one of many who proposed plans for future tank employment).[24] Nor is it to suggest that tank operations in the war should not be considered as part of the context in which theories of warfare developed in the inter-war years. But if we are to reach an understanding of what was achieved in using tanks during the war it is essential to focus solely on hard facts concerning tank employment and only on those tanks available at the time. When Fuller produced his paper it was not just a proposal, but a radical vision. It was precisely this visionary aspect that Fuller's first biographer, Anthony Trythall, has emphasized.[25] In producing 'Plan 1919', Fuller was concerned with the possibilities offered by a new and untried mark of a still relatively new weapon: not the Medium A or 'Whippet' tank – which was already in service when he wrote, nor with the Medium C, which was at least in the early stages of production – but with the next tank after that, the Medium D. This is why we must regard 'Plan 1919' in the manner in which Brian Holden Reid has, as 'the most famous unused plan in military history',[26] and

---

23 Fuller's original document was completed on 24 May 1918. Liddell Hart Centre for Military Archives, King's College London (hereafter, LHCMA), Fuller Papers I/TS/1/1/50. Subsequently circulated for discussion and amendment by the War Office, a considerably changed version entitled 'Memorandum on the Requirements for an Armoured Striking Force for an Offensive in 1919' was distributed in late July 1918. See Harris, *Men, Ideas and Tanks*, pp. 167-72, and Brian Holden Reid, *J.F.C. Fuller: Military Thinker* (London, 1987), pp. 48-55.
24 Childs, *A Peripheral Weapon?*, p. 156.
25 A.J. Trythall, 'J.F.C. Fuller: Staff Officer Extraordinary', in David French & Brian Holden Reid (eds.), *The British General Staff: Reform and Innovation, 1890-1939* (London, 2002), p. 156.
26 Reid, *J.F.C. Fuller: Military Thinker*, p. 48.

Photo 3: J.F.C. Fuller (1878-1966)

accept its marginal relevance to considerations of the operations in which tanks were used in the First World War.[27]

It is not the purpose of this chapter to focus solely on Fuller, but Trythall makes another telling, and relevant, observation concerning Fuller that is worth noting here: 'Extraordinary staff officers may be visionaries, but if the object of the staff is to *get the best possible things done* [my emphasis, BH], that attribute may not always be effective'.[28] Therefore, in leaving aside Fuller's 'visionary' work, it is in regard to his ability 'to get the best possible things done' that this piece gives due consideration, and well-deserved praise, to the Tank Corps' chief staff officer. So, it is with operational planning and analysis (and the role of Fuller – amongst others – in that process) that we must concern ourselves here, and not with operational theory.

---

27 See Harris, *Men, Ideas and Tanks*, p. 167, for a scathing attack on *Plan 1919* as an inappropriate use of Fuller's time and abilities in May 1918.
28 Trythall, 'Fuller: Staff Officer Extraordinary', in French & Reid (eds), *The British General Staff*, p. 156.

The Reality of Combat in British Tanks

Any examination of tank operations conducted by the BEF must also recognize that there were important practical limitations influencing the tactical employment of British tanks. These include issues related to the tank's design and technical specifications as well as the environment in which they were used – some aspects of which may be at least suggested here.

For a start, First World War British tanks were undoubtedly rudimentary war machines.[29] The extent to which conditions, particularly in the heavy tanks, influenced the crew's combat effectiveness is often not fully appreciated. Indeed, it was an important factor militating against effective co-operation by tanks with infantry in battle. In order to demonstrate this connection between ergonomics and performance it is appropriate to describe the tank's internal arrangement.

Each British heavy tank had a single crew compartment, the crew being 'a team of eight in a very cramped space'.[30] Space was cramped still further by the presence of the petrol engine which occupied practically all the inside space running from front to rear. In Marks I to IV, this was a six-cylinder Daimler-Knight, sleeve-valve 105-hp engine, which was seriously underpowered for the task of moving a vehicle weighing approximately 32.5 tonnes.[31] The engine generated considerable heat and carbon monoxide fumes. Although 'a fan sucked in fresh air through the radiator and helped to ventilate the stuffy interior', temperatures inside the tank averaged over 50º Celsius (125º Fahrenheit).[32] 'The tank soon became full of petrol and cordite fumes, but the crew dared not open a flap or loophole to get fresh air for fear of the enemy machine-gun bullets.'[33] The excessive heat frequently caused vomiting and exhaustion. Eight hours' continuous work was 'about the limit of a crew's endurance', after which they reportedly required forty-eight hours' rest.[34]

Undoubtedly, the circumstances in which the tank was conceived, designed and developed had a considerable influence on the tank's design. For example, the uncoordinated and fragmentary fashion of its development meant that a 'serious fault' in the system for transmitting motive power from the engine to the tank's tracks had been introduced during the design process.[35] The first tanks' weight had been expected to

---

29 Sound Archive, Imperial War Museums, London (hereafter, IWM Sound), 9752, Reel 8, Norman Dillon interview.
30 Basil Henriques, *Indiscretions of a Warden* (London, 1937), p. 116.
31 David Fletcher, *The British Tanks, 1915-19* (Marlborough, 2001), p. 46.
32 F. Mitchell, *Tank Warfare: The Story of the Tanks in the Great War* (London, 1933), p. 18. It should be noted that this was markedly cooler than the temperatures inside the German A7V.
33 Mitchell, *Tank Warfare*, p. 20.
34 The National Archives of the United Kingdom, Kew (hereafter, TNA), WO 95/92, 'Notes on Tank Operations April – [Ms. amendment: 'October'] 1917', n.d. [but presumably November 1917].
35 Captain D.G. Browne, *The Tank in Action* (Edinburgh, 1920), p. 20.

place great strain on the transmission, so supplementary (or 'secondary') gears had been introduced. These, according to David Fletcher, 'offered an alternative method of steering but … complicated the driving method alarmingly'.[36]

So, the earliest tank Marks were driven in the following manner. At the front of the tank sat the driver on the right. By his side was the officer in charge of the tank. According to the recollections of a former tank-crew member: 'Then there were two men at the back – one on each side of the rear portion of the tank.'[37] These were the gearsmen. Each 'had control of a gear lever … which would change the gear from one to two or neutral' so that, as one tank officer described:

> You could drive if you liked with one side of the tank in top gear and the other side in second gear – the result would be, of course that the tracks would move unevenly and the tank would swing in its movement and that was the chief method of turning. You had to put the clutch out and get the man at the back to put the appropriate gear in. It was a very tricky business.[38]

It was also very slow. This, in turn, seriously impacted on the tanks' ability to respond to battlefield situations (particularly infantry requests for assistance). Furthermore, when moving, the noise inside the tank largely precluded verbal orders. Instead:

> [t]he officer … would just tell the driver 'We want to turn to the right here by the side of this wood' and the driver would then issue his signal to his pal behind – usually by rapping on the engine cover with a spanner – two raps means bottom gear, one rap means top gear – that sort of thing. Others had whistles; others went by a series of shouts.[39]

In order, therefore, to perform these manoeuvres, '[t]he only way of altering direction was … to stop to put one track in gear and the other in neutral and then to go forward'.[40] Combat experience increasingly indicated that this was unsatisfactory since too many tanks were lost to German artillery when halted to turn.

The problems of steering were, therefore, a severe limitation on the tank's battlefield performance. As early as April 1917, the tank arm's senior commander in France, Colonel Hugh Elles, was well aware (prior even to their introduction in battle) that the new and improved tanks his units were about to receive were not markedly new or an improvement on earlier models. They still used the same transmission and steering methods as the Mark I and, as a consequence, what was termed the Mark IV was

---

36 Fletcher, *Landships*, p. 13.
37 IWM Sound, 9752, Reel 8, Dillon interview.
38 IWM Sound, 9752, Reel 8, Dillon interview.
39 IWM Sound, 9752, Reel 8, Dillon interview.
40 IWM Sound, 9172, Reel 5, Reginald Johnson interview.

clearly not the tank needed. In correspondence with his superior, Elles stated quite frankly:

> Mark IV machines will not do what we want; this has become quite plain from the Arras Battle. Our casualties in Tanks have been, as far as I can make out, ninety per cent due to the Tank being hit while stationary, to stop and swing and turn. I am very strongly of the opinion that we must have something faster and handier which can be driven by one man instead of four; and will not stop in heavily shelled ground …[41]

The advent of the Mark V heavy tank with its epicyclic transmission placed all control of the tank in one pair of hands.[42] The tank commander could now instruct the driver at his side to change direction, and expect a rapid response. This was an important development and greatly improved the tank's operational effectiveness.

Yet the Mark V was not introduced until mid-1918, so the Mark IV was to be the main British heavy tank for over a year after Elles originally detailed its shortcomings. Over a thousand Mark IV tanks were produced and three tank battalions were still equipped with them and used them in action to the end of the war. The chief reason was connected with issues of manufacture and supply. These questions of manufacture and supply have received good treatment by David Childs in his book *A Peripheral Weapon?* Their importance should not be underestimated. Production of adequate numbers of tanks depended on their inclusion in the industrial mobilization programme, but it was not until February 1916 that David Lloyd George reversed an earlier decision to avoid involvement in the production of the new weapon and incorporated tank supply into his Ministry of Munitions.[43] Without the Ministry's active involvement, the tank might have remained an experimental novelty.

Allied to this was the fact that so much industrial capacity was already taken up with production of other munitions, guns, aircraft and shipping, etc., that there was little spare available when the tanks were ready to go into full production. This issue of supply dogged the British throughout the war. The Medium A 'Whippet' tank and the Mark V did not appear in service until 1918 because it took that amount of time for industrial capacity to be found to produce the designs that battlefield experience had revealed were needed.

A useful indicator of the manner in which the tank was developed in the context of the existing priorities for British industrial capacity and the manufacture and supply of weapons and munitions is provided by the way in which the main armament was selected for the gun-armed tanks. For a variety of reasons, several of the

---

41 TNA, WO 158/814, Elles to Anley, 23 April 1917.
42 Fletcher, *Landships*, p. 31.
43 Ministry of Munitions, *History of the Ministry of Munitions. Volume II, Part I: Administrative Policy and Organisation* (London, 1921), p. 1.

preferred choices of main armament were unavailable. It was eventually agreed that the Admiralty would provide one hundred 6-pounder 57mm Quick Firing (QF) Hotchkiss guns. The other options considered and rejected were the 2.95-inch mountain gun and the Vickers-Maxim 2-pounder 'pom-pom'.[44] Swinton's own preference had been the 6-pounder gun being used for aerial defence. It is only necessary to point to the Zeppelin raids of 1915, and the considerable concern these attacks on the civilian population caused, to see why the latter was never a serious option. Effectively, the heavier-armed tanks – the so-called 'male' tanks – took pot-luck over their heavy weaponry but ended with what proved a more effective weapon than the 'pom-pom' for their 'pot-shots'. These 'long' 6-pounder guns were, however, in short supply and still in demand for the Royal Navy. Consequently, a new version was designed. Designated officially as the Ordnance Quick Firing 6-pounder six hundredweight Mark I, it had the advantage of being considerably shorter (by 112.7cm) than its predecessor. Combat experience had shown the latter to be easily clogged by mud as it traversed the shell-torn battlefields and prone to suffer damage from buildings both in the line and in the advance to starting positions.[45]

The choice of main armament of the 'female' tanks was also influenced to some degree by war production issues. In September 1916, the first machine-gun armed 'female' tanks had carried four .303 Vickers Mark 1 Machine Guns, together with approximately 31,000 rounds of .303 ammunition. Each Vickers had a rate of fire of 450 rounds per minute and combat experience undoubtedly demonstrated the effectiveness of these Vickers machine-gun armed tanks.[46] However, the Vickers was replaced in later Marks by the Lewis and Hotchkiss guns – each of which had a considerably reduced rate of fire and were, strictly speaking, automatic rifles rather than machine-guns. This seemingly retrograde step was actually a result of a variety of more sophisticated factors at work than any superficial analysis might suggest.

The Vickers as a 'medium' machine-gun weighing over 18 kilograms and, therefore, less man-portable than the alternatives, might be considered as the ideal armament for the tank. However, it was a weapon in growing demand as the BEF developed increasingly sophisticated tactics for its use (including employment of the guns in an 'indirect' or 'barrage fire' role),[47] whilst its use of belt-fed ammunition presented some

---

44 Capt. B.H. Liddell Hart, *The Tanks: The History of the Royal Tank Regiment and its Predecessors Heavy Branch Machine Gun Corps, Tank Corps and Royal Tank Corps 1914-1945. Volume One: 1914-1939* (London, 1959), p. 45.
45 David Fletcher, *British Mark IV Tank* (Oxford, 2012), p. 10.
46 One especially successful occasion was the work of D14, commanded by Second Lieutenant C.E. Storey, in the capture of Gird Trench, near Gueudecourt, on 26 September 1916, when over 400 yards of trench were capture and eight officers and 362 men were taken prisoner. See Hammond, 'Theory and Practice of Tank Co-Operation', pp. 83-4.
47 For more on the Vickers' burgeoning use, see Chris McCarthy, 'Nobody's Child: A Brief History of the Tactical Use of Vickers Machine-guns in the British Army, 1914- 1918',

stowage problems which certainly did not exist in the case of the 47- and 96-round drum magazines for the Lewis, for example. The gun-housings or 'sponsons' for the machine-gun armed Marks I, II and III, consequently, had to be very large to accommodate the water-cooled Vickers and its ammunition. Other weapon options negated the need for this, and the intention of standardising on one type of machine-gun was sensible.

However, the decision to switch to the Lewis Gun seems to have been principally based on lobbying by Lieutenant-Colonel Christopher Baker-Carr who, having established the BEF's Machine-Gun School at St. Omer in 1914, transferred to the tank arm as a battalion commander at the time of the force's expansion in late 1916, early 1917. The Lewis had technical issues when mounted in tanks that did not manifest themselves when in use in infantry or air combat. It was also, like the Vickers, in heavy demand elsewhere when selected for use in tanks. Nevertheless, it remained in tank service throughout 1917.[48] The Hotchkiss Portable machine gun, Mark I*,[49] by contrast, was originally intended as a light automatic weapon for cavalry units. Consequently, with the decline in the role of cavalry, significant numbers of these weapons were available for use in the Medium A 'Whippet', Mark V and Mark V* Marks. The production of semi-rigid steel ammunition belts consisting of linked 3-round strips, ensured one of its principle shortcomings identified in earlier trials was overcome.

With the Mark V's introduction in 1918, the 105-hp Daimler was replaced by a 150-hp Ricardo engine. This more powerful engine with its improved transmission system proved more capable of driving a 30 tonne tank and meant 'whereas one could walk more or less comfortably to keep pace with a Mark IV, one had to quicken one's step to keep up with [the Mark V]'.[50] But it too had its flaws. The new engine was noisier,[51] but the chief fault was that the radiators drew their air from outside the tank instead of from within. This considerably aggravated the poor conditions inside the tank, the engine producing both heat and carbon monoxide gas, which did not disperse rapidly in the confined interior.[52] Further problems arose when tanks had done many miles without their engines being overhauled. According to a report

---

Imperial War Museum Review, No. 8, 1993, and Paul Cornish, *Machine-Guns and the Great War* (Barnsley, 2009).
48 Fletcher, *British Mark IV Tank*, p. 10.
49 For example, IWM FIR 8083, Hotchkiss Machine Gun Mk 1*, <http://www.iwm.org.uk/collections/item/object/ 30032989> accessed 6 November 2013. 'The Mk I* version was produced for use in tanks … [and] replaced the original wooden butt with a pistol grip, and could feed cartridges from "belts" made from short, linked strips, each containing 3 cartridges, as well as from the standard Hotchkiss 30 round strip.'
50 Capt. D.E. Hickey, *Rolling into Action: Memoirs of a Tank Corps Section Commander* (London, 1936), p. 199.
51 The new engine had poppet valves instead of the sleeve-valves in earlier models. Hickey, *Rolling into Action*, pp. 191-2.
52 Fletcher, *Landships*, p. 35.

on operations towards the end of August 1918, large amounts of exhaust fumes got into the tanks 'owing to warping of the exhaust pipes and loosening of the joints generally'.[53] The Mark V (and its 'sister' tank the Mark V*) demonstrate clearly that in matters of tank design, as in other areas of warfare, the BEF's learning experience was not a consistent one.

So far, the focus has been on the way in which the technological limitations of the tank's engine, transmission systems and weaponry imposed on its crew's ability to fight. But other factors were important influences on their combat effectiveness. Because tanks had to operate in action with their flaps and loopholes closed, the crew were isolated:

> Nothing could be seen outside, nothing could be heard, while inside one half-shaded festoon lamp gave an eerie murky glimmer in the stygian gloom. The walls represented the limit of one's world and the crew of eight the population; one was completely isolated, existence depending on the skill of the driver and the wits of the officer. The tanks on the left and right might be seen but they existed merely as other worlds …[54]

Not surprisingly, 'In these conditions the crews fought [in] each action as a separate entity, relying on the mechanical efficiency of the machine and their own ready wits and stout hearts, and it is little wonder therefore that thoughts were directed mainly on self-interest rather than on broader tactical issues.'[55]

This sense of isolation was increased by the lack of a means for tank-to-tank communication. There were no radios and few attempts at visual signalling were effective. Command and control was, as a consequence, a particular difficulty and section and company commanders frequently followed their units into action on foot or on horseback, or rode inside one of their unit's tanks and communicated face-to-face and verbally with individual tank commanders during the action. It is surely a matter of considerable irony that Tank Corps officers found the horse so useful in the more mobile battles of 1918.[56]

---

53 TNA WO 95/113, '2nd Tank Battalion. Report on Operations of 23rd August, 1918', 25 August 1918.
54 TMARL, RH86 TC, Box 2, P.C.S. Hobart, 'Cambrai: A Complete Narrative'.
55 Documents Archive, Imperial War Museums, London, 72/7/1, Major-General H.L. Birks Papers, CAMBRAI and the attack on FLESQUIERES RIDGE.
56 One Tank Corps officer doing this provided the tank arm with its fourth Victoria Cross winner of the war. Lieutenant-Colonel Richard Annesley West DSO MC, Commanding 6th (Light) Tank Battalion, was killed during the morning of 2 September 1918 while forward with the infantry. West (who was on horseback) was present when a German counter-attack was launched. He rallied the British infantry and rode up and down in front of them giving encouragement. The counter-attack was defeated but West was killed by machine-gun fire. See Maj. R.F.G. Maurice (ed.), *The Tank Corps Book of Honour* (London, 1919), p. 73.

Practical Considerations in British Tank Operations 45

For the crews themselves, with the flaps closed, their vision of the battlefield was severely limited. As one crew member described:

> There were reflectors and sight-holes in the armour-plating through which to peep when the port-holes were closed. In the roof of the cabin in front, there was a hole for a small periscope. But in spite of these, one could see very little of what was going on outside, unless one made use of the port-holes and revolver loop-holes.[57]

In addition, the tank's rhomboidal shape meant that the commander and driver's vision to left or right was restricted by the protruding track 'horns'. Consequently, the former relied heavily on the four gunners (two to each sponson, on either side of the tank) to provide additional information on targets, etc. Again, the tank's internal communication problems had to be overcome: 'You couldn't talk to anyone inside a tank. You had to shout in their ear. There was a tremendous racket – not from the engine … but from the tracks and the rollers going round and the secondary gears.'[58] Although some Mark Vs were provided with speaking tubes, generally tank crews operated in conditions that greatly hindered their work as a cohesive unit.[59]

The gunners themselves were not in a significantly better position than the driver and commander regarding knowledge of the battle's progress:

> You could see nothing except just that little bit where the gun goes out. You could see nothing else when you were inside the tank … We had a limited view just along the sights of the gun. All we saw was their trench more or less. You couldn't tell whether you were shooting at anybody or not when you first went in. You fired generally along their trenches on each side.[60]

Such remarks help to explain to some extent occasions when British infantry suffered 'friendly fire' from tanks operating in their vicinity.[61] In order to make

---

57 Hickey, *Rolling into Action*, p. 50.
58 IWM Sound, 9752, Reel 8, Dillon interview.
59 LHCMA, Fuller Papers, I/TS/I/93, G.T.29/3/2, 'BATTLE NOTES No. 2. The following Notes have been compiled as the result of the experiences gained in the Tank Operations with the Australian Corps on July 4th 1918 at HAMEL. 60 Mark V Tanks took part in the Operation', 13 July 1918.
60 IWM Sound, 11042, Reel 4, Eric Potten interview.
61 One example occurred on the first occasion tanks were used in battle on 15 September 1916. When 47th Division attacked, one tank opened fire on the men of 1/6th London Regiment. See TNA, WO 95/2729. Another occurred at Ribécourt on 20 November 1917 during the battle of Cambrai when men of 9th Norfolks were also fired on by tanks helping them to clear the village. On this occasion, however, the infantry brigade commander was keen to stress that the tanks were not to blame. TNA, WO 95/1619 '71st Infantry Brigade No. G. 1455', 30 November 1917.

effective use of the 6-pounder guns with which the 'male' tanks were equipped, it was again necessary to stop the tank. However, to avoid German artillery fire, tanks fired on the move as far as possible. Even firing the gun was complicated by the noise in the tank:

> [You'd] more or less open the breach, put the shell in, close the breach and then you'd put your hands on the gun because when you were in a tank you didn't know whether it was your gun or the one on the other side [firing]. You put your hand on the breach block … and when it fired, it threw your hand off. Then you [knew you] had to reload it.[62]

Last but by no means least, it should also be mentioned that bullets or shell fragments striking the tank's exterior could cause splinters of hot, sharp metal (known as 'splash') to break off the inside walls. Consequently, many crew members in the first actions suffered eye or facial injuries. To counter this, crews were issued with steel, leather and chain mail face masks. These masks had eye slits which, when worn, could only have served to further inhibit the crew member's vision and could hardly have been conducive to a good awareness of events on the battlefield.[63]

The Cycle of Combat Experience

Given the difficulties previously outlined, it might seem even more remarkable that, in the course of a little over two years, British tank tactics developed, based on the use of tanks in combat, from an initial uncertainty about their possibilities to a sophisticated approach in the final months of the war. This degree of sophistication was such that different tank Marks were frequently used for different objectives and for tasks appropriate to their strengths and shortcomings. They were also used in a variety of roles as weapons of exploitation, mechanized supply carriers, armoured personnel carriers and mobile forward communication centres. The variety of roles in which tanks were employed and the occasions of their successful employment meant the tank became an important element (but not the key element) in the BEF's ability to achieve battlefield success in mid- to late-1918.

---

62   IWM Sound, 11042, Reel 4, Potten interview.
63   These masks are described in Eric Potten interview, IWM Sound, 11042, Reel 4, and IWM Sound, 10600, Reel 12, John Wainwright interview, and are clearly visible in contemporary photographs of tank crews. The IWM collection also contains excellent examples of these masks. See, for example, IWM EQU 1654, face mask, anti-splinter, tank crew<http://www.iwm.org.uk/collections/item/object/30013368> accessed 17 October 2013.

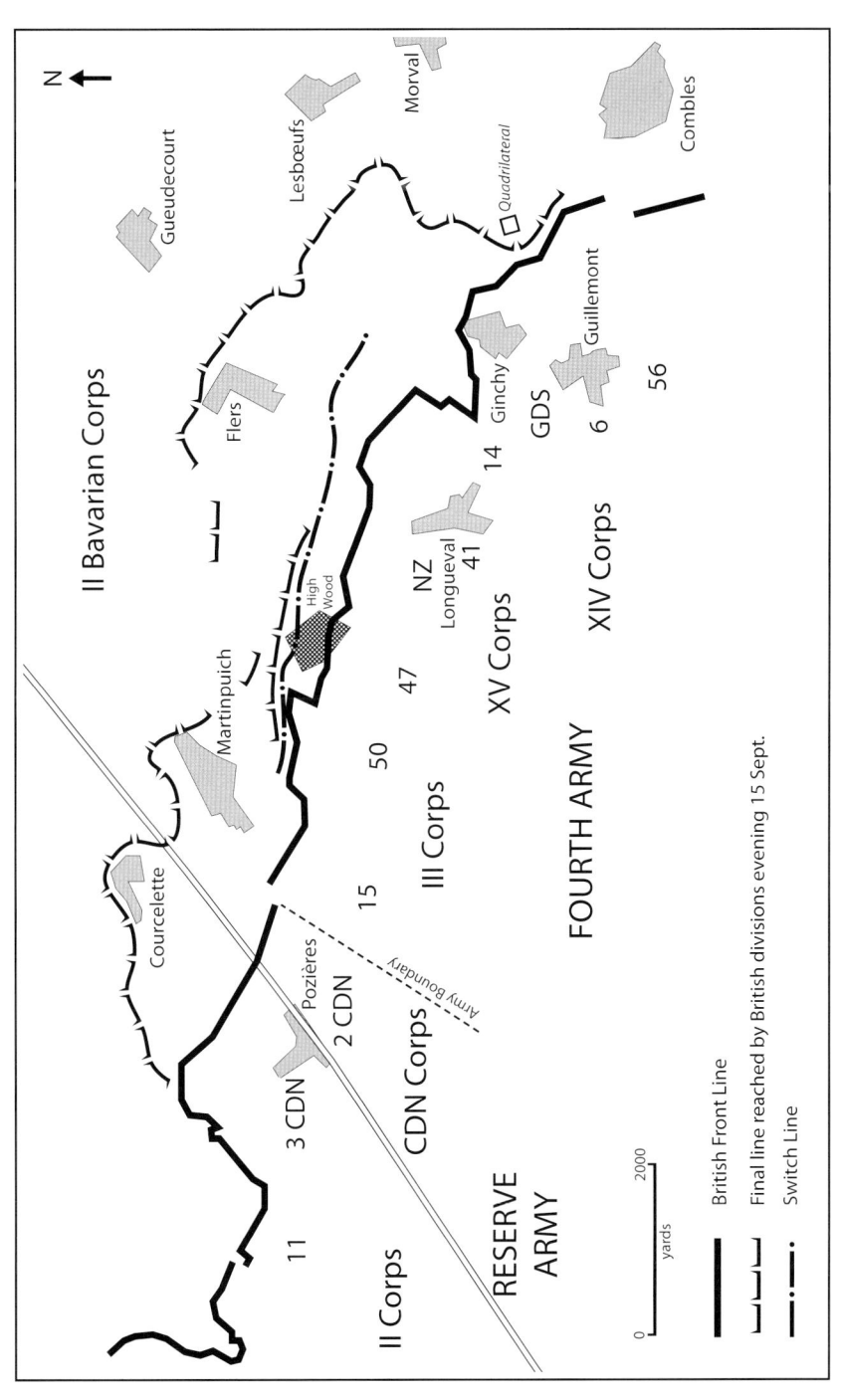

Practical Considerations in British Tank Operations 47

Map 1: Tanks at Flers–Courcelette, 15 September 1916

These developments, together with the introduction of appropriate equipment with which tanks could be 'accessorized'[64] to overcome any battlefield scenario they were likely to encounter, were all based on a continuous review cycle distilling the lessons of the fighting. Perhaps it is more accurate to depict this one cycle as a series of cogs – each in contact with the other. One cog was tactical, another mechanical, another related to the prioritization of the tank against other mechanical means of making war, and so on. Each turned and had an impact on the others.

This cycle of analysis and change began after the first occasion of tank use on 15 September 1916 when a survey of infantry commanders was instigated by GHQ, ascertaining their views on the performance of tanks.[65] These were eventually summarized by Lancelot Kiggell, Haig's Chief of Staff, in a pamphlet entitled *GHQ Notes on the Use of Tanks*, which was circulated throughout the BEF.[66] From the occasion of their first use, commanders of all formations from army down to battalion were encouraged to report on the action of any tanks assigned to co-operate with their unit in operations, just as they were invited to pass observations on, and suggest improvements in, the performance of the artillery and other arms. From these after-action reports, conclusions (although not necessarily the 'correct' ones) were drawn and incorporated into subsequent training and doctrinal publications. This was a sound and valuable process. However, it should not be taken as implying rigid, centralized control of tactical development.

Thus, for example, when Kiggell's *Notes* were circulated they were specifically designed as a device to ensure that information concerning the strengths and shortcomings of the new weapon was disseminated as widely as possibly amongst formations of the BEF – to inform and educate but not to dictate. It was information based on combat experience and was not theoretical. These *Notes* constituted the first steps in learning the lessons of tank fighting and the beginning of a continual cycle of action, review and refinement that was maintained until well after the war had ended.

When, at the end of 1916, the information in *GHQ Notes on the Use of Tanks* was refined and enhanced before incorporation into one of the official pamphlets (the 'S.S.' series) GHQ produced to disseminate tactical lessons throughout the BEF – in this

---

64 Such accessories included fascines, 'cribs', 'spuds' and unditching beams. Each is described and its purpose explained in Hammond, 'Theory and Practice of Tank Co-Operation'.
65 See TNA, WO 95/1913, Maj.-Gen. A.A. Montgomery to 15th Division, 19 September 1916. Whilst Trevor Pidgeon in his detailed study of the tank operations of 15 September 1916 sees Rawlinson as the survey's initiator, Byng, commanding Canadian Corps, also submitted a report on tank operations to Reserve Army HQ on 21 September. Presumably, therefore, the original request for a survey came from GHQ. TNA, WO 95/1047, 'Canadian Corps Report on Operations of Tanks', 21 September 1916. See also Trevor Pidgeon, *The Tanks at Flers: An Account of the First Use of Tanks in War at the Battle of Flers-Courcelette, The Somme, 15th September 1916* (Cobham, 1995), p. 200.
66 TNA, WO 158/236, 'GHQ Notes on the Use of Tanks', 5 October 1916. What appears to be another draft can be found in TNA, CAB 45/200.

case, *S.S. 135. Instructions for the Training of Divisions for Offensive Action*[67] – this might be said to be the point at which tanks finally joined the Army. Although concerned in general terms with the lessons of the Somme, *S.S. 135* contained a specific section regarding 'Action of Tanks'.[68] It also offered a structure for framing plans and operation orders, thereby covering the likely need for production of instructions relating to tanks in the projected battle.[69] *S.S. 135*'s essential quality was the practical application of lessons learned and it was held in high regard for this amongst divisional, brigade and battalion officers.[70] From this point forward, training and information concerning tanks was disseminated by the same means that doctrine and training publications informed the BEF concerning other aspects of its operational art. Indeed, it is possible to trace the clear path of this tactical guidance during the course of the war from its origins in the pre-war *Field Service Regulations* to the final doctrinal pamphlet *S.S. 135. The Division in the Attack* produced in November 1918.[71]

Hand-in-hand with this went the necessary process whereby the performance of the weapon itself – its mechanical, technical and environmental performance – was reported, reviewed and refined. For this purpose, the tank arm was responsible for the introduction of what became known as Tank Battle History Sheets, which each crew or its commander was required to complete after a tank had been engaged in action. The earliest version of this simple, but important, instrument was termed a 'Battle History Form' and was attached, as an appendix, to a document produced by Fuller in February 1917 entitled *Training Note No. 16*.[72] Whilst *S.S. 135* gradually circulated throughout the BEF, Fuller's *Note* represented the first clear distillation of the tank arm's own views on tank employment in battle. The Battle History Form, though actually only a typical variant of the 'instruments of analysis and evaluation' developed

---

67 *S.S. 135. Instructions for the Training of Divisions for Offensive Action* (London, December 1916).
68 *S.S. 135*, Section XIV, pp. 48-50.
69 *S.S. 135*, Section I, pp. 4-6.
70 'A really instructive Pamphlet dealing with the offensive and defensive action of a Division in modern warfare was issued around this time, and to the relief of all concerned it remained with very slight alterations a standard work for the Army.' Lt.-Col. W.C. Oates, *The Sherwood Foresters in the Great War 1914-1918: The 2/8th Battalion* (Nottingham, 1920), p. 89.
71 The author acknowledges with grateful thanks the invaluable assistance of Dr Andy Simpson regarding the development of British tactical doctrine and the applicability of the pre-war *Field Service Regulations* throughout the war. See Andy Simpson, *Directing Operations: British Corps Command on the Western Front 1914-18* (Stroud, 2006).
72 LHCMA, Fuller Papers, I/TS1/1/6, Training Note No. 16, Appendix A: Battle History Form. However, individual tank action reports had been produced by tank commanders as early as November 1916. See, for example, 'BATTLE HISTORY OF TANK NO. 544 – COMMANDED BY LT. H.W. HITCHCOCK.', 13 November 1916, in Monty Rossiter, 'A Tank at the Battle of the Ancre', *Stand To! The Journal of the Western Front Association*, No. 67, April 2003, pp. 30-31.

within the BEF in order to 'learn the lessons of the fighting', was to prove valuable to the senior commanders of the tank arm and, indirectly, the wider BEF.[73]

Fuller, as chief staff officer of what eventually became the Tank Corps, is unlikely to be remembered by posterity for such a routine document as *Training Note No. 16* and, yet, documents like this and his training notes issued prior to the Battle of Cambrai[74] helped enormously in the conduct of British tank operations and demonstrate his capabilities as a staff officer rather than a military theorist. What was exceptional about Fuller's staff work was not that it differed from the general trend set by staff of formations throughout the BEF by adopting fundamentally different techniques, but rather in the quality of what he produced and its applicability to the task in hand.

Of importance also was the work of the Tank Corps' own intelligence staff, chief amongst whom was Captain Elliot Hotblack.[75] The confidential reports of these men (and of Hotblack in particular), which were based on first-hand knowledge of the operations they were related to, were another very important mechanism, ensuring that essential technological and tactical suggestions were fed back as part of the continuing development cycle. By way of example, one such report on the fighting at Fontaine on 23 November 1917 during the Cambrai Offensive had a direct and clear influence on aspects of the Mark V*'s development prior to its appearance in 1918.[76]

---

73 Equally useful was a Daily Tank Log (Tank Corps Form TK22) in which crews recorded information relating to each tank's mechanical performance. There is an example in Mitchell, *Tank Warfare*, p. 103.

74 These can be found at TNA, WO 95/92, Training Note 'TANK AND INFANTRY OPERATIONS WITHOUT METHODICAL ARTILLERY PREPARATION' and 'NOTES ON INFANTRY AND TANK OPERATIONS', 30 October 1917. The former is also reproduced in full in *O.H., 1917*, Vol. 3, Appendix 9A, pp. 348-54.

75 Captain [later Major-General] Frederick Elliot ('Boots') Hotblack (1887-1979). A brewer before the war, Hotblack joined the Norfolk Regiment in 1915 prior to gaining a special appointment to the intelligence staff in France because of his skills as a linguist. He transferred to the Heavy Branch Machine Gun Corps (HBMGC) in 1916. He was awarded both the DSO and Bar and MC and Bar and was wounded five times in the course of his war service. Described by Fuller as a 'mixture of Abelard and Marshal Ney' (Bvt.-Col. J.F.C. Fuller, *Tanks in the Great War, 1914-1918* (London, 1920), p. xv), and by another Tank Corps colleague as a natural soldier whose 'sense of duty, his standard of discipline, his extreme efficiency, and his astonishing courage were an invaluable asset' ((Hon.) Evan Charteris, *H.Q., Tanks 1917-1918* (Privately printed, 1920), p. 88). His reconnaissance work, conducted at enormous personal risk, produced several important and influential reports on operations. See also Jim Beach, 'British Intelligence and German Tanks, 1916-1918,' *War in History*, 14 (2007), pp. 454-76.

76 The Mark V* tank developed in late 1917/early 1918 was provided with machine gun ball mounts on its rear cab. These machine guns could then be used against infantry in the upper storeys of houses. This had been a particular problem in village fighting during the Cambrai battle. See Fletcher, *The British Tanks, 1915-19*, p. 140.

Practical Considerations in British Tank Operations 51

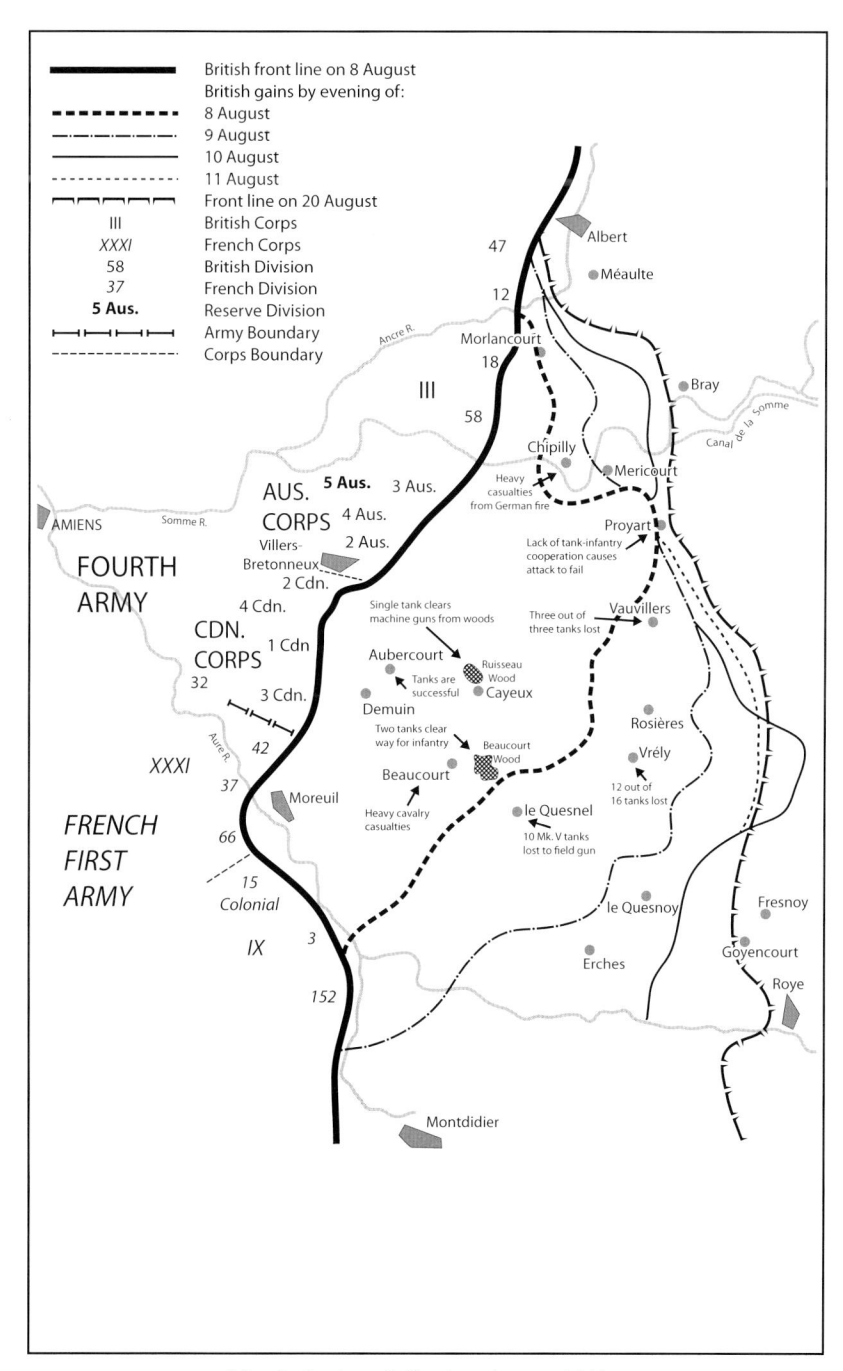

Map 2: Amiens Offensive, August 1918

The Planning and Preparation of Operations

An important constraint on tank operations, until recently given inadequate consideration in the historiography of the British tank arm, was the necessary preparatory work required prior to any tank operation. In particular, there was the detailed tactical reconnaissance both in front of *and* behind the British lines which was intended to ensure the tanks had clear and suitable routes into action. When a 'set-piece' attack was planned, its location was communicated down the chain of command as far as Tank Brigade HQs. Brigade Intelligence Officers, in turn, directed Battalion and Company Reconnaissance Officers to undertake detailed reconnaissance. This could be as much as three weeks or, as in the case of 4th Tank Brigade at Amiens in August 1918, only six days' beforehand and, in late 1918, an even shorter period still.[77]

This tactical reconnaissance may itself have been preceded by exploratory or strategic reconnaissance undertaken sometime before any action was contemplated and which was, therefore, to a degree, speculative. It examined such things as topography and geology as well as the enemy's defences.[78] Until the period of mobile warfare in late 1918, planning for most set-piece tank operations also featured this preparatory phase.

Immediately prior to the battle, routes for tanks to follow into action had to be marked out using tapes. Because of the necessity of disguising their presence, tank movement to start positions prior to the opening of an attack was conducted under cover of darkness. This necessitated provision of definite navigation aids for the tank commanders to follow and the elaborate and extremely hazardous laying of tapes by tank unit Reconnaissance Officers.

These preparations are an indication of the extent to which the tank arm itself accepted the restrictions imposed by 'trench warfare' and conformed to them. These rigid operational constraints were abandoned when opportunities arose in the latter half of 1918, but there was still a return to the more structured preparation of operations in planning for the set-piece attacks on the Drocourt-Quéant and Hindenburg Lines (September 1918) and the crossing of the River Selle (17-20 October). This was as much because of the nature of tanks available for operational use as a return to the commonly-understood methods developed in the trench-to-trench fighting of 1917.

---

77 Colin Hardy, 'Intelligence and Reconnaissance in the Tank Corps and its Predecessors on the Western Front, 1916-18' (unpublished MA diss., Birmingham University, 2013), p. 36.
78 This breakdown of phases of operational reconnaissance is well detailed in Hardy, 'Intelligence and Reconnaissance in the Tank Corps'.

Supply, Salvage and Logistics

Two other factors that constrained tank operations must be mentioned here. Both relate especially to 1918. The first is the question of supply and salvage, whilst the second is concerned with logistics. Production and supply problems undoubtedly had some influence on tank employment during the final war-winning offensives of the period known as 'the Hundred Days' (8 August – 11 November 1918). Repeated serious delays in the provision of spare parts for tanks had been an inevitable consequence of the tank's relatively lowly status in the 'production pecking order'.[79] Frequently the problem was not in the *quantities* of general spares being provided but in the provision of particular specialist items. The absence of key spares had already helped prompt the tank arm to create its own salvage units for the recovery of whole or part machines from the battlefield. By September 1918 the problem was severe.[80]

However, although the rate of repair of seriously damaged tanks rose rapidly in mid- to late-1918 (from 18 per week in late August to between 20 and 30 in early September and between 33 and 35 in late October),[81] it was increasingly the case that men normally engaged on repairs were transferred instead to the task of salvaging parts from abandoned machines because of the acute shortages of spares.[82] These two factors – the absence of sufficient supplies of all spares and the inadequate numbers of men available for both salvage *and* repair work – meant fewer tanks were available than might otherwise have been the case for operations in late 1918.

Of course, the Tank Corps' spares problem during the First World War was not unique. A recent study emphasizes that 'the ranging and scaling of parts for any equipment is difficult, especially when it is constantly modified,' as it was in the case of the First World War tank. It was 'a hugely complex problem to solve and remains so

---

79 See Childs, *A Peripheral Weapon?*, passim.
80 So severe, indeed, that the Tank Corps' chief technical officer, Lieutenant-Colonel Frank Searle, was pleading for spares even at the cost of production. See minutes of the sixth meeting of the Tank Board, 15 September 1918 in TNA, MUN4/6400. According to the official history of the Ministry of Munitions: 'The wastage of tanks [in the fighting of mid- to late-1918] had been five times as great as was anticipated, so that the stocks of spares were dangerously depleted.' Ministry of Munitions, *History*, Volume XII, Part III, p. 69.
81 These figures are quoted in Tim Travers, 'Could the Tanks of 1918 Have Been War-Winners for the British Expeditionary Force?', *Journal of Contemporary History*, 27 (1992), pp. 389-406.
82 Bryn Hammond, '"After Amiens": Technology and tactics in the British Expeditionary Force during the Advance to Victory, August – November 1918' in Gary Sheffield & Peter Gray (eds.), *Changing War: The British Army, the Hundred Days Campaign and the Birth of the Royal Air Force, 1918* (London, 2013), pp. 55-67.

even in the modern world where the British Army is committed to a very small scale deployment in comparison to that of the First World War'.[83]

Had more tanks been available in 'the Hundred Days', there were always very significant logistical barriers to their deployment to overcome. The influence of logistical factors on tank employment in the war's last months cannot be overstated.[84] An example to illustrate one aspect of this important subject is given here. The relatively rapid advance achieved by the BEF (compared with offensive operations of previous years) placed heavy emphasis on the re-establishment of railways. Whilst tanks could (and did) 'trek' (in the terminology of the period) under their own power along roads in the advance's wake before going into action, mechanical wear and tear (especially on their weakest link, the tracks) demanded that, wherever possible, tanks be transported by railway to assembly positions behind a newly solidified front-line. The repair or construction of such railways took time and made heavy demands on available manpower. Consequently, this practically ensured that tanks could only be deployed on a large scale in set-piece battles against established positions.

Conclusion

This chapter set out in the first instance to suggest that some of the often neglected aspects of British tank operations limited or otherwise defined the nature of those actions. Many factors relating to matters such as technology and environment dictated what was possible in combat, which should remind historians of the absolute necessity of engaging in detail with practical considerations of the type outlined here when advancing theoretical arguments about the BEF's use of weapons technology during the First World War.

In this connection, personal experience accounts (including oral history interviews), which are frequently considered to be flawed and partial views of strategy, high policy and the conduct and events of battle, hold real value as historical sources. The descriptions of 'hands on' use of weapons and other technologies are verifiable through examination of this equipment where it survives as, for example, museum exhibits.[85] Genuine insight regarding the practical limitations of a piece of 'kit' can only be provided by those who employed this equipment in battle. Theoretical considerations divorced from these practical factors are valueless if they rely on a misapprehension of a technology's capabilities. For this we can only *depend* on the words and opinions of those who actually used it.

---

83 John Pratt, 'An Analysis of the Effectiveness of Tank Maintenance, Repair and Recovery Work on the Western Front 1916 to 1918', unpublished MA diss., Birmingham University, 2013.
84 TMARL, Maj. S.G. Brockbank, 'History of the Central Workshops,' Chap. 2, p. 2.
85 Examples of the British main battle tanks of the war survive in the collections of the Tank Museum, Bovington (Marks I, II, III and Medium 'A'), the Museum of Lincolnshire Life, Lincoln (Mark IV), and Imperial War Museums, London (Mark V).

Practical Considerations in British Tank Operations 55

When considering tank deployment on the Western Front, it is necessary to emphasize here that factors affecting this were considerably more complex than the simple arithmetic of available tank numbers in France.[86] These factors have especial relevance to the question of whether tanks could have been used 'more efficiently' and made a greater contribution to an earlier and less costly Allied victory. Take, for example, the question of the number of British tanks available to the BEF in France on 12 August 1918 (the fifth day of the Amiens offensive), which forms part of Professor Tim Travers' consideration of the tank as a 'war-winning weapon' in 1918.

Although Travers is correct in identifying that significant numbers of tanks were still available to the BEF in France on the 12 August 1918, practical considerations do much to explain why they were not on hand for use on that front at that time. Firstly, and perhaps most obviously, neither GHQ nor the Tank Corps really had any intention of putting all their eggs in one basket by employing the entire strength of the British tank arm in a single operation. Instead, the four uncommitted tank battalions (7th, 9th, 11th and 12th) remained under the orders of 1st and 2nd Tank Brigades and were deployed in other sectors of the front held by the BEF.[87] One battalion, the 9th, had recently been in action with French units on 23 July.[88] Secondly, of these battalions, two (7th and 12th) were still equipped with the Mark IV whose obsolescence Elles had identified in mid-1917 and of whose shortcomings GHQ were certainly aware. Thirdly, even had the desire to deploy all the British tanks available in France in this initial offensive existed, the problems of transporting, supplying, and disguising the presence of, such a large number of additional tanks would have been immense. Cambrai had demonstrated this. Finally, as (presumably) an Army Reserve, according to Travers' vision of their possible employment, these tanks would have been held back some distance behind the British lines and, therefore, issues relating to their durability would presumably have affected their reliability in battle – especially had they been required to 'trek' forward several thousand yards before use.[89]

In order to make successful use of tanks, the BEF's senior commanders needed to educate themselves and the men of the formations they commanded about these factors and to give them due consideration in their operational planning. As in all other areas of operations conducted by the BEF, the process by which the 'lessons of the fighting' relating to tanks were learned was through the use of analytical means such as after-action reports and the more specialised Tank Battle History Sheets.

---

86 See Travers, 'Could the Tanks of 1918 Have Been War-Winners?', pp. 391-2.
87 Liddell Hart, *The Tanks*, pp. 177-8. Liddell Hart erroneously states that 1st Tank Brigade was not employed, as it 'was in the process of re-equipment and retraining with Mark Vs'. In fact, 7th and 12th Tank Battalions were equipped with Mark IVs until the end of the war.
88 TMARL, RH: 86 TC 9 Bn 237-253 [Courage] '5th Tank Brigade REPORT on OPERATIONS with IXth FRENCH CORPS. South of MOREUIL – July 23rd 1918', 29 July 1918.
89 Travers, 'Could the Tanks of 1918 Have Been War-Winners?', pp. 402-3.

As thorough as the process of operational analysis was, the education of the BEF concerning those aspects of past operations that had proved successful, and which might therefore prove successful in future operations, was neither clear nor straightforward. Nor could it be. Mistakes made in 1916 were repeated in 1918, and what proved useful in one context was irrelevant elsewhere. Finally, and above all, it is important to emphasize that the resilience and rugged adaptability of their German opponents does much to explain why there was never going to be a simple formula guaranteeing British success in operations – whether they involved tanks or not.

Acknowledgements

The author would like to thank Dr Andy Simpson, Mark Cook, Alan Jeffreys and Peter Hart for their assistance in the preparation of this paper, Colin Hardy and Major John Pratt for permission to refer to aspects of their recent Masters research, which greatly informed a more detailed understanding on my part of the issues of reconnaissance and tank supply and maintenance.

3

The Development of French Tank Warfare on the Western Front, 1916-1918

Olivier Lahaie

In August 1914, France had seventy-nine cavalry regiments in the field under the command of ten cavalry divisions. Most of these divisions were gathered within two corps.[1] During the first two months of the conflict, they conducted harassing reconnaissance and security missions, with occasional clashes with German Uhlans taking place. With the onset of the military stalemate, and the emergence of trench warfare, the French Army, too, was faced with the challenge of how to restore mobility to the battlefield. As a result of the new battlefield conditions, the tank, in the modern sense of the word,[2] appeared as one response. The purpose of this chapter is not to add to the many histories on the invention of the tank,[3] called at this time 'land battleship' in the French Army, but to explain the role played by Colonel (subsequently General) Jean Baptiste Estienne. This highly significant figure promoted tank development in France from its first achievements through to victory, in particular through the first Schneider and Saint-Chamond medium tanks.

The growing power of fire and the importance given to the infantrymen marked a turning point in the methods of fighting. Within this particular framework of trench warfare, in which machine guns and barbed wire prevailed, strategists understood

---

1 'N° spécial L'Arme blindée cavalerie', *Revue Historique des Armées*, 2/1984, p. 3.
2 Some historians would still hesitate to refer to the Schneider and Saint-Chamond vehicles as 'tanks' because they had no traversable turret. It could be argued that the term 'assault gun' is more accurate and, because of their weight, it would be more appropriate to consider them both as 'medium tanks' rather than 'heavy tanks', which was their designation between 1917 and 1918 when referred to in conjunction with 'light tanks'.
3 It could be reasonably asserted that the tank was developed on both sides of the Channel at the same time and in secret. Armour cooperation began in 1916, just after the introduction of this new weapon on the battlefield by the British.

that the horse cavalry had come to an end. Even the infantry experienced many difficulties in crossing barbed-wire defences under direct fire. Breaking the enemy defensive lines was at stake at this time for the 3rd Bureau of the *GQG* (*Grand Quartier Général*). The French thought extensive major attacks could enable them to achieve their objective.[4] Then the strategists decided that the breakthrough should be made by the cavalry units or other appropriate means. Indeed, technical developments had been continuous since the industrial revolution and the war made it possible to enhance this process further.

During the Artois and Champagne offensive operations in 1915, the artillery units showed their inability to provide the expected breakthrough because of, according to one French historian:

> the weak effectiveness of the explosive devices and artillery shells, as well as the one of the projectiles launched from the trench mortars. They were initially supposed to destroy the barbed wire entanglements through little targets, which resulted in major preparatory fire and large quantities of projectiles used. As a consequence, it required nearly one thousand shots of 75 mm shells, in order to open a 20 to 25 m breach in a standard barbed wire entanglement at a distance of 4 km.[5]

The major preparations of artillery fire impeded any hasty attack and led to heavy losses among the infantry. In addition, the enemy forces had time not only to assemble troops, but also to plug the gaps in their positions. The French Army's senior leadership considered, therefore, that 'technology was the only efficient way to contribute to the tactical mobility and movement required for victory'.[6]

At this point in the war, the death toll was very high for almost no territorial gain.[7] The greatest hope was the internal combustion engine, which had already been used in armoured cars and planes since the beginning of the twentieth century. Several inventions designed for shearing or crushing barbed wire were about to be proposed to a 'High Committee for Inventions', whose chairman was Paul Painlevé. But the more or less motorized and armoured prototypes (which were rather ineffective) were unable to pass beyond the stage of experimentation.[8]

---

4   Commandant Michel Goya, *La chair et l'acier: l'invention de la guerre moderne (1914-1918)* (Paris, 2004), p. 334.
5   Roger Pierre Laroussinie, *Mécanique de la victoire: la grande histoire des chars d'assaut* (Paris, 1972), p. 49.
6   Anon., *Traditions et historique de l'Arme Blindée et Cavalerie: tendances d'avenir*, cours d'arme n° 6 (Saumur: École d'application de l'arme blindée et de la cavalerie, 1980), p. 12.
7   In 1914 the French Army suffered more than 300,000 men killed in action, followed by 360,000 in 1915.
8   See, for example, 'Service Historique de la Défense', archives of the Ministry of War (hereafter, SHD – GR), 16 N 2131, 'Compte-rendu de destruction et ratissage des réseaux

Colonel Estienne and his 'Special Artillery'

Fortunately, Colonel Jean Baptiste Estienne (1860-1936) had already carried out studies for a combat vehicle. After his tertiary education at *L'école Polytechnique* (one of the most prestigious engineering schools), Estienne had chosen to join the Artillery. This brilliant and original officer – who could be ill-mannered and disrespectful to the hierarchy – considered mathematics as a form of intellectual entertainment. Taking inspiration from various articles from *La Revue scientifique*, he used science to tackle military questions. After a training period at the foundry in Bourges, 'his spirit found a large field of application to the changes imposed on the Artillery'.[9] At the beginning of the twentieth century, he invented a direction finder and a range finder. He was also the first person to advocate adjustments to artillery fire made by plane. He then developed individual body armour which was shrapnel and bullet proof.[10] Estienne had talked about the implications of barbed wire with fellow officers, who were aware of its use in the Balkan War (1912-13). He told them that not only was the barbed wire cleverly integrated into the defensive system of trenches, but also that means to overcome this obstacle needed to be considered.[11] So, one could believe that the idea of the battle tank came to his mind after these thoughts, as a report of the Artillery Studies and Experiments Inspectorate (*Inspection des études et expériences techniques de l'Artillerie*) claimed in December 1918.[12] However, this seems to have been a mistake. As Estienne explained after the war: 'The new weapon comes from a specific tactic relating to the use of tanks and has nothing to do with the numerous and sometimes very interesting barbed wire destructive devices'.[13]

In fact, Estienne the artilleryman realized as early as 23 August 1914 how devastating automatic weapons fire was against the infantry. Thus, he wrote in Charleroi:

> How can we advance facing machine-guns that we can't see? How can we approach them to look into them? …. How can we attack them to destroy all of them? We have to ensure for the front line fighters a safe, mobile and permanent shelter, from which they could challenge the enemy automatic rifles and defeat them. … Victory will be achieved by the one who will be the first to mount a cannon on a vehicle able to move on any ground.[14]

---

de fils de fer par caterpillars', 4 October 1917. The list of these unsuccessful attempts can be found in Laroussine, *Mécanique de la victoire*, pp. 49-55.
9   Ibid., p. 61.
10 Col. E.R. Ramspacher, Ingénieur général de l'armement (C.R.) Lavirotte, H. Lemarié, P. Beuchon & Col. G. Raphael, *Chars et blindés français* (Paris-Limoges, 1979), pp. 7-9.
11 Laroussinie, *Mécanique de la victoire*, p. 50.
12 Available at SHD – GR 16 N 2131, file 1.
13 Quoted in Laroussinie, *Mécanique de la victoire*, p. 57.
14 Quoted in Anon., 'La naissance des chars français', in *L'Encyclopédie des armes* (Paris, 1984), p. 605.

These ideas were, however, already taking root. At first, this inventive officer had thought to carry the infantrymen on board armoured trailers to ensure their protection. His vision had gradually moved towards an autonomous and protected motorized vehicle, also equipped with weapons. Then, Estienne, who was in command at this time of the 22nd Artillery Battalion in La Somme, came up with an innovative combat vehicle project. In a letter to Generals Maurice Janin[15] and Joseph Joffre, dated 1 December 1915, he wrote: 'I think it is possible to manufacture a mechanized vehicle equipped with a cannon, in order to carry, through any obstacle and under fire, the armed infantry and their equipment, at a speed of 6 km per hour.'[16] Estienne also claimed to have been chosen to develop his project. For its designer indeed, the future combat vehicle had not only to be armoured, to avoid the damage caused by shrapnel and machine-gun fire, but likewise tracked to get out of the mud or craters made by shell bursts.[17] It had also to be armed with a 37 mm cannon to silence strong-points. The 'land battleship' was born. It is interesting to note that it had originally been developed to break the enemy defensive system, which helps explains the concerns of that time.

On 12 December, Estienne was invited to the *GQG* located in Chantilly. He talked with the generals Janin, Philippe Pétain and Noël Édouard de Castelnau, and was received by the commander-in-chief in person. The inventor explained to Joffre the characteristics of the combat vehicle he had designed; he described to him the tactics he expected to use thanks to the arrival of the tank on the battlefield.[18] The commander-in-chief was very interested and decided to send him to Paris in order to look for industrial support. On 20 December, Estienne took advantage of this visit to the French capital to meet Major Ferrus, who was a member of the Automobile Department *(Service Automobile)*. Ferrus introduced him not only to Louis Renault, but above all Eugène Brillié, engineer of the Schneider Company in Le Creusot, who had already developed an experimental tracked vehicle mounted on the Holt Caterpillar. Back at Chantilly, Estienne reported the substance of these talks to Joffre. Brillié's project seemed feasible. Was it not the best way to create surprise on the battlefield, as well as the collapse of a portion of the German line? Needless to say, it would take some time before enough tanks were available to achieve this goal. As the automotive engineers thought it was possible, the project had to proceed. On 7 January 1916, following the suggestion of Estienne, the Under-Secretary to the Artillery *(Sous-secrétariat à l'Artillerie)* was entrusted by Joffre with the project, as well as with a certificate which would allow him to engage in testing. The commander-in-chief

---

15 Janin was then Adjutant-General at the French 'G.Q.G.' of Chantilly and especially responsible for the equipment.
16 Quoted in 'N° spécial L'Arme blindée cavalerie', p. 4.
17 The tracked suspension of the American Baby Holt tractor, used before war in agriculture and in the British heavy Artillery since 1915, had made a big impression on Estienne.
18 Refer to the summary of the presentation of Estienne in 'Collectif, Arme Blindée Cavalerie, de 1916 à nos jours', *Historama hors série* n°9, 1970, p. 42.

gave his agreement for the development of Schneider's project on 18 January.[19] As a result, three different kinds of French tanks were gradually developed: the Schneider and Saint-Chamond medium tanks and, finally, the Renault FT-17 light tank, all of which appeared during the Great War.[20]

On 26 March 1916, Estienne sent a project memorandum on the setting up of land battleship units to *GQG*. In August, he was promoted Brigadier-General. The following month, he was assigned to *GQG* in order to develop and command this new artillery department, which had emerged as a result of the invention of the tank. In September he named it *Artillerie Spéciale* (AS); it later became the 'Assault Artillery'.[21] However, the Automobile Department Directorate (*Direction du Service Automobile*) disapproved of this appointment, as its director had hoped to be tasked with the development of these tanks. Due to this man's disappointment, Estienne was to encounter many material and administrative troubles during the course of his work.

Estienne, who was responsible for the liaison between the armies and the Under-Secretary to the Artillery in everything concerning the land battleships, committed himself in a highly determined fashion to the challenge. After the design and technical development, he had to come up with some tactical ideas for the employment of tanks. In short, Estienne deserves the title of 'father of French tanks'. As far as a tank doctrine was concerned, everything at this point still remained to be created. Without any preconceived ideas, Estienne began his work. He planned to use the tanks on a large front to attack in coordination with the other arms of service. Even if the French high command did believe in the success of the land battleship, it was only assigned at that time tactical objectives (the crossing of German trenches, the capture of observation trenches and, in case of a deeper advance, capture of artillery positions). Indeed, its technical performance and autonomy were limited; therefore, it was not a strategic innovation. The tank was intended to be accompanied – or not – by the infantry, since the purpose was to take advantage of all the opportunities not only to surprise the enemy forces, but also to create a breakthrough by means of offensive shock action.[22] In a speech to the new crews, Estienne also stated:

> I do not want that we call [our vehicles] 'tanks'; we are French and must use French words. They have to be called *chars d'assaut*. In antiquity, the warriors fought on board tanks. You will do so. I have named our branch 'Assault Artillery' because, thanks to their fire power, *les chars* will engage themselves with the first line soldiers, instead of simply providing support to them.[23]

---

19 Ramspacher, et al., *Chars et blindés française*, p. 21.
20 For details on the Renault FT-17, see Tim Gale's chapter in this volume.
21 The abbreviation remained the same, 'A.S.' in French (SA).
22 The idea of the tank, 'especially designed to support Infantry', appeared later in the French Army.
23 Quoted in Laroussinie, *Mécanique de la victoire*, p. 82.

On 26 August 1916, the first memorandum on the tactical use of tanks was not only written by the 3rd Bureau (Planning and Operations) from *GQG*, but also dispatched to the armed forces. This dealt with Estienne's ideas on the subject.

The first tank team was set up on 7 October 1916.[24] On 24 October, Estienne was joined by two officers: the first was Colonel Monhoven, who became his 'Tactical Assistant', while the second was Major Doumenc employed as his 'Technical Assistant'. These two officers were artillerymen: the former came from the Colonial Artillery, the latter had graduated from the *L'école Polytechnique*, just as Estienne and Joffre had. Throughout the war and inside the 81st Heavy Artillery Regiment (*Depot Regiment* in Versailles), small units comparable to the artillery batteries were created (the *SA*), which were equipped with one of the two existing types of tanks, the Schneider and the Saint-Chamond.[25] The Schneider SA, established between 17 November 1916 and 2 June 1917, was numbered from 1 to 20 and constituted in *groupements* (battalions) from I to IV.[26] The Saint-Chamond SA – set up between 8 February 1917 and 1 January 1918 – was numbered from 31 to 42 and divided into groups from X to XIII.[27]

In the early part of 1917, the organization of Special Artillery was as follows: a battalion was composed of four *groups* (companies) and each company gathered four batteries (including one reserve). Each SA was under the command of a captain or a major and was equipped with four tanks. For identification purposes, 'the numbers of the groups were registered in Roman numerals and each battery was identified by an ace from playing cards [drawn with white paint]. Thus, the 1st battery had the Ace of Spades, the 2nd the Ace of Hearts, the 3rd the Ace of Diamonds and the 4th the Ace of Clubs'.[28] The manpower strength of the Schneider team was twelve officers, sixteen non-commissioned officers and 110 soldiers. The Saint-Chamond team was consisted of twelve officers, sixteen non-commissioned officers and 149 soldiers.[29] Each group had a Repair and Supply Platoon (*S.R.R.* in French) equipped with unarmed tanks, which were especially designed to carry equipment. The staff of this platoon was composed of three officers, eight NCOs and eighty-two soldiers.

The first crewmen were composed of volunteers, who gathered on 15 August 1916 in Marly-le-Roi, at a place called *Le Trou d'Enfer* (The Hole of Hell). It was a training centre newly opened to train the staff in driving over the course of two to three weeks. Then, they were sent to another camp in Cercottes[30] to attend manoeuvre and shooting courses. The tanks, which had just left the assembly lines, were also dispatched to this

---

24 Goya, *La chair et l'acier*, p. 337.
25 See below.
26 The three latest SA Schneider (18, 19, and 20) were finally dissolved and re-equipped with Saint-Chamond tanks, thus forming SA 40, 41, 42.
27 Bruno Jurkiewicz, *Les chars français au combat (1917-1918)* (Louviers, n.d.), p. 15.
28 Didier Guenaff & Bruno Jurkiewicz, *Les chars de la victoire: la Première Guerre mondiale dans l'Oise* (Louviers, 2004), p. 13.
29 Figures quoted in Ramspacher, et al., *Chars et blindés française*, p. 24.
30 This camp was opened 10 km north of Orléans on 30 August 1916.

camp so the first tank crews could be assembled. The camp in Champlieu[31] (inside the armed forces zone) constituted the final step in their instruction. There, the crewmen not only received combat training together with the infantry but also in mechanical maintenance before being transferred to the front. These technical courses were of paramount importance, since the crews entrusted their lives to their vehicles. Most of the AS men came from the artillery branch, but also from the Cavalry. Indeed, 'the stabilization of the front had decreased the cavalry engagement and several squadrons had been sent to the trenches or disbanded, in order to create some tank crews'.[32] The first AS doctrine, which encouraged the major hasty attack, perfectly suited the disposition of this second category of personnel.[33]

According to the military background of the company commanders, the soldiers were called 'gunners' or 'cavalrymen'. The special AS uniform consisted of an Adrian helmet with the Artillery or Infantry badge (according to the origin of the holder),[34] a thick, military, black leather-jacket for the drivers, designed not only to absorb shocks, but above all to provide protection from flames, as well as a pair of streamlined trousers clad by leather leggings or puttees and, finally, some studded combat boots. The beret and the left sleeve of the jacket were adorned with an embroidered badge representing a helmet without a plume, which surmounted two intersecting 18th century cannons.[35] Every soldier was also armed, so he could defend himself, with either a 'Ruby' 7.65 mm automatic pistol, or sometimes a '1892 revolver model' (8 mm), as well as a trench knife.[36] These weapons were attached to their regulation, tawny-leather belt. On 1 January 1917, Estienne wrote in his General Order No. 1: 'The AS has to be an elite troop, which will inspire admiration and trust in everybody through its single purpose'.[37] But the heavy losses in personnel did not allow the military authorities to preserve quality in recruitment. In April 1918, Estienne complained bitterly about the lack of skills of the staff who had been sent to him.[38]

On 18 December 1916, the Advisory Committee for the Assault Artillery (*Comité consultatif de l'Artillerie d'Assaut*) was created by Albert Thomas, who was the Under-Secretary of State for War (artillery and ammunition). The chairman was a member of the French Parliament, Louis Breton. He was specifically tasked to look into everything

---

31 On the commune of Orrouy, South of the Compiègne forest. This camp was created on 16 September 1916; and, Estienne established his command post there.
32 General Jean Compagnon, 'La chevauchée héroïque de Berry-au-Bac ; le chef d'escadrons Bossut (16 avril 1917)', in 'N° spécial L'Arme blindée cavalerie', p. 55.
33 Goya, *La chair et l'acier*, p. 340; and, Ramspacher, et el., *Chars et blindés français*, p. 24.
34 A special helmet was distributed in 1918, without a front visor and without crest, but reinforced by a pad of leather in order to protect the head against shocks on the armour. Crews wore a wool beret at rest.
35 It was embraced with metallic yarn for officers and fabric for the other staff, according to the description listed in a note written on 3 September 1917.
36 Jurkiewicz, *Les chars français au combat (1917-1918)*, p. 20.
37 Quoted in Ramspacher, et al., *Chars et blindés français*, p. 36.
38 Commandant F.J. Deygas, *Les chars d'assaut, leur passé, leur avenir* (Paris, 1937), p. 190.

that could improve this new artillery sub-component. At *GQG*, Estienne issued his 'General Order No.1' on 1 January 1917, followed on February 20 by an appendix, which specified the conditions for the use of tanks. The tank had to be engaged not only in hasty attacks, but also in supporting the infantrymen and working alongside them when crossing the enemy trenches (as long as they had followed the advance). If the infantry were unable to keep up with the pace of the tanks, the tank units did not wait for them but continued their advance. The tank crews were also tasked with destroying at short range the enemy machine-guns which had escaped the artillery barrage, but forward movement remained the priority.[39] At the end of March 1917, the AS had thirteen Schneider teams and two incomplete Saint-Chamond teams ready to be committed in Champlieu.[40] On the eve of the first employment in April 1917, it was decided to gather the SA in five temporary groups, then by May 1917 in eight fixed *groups*. There were four Schneider (I to IV) and nine Saint-Chamond groups (X to XIII).[41] By end of the year a number of reorganizations had taken place, which changed the AS structure completely.

After the Malmaison attack,[42] the teams were turned into three batteries composed of four tanks. An extra battery was available in reserve. Depending on availability, it was provided with two or three tanks. An AS HQ was also created for each Army Group. They were located in Mailly for the Central Army Group and in Martigny for the Northern Army Group. These command centres were each given two tank groups. Champlieu became a centre devoted to the general reserve, while Marly was closed. Cercottes served by September as a 'depot' centre, as well as an individual training and organization base.[43] 262 Infantry Regiment became a permanent infantry support unit.[44] On 29 December 1917, the provisional instructions on the use of assault tanks, the *Instruction provisoire sur l'emploi des chars d'assaut*, was issued. It was the first regulation published by the Operations Bureau at *GQG* and signed by General Pétain. This document encapsulated Estienne's ideas and set the AS rules of engagement, formalizing in this way the doctrine for infantry support.[45] Twelve Saint-Chamond teams were created in the camp located at Champlieu until February 1918.[46] In April, sixteen Schneider teams and six Saint-Chamond ones (as well as two light tank batteries) were gathered there.[47] In May 1918, eight tank regiments from 501 to 508 were set

39 SHD-GR 16 N 2142.
40 SHD-GR 16 N 2121, 'Notes du GQG sur l'A.S.', 8 January 1917 and 20 February 1917.
41 Ramspacher, et al., *Chars et blindés français*, p. 39.
42 This is dealt with below under the heading 'Other Combat Actions'.
43 Goya, *La chair et l'acier*, p. 350.
44 SHD-GR 16 N 2120, 'Rapport au sujet de la participation de l'A.S. aux opérations des 23-25 octobre 1917'.
45 It was still in force in 1936 and can be consulted at SHD-GR 14 N 13.
46 The full descent of the French tank battalions in 1918, too complex to be described here, can be found in *Historama hors série* n°9, pp. 48-50.
47 Ramspacher, et al., *Chars et blindés français*, p. 36.

up. They added a heavy group from the former Schneider and Saint-Chamond SA to the new light tank batteries and battalions. Thus the groups I, II, IV and X moved to the 501, 502, 504 and 505 SA Regiments (Renault). But 'most of the time, this assignment had no tactical impact. The heavy groups carried on fighting apart from their battalion'.[48] A ninth tank regiment (509) was created in autumn 1918.

The Schneider 'C.A.1' Tank

The first French tank was born of the successful meeting of Colonel Estienne and the engineer Brillié. The plans were ready by December 1915 and immediately shown to Joffre, who authorized the continuation of the development of the combat vehicle. The prototype, named 'artillery tractor' to keep it secret, was almost entirely constructed by hand in February 1916 by a team of ten iron workers from Billancourt. The leader was Second-Lieutenant Charles Fouché, a pre-war tractor merchant, who had become a caterpillar specialist at the 'Motor-Vehicle Technical Department' (Service Technique Automobile).[49] General Mourret, who was the Commanding Officer of this department, had appointed him to fix two Baby Holt tractor frames. The purpose was to build a vehicle composed of seven running wheels (instead of five) not only capable of crossing 1.50 m trenches, but able to crush barbed-wire entanglements, too.[50] After the success of this first stage, the new vehicle was subject to trials on 17 February at the polygon in Vincennes (among the guests, President Raymond Poincaré himself). A detailed policy for the Schneider tank was drawn up; on 21 February, the project was renewed in favour of Albert Thomas.[51] Nine other versions were manufactured in Le Creusot and then tested at 'The Hole of Hell'. Joffre ordered four hundred tanks from the Schneider Company. The delivery time was not to exceed seven months.[52] In March 1917, France already had 150 Schneider tanks; this number rose to 208 the following month. Nevertheless, thirty-four quickly became unserviceable due to a lack of spare parts. Twelve teams were therefore set up with the remaining ones.[53] 322 tanks were part of the armed forces in May 1917; 340 were delivered in July.[54] The final twenty-four machines were built in 1918.[55]

The Schneider 'C.A.1' tank was 6 m long, 2.50 m wide, and had a height of 2.39 m. It was a long vehicle put on 'a frame composed of two steel spars linked together by ties, with a front engine and a rear transmission. This frame was positioned on

---

48   Ibid., p. 40.
49   Ibid., p. 21.
50   Laroussinie, *Mécanique de la victoire*, pp. 73-6.
51   Ramspacher, et al., *Chars et blindés français*, p. 21.
52   SHD-GR 16 N 2120, letter from General Estienne to the War Minister, 26 June 1916.
53   Laroussinie, *Mécanique de la victoire*, p. 78; and, General Jean Compagnon, in 'N° spécial L'Arme blindée cavalerie', p. 55.
54   Ramspacher, et al., *Chars et blindés français*, pp. 22-3.
55   SHD-GR 16 N 2130, 'Point des livraisons de chars pendant la guerre', 1919.

two trucks thanks to springs. The trucks had three and four running wheels, which were rolling on the caterpillar tracks. The front truck supported a tension pulley. The tracks were between the sprocket at the rear and the tension pulley. They were made of thirty-four bases supported by rollers, which were mounted between two flanges.'[56] A type of ram had been placed at the front to be used as a support when the tank rocked into the enemy trench. This ram was also heightened by a rail designed for the pulling up of the barbed wire running on the parapets. At the rear there was a spoiler on which the tank was held up to assist it out of trenches after crossing. Despite these devices, an enemy trench could not be crossed which exceeded 1.50 m width.

The Schneider 60-hp, four-cylinder, petrol engine had a maximum speed of 1,200 revolutions per minute. Its ventilation was ensured by a hatch at the top of the vehicle, but it did not prove to be efficient. The fuel was supplied through a feed pump because the petrol tank had been placed at the front middle part of the vehicle, that is to say lower than the carburettor. 'The transmission system consisted of an inverted-cone-shaped clutch, a three-multiple-ratio gearbox and two secondary clutches acting each on a sprocket. Theses clutches made it possible not only to slow or stop the motor action to the right or left, but above all to get the direction change of the tank. All these mechanisms, mounted on running wheels, were operated by levers and pedals positioned near the driver's seat. The driver was at the front right side of the vehicle and on the right of the engine'.[57] The Schneider tank was equipped with a reversing device allowing the use of the three gear ratios backwards and forwards.[58] After the setbacks encountered during the attack of 16 April 1917,[59] it was considered safer to remove the rubber tubings feeding the engine with petrol. The aim was to limit the danger of fire inside the tank when it was hit by a shell. It was also decided to move the main petrol tank to the rear of the vehicle, as well as to protect it by a double wall.[60] It was prohibited for crewmen to place auxiliary gasoline cans next to the doors at the rear of the Schneider tank. Two auxiliary armoured 100 litre tanks were placed as an alternative at the rear of the vehicle. The engine ventilation was improved; the 245th Schneider tank produced was equipped with a starter, to make it possible to quickly react in the case of the engine stalling.[61] The tank moved at a maximum cruising speed of 6 km per hour and had a range of 48 km (30 miles). It was capable of climbing 45% slopes.

---

56 Anon., *Blindés: des origines à 1970. Profils et histoire* (Paris, 1976), Série Connaissance de l'Histoire, Special Issue n°3, p. 29; and *Historama hors série* n°9, p. 44.
57 Anon., *Blindés: des origines à 1970. Profils et histoire*, p. 29.
58 Guenaff & Jurkiewicz, *Le chars de la victoire*, p. 19.
59 This was the first commitment of French tanks to battle; it is described in the section 'French Tanks in Combat' below.
60 Inspecteur général Jean Molinié, *Les engins blindés du monde (1917-1967)* (Paris, 1981), 'n° spécial de *La Gazette des Armes*' n° 11, p. 10.
61 Lieutenant-colonel Paul Malmassari, *Les chars de la Grande Guerre* (Saint-Cloud, December 2009), Special Issue n°3 of *14-18 Le Magazine de la Grande Guerre*, p. 40.

The one block fighting compartment was placed in a superstructure made of hardened steel plates, clipped by rivets. Different windows and firing slits were designed for external observation. The crews got into the tank through a two-wing back-door. After the battle at Berry-au-Bac, 'a door was opened on the left flank. They also added an angled spotting scope, a suction pipe, as well as an acoustic tube.'[62] The crew consisted of an officer (the tank commander), an NCO and four soldiers (including a driver placed on the right-hand side, a gunner and two machine-gunners). It was protected against either 7.92 mm bullets fired at 150 m by *Mauser* rifles, or shell splinters. But the Germans had produced special bullets[63] to counter British tanks[64] and 13 mm anti-tank rifle. As a consequence, it was necessary to strengthen the Schneider vehicle armour even before distributing the tanks to the operational units. The armour was composed mainly of a 40 mm additional steel plate, which was riveted on the front of the vehicle and another 8 mm plate was placed on both sides of the vehicle. The maximum armour was thus increased from 11.5 mm to 19.5 mm. So, with the changes made to the petrol tanks, the Schneider vehicles built in the summer 1917 weighed an extra 500 kilos in comparison to the initial 12-ton model.[65]

The main armament was provided by a short, left-mounted, 75 mm cannon. This had been developed by the Schneider Company under the name of *75 mm blockhaus*. It had a horizontal breech and, unlike the military 1897 model, it was equipped with a screw breech.[66] This Schneider cannon fired explosive shells at a muzzle velocity of 200 m per second from an ideal range of 600 meters: 'its vertical sector was from below 10° to above 30° and the clearance in direction was 60°'.[67] The ammunition supply was ninety shells. The secondary armament consisted of two 'Hotchkiss 1914' 8 mm machine-guns fed by rigid strips composed of 4,000 rounds. They were mounted on some oscillating ball-mounts placed on each side of the vehicle. These machine guns were principally intended to rake the enemy trenches with fire as they were being crossed.

The last models of the Schneider tanks were delivered to the French Army in August 1918. The two other versions which had been proposed were not developed: the 'C.A. 2' model, which was to be equipped with a 47mm cannon mounted on a mobile turret, while the 'C.A. 3' model with a long frame was to have been equipped with a double turret. The poor mobility of the tank on rough ground, as well as the advent of the FT-17, these were most probably the arguments which dissuaded *GHQ* from pursuing their development.

---

62   Ramspacher, et al., *Chars et blindés français*, p. 26.
63   Perforating gun bullets with a steel core, the so-called 'S.M.K'.
64   They appeared on the battlefield at Flers on 15 September 1916.
65   For a total weight of 13.6 tons in order of battle.
66   Molinié, *Les engins blindés du monde*, p. 6.
67   Anon., *Blindés: des origines à 1970. Profils et histoire*, p. 29.

The Saint-Chamond Tank

Following the development of the Schneider tank, the Ministry of Armaments decided to develop another, improved model of tank; Albert Thomas placed an order for Saint-Chamond tanks, only informing Estienne and Joffre after he had done so. It was designed by another famous artilleryman, Colonel Emile Rimailho (1864-1954). He was the inventor of the famous 75 mm cannon. The prototype of this tank, built in Saint-Chamond by the Iron and Steel Works Company for the Navy at Homécourt (*Forges et Aciéries de la Marine d'Homécourt*), was ready in mid-1916 and available in September. In order to smooth ruffled feathers, Joffre ordered 400 vehicles. A pre-series version comprising fifty Saint-Chamond tanks was produced throughout the year. Work on the first mass-production tank commenced on 23 February 1917; manufacture was completed in December.[68] More powerful and better protected than the Schneider tank, the Saint-Chamond had also more impressive dimensions: it had a length of 8.83 m, a breadth of 2.67 m and a height of 2.34 m. Its major asset was its 75 mm cannon, designed by Colonel Rimailho.

The Saint-Chamond was equipped with a *Panhard and Levassor* 90-horse-four-cylinder-without-valve gasoline engine. It had a speed of 1,450 revolutions per minute. The Saint-Chamond seemed like an armoured wagon, with an angled shape, jutting out at both front and rear.[69] 'Compared to the Schneider vehicle, it was more comfortable inside, spacious and electrified. Moreover, the extent of the outside visibility was appreciated by the crews.'[70] The engine was connected to a 52 Kw dynamo, from which the two electric motors operated. It transmitted sufficient energy to propel the sprockets.[71] The suspension-system was inspired by the Baby Holt tractor, but the frame was longer that of the Schneider. Moreover, the caterpillar tracks had thirty-six bases. Due to its difficulties in moving over rough ground (such as its tendency to shed its caterpillar tracks when it took a bend), the decision was taken to widen the tracks from 326 to 500 mm. The movement gear, which was made of three pairs of bogies and suspended by helical springs, was rather weak.[72] Hence, the crewmen nicknamed the tank 'the elephant on the legs of a gazelle'.[73]

The vehicle moved at a maximum speed of 8.5 km per hour on road and at a maximum speed of 4 km over rough ground. It had a 59 km range thanks to its 250-litre tank. The vehicle was also capable of climbing 80% slopes. The 75 mm gun fitted to the early Saint-Chamonds was one designed by Colonel Rimailho, tanks manufactured later had the standard French field gun fitted, the M1897 model, which

---

68 Goya, *La chair et l'acier*, p. 339 ; SHD-GR 16 N 2130, 'Point des livraisons de chars pendant la guerre', 1919.
69 Anon., *Blindés: des origines à 1970. Profils et histoire*, p. 29.
70 Guenaff & Jurkiewicz, *Les chars de la victoire*, p. 24.
71 Crochat-Collardeau system.
72 Laroussinie, *Mécanique de la victoire*, p. 80.
73 Molinié, *Les engins blindés du monde*, p. 9.

Photo 4: St Chamond Tank

had enjoyed the approval of the French General Staff since its invention. As a result, the front of the tank had to be altered, so as to make it longer. On this second version, the higher roof had a sloping shape, in order to make it difficult for enemy infantrymen with grenades to clamber on to it. The opportunity was also taken to add an armoured cupola to increase protection for the driver.[74] Concerning the secondary armament, it consisted of four 8 mm machine-guns fed with rigid strips. Two of them were laterally mounted on a joint, while another was placed at the rear. The last machine-gun was on the right of the cannon, to shoot forwards. The tank was equipped with a cargo of 106 explosive shells, as well as 7,488 8 mm rounds. Like the Schneider vehicle, the armour was made of riveted steel plates. Its thickness ranged from 11.5 mm on the front and sides to 8 mm on the roof. The tank was manned by nine men, a tank commander, a driver, a gunner, a gun-loader, four machine-gunners and a mechanic.

As soon as the vehicle entered service, its crews started to complain about its technical unreliability.[75] To tackle its defects, and to compensate for the lack of spare parts, items from unrepairable tanks were retrieved. Estienne himself considered dismantling the latest 80 tanks, which were coming off the assembly lines, in order

---

74 In the first version, the driver had to open a hatch to put his head outside; thus, he had no protection if German infantrymen concentrated their fire on the hatches.
75 SHD-GR 1 K 91, 'Note résumant la question du matériel de l'Artillerie d'Assaut', [unsigned] 28 November 1916.

to provide material for the units.[76] In addition, some serious manufacturing problems were discovered. In particular, the caterpillar tracks were too narrow and the front of the vehicle too low and heavy. In combat, the craters caused by shells were a nightmare for the drivers because the front of the tank often became wedged in the ground. Aware of the lack of manoeuvrability of this tank, the Germans expanded their trenches beyond 1.80 m. In this way, they managed to stop the Saint-Chamond tank, since the frame became stuck on the parapets, while its caterpillar tracks, which were embedded inside the trench, turned in the gap, unable to gain traction. As a consequence, the beached tank became an easy target for the artillery. Subsequent versions were equipped with metallic rollers, placed under the front of the frame, in order to assist forward movement; the tracks were also widened. After the first combat actions, the number of visibility slots was increased, too. The engineers worked on the expulsion of fumes from inside the tank. Moreover, the power of the batteries was improved.[77] Time was spent on working on these different technical changes. On 31 March 1917, the SA only had forty-eight operational Saint-Chamond tanks.[78] With the thicker armour and the other alterations to the tank, its weight had increased from 19 to 24 tons (when fully equipped for battle).

French Tanks in Combat

Due to their relatively slow speed, the Schneider and Saint-Chamond tanks were well suited to accompany the infantry into battle. In addition, the thickness of their armour enabled them to launch attacks on positions fortified by barbed-wire and defended by machine-guns. However, their modest range made it impossible for them to exploit any break-through which might occur. This is the reason why Estienne decided quickly to build a light tank.[79]

Their first baptism of fire soon proved that these first assault tanks were far from perfect. In fact they made a lot of noise on the move and gave off some wreaths of black smoke when they accelerated. The crews were also obliged to spend half a day maintaining every vehicle after 25 km because the tank lacked mechanical reliability.[80] It was very dark inside the tanks; the crews found the noise and the heat unbearable. The petrol and cordite fumes, along with the exhaust gas made the air virtually impossible to breathe. Without any suspension, the Schneider and Saint-Chamond vehicles offered a rough time to the soldiers manning them on the battlefield. These tanks were also very sensitive to direct or indirect artillery fire, which represented

---

76 SHD-GR 16 N 2132, file n° 3, Letter from the Commander-in-Chief to the War Minister, 23 May 1917.
77 Ramspacher, et al., *Chars et blindés français*, p. 28.
78 Guenaff & Jurkiewicz, *Les chars de la victoire*, p. 13.
79 This was the Renault FT-17 tank; the first SA Renault appeared on 1 October 1917.
80 Col. Chedeville, 'Les chars de combat actuels et le haut commandement', *Revue Militaire française*, tome 3 (January-March 1922), p. 331.

the worst drawback. The roof was only a thinly armoured and the floor was barely armoured at all. The communication problems between the tanks (but also with the infantry) were obvious. Without any communication link, the crewmen needed either to mark sketch maps before the beginning of the action, or to hold flags out of the vehicles instead of speaking (most of them were not noticed, as the observation slits had been badly positioned); each battery took two carrier pigeons.[81] Fortunately, a few tanks were equipped with telegraphy radio sets on the eve of the Malmaison attack at the end of October 1917.[82]

After the initial surprise, the Germans adapted quickly to the tank threat. They started to shoot with their 77 mm cannon directly at the tanks. They also developed anti-tank techniques for their infantry. These attempts increased drastically the losses within the AS. In his memoir, a former tank commander recounted the horror of combat action:

> The gunners are waiting and look forwards. On the right, the machine gunner fires at the thickets. The one on the left is wiping his bloody face. Then the clash happens. A first shell falls on the bonnet, penetrates and explodes. It has reduced everything to pieces and has injured the crew projecting steel, oil, flesh and blood. No splinter has been lost. Five men have been mashed. What about the others? The front machine-gunner has been wounded. The right machine-gunner and the mechanic are knocked out against the armour. In the rear, the man is unharmed. A second shell is shot at the tank and crushes the machinery which squashes the rear machine gunner. The gasoline and the oil are pouring out. A flame has sprung up. It runs and is spreading. It has become a torrent of fire that rushes to the damaged front of the vehicle. Fire… Fire… A man ahead is escaping. The latch has fortunately given way. The door opens as the flames rush out. A torch has gone out with them, another one and a last one. Three people are on fire, screaming as they run. They have fallen, are burning and rolling around in pain.[83]

Of course, Estienne knew that his tanks had defects, but he had decided to use them in the interests of the war effort. 'The achievement means accepting imperfect work', he said.[84]

The first operational commitment of French tanks took place on 16 April 1917 during General Robert Nivelle's offensive, which aimed at breaking the German front between Reims and the channel connecting the Oise to the Aisne River. In this attempt to break through the German lines, 128 Schneider tanks, divided into three

---

81 Jurkiewicz, *Les chars français au combat*, p. 14.
82 Goya, *La chair et l'acier*, p. 349. See also below.
83 Lieutenant Corlieu-Jouve, *Ceux des chars d'assaut* (Paris, n.d.), p. 75.
84 Quoted in Laroussinie, *Mécanique de la victoire*, p. 47.

groups, were assembled. Due to various technical failures, only 121 vehicles were involved in the assault in the neighbouring areas of Berry-au-Bac on a 6-9 km uncovered plain located to the south-east of Le Chemin des Dames.

The first group (three teams, SA 3, 7 and 8, all told forty-eight tanks) was led by Major Chaubès and the second (five teams, SA 2, 4, 5, 6 and 9, eighty tanks) by Major Bossut.[85] Their mission was to support the advance of the 5th Army (including the 5th and 32nd Army Corps), which had to attack in the centre between Craonne and the Aisne River. Facing the tanks, which had to advance in the main Juvincourt-Guignicourt-Corbeny wood direction, were the 5th, 9th, and 10th Bavarian Divisions. These units were deployed 7 km in depth, occupying three successive major positions separated from 2 to 3 km from each other (plus a fourth one located approximately 9 km from the first position).[86] The objectives, which had been specifically assigned to the tanks, were the third and fourth German lines. These armoured groups had reduced close-support. Indeed, although their action was supported by twelve infantry divisions, there was only one cannon per 8 m of front. Bossut, who had gained Estienne's consent to conduct the attack, did not believe that an armoured success against the defensive position was possible. None of General Estienne's tactical requirements, which were released on 12 December 1915, had been taken into account;[87] in fact, Bossut failed to change the conditions for the employment of the AS.[88]

As there had been coordinated artillery barrages for several days, the tanks could not conduct a hasty attack. Moreover, the French troops were under the perpetual scrutiny of the observation posts, as well as the German artillery-observation aircraft. The first two enemy lines had been severely hit by artillery fire and nearly two-thirds of the German batteries seemed to have been reduced to silence. The Chaubès group attacked in column and was immediately stopped by a large trench, forming at this place the first enemy line. German artillery put it out of action. Twenty-five tanks out of fifty were destroyed, while six others broke down. The Bossut group, which had been reduced to thirteen tanks, managed to cross the first and second German lines under fire. It then fought for three hours against the third trench, waiting in vain for the arrival of the infantry. Due to the violence of the enemy's concentrated fire, it was finally forced to retreat.[89] Out of a total of eighty-two Schneider tanks which had been engaged, thirty-one had been hit and thirteen had been put out of action.

Thus, without being a complete failure, this tank attack had not produced the desired effect because the last Bavarian line had not been crossed and, thus, the

---

85 A third group, led by Major Lefebvre (SA 1, 10, 31), was not committed into action because of the failure of the first two groups.
86 Ramspacher, et al., *Chars et blindés français*, p. 42.
87 These can be found in Deygas, *Les chars d'assaut*, pp. 94-5.
88 See his letter to General Estienne quoted in General Jean Compagnon, in 'N° spécial L'Arme blindée cavalerie', p. 55.
89 For a full account of each SA commitment, see Ramspacher, et al., *Chars et blindés français*, pp. 46-54.

breakthrough was not achieved. The lack of surprise, the advance in full view of the German observation posts in Craonne, the propensity of the Schneider tank to catch fire, the lack of French counter-battery fire, as well as the difficulty of the infantry in advancing under hostile conditions, were the main factors explaining the poor results and heavy losses. Losses amounted to 25% of the crews from the *Artillerie Spéciale* and 43% of its tanks.[90] Out of fifty-seven tanks halted by artillery fire, only fifteen had received direct hits.[91] But thirty-five had caught fire because of the petrol cans which had been positioned next to the only doors of the Schneider vehicles to offer the chance of refuelling; the lack of protection for the petrol tanks had also contributed to tanks catching fire.[92]

This failure was obviously a dispiriting experience for those who survived. The intrepid and popular Louis-Marie Bossut (1873-1917) had received seven outstanding citations since the beginning of the war for actions conducted when riding a horse or driving a tank. He had commanded the first team of the Assault Artillery and, finally, was killed in this battle. His tank, which had been hit by a shell, caught fire, and he received a shrapnel wound in the chest. Bossut had been blown clear when his tank exploded. His crew was burnt to death while attempting to escape from the wrecked vehicle.[93] The posthumous mention of Bossut hinted at his vain impetuosity: 'After having given all his great heart as an intrepid cavalryman, he was gloriously killed after having led his tanks in a heroic ride towards the last enemy lines'.[94] If the valour of the crews was acclaimed by *GQG*,[95] the production of the Schneider tank was about to be suspended. Indeed, the hope placed in a powerful (and almost invulnerable) armoured attack had been disappointed. Some elite soldiers had been killed and much expensive material wasted. It took all the energy of Estienne (who wrote to the highest civilian and military authorities) – supported by the new Commander-in-Chief, Philippe Pétain, who actively defended the tank – to save the AS itself.[96]

---

90 180 men were killed, wounded or missing in action (33 officers, 28 non-commissioned officers and 119 soldiers) from an absolute total of 720; 76 tanks were destroyed, including 57 by fire; losses for the accompanying Infantry were 40%. Figures taken from: Ramspacher, et al., *Chars et blindés français*, p. 54; *Traditions et historique de l'Arme Blindée et Cavalerie: tendances d'avenir*, p. 13; and, Anon., 'La naissance des chars français' in *L'Encyclopédie des armes*, p. 620.
91 This information is according to a German report referring the engagement, and quoted in, 'Le baptême des chars d'assaut', article published in *Le Matin*, 13 April 1936.
92 SHD-GR 16 N 2124, 'Note du 3ème bureau du G.Q.G.', 17 June 1917.
93 This information is taken from the text of the address read by General Hallier, former leader of SA 2 and a witness of the scene, during the fiftieth anniversary of the first attack of French tanks on 16 April 1967.
94 SHD-GR 5 Ye 111 463, 'Dossier personnel du commandant Louis Bossut'.
95 SHD-GR 16 N 1686, General Order n°76, signed « Nivelle », 20 April 1917.
96 Pétain sent a letter to the Government in order to respond to an inquiry into the attack of Berry-au-Bac, intended to determine the future of the SA. SHD – GR 2121, 'Letter from the Commander-in-Chief to the Minister of War', signed 'Pétain', 2 June 1917.

Other Combat Actions of the Schneider and Saint-Chamond Tanks

The Saint-Chamond tank was first committed on 5 May 1917 during the attack against the Lafaux Mill (Moulin de Laffaux). During this employment, the tank experienced difficulty in moving over rough terrain; this was the reason why changes had to be made to its design. The tank attack launched by Lefebvre's group against three German defensive lines was smaller than the one at Berry-au-Bac. There were only forty-one tanks committed (nineteen Schneider tanks from SA 1 and ten and twelve Saint-Chamonds from the SA 31 and 32). They were also supported by two infantry divisions, as well as one cannon per 22 m of front. The observation and fighting aviation provided additional support. The final objective was not only to enable the 6th Army to retreat from Reims, but also to accomplish the capture of Le Chemin des Dames. This time it was a full success, mainly because the Germans had accepted the need to abandon Laffaux, which was a stronghold. On this occasion, 'the doctrine on the use of tanks was based on direct support and comprised a common mission given to the chosen infantry units, but on routes, towards objectives and at a speed tailored to the capabilities of the tanks. They supported the infantry by lateral manoeuvres to outflank, as well as to fall back on the enemy rear. For close protection, they were covered by an infantry battalion endowed with a highly offensive spirit, that is to say the 17th Light Infantry Battalion (*17ème Bataillon de Chasseurs à Pied*)'.[97]

Bossut had had the idea of creating this battalion, in order to improve combined arms cooperation. Learning from the unfortunate experience at Berry-au-Bac,[98] Estienne had prohibited the troops to advance in column, but instead recommended the team formation.[99] The German artillery indirect fire was, therefore, less effective. If the percentage of casualties was comparable to the action on 16 April, only five tanks were hit (of which three were lost).[100] This rather limited action had presented the opportunity to restore confidence in the AS.[101] According to an eye-witness one month later, 'In Mailly, our favourite pleasure is to observe the caterpillar tractors manoeuvre, in other words, what will become the tanks. We look at them plunging into a large pit and climbing unbelievable slopes under the eyes of politicians, among them Poincaré, Clemenceau, etc. The show is encouraging for the future of the war; it's a real pleasure.'[102]

---

97 Anon., *Traditions et historique de l'Arme Blindée et Cavalerie ; tendances d'avenir*, p. 13.
98 SHD-GR 2120, 'Rapport au sujet de la participation de la 5ème Armée des groupements Bossut et Chaubès de l'Artillerie d'Assaut (16 avril 1917)', GQG/3ème bureau, [signed] 'Estienne', 28 April 1917.
99 SHD-GR 2121, 'Projet pour l'emploi tactique des chars', GQG/3ème bureau, [signed] 'Gal Estienne', 1 May 1917.
100 SHD-GR 16 N 2120, box n° 3, file n° 4, 'État des pertes en chars et personnels', G.Q.G., 9 September 1919.
101 Goya, *La chair et l'acier*, p. 347.
102 Louis Maufrais, *J'étais médecin dans les tranchées* (Paris, 2008), p. 273.

From 23 to 25 October 1917, an attack conducted by the groups I and X against La Malmaison was launched to seize the Chemin des Dames ridge. Forty Schneider and twenty-three Saint-Chamond vehicles (SA 8, 11, 12, 31, 33), supported by five infantry divisions as well as one cannon per 6 m front, fought brilliantly, causing the Germans to abandon the position. The operation was considered as 'a good detailed example of common mass action. The tanks were put under the orders of small infantry units and had to attack the same objectives, on the same route and at the same rhythm of advance'.[103] To save time, the infantry had been specifically in charge of assisting the tanks when they crossed the trenches. The French artillery lengthened its fire in accordance with the advance. The German artillery was surprised by the strength and speed of the armoured advance. As a consequence, it was unable to retreat in time. The enemy troops were completely demoralized as they had lost 70,000 men (including 11,200 prisoners) because they had not been able to commit their reserve units. Still, '[t]he autumn 1917 fights confirmed the vulnerability of the heavy tanks on a ground full of obstacles. Out of sixty-three committed tanks, twenty-seven [including eight Saint-Chamond tanks from the SA 33] did not overcome the first French lines. Fifteen others broke down in the German position and only twenty-one played an effective role'.[104] The AS suffered twenty killed and sixty-two wounded.[105] By the end of 1917, the Schneider and Saint-Chamond tanks had been committed on 231 occasions, with an average loss rate of 40% each time.[106]

The German offensives in 1918 placed the French tank units in an unprecedented defensive role. When the first offensive was launched in March, 'there were 245 Schneider tanks [sixteen companies] and 222 Saint-Chamond vehicles [twelve companies] available'.[107] Two Army Group HQs of the AS remained in Mailly and Martigny-les-Bains: the AS of the Northern Army group (*Groupe d'Armées du Nord*, groups IV and IX) in the first camp and the AS of the Eastern Army group (*Groupe d'Armées de l'Est*, groups II and X) in the second one. The groups I, III, XII and XIII remained in Champlieu, to set up a general reserve under the orders of Colonel Monhoven. If the crews were experienced, the equipment was in a bad condition. On 4 April, the groups I and III were urgently committed and failed to stop the German advance.[108] From 5 to 7 April the SA 2, 3 and 4 were gathered to the south of Amiens in the rear of the 1st and 3rd French Armies, in order to provide assistance in the defence of the French second line. To support the overall plan, one AS GHQ was set up in each army.[109] On 7 and 13 April, the SA 10 and 3 were committed with

---

103 Anon., *Traditions et historique de l'Arme Blindée et Cavalerie: tendances d'avenir*, p. 13.
104 Anon., 'La naissance des chars français', in *L'Encyclopédie des armes*, p. 620.
105 Jurkiewicz, *Les char français au combat*, p. 58.
106 Goya, *La chair et l'acier*, p. 350.
107 Lieutenant-colonel Perré et capitaine Le Gouest, 'Chars et statistiques', *Revue d'infanterie*, n° 514, 1 July 1935, p. 81; and, Ramspacher, et al., *Chars et blindés français*, p. 55.
108 Ramspacher, et al., *Chars et blindés français*, pp. 55-56.
109 Goya, *La chair et l'acier*, p. 351.

considerable losses in the Park of Grivesnes and the Senecat Wood (eight killed, seven wounded and three tanks destroyed from six committed in the first action; one officer killed, six officers wounded or missing in action, a further ninety wounded and three tanks destroyed out of twelve committed in the second).[110]

The SA command, dissatisfied with the role that had been given to the tanks, considered that the action on 7 April had been a failure. Its criticism was, however, less categorical after the action on 13 April because the French infantry had conquered the wood. In order to face the enemy offensives in May, the French command withdrew the tanks from the *groups* located at the divisional level and placed them at the army corps level. It was essential to be able to gather at least seventy tanks in a short time to plug the gap. (In fact, after their release from the assembly lines, the FT-17 light tanks were subsequently committed with heavy tanks in their first combat action on 31 May.) On 27 and 28 May, in coordination with the Americans, three batteries from the SA 5 (twelve tanks) attacked the eastern part of the Saint-Éloi Wood and assisted in the conquest of Cantigny. Only three men from the SA were killed in action, with two tanks destroyed.[111]

During the Matz battle from 11 to 13 June, the groups X (SA 33 and 36), III (SA 1, 6, 10, 15), XII (SA 37, 38, 39) and XI (SA 32, 34, 35) counter-attacked without artillery preparation. Despite the surprise, the losses were heavy. Seventy-two tanks out of the 147 committed were destroyed. Sixty-three men were killed, 235 wounded, with ninety-one reported missing. 'The group X, most exposed to the direct fire from the German artillery, suffered the loss of nineteen tanks out of the twenty-four (79%). The group III lost 68% of its tanks. The group XII lost 39% and the group XI, less involved in the battle, declared the loss of 11% of its tanks'.[112] So, the result of this armoured counter-attack was mixed, although the German push towards Compiègne had been stopped. This action became the last one in which the Schneider and Saint-Chamond vehicles fought without the reinforcement of the light tanks. On 13 June, four Schneiders fought in the Merlies Wood.

On 9 July, sixteen Schneider tanks from the SA 16 and 17 managed to conduct a successful attack on the road from Montdidier to Compiègne, between Gournay and Antheuil-Portes. Nine days later, 190 Saint-Chamond and 125 Schneider vehicles, divided into eight *groups* (SA 5, 13, 17, 35, 36, 40, 41, 42) attacked with 585 light tanks from the Villers-Cotterêts forest to support the counter attack of the 6th, 9th and 10th Armies between the Aisne and the Marne Rivers. The fighting lasted until 27 July. Out of more than 1,200 actions, about 40% of the Schneider and Saint-Chamond tanks had been destroyed. Nearly 900 crewmen were killed, wounded or

---

110 Figures quoted in Ramspacher, et al., *Chars et blindés français*, p. 57.
111 Ramspacher, et al., *Chars et blindés français* p. 58; and, Jurkiewicz, *Les chars français au combat*, p. 63.
112 Guenaff & Jurkiewicz, *Les chars de la victoire*, pp. 97, 99.

missing in action, despite the lessons learnt from the previous battles and the continuing efforts at improving organization.[113]

From 8 to 18 August, a Schneider group (thirty-two tanks) was committed along with light tanks near Montdidier. From 20 August to 16 September, twenty-eight Saint-Chamond and twelve Schneider vehicles fought along with the FT-17 light tanks on the Somme. 50% of the Schneider tanks were put out of action. At this time, the U.S. troops were supported by some Saint-Chamond tanks.

On 12 and 13 September 1918, two Saint-Chamond groups (twenty-five tanks belonging to the SA 34 and 35) and two Schneider groups (thirty-six tanks belonging to the SA 14 and 17) took part in the reduction of the St. Mihiel salient, a battle led by General John J. Pershing. On this occasion, a single tank was lost because the French tanks had a more limited role, having been hampered by traffic jams just before the attack.[114]

From 26 September to 8 October, six groups (seventy-seven Schneider and twenty-five Saint-Chamond tanks) fought side by side with the Americans in the Argonne (Romagne-Montfaucon) and in Champagne. In this action, losses in personnel reached up to 60% of the crewmen and some battalions even lost all their officers.[115] On 30 September, three Schneider teams (twenty-four tanks) supported the attack of the 5th Army between the Vesle and Aisne Rivers; they could not advance beyond three hundred metres and lost 25% of their crews. The Saint-Chamond tanks were not committed again in action until after 6 October 1918.[116]

If the Schneider and Saint-Chamond tanks continued to be employed until the end of the war, their performance was marginal compared to those of the light tank battalions (*Bataillons de chars légers*) which had just been created. The monthly number of combat actions of these medium tanks thus fell from 200 in June and July to less than ninety in September and November 1918.[117] To limit the effects of the shortage, the number of tanks inside the teams was reduced or light tanks were incorporated within them. In November 1918, there were only seventy-two medium tanks in action and most of them had been disarmed to be used for the transportation of equipment. However, it was planned to use the last Schneider and Saint-Chamond tanks which were still operational in the offensive which was intended to take place in Lorraine by 14 November 1918.

---

113 SHD-GR 16 N 2120 box n° 3, file n° 4, 'État des pertes en chars et personnels', G.Q.G., 9 September 1919.
114 Goya, *La chair et l'acier*, p. 357.
115 Figures quoted in *Historama hors série* n° 9, p. 54.
116 Malmassari, *Les chars de la Grande Guerre*, p. 98.
117 SHD-GR 2130, file n° 2, 'Note sur l'Artillerie d'Assaut', n.d., unsigned. FT-17 tanks were sent into action 1,640 times in the same period.

Conclusion

In December 1916, reaching the same conclusions as the British, Estienne had made up his mind on the development of a tank which was lighter than the Schneider and Saint-Chamond machines. The need for rapid mass production was entrusted to Louis Renault who had designed the prototype of the FT tank in April 1917. Particularly successful and versatile, as well as inexpensive to produce, this tank quickly overshadowed its predecessors, remaining 'the tank of victory' in the collective mind. During the war, the Schneider and Saint-Chamond tanks were committed 1,064 times in action, approximately three times less than the light tanks; 308 tanks were completely destroyed.[118] According to one set of figures, among the Schneider crewmen, thirty-eight officers and twenty-eight NCOs were killed, while twenty-two officers and twenty-three NCOs from the Saint-Chamond crews perished. In total, 209 soldiers were killed in the Schneider and 140 in the Saint-Chamond units.[119]

General Estienne was awarded to the rank of *Commandeur de la Légion d'honneur* on 2 August 1918, with the following citation:

> This General Officer is very intelligent and equipped with exceptional values. He has numerous bright ideas. The spirit and faith with which he was able to defend and make a success of his ideas has offered the most eminent services to the common cause. He has entirely set up and organized, ignoring the prevailing difficulties, the wonderful combat device called the Assault Artillery. He turned it into a powerful weapon, whose strength has been valuable and contributed to a large part to the success of the French armies in the second half of July 1918. He is also a brave soldier, as well as an outstanding technician. He may be proud of his work.[120]

It is remarkable to note, as stated in this citation, that the Assault Artillery offered great support in 1918, i.e. at the moment when it was committed in the opposite fashion from the initial ideas of its creator. The Assault Artillery was engaged at that time above all in small offensive fights, but during large-scale defensive actions.

During the Great War, the simultaneous development of two different medium tank models, but also the rivalry between the French GQG (with Estienne and the Schneider tank) and the Ministry of Armaments (with Albert Thomas and the Saint-Chamond tank), as well as the Automobile Department (*Direction du Service Automobile*), which did not want to accept Estienne assigned to GQG in order to

---

118 Figures quoted in Ramspacher, et al., *Chars et blindés français*, p. 75.
119 SHD-GR 2166 , 'État des pertes de l'A.S. (1917-1918)', G.Q.G./1er bureau, unsigned, 1919.
120 Archives Nationales, fichier LEONORE, dossier LH/909/20 (Général Jean Baptiste Estienne).

command the SA, led to a waste of resources which proved harmful to the rapid creation of the tank teams. It accentuated the lack of spare parts and material, too, which affected the operational capability of the units.[121] This evil was enhanced by the order of 850 tracked artillery tractors placed by General Nivelle. In December 1917, Estienne wrote to the Ministry of War to inform it of the supervision of the SA realized by the Automobile Department. 'It kept on triggering everlasting difficulties', he stated. Clemenceau, who had faith in the tanks, had appointed Abel Ferry to carry out an investigation of the matter.[122] Based on the findings of the MP-soldier, and in an effort to prevent the disorder which was so harmful to the war effort, Clemenceau decided to establish through a Decree of 8 January 1918, a 'Directorate for Assault Artillery' under the Artillery Command. The manufacturing aspects alone remained under the responsibility of the Ministry of Armaments. In May 1918, *Le Tigre* was convinced by Estienne's arguments and decided that only the President of the Council and Minister of War had now the authority over all matters related to tanks.[123]

This rationalization effort, however, did not solve the lack of spare parts. On 1 April 1918, the Assault Artillery had as many unavailable or damaged tanks as the machines it had lost in action since its creation.[124] At the armistice, France possessed no more than 200 medium tanks out of the 800 which had been manufactured, due naturally to combat losses, but primarily because it was not possible to perform the necessary repairs on the damaged tanks. But trench warfare had ended – and victory had been achieved – thanks to the massive use of light tanks. So, ultimately, no-one thought seriously about the causes of the failures which had occurred.

---

121 Goya, *La chair et l'acier*, pp. 336, 338.
122 Ferry was the French Deputy of Vosges and a Commissioner to the armed forces.
123 Ramspacher, et al., *Chars et blindés français*, p. 12.
124 Le Gouest, 'Chars et statistiques', p. 81.

4

From the *Bremerwagen* to the A7V: German Tank Production and Armoured Warfare, 1916-1918

Ralf Raths

While the German *Panzerwaffe* which secured many of the victories of the *Wehrmacht* in the Second World War is still of great interest to historians, there has been no corresponding attention paid to its predecessor in the Great War.[1] But analysing the history of successes and failures of German tanks in the First World War promises to be extremely rewarding for the researcher. While at first glance it appears to be a classic case study of an army failing when confronted with technological as well as organizational challenges,[2] a close look, however, reveals rather more complex mechanisms at work behind the processes of experimentation, procurement and employment of tanks in battle by the Imperial German Army in the final two years of the Great War.

In order to explain what was a very complex and tangled story, several different approaches will be combined. Since the main part of this account needs to deal with the departments that were involved in the development of the tank and the relations between them, Jeremy Black's idea of concentrating on the organizations themselves will be taken into account. According to Black, military organizations 'can be understood in a double sense, first, the explicit organisation of the military – their unit and command structures – and, secondly, organisation as an aspect of, and intersection and

---

[1] At the same time, this fascination has concentrated mainly on operations and technology. Tank production is as neglected for this period, although an exception is Hartmut Knittel, *Panzerfertigung im Zweiten Weltkrieg. Industrieproduktion für die deutsche Wehrmacht* (Osnabrück, 1995).

[2] Walther Albrecht, *Gunther Burstyn (1879-1945) und die Entwicklung der Panzerwaffe* (Osnabrück, 1973), p. 101.

interaction with, wider social patterns and practices.'[3] The latter allows linkage with the useful cultural model concerning the connection of theory and reality of warfare that has been developed by John Lynn. It elegantly explains the mutual influence of the idea of how war should be fought, on the one hand, and the reality of warfare on the other.[4] As will be shown, this model is easily applicable in the case of German tank production in the First World War. But, as interesting as these approaches may be, one cannot investigate tank development and operations without considering the technology itself.[5] Although the role of technology will not be overemphasized in the way it has been by some historians,[6] it will still be a central factor. It should, of course, be borne in mind that technology always has to be seen within the complex structure of a military organization, which inevitably includes a range of cultural and social parameters.[7]

Before 1916 the German Army was not completely unaware of the idea of combining an engine, a weapon and armour to create a fighting vehicle. However, after considering many technical, financial and tactical factors, the decision was reached to use motor vehicles not as fighting vehicles (let alone all-terrain), but rather for logistics, and even then only on roads.[8] This changed somewhat with the advent of trench warfare. Many horses died of exhaustion or in battle, while fodder also ran short. The terrain in the West got worse and brought the remaining horses to their limits, the payloads became even heavier, with bigger artillery pieces and greater quantities of ammunition. Hence, the first step toward tanks was to consider lorries for logistics on the battlefield. As the terrain was challenging, several concepts of (unarmed and

---

3   Jeremy Black, 'Military Organisations and Military Change in Historical Perspective', *Journal of Military History*, 62 (October 1998), p. 871.
4   John A. Lynn, *Battle: A History of Combat and Culture from Ancient Greece to Modern America* (Cambridge, 2004), pp. 359-70.
5   Although the role of the tank as an actual battle winner is still disputed, a technological perspective cannot be completely neglected. George Raudzens, 'The Measurement of Technological Determinism in Military History', *Journal of Military History*, 54 (1990), p. 422.
6   One such historian is Martin van Creveld, who has gone so far as to claim that 'war is completely permeated by technology and governed by it'. Martin van Creveld, 'Technology and War I: To 1945', in Charles Townshend (ed.), *Modern War* (Oxford, 2005), p. 203.
7   Max Boot, *War Made New: Technology, Warfare and the Course of History, 1500 to Today* (New York, 2006), p. 15; and, Heinrich Walle, 'Die Bedeutung der Technikgeschichte innerhalb der Militärgeschichte in Deutschland, Methodologische Betrachtungen', in Roland G. Foerster & Heinrich Walle (eds.), *Militär und Technik. Wechselbeziehungen zu Staat, Gesellschaft und Industrie im 19. und 20. Jahrhundert* (Herford & Bonn, 1992), esp. p. 25.
8   Heinrich Kaufhold-Roll, *Der deutsche Panzerbau im Ersten Weltkrieg* (Osnabrück, 1995), p. 25.

unarmoured) tracked vehicles were tested from 1915 onwards.[9] Yet it was not until the appearance of the first British tanks on the battlefield in September 1916 that German tank development began. In tracing the history of German tank production and attitudes to armoured warfare, this contribution will adopt a strictly chronological approach, examining what can be seen as four distinct phase.

Initial Reactions and First Steps (October 1916 – March 1917)

The first encounter with Allied tanks on 15 September 1916 acted as a catalyst for the development of German tanks.[10] The first steps which resulted from this initial reaction can be traced clearly. Over two weeks later, on 2 October 1916, the Headquarters of 1st Army sent a report about the tanks to the *Oberste Heeresleitung* (German Supreme Army Command, or OHL). The Army HQ commented that this new weapon was 'potentially noteworthy'.[11] This report can be seen as the starting point of German tank development. This process had so many participants that the most important (at least for the first phase) will need to be outlined briefly before turning to subsequent events.

One of the main participants was the Prussian Ministry of War. The Ministry of War was the central authority for everything except actual operations, so it organized the structure, equipment, weaponry and everything else.[12] Tank development and production was thus a task for this ministry. The General War Office (*Allgemeines*

---

9 Wolfgang Schneider & Rainer Strasheim, *Deutsche Kampfwagen im 1. Weltkrieg. Der A7V und die Anfänge deutscher Panzerentwicklung* (Friedberg, 1988), p. 4. See also Peter Chamberlain & Chris Ellis, *Tanks of World War I: British and German* (London, 1969), pp. 54-9.
10 For interesting accounts, see: Patrick Wright, *Tank: The Progress of a Monstrous War Machine* (London, 2000), pp. 38-53; and, Douglas Orgill, *The Tank: Studies in the Development and Use of a Weapon* (London, 1970), pp. 20-22.
11 Bundesarchiv, Koblenz (hereafter, BA), RH 61/1019, Generalmajor a.D. [Erich] Petter, Kampfwagen-Abwehr im Weltkriege 1914-1918, bearbeitet im Auftrage der Inspektion der Kampfwagentruppen, unpublished MS, Berlin, 1932, p. 2. The works of *Generalmajor* Erich Petter, two very detailed studies dating from 1932, are one of the main sources on German tank development in the First World War, since many documents which he used were lost in the fire at the *Heeresarchiv* in Potsdam in April 1945. Luckily, Petter understood his work not so much as historiography, but more as a collection of important data. For Petter's value as a source, see Alexander Fasse, 'Im Zeichen des "Tankdrachen": Die Kriegführung an der Westfront 1916-1918 im Spannungsverhältnis zwischen Einsatz eines neuartigen Kriegsmittels der Alliierten und deutschen Bemühungen um seine Bekämpfung', PhD diss., Humboldt Universität Berlin, 2007, p. 40.
12 Wiegand Schmidt-Richberg, 'Die Regierungszeit Wilhelms II.', in Militärgeschichtliches Forschungsamt (hereafter, MGFA) (ed.), *Deutsche Militärgeschichte 1648-1939*, III.V (Munich, 1983), pp. 53-4, 67. The German Army had, strictly speaking, a federal character and was composed of different contingents from the federal states. Three of these states had their own war ministries (Bavaria, Saxony and Württemberg), but the Prussian Ministry of War was without doubt the leading authority and acted informally as the

Kriegs-Departement) with its numerous sub-departments was the executive section. Since a Tank Department was never created, many departments of the War Office had to work together on tank design. These were A2 (the department of infantry, A for *Abteilung*, meaning department), ANch (Nch for *Nachrichten*, therefore intelligence and communication), A4 (field artillery), A5 (*Fußartillerie*; in earlier times artillery for fortification warfare, but basically all heavy and super-heavy artillery in the years before the Great War) and A6 (combat engineers). Most important was the department A7V (*Verkehr*) – the department for motor transport, which had the task to organize 'the whole field of motor vehicles'.[13] A7V cooperated with several testing commissions, which handled the technical parts in the development and testing of material. Commissions existed for vehicles (VPK, *Verkehrprüfungskommission*), for rifles and machine-guns (GPK, *Gewehrprüfungskommission*) and for artillery (APK, *Artillerieprüfungskommission*). At this point, it ought to have become clear that the organizational structure within the Ministry of War alone was overly complex.[14] At least nine different groups had to work together on tank design – and this conglomerate was just one of the participants in the overall process.

The 'opponent' was the OHL, and within it two departments in particular. The department OI (*Operationsabteilung*, department of operations), in which the section OIc under Major Alfred von Vollard-Bockelberg had to deal with all operational aspects of planes, motor vehicles of all kinds and, when the matter arose, tanks. Given the size of the section's task, it is tempting to say that is perfectly understandable that the new weapon was not high on its list of priorities when it first became involved.[15] The other important department of the OHL was the OII which officially dealt with 'economic questions regarding operations'. This basically meant the providing of material in all forms, so this department was a very important and powerful institution. The section OIIb specialized in the provision of weaponry and the assessment of inventions. It was also of the utmost significance that this section's leader, Max Bauer, had excellent personal connections to German heavy industry. He was a central figure in the development and procurement process.[16]

There could have been one element which connected these agencies – the Inspector General for Traffic and Transportation. Established in 1911, this department had just one problem – it was required to deal with everything to movement throughout army, while it had nearly no men and no respect among its peers. As a result, it did not

---

Ministry of War for the whole German Empire. Personnel policies were not, however, dealt with there, rather in a special office, the *Militär-Kabinett*.
13 Heinrich Kaufhold-Roll, *Panzerbau im Ersten Weltkrieg*, p. 29.
14 Although, formally, the PKs were only associated to the Ministry of War, they can be regarded as 'part of the Ministry team'.
15 Heinrich Kaufhold-Roll, 'Die Entstehung des Schweren Kampfwagens (A7V)', in Komitee Nachbau Sturmpanzerwagen A7V (hereafter, Komitee Nachbau) (ed.), *Sturmpanzerwagen A7V. Vom Urpanzer zum Leopard 2* (Herford & Bonn, 1990), p. 30.
16 Ibid., p. 31.

participate in the development of the tank.[17] The clash between the Prussian Ministry of War and the OHL over the question of the tank was part of a wider struggle. As the war progressed, the OHL tried to centralize and concentrate as much responsibility as possible in its own offices at the front, far away from the authorities at home. The Ministry of War, like many other agencies, tried to fight these trends in wartime management.

With reference to the 1st Army report sent to the OHL on 2 October 1916, the Prussian Minister of War Adolf Wild von Hohenborn, who had received a copy, made the following note: 'Deserves serious attention despite some failures. We shall not be outwitted in any form!'[18] On 11 October 1916, the OHL sent a note (along with descriptions and drawings of the British tanks from the front) to the Ministry of War which shows no divergence from this view: 'Without overestimating the appearance of these fighting vehicles, some results cannot be denied. By all means an improved vehicle would be an effective weapon. I therefore see it as necessary that the construction of such a vehicle is started immediately ... As soon as a useful model is found, mass-production of such vehicles ought to be started.' The Minister of War added a handwritten comment: 'He can be informed that we are already dealing with this matter. Solution is urgent – and important!'[19] On the very same day, the Minister of War contacted his department A7V and wrote: 'Personal messages from the front encourage my opinion that we have a respectable opponent in the enemy's armoured vehicles, which can – improved and increased in numbers – become a serious disadvantage for us in the spring. The finalizing of a German model is highly urgent.'[20] On 23 October 1916, the OHL sent the Ministry of War more drawings, descriptions and the information, pointing out France was working on tanks, too. The OHL asked for an acceleration of construction and mass-production so that the armies at the hotspots of the front could be equipped with these vehicles as soon as possible. The War Minister agreed once again.[21]

At this point, approximately one month after the appearance of British tanks, there is no sign of the reactions which have been claimed to have followed – indeed, there is no evidence in the available source material of laziness, technophobia, or an underestimation of the new weapon. The Ministry of War and OHL were both alert and active: both agencies were able to think over the wider perspective, since they realized that they were dealing with a long-term development and procurement project. As both agencies agreed that time was of the essence, the army turned to the projects which

---

17 Ibid., p. 53.
18 BA, RH 61/1020, Petter, Kampfwagen-Abwehr, p. 3.
19 BA, RH 61/1021, Entwicklung und Auslieferung des A7V Panzerwagens (1941-1942), KM. Verkehrsabteilung – A7V – I.4.8 (hereafter, Entwicklung und Auslieferung), Nr. 28, Heft 1, Bl. 22, and, OHL to Ministry of War, Infantry Dept., 11 October 1916.
20 BA, RH 61/1019, Generalmajor a.D. [Erich] Petter, Die technische Entwicklung der deutschen Kampfwagen im Weltkriege 1914/1918, unpublished MS, Berlin, 1932, p. 14.
21 Ibid., p. 15.

were already in progress – prototypes for all-terrain lorries. At this point, a range of types were all in various states of completion, although some were still on the drawing board, others in the form of small-scale models, or genuine prototypes. These models had been developed by private industry, big automobile or machinery firms, small companies or even individual engineers, all hoping that the army would order a large number of their vehicle once the design had been approved.

The models' range started with the absolutely absurd 'Goebel Land Cruiser' (*Landpanzerkreuzer*) which had been under development since 1913 and would have had dimensions of 118ft in length, 17ft width, 17ft height and a weight of 550 tons.[22] Another strange, but more realistic design was the *Treffas-Wagen*,[23] which was basically a cabin between two really big wheels, stabilized by a rear wheel. Ten were ordered by the German Army for testing but, since the prototype tended to dig itself in while attempting to cross trenches, the order was quickly reduced to one. The *Zechlin-Wagen* was another exotic design, based on parallel revolving vats (*Schreitkufensystem*), but, although it was tested between early 1916 and June 1917, it never functioned properly. The same goes for another vats-system, the *Steil-Wagen*. More realistic models were the *Dür-Wagen* and the *Orion-Wagen*, vehicles based on crawler tracks. The most promising concept was the *Bremerwagen*, which merits further attention because it was seen as the first potential tank by the army in the winter of 1916.

On 17 July 1915, the Ministry of War had assigned the task to design an all-terrain lorry (*Überlandwagen*) to an engineer, Hugo Bremer. His approach seems uninspired today. He simply took a lorry and replaced each wheel with tracks. But what may sound straight-forward was not that easy in 1915. While usable track systems were indeed at least thirty years old at this point, they were in no way common in Germany. On the other hand, there were many other ideas how a vehicle theoretically could be made suitable for all types of terrain, so a difficult decision had to be made.[24] Indeed,

---

22 Chamberlain & Ellis, *Tanks*, p. 54. The idea was dismissed in May 1917, but, interestingly enough, the Crown Prince himself had interest in this project and arranged another exhibition of a model in June 1917. For interesting thoughts regarding the mixture of technological progress and utopian ideas in this period, see Michael Salewski, 'Geist und Technik in Utopie und Wirklichkeit militärischen Denkens im 19. und 20. Jahrhundert', in Foerster & Walle (eds.), *Militär und Technik*, pp. 73-97.
23 Today *Wagen* in German usually means a normal car, but in the First World War it could describe practically any motor vehicle. The German names for tanks changed over the years, but they usually incorporated the term *Wagen*. The first was *Sturm-Panzerkraftwagen*, which can roughly be translated as 'armoured assault motor vehicle', the last was simply *Schwere Kampfwagen*, which means 'heavy fighting vehicle'. The term *Kampfwagen* was in use until 1945 within the term *Panzerkampfwagen*, but has not been revived in the *Bundeswehr*, the post-1945 German armed forces.
24 Kenneth Macksey & John Batchelor, *Tank: A History of the Armoured Fighting Vehicle* (London, 1970), pp. 14-15. Macksey and Batchelor speak of (and show) 'a continuous flow of different devices, intended for the same purpose, [that] had been proposed and built.'

the actual combining of the lorry chassis, the engine and the tracks was a technical challenge all of its own.

Coincidentally, the *Bremerwagen* had its first demonstration in front of Ministry of War officials on 6 October 1916 – only four days after the first report on tanks. But the model proved a failure. The engine was underpowered, the steering was practically non-existent, but A7V of the Ministry of War ordered twenty test vehicles anyway. The reason was that the OHL wanted tanks at the front fast, so A7V decided to at least explore and improve the *Bremerwagen* simply because it was available. It was at this point that the first institutional friction occurred. On 23 January 1917, the infantry department A2 decided to establish two units (*Sturm-Panzerkraftwagen-Abteilungen*) of five *Marienwagen* (improved and armoured version of the *Bremerwagen*)[25] each. The *Marienwagen* was still unarmed, unfit for service and the units were considered as part of the infantry branch. A7V, A2 and OHL were clearly not communicating here, and these problems continued. For the next few weeks, the OHL demanded tanks for the front and the Ministry of War reported that the *Marienwagen* was under development. But when members of the OHL saw these (still unfit) vehicles for the first time at a demonstration on 12 March 1917, they were disappointed;[26] they consequently revoked the order to form the *Marienwagen* units on 3 April 1917.[27] Yet, as the first demonstration on 6 October 1916 had been rather unconvincing, a parallel and much more important project had been started: the development of the A7V tank, codenamed after the War Ministry department responsible.

On 30 October 1916, a conference was held that brought together the important participants in this project: A7V, the VPK, GPK and APK, and members of the VDMI, the *Verein deutscher Motorfahrzeugindustrieller* (Association of German Motor Vehicle Industrialists). The members of the VDMI represented industry, including delegates from Daimler, Dürkopp, NAG, Benz, Büssing and Hansa-Lloyd. Due to the pressure of time, the group dismissed an open call for tender, which was no great sacrifice since many of the big companies were already at the conference. The VPK was the official contractor, supported by the APK and the GPK, and a Technical Commission that consisted of engineers from private industry. This Technical Commission carried an impressive list of names: Prof. Hofmann of Büssing, *Geheimrat* von Opel of the Opel company, *Kommerzienrat* Junck of NAG, *Direktor* Horch of Audi, *Ober-Ingenieur* Link of Daimler and *Direktor* Winkler (no company name is given in the surviving record of the meeting).[28] There were no representatives of the OHL involved in this

---

25   Schneider & Strasheim, *Deutsche Kampfwagen im 1. Weltkrieg*, p. 4.
26   BA, RH 61/1021, Entwicklung und Auslieferung, Nr. 28, Heft 1, Blatt 179, OHL to Ministry of War, 15 March 1916, noting, 'The vehicle seems to perform well as a lorry; as a tank it suffices not.' [Underlining in original, RR]
27   Kaufhold-Roll, *Panzerbau*, pp. 37-9.
28   BA, RH 61/1019, Petter, Technische Entwicklung, pp. 19-22.

project. A catalogue of technical parameters was determined which the new design had to fulfil.[29]

From the purely technical perspective, even relatively small details were proving difficult. In the first phase of the development programme, the VPK tried to secure a usable track system. But, since they were not able to find a single system in the German Empire, they had to examine a track system that the Austro-Hungarian Army had coincidentally shown in Berlin at this time. The VPK had to contact the company which had built this model, Caterpillar-Holt; it was brought to Berlin from Budapest, together with a Hungarian driving-instructor who knew how to operate it. But this initiative paid off. The track-system was successfully modified to become the basis of the A7V – and the German Empire had to pay Caterpillar-Holt for using their patented system.[30] Since the VPK had to rely on industry for every part of the A7V, the list of firms who were part of the project was extensive. By early January 1917, there were sixteen firms involved in the construction of the tank.[31]

On 15 November 1916, the OHL made the task even more complex. It was decided the A7V chassis needed to be suitable for two tasks: to carry armour and weapons, hence making it a fighting vehicle; *and* it had to be able to operate as an all-terrain-lorry – if no armour and weapons were carried.[32] Although many aspects of the project took time, the A7V was constructed with astonishing speed. The engineers began planning on 28 November 1916, finishing the plans on 22 December 1916. The first chassis (with a wooden mock-up) was ready on 16 January 1917; the first demonstration was held on 30 April 1917.[33] One has to bear in mind that no preliminary work in this field of engineering had taken place; likewise the engineers were not in a position to copy a captured machine since the first British tank was captured on 12 April 1917, three months after the first tests of the A7V chassis.

It is at this point, however, that the first wrangles began. VPK planned from the beginning to order at least 100 A7Vs, arguing that only correct tactical employment for such a complex and expensive weapon was to use them in great, concentrated masses – ideally with the advantage of surprise in the first operation. On 31 March 1917, VPK even suggested increasing the number to be ordered to 200. However, between mid-December 1916 and mid-January 1917, the OHL changed its mind.

---

29 Schneider & Strasheim, *Deutsche Kampfwagen im 1. Weltkrieg*, p. 8.
30 Kaufhold-Roll, *Entstehung*. p. 57.
31 BA, RH 61/1021, Entwicklung und Auslieferung, Nr. 28, Heft 1, Bl. 244, VPK to Allgemeines Kriegsdepartment, 3 January 1917, Liste der Firmen für A.7.V.-Wagen, p. 2.
32 This is not to be confused with modern modular concepts, with changing configuration from task to task. The idea was to develop a track-based standard chassis that fit both tasks and formed the base for a production line of tanks and a production line of all-terrain lorries. Once one A7V was built as a tank or a lorry it was permanent. The same multi-role idea was applied to the *Orion-Wagen*. BA, RH 61/1021, Entwicklung und Auslieferung, Nr. 28, Heft 1, Bl. 301, VPK to A7V, 13 February 1917, Orion-A7V-Wagen.
33 Kaufhold-Roll, *Panzerbau*, p. 45.

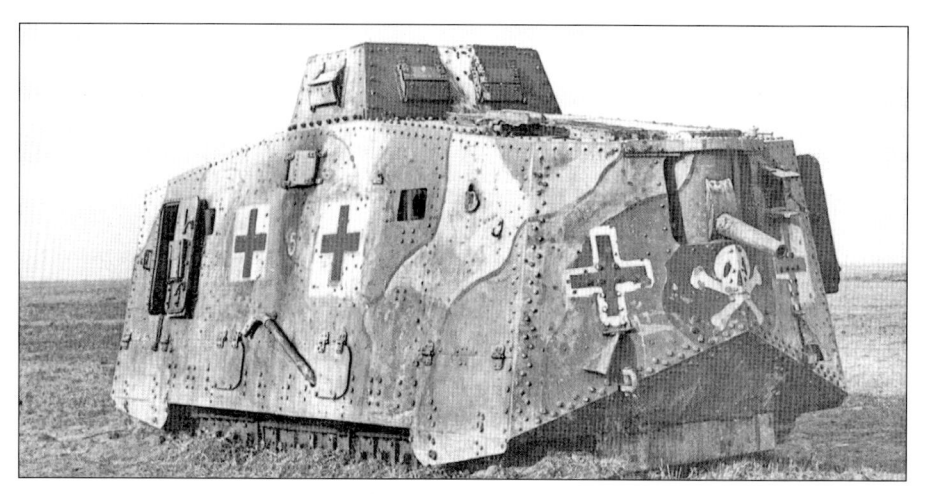

Photo 5: A7V, 1918

On 21 January 1917, it instructed that only ten of the 100 planned A7Vs should be produced as tanks, the remaining ninety were to be produced as all-terrain lorries. Although the number of tanks was raised to twenty-five on 16 February 1917, and VPK had new hope for a short time, things went from bad to worse. On 6 April 1917 OHL then denied that tanks had been put on the highest priority list for resources.[34]

Since the German tank development programme had started shortly after the beginning of the rigid Hindenburg programme of August 1916, not being on the rank one list (out of three ranks) meant that there was practically no chance of getting enough construction materials to build the tanks quickly, or, indeed, to build them at all. This had been a problem even from the beginning of the development of the A7V. On 12 December 1916 the VPK had sent a letter to the department A7V, complaining that the firms which had been urgently asked to deliver and process material were uncooperative, so much so that not even a single prototype would be ready for spring 1917. Hence, they asked that the Minister of War should decree that the relatively small amounts of material should be of the highest priority.[35] The VPK even proposed that industrialists whose firms would significantly speed up the A7V project could be

---

34 BA, RH 61/1021, Entwicklung und Auslieferung, Nr. 28, Heft 2, Blatt 42, Telegram from OHL to Ministry of War, 6 April 1917.
35 One should not think of the weight of one A7V prototype here, because due to bureaucratic processes the VPK already had to plan the construction of all vehicles at this point. The VPK therefore ordered 111t aluminum, 35.47t copper-tin-alloy, 5.1t copper, 2.3t nickel, 1.21t messing and small amounts of other metals. According to the VPK, this was already the absolute minimum ('das Minmum …, von dem irgendwelche Abstriche unmöglich sind.'). BA, RH 61/1021, Entwicklung und Auslieferung, Nr. 28, Heft 1, Bl. 272, VPK to Allgemeines Kriegsdepartment, 3 January 1917, A.7.V.-Wagen, pp. 1-2.

awarded an official decoration. That would have been a rather unusual step, and the VPK knew that, but they expected a notable quickening of pace as a result.[36] On 15 February 1917, the OHL put the tanks on priority two list, but added that this could change once the finalized A7V had been tested.[37] The VPK stressed repeatedly that this classification was in direct contradiction to the statements of the OHL and the Ministry of War about the urgency of the tank problem.[38]

Yet, at the same time, the OHL started to harass the A7V engineers with new demands regarding the design of the tank. In February 1917, for example, it requested that the A7V should be safe against direct hits from field artillery from all sides – and not only on the frontal armour, which had been the specification until then. The VPK answered that, since the tank would have to carry a reduced number of weapons, this would violate one of the central doctrines of the German Army: 'Wirkung geht vor Deckung' (in essence, 'The effect of firepower is more important than protection').[39] Now, this argument is a very interesting one. What we see here are engineers in conflict with the operations department of the army,[40] who were using not a technical but a tactical argument to make their point. The doctrine which was cited represented one of the core ideas behind tactical thought in the German Army – it could not just simply be passed over by the OHL.[41] It was an even more convincing argument, since it was felt throughout the whole army, including the OHL, that trench warfare was the exact opposite of how war should be fought.[42] So using this argument in this context had a subtle subtext: if the OHL were to violate this core doctrine in the design of the tank, which was intended to break the stalemate, this would mean it would be violating it *again* – a repeat of November 1914, when the first trenches were built. In other words, this note from VPK to OHL was bordering on the poisonous. The OHL reacted accordingly: there was to be no discussion – either VPK created such an artillery-proof A7V, or there would never be more than ten A7Vs. VPK gave in and, on 28 February 1917, delivered plans for the new armoured fighting vehicle. We do not know what the reaction of the OHL was.

In March 1917, OIc within the OHL had a new idea. VPK was ordered to copy the concept behind the British tanks and build a rhomboid version of the A7V (designated

---

36 BA, RH 61/1021, Entwicklung und Auslieferung, Nr. 28, Heft 1, Bl. 179, VPK to A7V, 12 December 1916, A.7.V.-Wagen. Materialbeschaffung, p. 2.
37 BA, RH 61/1021, Entwicklung und Auslieferung, Nr. 28 Heft 1, telegram from OHL to War Office, 15 February 1917.
38 For example, BA, RH 61/1021, Entwicklung und Auslieferung, Nr. 28, Heft 1, Bl. 333, VPK to Allgemeines Kriegsdepartment, 12 March 1917.
39 BA, RH 61/1019, Petter, Technische Entwicklung, p. 28.
40 The reputation of the General Staff was extremely high. The soldiers serving there were sometimes referred to as *Halbgötter*, meaning 'demi-gods'. Gordon Craig, *Deutsche Geschichte 1866-1945. Vom Norddeutschen Bund bis zum Ende des Dritten Reiches* (Munich, 1989), p. 152.
41 Ralf Raths, *Vom Massensturm zur Stoßtrupptaktik. Die deutsche Landkriegtaktik im Spiegel von Dienstvorschriften und Publizistik 1906 bis 1918* (Freiburg i.Br., 2009).
42 Lynn, *Battle*, pp. 361-2.

A7V-U, U meaning *Umlaufkette*, encircling track) to test whether this variant possessed any advantages.[43] VPK again declared that this project would be pointless, but this time they did not want to risk a new quarrel. They designed and actually built one A7V-U. The design, however, only seemed to possess negative features. Thus, after a dynamic start in the winter of 1916, the OHL completely changed its mind regarding the tank question in the first quarter of 1917. It reduced the numbers of planned tanks, cut resources to the project, and even ended up in a direct confrontation with its chief contractor, VPK.

Fading from the Spotlight (March 1917 – December 1917)

In considering what had gone wrong towards the end of the first stage of German tank development, several points need to be considered. The first one was down to the strategic direction of the war: the concentration on unrestricted submarine warfare from 1 February 1917 changed the priorities in the OHL. The second was a changing perception of tanks: since September 1916 the shock of the first encounter with British tanks had largely worn off. German anti-tank measures appeared to be working quite well,[44] while the tanks themselves were not performing particularly impressively, both technically and tactically.[45] British tanks could usually be stopped at the tactical level which meant that the OHL feared operational effects less and less. The unimpressive debut of the French tanks on 16 April 1917 reinforced these views.[46] And here the third factor came into play: building tanks would have consumed considerable resources, and in a situation in which materièl and personnel were becoming scarcer.

Following the First World War, a controversy took place in Weimar Germany as to whether the country had allocated resources wisely in its attempt to build tanks. This question continues to be discussed by historians, although with less ferocity than it was debated in the 1920s.[47] But whether the German Empire was able to afford to build tanks in early 1917 is not really the point here. The issue is that the OHL without doubt had few resources and none to waste. Hence, the decision to redirect resources to a new project would have had to have been justified by the prospect of a weapon with war winning qualities. Yet, up to this point the only tank prototypes the

---

43 Chamberlain & Ellis, *Tanks*, p. 67.
44 For German anti-tank development, see the authoritative work by Fasse, 'Tankdrachen', pp. 682-6.
45 Gerhard Förster & Nikolaus Paulus, *Abriss der Geschichte der Panzerwaffe* (Berlin (Ost), 1977), pp. 19-20.
46 Maxwell Hundleby & Rainer Strasheim, *The German A7V Tank and the Captured British Mark IV Tanks of World War 1* (Sparkford, 1990), p. 30.
47 Alexander Fasse makes the interesting point that, regardless of whether Germany could have built a large number of tanks or not, there was no fuel to run them in 1918. Fasse, 'Tankdrachen', p. 676.

OHL had seen were the *Bremerwagen*, which had performed poorly.[48] Given that the already technically mature submarines seemed to possess war-winning potential,[49] while the Allied tanks were performing unimpressively, the OHL had perfectly sound reasons not to make the development of tanks a top priority. A fourth reason is usually forgotten but also has to be taken into account. The OHL had another huge task to take care of at this point: the complete revision of the tactical defensive doctrine and its implementation within the army before the spring of 1917.

As Timothy Lupfer has pointed out, the theoretical part had already taken months to revise – and crucial months these were, from September until early December 1916, precisely the key months of the tank crisis. The more time-consuming task of disseminating the doctrine throughout the army had begun in the winter of 1916-17, which was a period of reorganization and standardization. This phase from December 1916 until April 1917 led to an army 'that in only seven months, despite severe economic and manpower constraints, was organized, trained, equipped, and led according to new defensive principles.'[50] Since the rather poorly staffed OHL was in charge of this gigantic task,[51] and insisted on continuous feedback, it seems likely that there will have been little opportunity for them to become involved in the tank issue. Whether this was the result of a circumspect decision made by the OHL, or whether the organization was simply overwhelmed by the level of work, remains an open question. At any rate, it is clear that the widespread reform of German defensive tactics essentially strangled tank development in early 1917.

Nonetheless, the OHL began to approach tank construction in a fresh way by attempting to centralize all authority under its own roof, mainly as a result of a struggle which had been going on for months and which was to be solved in early 1917. As motorized transport was becoming more essential to the progress of the war, the OHL tried to take control of this field, too, and instigated a reorganization. This collided with various authorities on the home front, particularly with the Ministry of War because the chief prize was control of the key agency *Inspektion des Kraftfahrwesens* (Directorate of Motor Transport, abbreviated *Ikraft*). However, since *Ikraft* was located in the *Reich* it could not be placed under the command of a frontline authority, like the OHL. Still, as the OHL had been growing in influence, especially under the leadership of Paul von Hindenburg and Erich Ludendorff, it was willing to risk a confrontation with the Ministry of War.[52]

48   Hundleby & Strasheim, *German A7V Tank*, p. 30.
49   At any rate, this was an assumption based on the calculations made by the navy, which stated that the submarines would win the war within five months. David Stevenson, *Der Erste Weltkrieg 1914-1918* (Düsseldorf, 2006), pp. 316-7.
50   Timothy Lupfer, *The Dynamics of Doctrine: The Changes in German Tactical Doctrine During the First World War*, Leavenworth Papers No. 4 (Fort Leavenworth, KS, U.S. Army Command and General Staff College, 1981), pp. 24, quote, 11.
51   Ibid., p. 24.
52   BA, RH 61/1019, Petter, Technische Entwicklung, pp. 33, 148.

The power struggle had started several months before the tank question had emerged, but its conclusion took place in the critical period of winter 1916. The OHL emerged victorious and a new position was created on 16 December 1916, the *Chef des Feldkraftfahrwesens* (Head of Field Motor Transport, abbreviated *Chefkraft*). The timing here is interesting, since the creation of *Chefkraft* occurred in a period in which motor transport became of the highest importance due the tank issue. In fact, at the moment when the Ministry of War gave in, it completely 'abandoned its influence on testing and purchasing in the field of motor transport'. Such a process surely caused disgruntlement. But even worse was that it led to organizational friction. For example, up until May 1917 there were two parallel (and competing) testing departments – the testing department of *Ikraft*, known as *Vakraft* (*Versuchsabteilung des Kraftfahrwesens*, testing department of motor transport), that was controlled by *Chefkraft*, and the well-known VPK that somehow secured a form of autonomy until May 1917 when it was put under *Vakraft*'s control.[53]

Hence, by the beginning of 1917, a new player had emerged and the balance of power had shifted. The A7V project of the Ministry of War continued on a small scale, but the OHL was the dominant participant from this point on. However, *Chefkraft* then took a most interesting step. On 31 March 1917, a month before the first demonstration of the A7V, *Chefkraft* sent the plans of a new tank design to the Ministry of War![54] The plans were accompanied by a note stating that the OHL placed a high value on it. The Ministry of War naturally tried to stop this new project – on the one hand, to concentrate efforts on the production of its own A7V, on the other, to cause no irritation to industry by switching priorities. But *Chefkraft* pushed this new project forwards – named the *K-Wagen*.

The *K-Wagen* was a gigantic construction. The final design had a weight of approximately 125 tons, a length of 13 metres, four 77 mm cannons and seven machine-guns, driven by 1300-hp. This design had completely new dimensions, so the engineers could not use their experience from motor-car construction. The chassis was built as a bridge-element, submarine clutches were considered by the designers, while the engines had to be taken from ships. The whole tank was to have been transported in three parts by train since it would not fit on any rail track in one part; in fact, it had to be distributed between fifteen lorries, then assembled 6 km behind the frontline using specially designed truck cranes. The leading German tank engineer, Vollmer, who also was the chief designer of the A7V, mentioned as early as May 1917 that the construction was impractical, and even *Vakraft*, *Chefkraft*'s own testing department, wrote on 18 October 1918 that the *K-Wagen* was ironically only usable in a war of

---

53 Ibid.
54 Although the Ministry of War had lost areas of responsibility over the years, the official channels of course still required the inclusion of this authority at numerous levels.

position and thus was unlikely to be successful in the current type of war.[55] It was a crawling fortress. While there are some critical statements to be found, it is not really clear why this design had any proponents at all. *Chefkraft* later stated that the *K-Wagen* was designed to solve tactical tasks for which the A7V was unsuitable and, therefore, was rather an addition and not a replacement. But this argument was not very convincing.[56] It is most likely that the anti-tank successes of the German Army were indirectly responsible for this design.[57] The OHL concluded from these successes that a tank had to be completely impenetrable in the face of artillery fire if it were to have any chance of survival on the battlefield – hence the demand to create thicker armour for the A7V in February 1917. From this point of view, the *K-Wagen* had one decisive advantage over the A7V – it would survive on the battlefield. Nevertheless, even if the *K-Wagen* possessed advantages, one would have expected some reservations to be expressed by the developers about such a problematic design, at least from the civilian engineers who formed the technical commission.[58] But, at this point, culture and socialization came into play which prevented any worries being expressed: 'A civil member of the commission countered members, who looked on the project of the *K-Wagen* with displeasure, with the exclamation that what His Excellency von Hindenburg wishes had to be executed'.[59]

To recapitulate: by the end of March 1917, several tank projects were in the making (the A7V, the A7V-U and the *K-Wagen*). All-terrain lorries were still being tested with the intention that they might be turned into tanks later, including, amongst others, the *Treffas-Wagen* and the *Orion-Wagen*. Regarding this diversity it is important to look once again at the organization of the German Army. Industry undoubtedly had to be involved in tank development,[60] but there was still no official communications route between the army and industry. Theoretically, A7V would have been the primary department for such negotiations, but it was not clear how such negotiations could be initiated. On occasions industry approached the army, sometimes vice-versa. Then practically everybody talked with everybody. When a civilian design was rejected by an army department, civil engineers often simply approached another department. When the idea of an army department was rejected by a higher department, the development was continued secretly. And, when a design was accepted and needed to be developed, some army officials used their personal contacts in private companies to reach agreement on a contract.

---

55 '… nur für den Stellungskrieg geeignet.' BA, RH 61/1019, Petter, Technische Entwicklung, p. 55.
56 BA, RH 61/1019, Petter, Technische Entwicklung, p. 38.
57 Fasse, 'Tankdrachen', p. 685.
58 *Vakraft* included engineers from Daimler, Adler, Loeb, NAG, Siemens, Benz, Büssing, Audi, Opel, Körting and Deutz, which was even more companies than in the A7V commission.
59 BA, RH 61/1019, Petter, Technische Entwicklung, p. 48.
60 Walle, *Sturmpanzerwagen*, pp. 14-15.

On 14 May 1917, a demonstration of all models was held for the OHL near Mainz, followed by a discussion that led to some key decisions. First of all, two A7V units were to be established,[61] each consisting of five tanks and the necessary support vehicles, personnel, and so on. Since 100 percent reserves were seen as imperative, the number of A7V chassis to be armoured was raised from ten to twenty. More tanks would need to be produced if the first units proved themselves. Although, in this way, at least twenty A7V tanks would be built later, it was a clear and final defeat for VPK since the concept of mass employment, so important to VPK, was dismissed. On the other hand, the construction of ten *K-Wagen* was to be authorized in the near future.[62] The *Treffas-Wagen*, along with many other designs, was finally dismissed; the *Orion-Wagen* survived the demonstration, but required further development.[63]

Over the next few months, all the teams worked on their designs, but, due to technical problems and the fact that tanks were still a low priority, work progressed slowly. It is important to stress at this juncture that, although the OHL allowed some tanks to be built in May, the programme nearly came to a complete halt in the following months since the OHL did not make the necessary resources available. For example, on 11 June 1917, even *Chefkraft* (part of the OHL itself) changed its mind and also wanted to order 100 more A7V chassis, in the same way as VPK had been demanding since 31 March 1917. However, on 8 July 1917, this idea was rejected. A7V continued to enforce this plan, but received a negative answer from *Takraft* on 13 July 1917, on account of scarce resources, namely aluminium and tin.[64]

The second major change came with the tank battle of Cambrai, which began on 20 November 1917. The OHL informed *Chefkraft* and the Ministry of War: 'The recent battles of the 2nd Army showed again the large moral and tactical impact of tanks in battle.'[65] The OHL now wanted to speed up the tank programme. While the *Orion-Wagen* was abandoned (a decision which led to a law suit),[66] on 7 December 1917 tanks were placed on the first priority list for resources (at least for steel and iron); on 13 December 1917, ten additional 'units of armour' were permitted up to thirty-eight in

---

61 This did actually not happen until 29 September 1917. BA, RH 61/1019, Petter, Technische Entwicklung, p. 42. A third unit was permitted on 6 November 1917. These *Abteilungen* were established as parts of the motor transport corps, not as a branch in their own right. Hundleby & Strasheim, *German A7V Tank*, p. 34.
62 This actually did not happen until 28 June 1917. BA, RH 61/1019, Petter, Technische Entwicklung, p. 45.
63 The Orion already was a good design, but had one problem: it used a form of pedrail system with eighteen track 'feet' on each side, with steering provided by a steel wheel at the front. The 'feet' tended to get stuck in barbed wire.
64 BA, RH 61/1021, Entwicklung und Auslieferung, Nr. 28, Heft 2, Bl. 141, Takraft to A7V, 13 July 1917, A7V Wagen.
65 BA, RH 61/1019, Petter, Technische Entwicklung, p. 56.
66 BA, RH 61/1019, Petter, Technische Entwicklung, p. 101.

total;[67] and, the 100 percent reserve was given up to get more tank units to the front quickly with the existing vehicles.[68]

However, this attempt at rationalization was thwarted when a parallel development was started. Engineer Vollmer had been thinking about light tanks since May 1917 and autonomous developments such as the *Leichter Kampfwagen* (LK). The basic idea was to mount relatively thin armour, tracks and a machine-gun on cars which had been taken out of service. These vehicles would not be that well protected but, compared to heavy tanks, fast, agile and easy to build.[69] *Chefkraft* and Vollmer worked together on this project from September 1917 onwards, but on 17 January 1918 the OHL rejected this type of tank as too easy to destroy. *Chefkraft* did not stop the project at this point, rather they actually tried to develop an LK with the same speed and agility, although with thicker armour.

The A7V at War: Organization and Operations (January 1918 – November 1918)

Around early January 1918, the first A7V units entered service. The first A7V was ready in late October 1917 – roughly a year after the original development work had started. On 5 January the first unit was ready, the second unit following on 22 March, and the third on 28 March 1918.[70] An individual unit had seven officers, 171 soldiers, five tanks, two cars, one motorcycle and four lorries.[71] Soldiers were recruited from the traditional branches – artillery for the 5.7 cm gun, motor transport corps for the drivers, infantry for the machine-gunners, and so on. According to the one historical account of German tanks in the Great War, there was initially no need for recruitment: 'Replacements were covered by numerous volunteers. The reason for this interest may be seen in the novelty of the weapon, the longer recreation phases between operations, the chance for promotion or decoration and, not least, in the good rations.'[72] Later, *Chefkraft* directly ordered soldiers to the tank units – apparently the novelty had worn off.[73] Yet, although the performance of all the soldiers was judged as satisfactory

---

67 The OHL had already raised this number by eight to twenty-eight on 17 October 1917. The reason for this step is unclear. BA, RH 61/1021, Entwicklung und Auslieferung, Nr. 31, Heft 1, Bl. 102, Chefkraft to A7V, 17 October 1917, A7V-Panzerwagen.
68 Captured tanks were placed under *Chefkraft*'s command at this point to form its own units. These units, which went in service from 8 March 1918, formed by far the largest part of the German tank corps in the First World War, but cannot be examined in detail here. On this, see Fred Koch, *Beutepanzer im Ersten Weltkrieg. Britische, französische und russische Kampf- und Panzerwagen im deutschen Heer* (Freiburg, 1994).
69 This emphasis on simplicity had been the norm in France and Britain since the beginning of their tank development programmes. Macksey & Batchelor, *Tank*, pp. 20, 26.
70 BA, RH 61/1020, Petter, Kampfwagen-Abwehr, p. 192.
71 Uwe Böhm, 'Der Aufbau der deutschen Kampfwagentruppe im Ersten Weltkrieg', in Komitee Nachbau (ed.), *Sturmpanzerwagen A7V*, pp. 160-2.
72 Ernst Volckheim, *Die deutschen Kampfwagen im Weltkriege* (Berlin, 1923), p. 20.
73 Böhm, *Aufbau*, p. 162.

in contemporary sources, perhaps they could have performed better. As one historian noted recently: 'Finally, unlike the British (and later the Americans), the Germans did not form a tank corps. ... Thus they lacked the spirit and self-esteem of the Allied tank men.'[74]

However, once the first unit had received personnel and material, it still required training. It was transferred to a training site in Sedan, in France, where the *Führer- und Generalstabskurs* (Leaders and General Staff course) took place. To quote a very good analysis of this step: 'It is permissible to speculate that the OHL hoped for some tactical ideas to be produced by the training course for the use of the ATDs [assault tank detachment, RR]. The OHL itself still had no significant concept of its own'.[75] The unit failed to satisfy its instructors. In fact, it was declared to be non-operational because of technical problems and, above all, the failure to create a generally homogeneous unit. It was then transferred to *Sturmbataillon 5* for six weeks – the battalion of the famous Willy Rohr. Here the tank crews had to take part in the standard storm troopers' infantry training to develop unit cohesion. It was only later that tanks were incorporated into the training regime.[76] It is interesting that the infantry officers had few reservations about running a training course for soldiers of an entirely new arm of service. The general German tactical principles were simply applied to this new weapon system.

However, the subsequent verdict of the OHL was negative. On 25 February 1918, Erich Ludendorff visited ATD 1 to form an impression of its potential. The unit cooperated with assault infantry during this demonstration and had to cross terrain of increasing difficulty. A letter from *Chefkraft* to A7V summed up the OHL opinion of the event, noting that the A7V had fulfilled the demands that were articulated in the original specifications list of November 1916, but that the battlefield had significantly changed since then. The A7V would never be able to master the battlefields of 1918, since it had two problems which could not be solved – the low nose and the fact that the armour was mounted on the chassis. Both these problems were clearly the product of the multi-role design, *Chefkraft* argued, both could not be solved and both reduced the efficiency of the tank so much that this model could not be used as the main fighting vehicle of the army.[77]

While *Chefkraft* certainly made some valid points in this communication, these may have been exaggerated to promote their own projects, the *K-Wagen* and the LK light tank, since Willy Rohr, regarded as a master tactician at this time, had come to a different judgement only a few days earlier, on 24 February 1918. He agreed that the A7V would need suitable terrain, but that the tank then would be an effective

---

74 Chamberlain & Ellis, *Tanks*, p. 66.
75 Hundelby & Strasheim, *German A7V Tank*, p. 98.
76 Hundleby & Strasheim, *German A7V Tank*, p. 100; BA, RH 61/1020 and Petter, Kampfwagen-Abwehr, p. 185.
77 For technical details, BA, RH 61/1021, Entwicklung und Auslieferung, Nr. 31, Heft 1, Bl. 288/9, Chefkraft to A7V, 2 March 1918.

instrument at the tactical level.[78] The case was settled, however. On 27 February 1918, even before its first mission, the A7V project was dead and buried. The OHL decided that only the twenty A7V which had already been built should go in service – three units with five tanks each, five as a central reserve; the whole group was linked to the logistics of the 1st Army.[79]

All tank units were stationed in Charleroi, where they were quartered in the *Bayerische Armee-Kraftwagen Park 20* (Bavarian Army Motor Vehicle Park 20), a central hub, divided into four departments, with modern workshops and its own salvage unit.[80] Charleroi was also the headquarters of the *Kommandeur der Panzerwagen-Abteilungen* (commander of tank units), a position that was created in May 1918. This commander was directly subordinate to *Chefkraft*.[81] The OHL itself, however, made the decision whether the tank units were to be employed; these decisions were always based on an investigation of the potential operational area, the results of which were communicated to the OHL via telephone or telegraph. If the OHL permitted the operation, the whole tank unit was transported to the area by train. Loading the whole unit could be achieved in less than two hours if necessary.

While the tanks were being transported, the infantry and artillery in the operational area had already prepared the terrain. Trenches were filled up, passages were prepared through the barbed wire, with an effort to maintain secrecy. If the terrain was still not suitable despite the exploration and the preparation, the leader of the tank units was explicitly required by the manual to inform the responsible superiors.[82] The tanks arrived and were off-loaded at night; if this was not possible, aircraft were ordered to secure the airspace over the improvised train station. The tanks were then hidden beneath trees, in barns, or under artificial camouflage, until the operation commenced.[83] The tanks were even hidden from their own troops where possible to avoid endangering the operation. Movement was only allowed at night, the traces of the tracks had to be eradicated, and sounds had to be minimized as far as possible – or to be drowned out by artillery fire.

The tactical principles for the operations were not very elaborate compared to the manuals of the artillery or the infantry at this juncture. The rules for an attack were simple. The main task was to support the infantry by (literally) rolling over enemy

---

78   Kaufhold-Roll, *Panzerbau*, p. 82.
79   BA, RH 61/1019, Petter, Technische Entwicklung, p. 80.
80   In total, there were nearly 700 people working there: four officers, forty NCOs, 350 soldiers and 250 Belgian civilians. BA, RH 61/1019, Petter, Technische Entwicklung, p. 91.
81   Ibid., p. 92.
82   *Anleitung für die Verwendung von Sturm-Panzerkraftwagen-Abteilungen* [Manual for the Employment of Assault Armoured Vehicle Units] of 18 January 1918, §5, reproduced in Edelfried Baginski, 'Einsatzgrundsätze deutscher Kampfwagen im Ersten Weltkrieg', in Komitee Nachbau (ed.), *Sturmpanzerwagen A7V*, pp. 197-8.
83   Volckheim, *Kampfwagen*, pp. 13-14.

positions, pinning down the troops there, and repelling counter-attacks. If the enemy units were weak, the tanks were to attack using surprise and break through the positions from the flank, thus maximizing their impact. The contact between infantry and tanks was never to be broken, since tanks could make an impact, but never hold ground on their own.[84]

Whether the tanks were in front of, amongst, or behind the infantry was dependent on the particular operation, but usually they drove in the vanguard of the first wave. The artillery had to leave corridors in the operational area, so that the tanks would not encounter heavily shelled terrain. If that was not possible, or the terrain was very rough naturally, the tanks were accompanied by combat engineers. Using smoke was a common tactic for the tanks to avoid being seen by enemy artillery, or to get out of their zones of fire. If this did not work, the manual stated that simulating that the tank had been knocked out might work for a period. The instructions for defensive operations were sparse. Tanks were to be held back as a mobile reserve and used for blocking enemy breakthroughs, conducting counterattacks or attacking enemy tanks. Basically, they fought the same way as during an attack.[85] If a tank had to be abandoned, the crew were to remove the machine-guns and usable parts and then take part in the battle as an assault unit, or in a defensive position, depending on the tactical situation – but defensive actions were not to be conducted near the tank since these big objects tended to draw artillery fire.[86]

The A7V tanks saw action on several occasions but never made a more than, at best, a tactical impact.[87] The first action took place on 24 March 1918 at St. Quentin – eighteen months after the army's first encounter with Allied tanks. Only *Abteilung* 1 was ready, and, as Hundleby and Strasheim put it: 'Nobody could expect decisive result from the use of these five A7V tanks (and the five Mark IVs of ATD 11). Therefore, the whole action was nothing but another trial, this time with a real enemy and live ammunition.' Still, although two of the four attacking tanks broke down

---

84 Combat experience demonstrated later that it was not the tanks which were faster, it was rather the infantry. An addendum to the manual, published on 19 May 1918, stated: 'On longer distances the speed of the tanks is not sufficient to keep up with the infantry. The infantry must not be held up in such cases by the temporary falling back of the tanks, but has to fulfil its tasks as fast as possible regardless of the advance of the tanks.' *Merkblatt für das Verhalten der Infanterie beim Zusammenwirken mit Panzerwagen* [Notes on the Conduct of Infantry when Co-operating with Tanks] of 19 May 1918, reproduced in Baginski, 'Einsatzgrundsätze deutscher Kampfwagen', p. 199.
85 This conformed to the general principles of the German defensive doctrine in this period, which was based on the idea of incorporating the spirit and the principles of the attack when on the defensive. Lupfer, *Dynamics*, p. 16; and Raths, *Massensturm*, pp. 189-201.
86 *Anleitung*, reproduced in Baginski, 'Einsatzgrundsätze deutscher Kampfwagen', p. 199.
87 For an overview, BA, RH 61/1012, Forschungsarbeit Archivrat Hildebrandt: Kampfwagentruppe und –abwehr im Ersten Weltkrieg (1931), Anlage 4c, 5-7. For accounts of all operations, G.P. von Zeschwitz, *Heigl's Taschenbuch der Tanks* (Munich & Berlin, 1938), pp. 121-55.

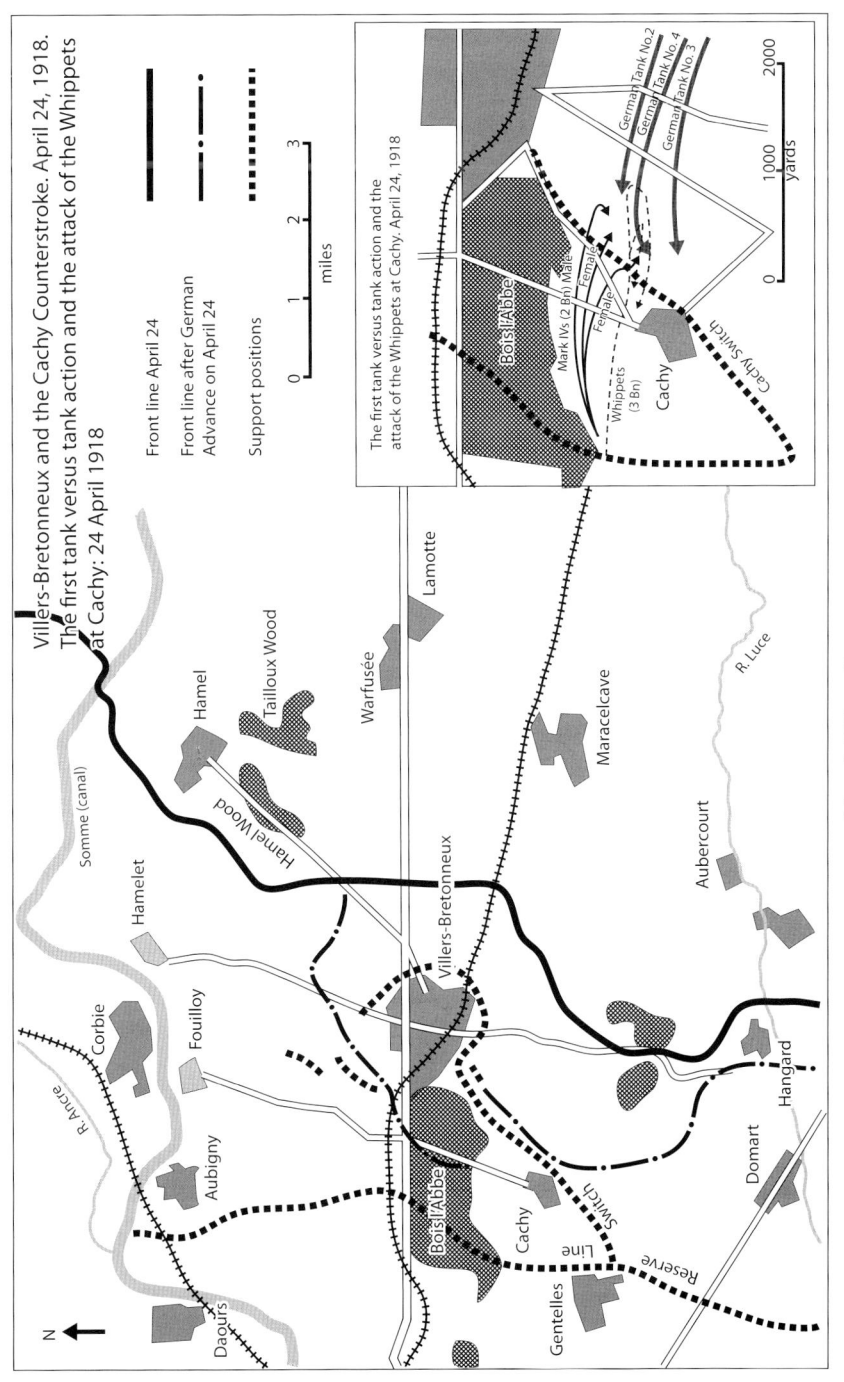

German Tank Production and Armoured Warfare 99

Map 3: Villers Bretonneux

quickly, and although the remaining two had serious problems to find a way through the fog, barbed wire and other obstacles, they cooperated well with the soldiers of Infantry-Division 36, reached the enemy trenches and returned the 'tank shock' to its inventors. The soldiers manning the trenches fled and more than 150 soldiers were subsequently captured; the tanks reached their designated objectives on time, making the mission a success.[88]

The next operation would have been on 8 April, but, when the tanks arrived at the operational area, the attack was already going very well and it became quickly apparent that they were not required.[89] Another unit was ordered to the 6th Army to participate in an attack near Armentieres on 9 April, however this unit as well as the accompanying unit of captured tanks never even reached their starting positions because both units had become stuck in a ravine. They were not only unable to reach the frontline, they even hindered other units.[90]

The next operation turned out to be the biggest success in the history of German tank units in the war: Villers-Bretonneux on 24 April 1918.[91] The 2nd Army wanted to straighten a salient at the front and deployed several infantry divisions, more than 1,200 artillery pieces and over 700 aircraft for the operation; and, it explicitly requested all three tank units. The terrain was ideal for the A7V[92] and fourteen tanks reached the operational area. When the attack began, the tanks advanced with the infantry, but the terrain was so good that this time the tanks advanced too fast and lost touch – they even had to turn around to re-establish contact.[93] The tanks fulfilled their tasks successfully; moreover, the first tank-versus-tank action occurred. Near Cachy the A7V *Nixe* was engaged by one male and two female Mark IV tanks – it is

---

88 Hundleby & Strasheim, *German A7V Tank,* p. 102.
89 Ibid., p. 109. The same interpretation can be found at BA, RH 61/1012, Forschungsarbeit Archivrat Hildebrandt, Anlage 4c, pp. 14-21.
90 Zezschwitz, *Heigl's Taschenbuch,* p. 123.
91 For a detailed account, BA, RH 61/1012, Forschungsarbeit Archivrat Hildebrandt, pp. 14-21.
92 According to one historian, there were 'dry fields and meadows, hardly any obstacles and nearly no trenches, only sporadic shell-holes'. Klaus Paprotka, 'Taktische Einsätze der Sturmpanzerwagen A7V im Jahre 1918', in Komitee Nachbau (ed.), *Sturmpanzerwagen A7V*, p. 224.
93 Volckheim, *Kampfwagen*, p. 23. Turning around to reestablish contact could be, in fact, a dangerous manoeuvre. During a minor action on 30 August 1918, several A7V also had to turn back after they lost contact with their infantry units. But they lost their way and the Bavarian infantry they approached had no knowledge of the tank operation – one could observe that at least the security precautions had been successful. Unfortunately, the Bavarians were unable to identify the A7Vs as German tanks, as they never had seen or perhaps even heard of such vehicles before, so they ordered their artillery to knock them out. Two tanks were hit, although no crew members were killed as a result. Hundleby & Strasheim, *German A7V Tank*, p. 143.

unlikely that there was a 'victor', since all tanks left the battlefield severely battered.[94] The next clash, fought in the same area slightly later, does provide a clear winner. One A7V (named 'Siegfried') prevailed against seven Whippets in a 20-25 minutes long battle, destroying at least one, immobilizing two others and driving the remaining four from the battlefield.[95]

As soon as one unit was ready for action again, it went into combat.[96] After Villers-Bretonneux, *Abteilung* 2 was in action on 31 May 1918 near Reims and experienced the exact opposite. The terrain was unfavourable and the reconnaissance poor – the whole unit drove head-on into a position probably of two complete batteries of field artillery. Immediate retreat was the only option.[97] *Abteilung* 1 went to battle on 1 June 1918 near Reims, too, and again (with *Abteilung* 3) on 9 June 1918.[98] On 15 July 1918, *Abteilung* 1 and 2 were in action near Reims again;[99] on 31 August 1918, both were operating near Cambrai. On 7 October 1918, *Abteilung* 3 was about to start a mission when a river that had previously been reported as 'no obstacle for tanks' turned out to be a deep and broad river and the action had to be cancelled. The last combat action was conducted on 11 October 1918 near Iuwy, a completely defensive mission.[100]

The final balance sheet of these German tanks operations is ambivalent. On the one hand, the material, the personnel and the units as a whole were able to operate successfully. On the other hand, technical problems were omnipresent and, as soon as the terrain became rough, the A7Vs got into trouble. The main problem, however, was poor reconnaissance and the dispersal of the limited number of vehicles, combined with rather diffuse ideas as to what tanks should achieve. These were not tangible problems for the tank units, more of the divisions and armies that used them. But then again these armies and divisions were part of the same German military system. Put succinctly, German armoured warfare as it was conducted at the tactical level was

---

94 Paprotka, 'Taktische Einsätze', p. 225; Hundleby & Strasheim, *German A7V Tank*, p. 120; BA, RH 61/1020, Petter, Kampfwagen-Abwehr, p. 241. According to Foley, 'There is something strongly symbolic about the fact that the first tank vs. tank action in the history was initiated by No. 1 Tank of No. 1 Section "A" Company, 1st Battalion Tank Corps.' John Foley, *A7V Sturmpanzerwagen* (London, 1967), p. 2.
95 Hundleby & Strasheim, *German A7V Tank*, p. 122; Paprotka, 'Taktische Einsätze', p. 226.
96 Volckheim, *Kampfwagen*, p. 25.
97 Hundleby & Strasheim, *German A7V Tank*, p. 128; Paprotka, 'Taktische Einsätze', pp. 229-231; Volckheim, *Kampfwagen*, p. 25; and, Zezschwitz, *Heigl's Taschenbuch*, pp. 131-3.
98 Zezschwitz, *Heigl's Taschenbuch*, pp. 134-40.
99 For an interesting description of this action, see Alfred Stenger, *Der letzte deutsche Angriff, Reims 1918* (Oldenburg i.O., 1930). Since this book is not specifically about the tanks but an account of the battle itself, it places the role of the tanks within a broader perspective.
100 Volckheim, *Kampfwagen*, p. 27. At this point the three *Abteilungen* had already been merged into one unit to reduce the baggage. BA, RH 61/1019, Petter, Technische Entwicklung, p. 123.

successful up to a point, yet the integration of the units as part of operational plans was a failure, not to speak of the strategic dimensions to tank production and deployment.

Technology, New Models, New Dimensions (August 1918 – November 1918)

In the field of technology, the final product of the German tank development programme ought not to be dismissed out of hand.[101] The biggest disadvantage was clearly its lack of trench-crossing ability. Although the A7V could cross trenches up to 2 m, it was lost in heavily shelled terrain. The reason was its 'low nose'. Since the A7V chassis was designed to be able to carry a superstructure for fighting (armour, gun, machine guns), as well as for transportation (flat cargo area), it had to protrude from the tracks horizontally – this was the only solution given the significant payload it had to carry. Still, what was good for the transportation version was bad for the fighting version. The protruding part at the front, the 'low nose', bumped into obstacles before the tracks could reach them and the tank was stopped, literally, 'in its tracks'. The A7V could, therefore, only operate in terrain that was not too heavily shelled. But this problem was not exclusive to the A7V – the French *Char d'assaut St. Chamond* had exactly the same problem, but even worse. The A7V was a complex piece of machinery and the vehicles suffered many mechanical failures during operations; still, the early British tanks had had similar problems. The A7V was never developed further, so it would be pointless to compare the technically superior Mark V with what was, in effect, the German 'Mark I A7V'.

On the other hand, the A7V also had some technical plus points. It was a relatively fast and agile vehicle on suitable terrain; its tracks were largely protected by armour and hence far less vulnerable than the tracks of the British tanks, while the angled armour plates improved the overall level of protection. Chamberlain and Ellis may have summed up German tank technology in the First World War best when they remarked that the problem of the A7V was not that it had too many negative features, but more that it performed weakly in, of all areas, the most important requirement of a Great War tank – stability and trench-crossing ability.[102]

One particularly interesting feature of the A7V was the number of crew members. Although not significantly larger than a British tank,[103] the A7V had far more crew members. Dependent on the task it was given, there were sometimes over twenty

---

101 For technical details, BA, RH 61 /1021, Entwicklung und Auslieferung, Nr. 28, Heft 2, Bl. 202f., Vakraft to A7V, 5 January 1918, A7V-Wagen.
102 Chamberlain & Ellis, *Tanks*, p. 64. According to Foley, 'The greatest shortcoming, however, was in its obstacle-crossing capacity. The limited span of the underhung tracks and the scanty ground clearance (40mm) made negotiating obstacles extremely difficult.' Foley, *A7V*, p. 5.
103 Both about 30t, both about 8m length, the German tank was a little higher, but the typical British tank was broader. Both had a comparable number of weapons; the British machines had six weapon stations, the A7V had seven.

soldiers crammed into the hellishly hot, loud and fume-ridden vehicle: one commander, one driver, three men on the main gun, two engineers, twelve men on six machine guns, one or two couriers, sometimes even specialists for the carrier pigeons. These crew members were taught to change stations in the tank if necessary, a principle that was also used in the infantry. But training always remained a central problem for the German tank units. While the British and French tank corps had enough vehicles to train properly, the Germans were not afforded this opportunity. Driver training was only possible on vehicles which clearly did not have the characteristics of a tank. The first time the driver actually got his hands on an A7V was in France, either in Charleroi, the central base for the tank units, or directly at the front.[104] The same applied to the other members, so the training of the German tank crews was always more improvised than that of their British or French counterparts.[105]

The actual experience inside an A7V did not differ much from that of Allied tank crews. It was extremely loud, hot (over 60°C were not unusual), fume-filled, and there was no room to move. The usual effect of longer operations (the A7V could travel about 25-30km, dependent on the terrain),[106] were headaches, nausea, heart problems, even delirium and fainting. Sometimes crews left the tank while on the battlefield to get fresh air – this tells us a great deal about the conditions they worked under.[107]

Yet, while the A7Vs were still fighting the Allies, the tank developers continued fighting each other. In May 1918, the OHL began to reconsider light tanks as the French models had performed quite well. At this point, there were at least two projects. *Chefkraft* was still developing the LK II,[108] the improved version of the first light tank model. But a parallel project had been started in early 1918. Colonel Max Bauer from OIIb had used his excellent contacts to industry and had developed a light vehicle together with Krupp, the so-called *Krupp-Protze*, a mixture of light tank and motorized limber, quite deliberately without informing *Chefkraft*. The concept behind this vehicle was that it would not only be combat effective in its own right, it would also be capable of pulling a field gun for the infantry (*Infanterie-Geschütz*) to maximize the effect of the combined arms team. When the OHL decided in mid-1918 to reconsider light tanks, they preferred Bauer's design, despite obvious disadvantages compared with the LK II.

In August 1918, the third great change in German tank politics (after April 1917 and November 1917) occurred. Following the 'Black Day of the German Army' on

---

104 Böhm, *Aufbau*, pp. 162, 165.
105 Kaufhold-Roll, *Entwicklung*, p. 27.
106 Volckheim, *Kampfwagen*, p. 21.
107 Ludwig von Eimannsberger, *Der Kampfwagenkrieg* (Munich, 1934), p. 43.
108 Martin van Creveld is, of course, correct when he writes, 'War, however, is an imitative activity.' Van Creveld, *Technology and War*, p. 221. But the LK was not a copy of the Whippet as one often reads, for instance, in Chamberlain & Ellis, *Tanks*, p. 69. That both vehicles looked alike was simply coincidence. The Whippet appeared on the battlefield four months after the LK design project started.

8 August 1918, the OHL decided that radical steps needed to be taken. Colonel Bauer was appointed as the responsible authority for tank questions at the OHL and, surprisingly, with the agreement of the Ministry of War, he started to develop a tank production programme of completely new dimensions for the year 1919. The *K-Wagen*, the A7V-U (which was being reconsidered after February 1918) and A7V were completely erased from the programme. *Vakraft* had to develop a completely new, far more modern, heavy tank – the *Oberschlesienwagen*.[109] This tank was planned to become the standard heavy tank. However, although a role was still envisaged for them, heavy tanks were no longer the centrepiece of German tank production in 1918. Instead, the *Krupp-Protze* and the LK II were to be produced in massive numbers. For that purpose, tank production became the top priority in the process of resources distribution. On 23 October 1918 these ideas were articulated in the official *Kraftwagen-Beschaffungs-Programm* (motorized vehicles supply programme). This foresaw the production of 800 LK II by the spring of 1919 alone, although earlier views from the Ministry of War, which influenced the programme, even spoke of 4,000 light tanks and 400 modern heavy tanks by the end of 1919.[110] The programme also included ideas to revive the long forgotten *Marienwagen* in a new version and to mount 5.7 cm field guns on lorries to create anti-tank trucks.[111]

The plans for mass-production of tanks were far from realization. Although the idea of concentrating on two or three models and mass-producing them was good, it came far too late. At this juncture in the war, the German Army was becoming more desperate by the day. The final proposal makes this clear. On 6 November 1918, the Ministry of War submitted a plan to install 2 cm canons on civilian cars to create improvised anti-tank units. The OHL rejected the idea. Thus, after little more than two years the attempt to create a German tank force came to an ignominious end shortly before the armistice in November 1918.[112] Practically no tanks were built in Germany during this final phase, while the Allied powers built thousands of them – in many ways, a difference which points to many of the reasons why Germany lost the war.

---

109 A call for tender for this project was made in June 1918. Although many companies were interested, the OHL decided to take a design that had been developed by *Chefkraft* – the aforementioned *Oberschlesienwagen*. The design itself was actually impressively modern: it resembled in many ways more a tank of the 1920s than one of the Great War era. Heinrich Kaufhold-Roll, 'Die Entwicklung von Technik und Taktik im Ersten Weltkrieg', in Komitee Nachbau (ed.), *Sturmpanzerwagen A7V*, p. 118.
110 BA, RH 61/1021, Entwicklung und Auslieferung, Nr. 28, Heft 2, Bl. 290, A7V to OHL, October 1918 [no day given, RR].
111 BA, RH 61/1019, Petter, Technische Entwicklung, pp. 111-3.
112 Most A7V were destroyed or captured, the captured tanks were mostly re-captured or given back. Nevertheless a strange, somehow massively modified version of an A7V called *Heidi* and some captured tanks were used during the Revolution, on the side of the government. Uwe Larsen, 'Geschichte der Sturmpanzerwagen A7V von 1918 bis jetzt', in Komitee Nachbau (ed.), *Sturmpanzerwagen A7V*, pp. 273-5.

Conclusion

What were the reasons, then, for a series of German decisions which had a fundamental impact on a flawed programme of tank design and production between 1916 and 1918? In many ways, there was often a concrete military or economic logic to German decision-making. The OHL always studied very carefully the reports from the front and here the tank question was no exception.[113] But after the first shock of the Allied employment of tanks had subsided, these reports formed the basis for the decision not to push the tank programme. While anti-tank warfare was tough and involved casualties in men and material – it proved an effective counter to the threat.[114] Hence, as long as the front demanded German tanks, the OHL tried to mass-produce them quickly; yet, once the frontline troops got used to tanks and learned to combat them, the OHL preferred to concentrate on other issues. Although this had its own rationale, it seems to show a major flaw in German military thinking at this time. The OHL concentrated so much on acute tactical and operational problems that the long-term perspective was neglected. However, it could be argued that the OHL's initial analysis was proved correct because few historians have judged tanks to have been the decisive element of the Allied victory, although a debate still rages as to what extent Allied tanks contributed to victory.[115]

There are, however, problems with this interpretation. If the decision was correct not to overestimate the tanks, and if that decision was made based on military and economic reasons, the question arises as to why the tank programme was continued on such a small scale. It was inevitable it would consume resources, yet with a result which was more than questionable. The situation was aggravated by the constant mood swings of the OHL regarding the tank issue. The degree of support for the half-hearted programme was changing all the time. Sometimes the OHL encouraged tank development and sometimes it blocked the programme, with the consequence that the effort was crippled. If this is taken into account, then the picture changes dramatically. From this perspective, the OHL did not make the right decision – it made no decision at all. On the one hand, it allowed tank development to continue as a form of safety net, on the other it provided virtually no resources and did not coordinate the process efficiently; the respective emphasis apparently only depended on the particular strategic and operational situation at any one time. Then again, such policy shifts could be observed in the Allied armies – the British Tank Corps itself experienced a phase of stagnation over several months because of disinterest on part of the army, although it subsequently changed its mind.[116]

---

113 Lupfer, *Doctrine*, p. 9.
114 Fasse, 'Tankdrachen', pp. 683-5.
115 Fasse, 'Tankdrachen', pp. 28-35; Martin van Creveld, *The Changing Face of War: Lessons of Combat, from the Marne to Iraq* (New York, 2006), p. 76.
116 Kaufhold-Roll, *Entwicklung*, pp. 24, 27; and, Förster & Paulus, *Geschichte der Panzerwaffe*, p. 15.

However, the deliberate parts of the decision were of course just one factor in the process. The organizational structure within which German tank development and production was managed was a system, with many different centres of power which, at any one time, worked independently of each other, in different directions, parallel, often in an uncoordinated fashion, or even in a contradictory way, thus drastically reducing the freedom of action for each agency involved. This fact covers both of Jeremy Black's definition of military organizations. The 'explicit organization' in this case is polycratic and chaotic with overcomplicated structures, failing channels of communication and insufficient coordination. At the same time, the 'wider social patterns and practices' were nothing less than the *Federkrieg*, to use Petter's characterisation, a war of pens. Every faction tried to secure as many resources and as much influence as possible while working to undermine the other groups. This inherently competitive system leads to the question as to how well a design and procurement regime would have worked if the OHL had not changed its mind in early 1917. It is not implausible that there would still have been heavy organizational friction. On the other hand, it is important to bear in mind that the quarrels over the tank question between departments, factions and individuals also occurred in the Allied war economies. The Ministry of War in France and the General Staff also competed over different tank models.[117] So, it is legitimate to ask whether we are dealing here with a specifically German style of military management.

The final aspect which has to be considered concerns the aforementioned cultural dimensions. The Germans had a fairly clear idea of what John Lynn has called the 'discourse of war', that is, how war should be fought. It was what Robert Citino has referred to as 'the German way of war'. Put succinctly: 'Prussia-Germany tried to keep its wars short, winning a decisive battlefield victory in the briefest possible time.… No other country took this trend to such extremes. Prussian armies virtually always tried to get onto the flank or into the rear of their adversaries, not just with one cavalry unit or two, but with the entire force.' And, in addition: 'The Prussian army attacked.… This preference extended from the staff to the field officers all the way down to the tactical level.'[118]

The 'reality of warfare' is how a war is actually fought and that reality is often quite different from the 'discourse of war'. The reality in the years 1914-1918 was surely the complete opposite of the German ideal, at least in the West. And, even though the German Army was far from technophobic and, although the tank was a potential tool to re-adjust the reality of war to the 'discourse of war' by reviving the German way of war, a war of movement, it was at the same time the manifestation of everything the German Army regarded as alien: soulless war material, without morale, the human element or spirit, no different from the 'spiritless' trench warfare they

---

117 Kaufhold-Roll, *Entwicklung*, p. 27.
118 Robert M. Citino, *The German Way of War from Thirty Years' War to the Third Reich* (Lawrence, KS, 2005), pp. 306-12.

had been trying to overcome.[119] It took considerable mental flexibility for a German officer to gain inner distance to this deeply ingrained 'culture of warfare'[120] and, therefore, real proponents of the tank were relatively rare – even rarer than in the Allied armies. In short, this analysis of German tank development has suggested that the German approach to tank design and production was not dramatically different from the French and British: the military, economic, social, political, organizational and cultural parameters were only slightly different to those of the Allies, causing the outcome – the decision *not* to mass-produce tanks.

---

119 'It is difficult to say exactly when "modern" war began, but it was apparent by the end of 1915 that pre-war assumptions were false. ... The "human solution" was not enough. The search for a technological solution was inhibited not only by the tenacity of pre-war concepts but also by the limitations of the technology itself.' John Bourne, 'Total War I: The Great War', in Townshend (ed.), *Modern War*, pp. 131-2.
120 According to Wilson, 'Change in European Warfare was not driven exclusively by technological advance, but filtered through shifting cultural perceptions of how armies should be organized and how war should be fought.' Peter Wilson, 'European Warfare 1815-2000', in Jeremy Black (ed.), *War in the Modern World since 1815* (London & New York, 2003), p. 201.

5

Scouting for Brigands: British Tank Corps Reconnaissance and Intelligence, 1916-1918

Jim Beach

Looking back on his time as chief staff officer of the Tank Corps, the renowned armoured warfare theorist J.F.C. Fuller famously described them as a 'band of brigands'.[1] A recent historian has built upon this description, positing them as a 'futuristic unit' that challenged the army's military and social norms.[2] Unsurprisingly, the corps' innovative use of cutting edge technology has been of perennial interest to military historians. In particular, the contribution of tanks to the British Expeditionary Force's (BEF) way of war has been much discussed and frequently contested.[3] Whatever the rights and wrongs of this debate, it is clear that the use of tanks on the Western Front generated quite specific information requirements. This chapter will explore the ways in which those needs were addressed and, in so doing, will highlight this important

---

1   J.F.C. Fuller, *Memoirs of an Unconventional Soldier* (London, 1936), p. 87. The Tank Corps was known officially as the Heavy Branch of the Machine Gun Corps until July 1917. For simplicity, their later nomenclature has been used throughout this chapter: A.F. Becke, *History of the Great War: Order of Battle*, Vol.4 (London, 1944), pp. 267-83.
2   Christy Campbell, *Band of Brigands: The First Men in Tanks* (London, 2007), pp. 258-60.
3   The following are important milestones in the academic literature: Shelford Bidwell & Dominick Graham, *Firepower: British Army Weapons and Theories of War, 1904-1945* (London, 1982), pp. 131-46; Tim Travers, *How the War was Won: Command and Technology in the British Army on the Western Front, 1917-1918* (London, 1992); J.P. Harris, *Men, Ideas and Tanks: British Military Thought and Armoured Forces, 1903-1939* (Manchester, 1995), pp. 1-194; J.P. Harris, 'The Rise of Armour', in Paddy Griffith (ed.), *British Fighting Methods in the Great War* (London, 1996); David Childs, *A Peripheral Weapon: The Production and Employment of British Tanks in the First World War* (London, 1999); J.P. Harris, 'Haig and the Tank' in Brian Bond & Nigel Cave (eds.), *Haig: A Reappraisal 70 Years On* (Barnsley, 1999); Bryn Hammond, 'The Theory and Practice of Tank Co-operation with other Arms on the Western Front during the First World War', PhD thesis, University of Birmingham, 2005.

dimension to tank operations. Of course, it must be acknowledged that the Tank Corps' reconnaissance work and chief intelligence officer have both made recurring appearances in the organization's histories;[4] but this chapter tries to take a step forward, drawing the strands together and placing these activities in the context of a wider intelligence system. For those with an interest in intelligence more generally, the corps also provides an interesting case study within a technology-driven military environment. Similarly, it offers a useful sidelight upon the relationship between reconnaissance and intelligence during a period of doctrinal flux. Building upon recent work on BEF intelligence,[5] the chapter is structured thematically; it examines in turn the policy, personnel, processes, and products of Tank Corps reconnaissance and intelligence.[6]

The Reconnaissance Imperative

Although incremental improvements were made as the war progressed, the first British tanks were slow moving, difficult to operate, and had a very limited radius of action. These basic technological constraints generated a multitude of challenges for the tank crews and those seeking to work alongside them.[7] As Bryn Hammond has argued, understanding these 'practical factors' of tank usage should underpin any analysis of their military effect.[8] One specific limitation was the tank's severely restricted visibility, particularly when moving under threat of hostile fire. As an early history explained, tank commanders were 'entirely dependent upon their maps [and] compass[es], and upon the information which a preliminary reconnaissance of the ground had given them'.[9] At first, in September 1916, this need for reconnaissance was overlooked. As one tank commander recalled, he was simply presented with 'a map showing … pre-conceived tank routes which had been arbitrarily fixed'.[10] Looking back, another mused about how much more effective the tanks might have been 'if

---

4 Clough & A[mabel] Williams-Ellis, *The Tank Corps* (New York, 1919), pp. 29, 75-76, 80; [Evan Charteris], *HQ Tanks, 1917-1918* (Privately printed, 1920), pp. 87-88; Douglas Browne, *The Tank in Action* (London, 1920), pp. 30, 40, 53; J.F.C. Fuller, *Tanks in the Great War* (New York:, 1920), pp. xv, 59; [Anon.] 'The Organization and Administration of the Tank Corps during the Great War, 1916-1918', *Army Quarterly*, 2 (1924), p. 300; Basil Liddell Hart, *The Tanks*, Vol.1 (London, 1959), p. 88.
5 Jim Beach, *Haig's Intelligence: GHQ and the German Army, 1916-1918* (Cambridge, 2013).
6 For a discussion of this approach to the history of intelligence organizations, see Jim Beach, 'No Cloaks, No Daggers: The Historiography of British Military Intelligence', in Christopher Moran & Christopher Murphy (eds.), *Intelligence Studies in Britain and the United States: Historiography since 1945* (Edinburgh, 2013), pp. 204, 212.
7 'Tanks were inefficient in ergonomic terms and their means to effect co-operation with other arms remained primitive and unsatisfactory throughout the war'. Hammond, 'Theory and Practice', p. 406.
8 Hammond, 'Theory and Practice', p. 380.
9 C. & A. Williams-Ellis, *Tank Corps*, p. 29.
10 The National Archives of the United Kingdom, Kew (hereafter, TNA), CAB 45/134, Holford-Walker to Edmonds, 22 April 1935, cited in Hammond, 'Theory and Practice',

only we had been able to reconnoitre'.[11] Therefore one of the key lessons from their initial usage was, as Fuller put it: 'That tank operations require the most careful preparation and minute reconnaissances in order to render them successful'.[12] So, when the tanks made their next significant battlefield appearance, in November 1916, 'the absolute necessity of good reconnaissance had been recognised'.[13] Then, in February 1917, Fuller codified this reconnaissance imperative as one of the three main elements needed for tanks to operate effectively with the infantry.[14] This prioritization was vindicated by later experiences. As one tank brigade put it succinctly in mid-1917, 'reconnaissance work for the successful employment of tanks is extremely important' but they also noted that such work was 'very difficult'.[15]

Having establishing that good reconnaissance was required by the 'circumstances peculiar to tank operations',[16] the new corps decided that it needed its own system to generate and manage that information. One tank chronicler drew a parallel with the Royal Flying Corps in this need for a unique capability 'run on individual lines'.[17] This entity became known as the reconnaissance branch or service. Within the early literature, and so presumably also at the time, there was a lack of precision as to its nomenclature and 'intelligence' was often used synonymously with 'reconnaissance'. In trying to explain its purpose, the corps' first historian described it as a 'Reconnaissance Service' which was 'a specially adapted branch of "Intelligence"'.[18] This apparent ambiguity needs to be explored within the context of contemporaneous doctrine.

Prior to the First World War the primary means of scouting the ground ahead and locating an enemy was with cavalry, latterly augmented by aircraft.[19] This reconnaissance system was controlled by the operations staff and the output was then taken by the intelligence staff and overlaid with information from their sources to address more complex questions, such as enemy intentions. This primacy of reconnaissance

    p. 60. For the production of these maps, see Peter Chasseaud, *Artillery's Astrologers: A History of British Survey and Mapping on the Western Front, 1914-1918* (Lewes, 1999).
11 Basil Henriques, *The Indiscretions of a Warden* (London, 1937), p. 119.
12 Fuller, *Tanks*, p. 59.
13 Browne, *The Tank*, p. 40.
14 The others were clearly defined objectives and two-way communication. Liddell Hart Centre for Military Archives, King's College London (hereafter, LHCMA), Major-General J.F.C. Fuller Papers, I/TS1/1/6, 'Training Note No. 16', February 1917, cited in Hammond, 'Theory and Practice', p. 99.
15 TNA, WO 95/101, SZ101/82, 2nd Brigade, 'Summary of Tank Operations, Battle of Messines', 22 June 1917.
16 Browne, *The Tank*, p. 30.
17 Ibid., p. 46. The RFC had a small intelligence organization focused upon the German air service on the Western Front. Beach, *Haig's Intelligence*, p. 43.
18 C. & A. Williams-Ellis, *Tank Corps*, p. 80.
19 For a discussion of pre-war reconnaissance and intelligence, see Beach, *Haig's Intelligence*, pp. 13-19.

was inverted by the stagnation of trench warfare; the physical location of the enemy becoming a relatively straightforward question, while the increasing complexity, intensity, and destructiveness of warfare generated a raft of fresh enemy information requirements that could only be answered through the intelligence sources. The sheer scale of the military endeavour also generated a vast amount of information that needed to be processed by an increasingly sophisticated analytical system. From these circumstances, by 1918, a very distinctive intelligence function had emerged to manage collection, collate data, conduct predictive analysis, and disseminate products at all levels within the BEF.

For the Tank Corps the distinction between reconnaissance and intelligence work was less clear-cut, and can be explained in terms of their standard usage. In an attack a tank unit was faced with a two key problems: first they had to get the tanks to appropriate starting positions and, second, they had to direct them effectively against enemy positions. Both actions needed to be done efficiently and by late 1917 it was recognised that any preliminary movement ought to be done as secretively as possible. Early on the significant physical and technological challenges meant that the priority was getting the tanks to the start line by the best routes. Naturally, information gathering in support of such moves was focused within friendly territory and, to begin with, this work was conducted by a small cadre of specialist officers. Like the corps, this group grew and, as the war progressed, such expertise became more widely disseminated to the point where route reconnaissance within the British lines was a skill expected of all tank commanders. More challenging was to create an understanding of what lay beyond the frontline. This needed an additional synthesis from sources such as air photography, captured maps and documents, local knowledge from civilians, prisoner testimony, and personal reconnaissance.[20] Although this second phase might best be described as 'intelligence' work proper, for a tank company moving from the railhead, to lying up positions, then on to the start line, and onwards into hostile territory, the journey was a single operation. Therefore the use of 'reconnaissance' as an umbrella term for all information-gathering was logical if potentially confusing to a modern reader.[21]

Working for a 'Legend'

In early 1918 one of the tank brigade Intelligence Officers (IO) wrote to the corps' General Staff Officer (Intelligence), Elliot Hotblack, telling him that: 'You claim a certain gleam of reflected glory from honours gained by your IOs, [but] I needn't tell you how they feel about their [GSO2(I)] – it's a wonderful thing to have a "Legend"

---

20   C. & A. Williams-Ellis, *Tank Corps*, p. 29.
21   For example, in some documents brigade Intelligence Officers are sometimes referred to as Reconnaissance Officers.

at the head of one's department!'[22] At first glance this may appear sycophantic, but Hotblack's reputation warranted the accolade as he was probably one of the most celebrated intelligence officers within the BEF.[23] Before examining the intelligence personnel collectively, we must pause to look at him individually. When he joined the tanks at the end of September 1916,[24] Hotblack was a junior intelligence analyst at General Headquarters (GHQ).[25] Twenty-nine years old, he had been born into a family of brewers, was educated in Switzerland, and had joined the army's new Intelligence Corps in September 1914.[26] Unlike some of his rather unmilitary peers, Hotblack thrived, was promoted to captain, mentioned in despatches, and awarded the Military Cross (MC).[27] Parenthetically, it is interesting to see that John Charteris, the head of BEF intelligence, sent one of his best officers to the nascent organisation and this is a strong indication of GHQ endorsing its development as a combat arm.[28]

Hotblack had a good start with the tanks. In November 1916 he won the Distinguished Service Order (DSO) for leading a tank into action by walking in front of it under enemy fire.[29] As one of his subordinates later put it, this was 'an inspiring deed … demanding skill as well as courage' and so 'set the tone' for subsequent tank reconnaissance work.[30] Hotblack continued to put himself in harm's way; he was wounded five times before the armistice,[31] as well as receiving bars to both his MC and DSO.[32] Fuller described him as 'conscientiously' fearless and this assessment is partly corroborated by Hotblack's testimony to the post-war enquiry into 'Shell Shock', where he argued that men's minds should be trained to expect and then

22   Tank Museum Archives & Reference Library (hereafter, TMARL), F.E. Hotblack Papers, Williams-Ellis to Hotblack, 5 January [1918]. Emphasis in original.
23   This renown explains why he was painted for an official portrait: William Orpen, *Major FE Hotblack DSO MC* (1917), ART3007, Imperial War Museum. For Orpen's work at this time, see Robert Upstone, *William Orpen: Politics, Sex & Death* (London, 2005), pp. 34-46.
24   Hotblack was initially a Staff Captain, becoming GSO3 (Intelligence) when the headquarters was reorganized at the end 1916, and then GSO2 in August 1917. *Quarterly Army List* (hereafter, *QAL*), October 1919, 1074a; TNA, WO 95/91, HQ Tank Corps war diary, 30 March 1917.
25   Imperial War Museum, Kirke Papers, Diary, 28 September 1916; *QAL*, October 1919, 1074a.
26   For an analysis of the Intelligence Corps' officers, see Beach, *Haig's Intelligence*, pp. 66-85.
27   *London Gazette*, 18 June 1915, 3 June 1916.
28   Hammond, 'Theory and Practice', p. 92. Hotblack recalled that Charteris had told him that 'the Tanks had a great future and ... Haig was backing them'. TMARL, Hotblack Papers, Hotblack to Martin Gilbert, 28 November 1968.
29   *London Gazette*, 10 January 1917; *Daily Mirror*, 11 January 1917; *The Graphic*, 20 January 1917; C. & A. Williams-Ellis, *Tank Corps*, pp. 74-5; Browne, *The Tank*, p. 40; TMARL, Hotblack Papers, [undated ms note] 'Tank Reconnaissance'.
30   C. & A. Williams-Ellis, *Tank Corps*, pp. 75-6.
31   TNA, WO 95/91, HQ Tank Corps war diary, 9 April & 7 July 1917; TMARL, Hotblack Papers, typescript diary, 15 May, 29 September 1917; C. & A. Williams-Ellis, *Tank Corps*, pp. 376-7.
32   *London Gazette*, 18 February 1918, 14 February & 30 July 1919.

overcome fear.³³ Fuller also portrayed him as a combination of Napoleon's famously reckless commander, Marshal Ney, and Abelard the philosopher.³⁴ He also seems to have been ubiquitous throughout the Tank Corps' major operations. For example, their 1917 war diary provides constant evidence of his liaison with major headquarters and personal reconnaissance of forthcoming battlefields.³⁵ Given the risk of capture, Hotblack's later frontline forays might be judged as rather reckless for a senior staff officer, but it seems clear that they cemented his reputation within the wider organization.³⁶ Recent research has also suggested that, in early 1918, he was the BEF's lead in analysing the emerging and fragmentary intelligence on the development and deployment of German tanks.³⁷

Taking a step back, Hotblack perhaps personifies the Tank Corps' unusual mixture of reconnaissance and intelligence work. Comfortable dealing with both the mud of No Man's Land and the minutiae of reports, he simultaneously embraced both old and new conceptions of intelligence. As discussed, before 1914 reconnaissance dominated the procurement of information about an enemy. A hangover from this could be discerned during the First World War whereby a distinction was made between 'outdoor' and 'office' intelligence work.³⁸ The former was more traditional and privileged personal reconnaissance activities. As the pre-war doctrine explained:

> Outdoor work [ought] to be observed … The spectacle of an Intelligence man entering the camp in the early morning on a tired horse tends to raise … [intelligence] in the esteem of the army and there will always be occasions when the display of a little personal gallantry, or the cheerful endurance of exceptional fatigue or discomfort, on the part of Intelligence officers or men, will have a good effect in inspiring that confidence which is required.³⁹

The Edwardian officer corps was imbued with the experience of 'small wars' across the Empire, most recently the Boer War which triggered a range of military reforms.⁴⁰

---

33   Fuller, *Memoirs*, p. 89; Cmd 1734, *Report of the War Office Committee of Enquiry into "Shell Shock"* (HMSO: 1922), p. 76. Apparently he was 'obsessed with bravery'. TMARL, Hotblack Papers, Notes by Colonel W.J. Hotblack, 10 May 1988.
34   Fuller, *Tanks*, p. xv.
35   TNA, WO 95/91-92, HQ Tank Corps war diary, 6, 24 May, 2 July, 8 August, 9, 15 September & 6 October 1917.
36   TMARL, Hotblack Papers, Elles to Military Secretary, 25 August 1918.
37   Jim Beach, 'British Intelligence and German Tanks, 1916-1918', *War in History*, 14 (2007), pp. 454-75.
38   Beach, *Haig's Intelligence*, pp. 65-6.
39   David Henderson, *Field Intelligence: Its Principles and Practice* (London, 1904), p. 3.
40   For the impact of the Boer War, see: John Gooch, 'Britain and the Boer War', in George Andreopoulos & Harold Selesky (eds.), *The Aftermath of Defeat: Societies, Armed Forces and the Challenge of Recovery* (London, 1994), pp. 40-58; Edward Spiers, 'Between the South African War and the First World War, 1902-1914', in Hew Strachan (ed.), *Big*

From these conflicts reconnaissance work had been distilled into books such as Robert Baden-Powell's *Aids to Scouting for NCOs and Men* (1899) which famously developed into *Scouting for Boys* (1908). Without delving too far into contemporaneous notions of military masculinity,[41] it can be argued that conducting reconnaissance in trench warfare was an inherently 'manly' activity as it exposed the participant to a high degree of physical risk, in contrast to the new wave of 'indoor' intelligence work. As one tank brigade explained: 'The Battalion Reconnaissance Officer [ought] to devote a greater amount of his time to outdoor work. Knowledge gained from reports and photographs, unless well supported by personal reconnaissance [do] not carry conviction.'[42] The Tank Corps' information practitioners therefore had to be reasonably competent at analytical work, but their forte was to found in and around the frontlines doing their own collection. Hotblack's unusual combination of intellectual prowess and personal bravery thus made him an ideal intelligence leader in this context.

Intelligence Officers and Reconnaissance Officers

In December 1916, three months after despatching Hotblack, GHQ began to trawl for more Intelligence Corps officers to serve with the tanks.[43] This process anticipated the creation of three tank brigades,[44] with the first officers arriving shortly after their

---

    Wars and Small Wars: The British Army and the Lessons of War in the 20th Century (London, 2006), pp. 21-35; Spencer Jones, *From Boer War to World War: Tactical Reform of the British Army, 1902-1914* (Norman, 2012). For general discussions of the army's officers, see: Keith Simpson, 'The Officers', in Ian Beckett & Keith Simpson (eds.), *A Nation in Arms: A Social Study of the British Army in the First World War* (Manchester, 1985), pp. 63-96; Gary Sheffield, *Leadership in the Trenches: Officer-Man Relations, Morale and Discipline in the British Army in the Era of the First World War* (London, 2000), pp. 29-40; Timothy Bowman & Mark Connelly, *The Edwardian Army: Recruiting, Training, and Deploying the British Army, 1902-1914* (Oxford, 2012), pp. 7-40.

41 For introductions to this area, see: Margaret Randolph Higonnet, Jane Jenson, Sonya Michel & Margaret Collins Weitz (eds.), *Behind the Lines: Gender and the Two World Wars* (London, 1987), pp. 2-3; Leonard Smith, 'Masculinty, Memory and the French First World War Novel', in Frans Coetzee & Marilyn Shevin-Coetzee (eds.), *Authority, Identity and the Social History of the Great War* (Oxford, 1995), pp. 251-2; Joanna Bourke, *Dismembering the Male: Men's Bodies, Britain and the Great War* (London, 1996), pp. 11-30; Michael Paris, *Warrior Nation: Images of War in British Popular Culture, 1850-2000* (London, 2000), pp. 110-45; George Robb, *British Culture and the First World War* (London, 2002), pp. 33-6; Jessica Meyer, *Men of War: Masculinity and the First World War in Britain* (London, 2009), pp. 1-13.

42 TNA, WO 95/104, GS577, 3rd Brigade, 'Summary of Tank Operations, 31 July 1917' [August 1917].

43 Library & Archives Canada (hereafter, LAC), Lt.-Col. Charles Mitchell Papers, MG30-E61, [ms notes on] GHQ Intelligence conference, 30 December 1916, Vol.14.

44 1st & 2nd Brigades (February), 3rd Brigade (April); three more were created in 1918. Becke, *Order of Battle*, pp. 269, 273, 275.

headquarters were established.⁴⁵ Again, this deployment suggests Charteris' desire to support the new corps.⁴⁶ These posts constituted one percent of the Intelligence Corps' officer manpower and were formalized in the organization's establishment tables.⁴⁷ The priority given to this commitment is demonstrated by the fact that experienced officers were specified, making the tank brigades roughly equivalent to an army corps in this regard.⁴⁸ Formal documentary evidence of the brigade IOs' duties has not been found, but an indication can be extrapolated from the work undertaken by the intelligence section at Tank Corps headquarters.⁴⁹ This included reconnaissance, intelligence liaison with frontline formations, collation of enemy information, procurement of maps and air photographs, counter-intelligence, and the training of subordinates. These officers appear to have been closely integrated into the brigades' operational processes. In the planning and conduct of attacks in April and July 1917, one brigade's IO was an almost constant companion to his commander.⁵⁰ In August the same commander credited his IO with planning one of his battalion's attacks.⁵¹ Similarly, for four months in 1918, another brigade's IO stood in as chief of staff.⁵² In both of these examples, the Intelligence Corps officers were given a great deal more responsibility than was common in other headquarters.⁵³

Because of the small number of officers and the very fragmentary survival of personnel records, it is impossible to discern any clear patterns in their selection for these roles.⁵⁴ However, two of the original IOs are fairly well-known. The first is

45 TNA, WO 95/97, Lt. Clough Williams-Ellis, 1st Tank Brigade war diary, 23 February 1917, WO 95/101, Capt. Thomas Nelson, 2nd Tank Brigade war diary, 5 March 1917, WO 95/104, Capt. Francis Alker, 'War History of 3rd Tank Brigade' [December 1918].
46 In this regard, it is perhaps interesting that when one of the first brigade IOs was killed in April 1917, a replacement was found immediately. TNA, WO 95/101, Capt. Ronald Cazalet, 2nd Tank Brigade war diary, 9, 13 April 1917, WO 339/21899, personnel file.
47 TNA, WO 158/962, IC/7084, Charteris to GSO(b), 19 August 1917. This establishment table also assigned two Intelligence Corps officers to HQ Tank Corps to assist the GSO2 & 3 (Intelligence).
48 The Intelligence Corps' officers were graded (in descending order) from 1st to 4th Class Agent. Beach, *Haig's Intelligence*, pp. 78-9. The 1917 establishment table required that a 2nd Class Agent be assigned to tank brigades while corps had five officers, two of which would be 2nd Class. By way of comparison, an infantry division had a single 3rd or 4th Class Agent.
49 TNA, WO 95/91, 'Duties of General Staff, Heavy Branch' [April 1917], WO 95/91, HQ Tank Corps war diary, 13 February 1918 & Appendix 10, 'Duties of General Staff, Tank Corps'.
50 TNA, WO 95/97, HQ Tank Corps war diary, 11-26 April, 11-19 July 1917.
51 Christopher Baker-Carr, *From Chauffeur to Brigadier* (London, 1930), p. 252, cited in Hammond, 'Theory and Practice', p. 165.
52 TNA, WO 95/104, 24 June to 19 October 1918, 'War History of 3rd Tank Brigade', [December 1918]. His intelligence role was backfilled by a battalion RO.
53 Beach, *Haig's Intelligence*, pp. 82-3.
54 In addition to Cazalet mentioned above, a personnel record is extant for Captain David Lindsay, who was with No.1 Tank Group at the end of the war. TNA, WO 339/52963,

Tommy Nelson, a forty year old pre-war publisher. A lover of outdoor adventure, he had played rugby for Scotland and possessed 'granite common sense'. John Buchan, his close friend and business partner, dedicated the famous thriller *The Thirty-Nine Steps* (1915) to him. Nelson had come to France with his yeomanry squadron in late 1915 and in 1916 undertook staff and then observation work at divisional and corps level. In early 1917 Buchan had suggested he volunteer for the tanks and Nelson was killed by a shell while accompanying Hotblack at Arras in April.[55] The other 'original' was Clough Williams-Ellis, renowned subsequently as the architect who created Portmeirion. The son of an academic-turned-cleric,[56] Williams-Ellis was an unusual character who joined the army in September 1914 at the age of thirty-one and transferred from the Welsh Guards to the Intelligence Corps in July 1916.[57] Posted to the Ypres Salient, he channelled his fertile mind into the creation of complicated sledge-mounted 'man-traps' that were to be 'baited with dummy ... corpses' and which would, when triggered, release a flare thus prompting the unfortunate German soldier to be dragged by wire hawser into the British lines.[58] These traps did not become operational and an explanation for Williams-Ellis being allowed to indulge in such experiments can be found in the fact that one of his superiors was a close friend of his father-in-law.[59] In November 1916 a new head of intelligence arrived at the headquarters and he was less amused. Although he conceded that Williams-Ellis was full of ideas, he also thought him to be aggressive, conceited, and erratic.[60] Around this time Williams-Ellis presented himself uninvited at Tank Corps headquarters and, after tea and toast with the corps commander, 'came away a hot tank partisan' seeking an immediate transfer.[61] Renowned as an artistically-inclined officer accessorized with

and WO 95/95, A3/417/16, HQ Tank Corps to Brigades, 7 November 1918. In addition, Capt. H.H. Hindmarsh in No.2 Group had been employed previously in X Corps Intelligence. LAC, MG30-E61, Mitchell Papers, Vol.14, 'Second Army Intelligence – General Staff Officers and Intelligence Corps Officers', November 1917.

55 *London Gazette*, 6 July 1906; TNA, WO 374/50213, personnel file, WO 95/2233, Lothian & Border Horse war diary, 24 February 1916; 'Captain T.A. Nelson', *Times*, 17 April 1917; TMARL, Hotblack Papers, Hotblack to 'Madame', 18 April 1917; John Buchan, *These for Remembrance* (London, 1919; reprinted, 1987), pp. 14-17; Hew Strachan, 'John Buchan and the First World War: Fact into Fiction', *War in History*, 16 (2009), p. 301.
56 'Williams-Ellis, John Clough (1833-1913)', Welsh Biography online <http://wbo.llgc.org.uk> accessed 29 January 2013.
57 TNA, WO 339/20340, Intelligence Corps casualty form.
58 Clough Williams-Ellis, *Architect Errant* (London, 1971), p. 122; letter to Beatrice, 18 November 1916, in Jim Beach (ed.), *The Military Papers of Lieutenant-Colonel Sir Cuthbert Headlam, 1910-1942* (Stroud, 2010), p. 149. Another example of his inventiveness was a system of military memory training. [Clough Williams-Ellis], *Reconography: Simplified Reconnaissance Sketching* (London, 1919).
59 John St Loe Strachey, *The Adventure of Living: A Subjective Autobiography, 1860-1922* (London, 1922), p. 349.
60 Letters to Beatrice, 13, 18 November 1916, in Beach (ed.), *Headlam*, pp. 148-9.
61 Williams-Ellis, *Architect*, p. 125.

a shepherd's crook, after serving eighteen months as a tank brigade IO he replaced Hotblack when the latter went on a staff course.[62] Thus 'accidentally a staff officer' at the armistice, he was tasked with writing the first history of the Tank Corps.[63]

Subordinated to the tank brigades were tank battalions with, from April 1917, their own Reconnaissance Officers (RO) ranked as captains.[64] This designation was replicated at company-level with an equivalent or lower rank.[65] Whereas the brigade IOs were posted from the Intelligence Corps, these ROs were recruited internally. Although this meant they had limited connections with the wider intelligence system, they did have practical experience of conducting tank operations. As Christy Campbell has colourfully described them, the Tank Corps' personnel were 'a ragbag of volunteers' and 'its officers were city clerks and junior solicitors, its engineers had been bus garage managers; the caste system of the old army was irrelevant'.[66] Therefore it could be argued that, by diversity of background and self-selection, this recruitment pool contained those already predisposed towards unorthodoxy and innovation.[67]

The reconnaissance imperative had prompted the creation of this separate stream of tank officers and, unsurprisingly, they often remained in these roles. For example, in early 1918 Douglas Browne became a company RO replacing an officer who had moved up to become the battalion RO. Later that year Browne became RO for another battalion.[68] Although there were obvious benefits to this specialization, it was also recognized quite quickly that all tank commanders needed reconnaissance expertise. As early as April 1917, an analysis of training needs noted that: 'The value of personal

62 TMARL, N.M. Dillon Papers, 'Record of N.M. Dillon', n.d.; TNA, WO 95/91, HQ Tank Corps war diary, 16 October 1918.
63 C. & A. Williams-Ellis, *Tank Corps*. Anxious to get home, he arranged to write it back in Britain where Amabel, his author wife, 'did almost all the writing whilst I fed her with [documents]'. Williams-Ellis, *Architect*, p. 129.
64 For a detailed examination of the work of battalion and company ROs, see Colin Hardy, 'Intelligence and Reconnaissance in the Tank Corps and its Predecessors on the Western Front 1916-18', MA diss., University of Birmingham, 2013. I am grateful to Colin for giving me a copy of his work.
65 TNA, WO 95/91, 'Headquarters of a Battalion of Heavy Branch, Machine Gun Corps' & 'Company, Heavy Branch, Machine Gun Corps', 21 April 1917. For snapshots of the rank mix at company-level, see TNA, WO 95/101, 2nd Brigade, 'Operations with Second Army', 7 June 1917; Appendix E to SZ187/54/22, 2nd Brigade, 'Report on Tank Operations, 31 July 1917', 21 August 1917. When looking back upon this arrangement within companies, one tank battalion felt that lieutenants sometimes had insufficient status when liaising with frontline units. TNA, WO 95/112, 13th Tank Battalion, 'War Experiences', n.d.
66 Campbell, *Brigands*, pp. 258, 260.
67 Again, a small number of potential targets and limited archival survival have yielded an insufficient sample to discern any recruitment or employment patterns. TNA, WO 339/1885, John Jinks, WO 339/66459, Walter Demuth, WO 339/67636, Cyril North, WO 339/68292, Bertrand Carter, WO 339/80634, Angus Whyte.
68 7th & 12th Battalions. Browne, *The Tank*, pp. 308, 495.

reconnaissance by ... commanders and drivers is most necessary. [Tank] commanders must take great responsibility in the selection of routes and not leave that selection entirely to company [ROs].'[69] This became a continual requirement and, at the war's end, two tank brigades bemoaned the fact that there had been a 'tendency ... to keep reconnaissance rather as a thing apart' or to 'regard [ROs] as a separate caste' whereas 'the idea should be inculcated that every individual is his own best reconnaissance officer'. As one of them put it, the primary function of the RO should be as a 'specially trained' instructor in reconnaissance work, imparting his knowledge to his battalion or company.[70] In 1918 such dissemination of reconnaissance knowledge expanded considerably, particularly during the first three months when the Tank Corps, like the rest of the BEF, stood on the defensive.[71] Preparations to meet the impending German offensive with counter-attacks necessitated fresh reconnaissances of large swathes of the British rear areas and so provided opportunities for ROs and others to hone their skills.[72] More formal training also took place. One brigade ran a fourteen day 'reconnaissance school' while another ran a one-week course for battalion and company ROs.[73] The latter's main purpose was to train them to impart knowledge to tank crews in a 'concise and profitable' manner, but the get-together also allowed them to share experiences from operations in 1917, harmonize their methods, and make preparations for lower level training. Williams-Ellis outlined the syllabus of a generic five-day course as consisting of lectures, basic map work, 'visualising country from a map', sketching, night guiding, practical reconnaissance of areas and routes, and examination of air photographs.[74] There is also strong evidence of this training continuing into the summer of 1918 until the BEF resumed the general offensive in August.[75] Furthermore, at some point in early 1918 a centralized reconnaissance school was established at Le Tréport on the channel coast.[76]

69   TNA, WO 95/91, Superintendent of Training, Bovington, 'Report on the Tank Operations in the Battle of Arras', 23 April 1917.
70   TNA, WO 95/112, 3rd Brigade, 'War Experiences', n.d., WO 95/104, 5th Brigade, 'War Experiences', n.d.
71   C. & A. Williams Ellis, *Tank Corps*, pp. 207, 238.
72   TNA, WO 95/108, G111/7, 4th Tank Brigade, 'Notes on Reconnaissance of Forward Areas', 10 February 1918; 4th Tank Brigade, 'Notes on Conference', 16 February 1918; Browne, *The Tank*, pp. 324-5.
73   TNA, WO 95/104, 'War History of 3rd Tank Brigade' [December 1918], WO 95/108, 4th Tank Brigade Training Memorandum No.4, 'Reconnaissance', 14 January 1918.
74   C. & A. Williams Ellis, *Tank Corps*, p. 239.
75   TNA, WO 95/108, G108/3, 4th Tank Brigade Training Memorandum No.6, 'Gunnery – Reconnaissance – Gas', 11 May 1918, WO 95/102, 2nd Brigade to Companies, 'Training', 28 July 1918.
76   Browne, *The Tank*, pp. 313, 340.

Teeing up the Tanks

Within the historiography there is a strong suggestion that reconnaissance and intelligence processes made an important contribution to the execution of tank operations. Williams-Ellis observed that he and his peers were responsible for 'the preliminary survey of the proposed battle site' to determine 'where and how tanks could best operate'.[77] Fuller suggested a wider remit, stating that they played 'an all-important part, not only before the battle, but during it, and immediately after it'.[78] The vital preparatory phase was often quite lengthy; as one battalion commander put it:

> The work of the tank on the day of battle, was the final effort of several weeks of preparation and organisation. Elaborate reconnaissance and intelligence work had to be accomplished. Routes … had to be prepared … The terrain over which the tanks were to operate, on the day of battle, had to be carefully surveyed.[79]

Looking back, one RO noted the 'infinite amount of work and forethought' required and felt that 'success or failure hung upon the tank commanders' familiarity, from thorough coaching beforehand, with the ground they had to cover'.[80]

The lack of meaningful reconnaissance in 1916 has already been noted, therefore the first test of the new system came at the Battle of Arras in April 1917.[81] Tank Corps headquarters had conducted their initial reconnaissance in February, with the tank units deploying their ROs three weeks before the attack.[82] After liaising with front-line corps, they conducted analysis of air photography, marked routes with tape, and arranged route clearances with local engineer units, arranging for trench to be filled in and any cables to be buried or raised. After the battle it was felt that such route work within the British lines was not a good use of ROs' time and it was suggested that, in future, the task should fall to tank commanders. This division of labour was summed up in a later Tank Corps report which said that 'the work of the [ROs] lies beyond the enemy's front line; they should not be employed on our side of it'.[83] In the days prior to the attack the ROs also accessed the local observation post system, in order to show

---

77   C. & A. Williams-Ellis, *Tank Corps*, p. 29.
78   Fuller, *Tanks*, p. 106.
79   A.H.T. Somers, *The War History of the Sixth Tank Battalion* (Edinburgh, 1919), pp. 130-131, cited in Hammond, 'Theory and Practice', p. 397.
80   Browne, *The Tank*, p. 45.
81   Jonathon Nicholls, *Cheerful Sacrifice: The Battle of Arras 1917* (London, 1993).
82   Except where indicated, this information has been drawn from TNA, WO 95/91, SG52/59, HQ Heavy Branch MGC, 'Summary of Tank Operations, 1st Brigade Heavy Branch, 9 April to 3 May', 17 May 1917, WO 95/97, HQ Heavy Branch, 'Summary of Tank Operations, 1st Brigade, April-May 1917', 17 May 1917.
83   TNA, WO 95/92, 'Notes on Tank Operations, April to October 1917' [October 1917]. The point was reiterated in 1918. TNA, WO 95/93, 3rd Tank Group, 'Tactical Experiences of all the past Tank Corps operations' [1918].

parties of tank commanders the ground ahead.[84] However, as Hammond has highlighted, in one sector poor route reconnaissance meant the loss of five tanks before the attack had even started.[85] When it commenced the ROs reported their initial observations and then 'reconnoitred the country ahead', acted as guides to tanks, and supplied information to those that reached 'rallying points'.

In June the tanks were back in action, this time at the Battle of Messines.[86] As with Arras, this was a long-planned operation and three months before the Tank Corps had commenced the reconnaissance.[87] This time their work also included liaison with Second Army's counterintelligence officer to obtain information, presumably from civilians, about the country within the German lines.[88] The experience of this attack reinforced 'the extreme importance of detailed reconnaissance of the ground'.[89] It is also noticeable that the after-action analysis suggested further refinements to the reconnaissance process. One brigade noted the importance of decentralization, liaison with varying levels of headquarters in the line, and also the necessity of creating a standard filing system to prevent duplication of effort in obtaining information. It also cautioned against the natural instinct to focus preliminary reconnaissance work on the first, shallower objectives rather than the subsequent, deeper ones,[90] and subsequently their battle instructions stressed the necessity for forward reconnaissance to be undertaken during the attack.[91]

From a reconnaissance and intelligence perspective, the next engagement, the Third Battle of Ypres was an almost textbook operation that consolidated the procedures adopted earlier in 1917.[92] A 'great mass of information' was made available to the tank commanders and they had 'ample time' to familiarize themselves with the

---

84 For a summary of the BEF's frontline observation system, see Beach, *Haig's Intelligence*, pp. 91-3.
85 C. & A. Williams-Ellis, *Tank Corps*, pp. 52-3, cited in Hammond, 'Theory and Practice', p. 109.
86 For a brief summation, see Robin Prior & Trevor Wilson, *Passchendaele: The Untold Story* (London, 1996), pp. 55-66.
87 TNA, WO 95/91, Tank Corps to Second Army, 23 March 1917, cited in Hammond, 'Theory and Practice', p. 136.
88 TNA, WO 95/101, SZ101/82, 2nd Brigade, 'Summary of Tank Operations, Battle of Messines', 22 June 1917.
89 TNA, WO 158/298, Second Army to GHQ, 'Notes on the Employment of Tanks in the Battle of Messines', 25 June 1917, cited in Hammond, 'Theory and Practice', p. 136.
90 TNA, WO 95/101, SZ101/82, 2nd Brigade, 'Summary of Tank Operations, Battle of Messines', 22 June 1917.
91 TNA, WO 95/101, SZ187/39, 2nd Brigade, 'Notes on Conferences, 14-15 July', 17 July 1917.
92 C. & A. Williams-Ellis, *Tank Corps*, p. 133. Except where indicated, this information has been drawn from TNA, WO 95/97, BMS/282/77, 1st Brigade, 'Summary of Tank Operations, 31 July 1917', August 1917, WO 95/104, 2nd Brigade, 'Preliminary Instructions No.1 for the Offensive', 22 June 1917, GS577, 3rd Brigade, 'Summary of Tank Operations, 31 July 1917' [August 1917].

ground.[93] Headquarters Tank Corps had started the work in May, with the brigade IOs following shortly after and liaising with local corps headquarters. The IOs then inducted the battalion ROs who tapped into the frontline divisions before familiarizing their company ROs with the ground.[94] Route reconnaissance in friendly areas was delegated to 'assistant' ROs and, because of the relatively flat topography, air photographs were more helpful than direct observation. That said, one battalion RO reconnoitred No Man's Land up to the German wire. Overall, Fuller felt that 'the distribution of information was more rapid than it had been on previous occasions [with] constant discussions between the brigade and battalion [ROs]',[95] while one brigade attributed the success of the tanks in reaching their objectives to 'the excellence of the reconnaissance' and the close collaboration between company ROs and tank commanders. But flawless reconnaissance was not enough to ensure battlefield success. Although one post-war history suggested that the tanks were allowed to 'drown ineffectually in a morass', the same author noted that during the July reconnaissance the weather was good and 'the surface soil dry and crumbling'.[96] One tank brigade's after-action report conceded that the poor weather had created difficulties with marshy ground but that the routes selected were the 'best available'.[97] As Hammond has concluded, it was actually the channelling of the tanks by the defended remains of woods, not the mud, which doomed them to failure at Ypres.

In November 1917 came the Tank Corps' most celebrated engagement, the Battle of Cambrai.[98] As is well known, the reconnaissance processes for this attack were deliberately curtailed. As one history put it, 'four times as many tanks as went in on the first day at Ypres were to be employed … [yet] there had been little time for preparation and less for reconnaissance'.[99] The IOs of the brigades were informed of the operation four weeks prior to the attack, with the battalion ROs told a few days later.[100] Although the normal cascade of reconnaissance visits commenced, they were carefully managed and company ROs were kept in the dark until two weeks before, with the tank commanders told a week later. This meant that there was insufficient time to collate the available intelligence, but the 'rolling character' of the terrain meant that observation was straightforward and this partly compensated.[101] The reason behind

---

93   Browne, *The Tank*, pp. 112-3.
94   TMARL, Basil Henriques Papers, pass issued by HQ Fifth Army, 24 June 1917.
95   Fuller, *Tanks*, p. 118.
96   Browne, *The Tank*, p. 103.
97   TNA, WO 95/101, SZ187/54/22, 2nd Brigade, 'Report on Tank Operations, 31 July 1917', 21 August 1917.
98   Bryn Hammond, *Cambrai 1917: The Myth of the First Great Tank Battle* (London, 2008).
99   Browne, *The Tank*, p. 262.
100 TMARL, Henriques Papers, pass issued by HQ 36th Division, 3 November 1917.
101 TNA, WO 95/98, Appendix A to BM/390/94, 1st Brigade, 'Summary of Operations, 20-23 November 1917', December 1917, WO 95/104, GS No.1140, 3rd Brigade, 'Report on Operations with Third Army, 20-27 November 1917', 22 December 1917.

this procedural compression was the desire to obtain full surprise with the attack.[102] The question of maintaining secrecy had arisen before with tanks but, as one brigade pointed out with regard to the Messines operation:

> Secrecy is essential, but very little information can be obtained from the officers in the line unless Reconnaissance Officers disclose their identity. Every help was given them on learning that they belonged to [the] tanks.[103]

Therefore at Third Ypres only the most straightforward security instructions were given, such as no marked maps to be taken into frontline trenches, nor should officers expose themselves unnecessarily during reconnaissances.[104]

Before Cambrai the pendulum swung the other way; badges were removed, cover stories were concocted and, at one point, battalion commanders and their ROs were 'mutually unaware' that the other had been briefed about the operation.[105] As Williams-Ellis recalled: '[Officers'] drivers were carefully primed with cock-and-bull stories … [ROs] slunk about, above all avoiding headquarters and those other social centres which etiquette enjoins must be first called upon by all who visit other peoples' trenches'.[106] It would seem that this experience instilled good habits into the Tank Corps and, in later operations, the need for secrecy became a common feature. Insignia were removed from uniforms and vehicles and false ones substituted, reconnaissance parties were limited to essential personnel only and sometimes only pairs, all ranks were educated as to the importance of discretion, and the standard cover story – drawing on genuine activities in the early months of 1918 – was that the defensive use of tanks was under consideration.[107]

The corps' next major offensive, the Battle of Amiens in early August 1918, was modelled upon Cambrai's procedures.[108] There was insufficient time for detailed

---

102 Subsequent intelligence suggested that the Germans did have some forewarning of the offensive but were taken aback by its scale and method. Beach, *Haig's Intelligence*, p. 265.
103 TNA, WO 95/101, SZ101/82, 2nd Brigade, 'Summary of Tank Operations, Battle of Messines', 22 June 1917.
104 TNA, WO 95/101, 2nd Brigade, 'Preliminary Instructions No.1 for the Offensive', 22 June 1917.
105 TNA, WO 95/98, BMS/282/77, 1st Brigade, 'Summary of Tank Operations, 31 July 1917', August 1917, WO 95/104, GS No.1140, 3rd Brigade, 'Report on Operations with Third Army, 20-27 November 1917', 22 December 1917.
106 C. & A. Williams-Ellis, *Tank Corps*, p. 170.
107 TNA, WO 95/99, 1st Brigade, 'Secrecy', 15 August 1918, Appendix B to BMS/106/29, 1st Brigade, 'Report on Operations, 21-25 August 1918', 29 August 1918, WO 95/108, 2nd Brigade, 'Instructions No.2: Reconnaissance & Secrecy', 17 August 1918, WO 95/102; G400/16, 4th Brigade Instruction No.8, 'Secrecy', 25 September 1918.
108 Browne, *The Tank*, p. 355.

Photo 6: Tank column, Amiens, August 1918

reconnaissance but most tank commanders did get a chance to observe the ground.[109] Although the first day was a great success, as Hammond notes, like Cambrai, the subsequent attacks were 'poorly co-ordinated [and] without adequate time for preparation and reconnaissance'.[110] The battle marked the opening of the BEF's victorious 'Hundred Days' campaign.[111] The Tank Corps was an important participant in its various battles but, as Jonathan Boff has argued, it was spread thinly, badly worn down, and struggled to keep up with the tempo of operations, particularly in any series of hastily arranged attacks.[112] With regard to reconnaissance work in this campaign, one can discern a reasonably functioning system. For example, after an attack in mid-August, one brigade noted restricted opportunities for tank commanders' prior observation but that benign terrain and 'thorough coaching by their company [ROs]' meant

---

109 TNA, WO 95/112, Appendix G to 5th Brigade, 'Report on Operations with Australian Corps, 8-15 August 1918', 23 August 1918.
110 Hammond, 'Theory and Practice', p. 308.
111 For overviews, see: Elizabeth Greenhalgh, *Foch in Command: The Forging of a First World War General* (Cambridge, 2011), pp. 407-494; and, Jonathan Boff, *Winning and Losing on the Western Front: The British Third Army and the Defeat of Germany in 1918* (Cambridge, 2012), pp. 22-38.
112 Boff, *Winning and Losing*, pp. 140-3.

that 'all officers went into battle with [an] <u>adequate</u> idea of what lay before them'.[113] Such an expectation of sufficient, rather than exhaustive, information would have been the best that tank commanders could have hoped for in this period. Surveying the various after-action reports from September through to November, the picture is one of a few days' reconnaissance at best; more common are attacks launched with 'extremely hurried' reconnaissance, or none at all.[114] An exception to this pattern is the famous attack across the Canal du Nord at the end of September. In that operation six days were spent on reconnaissance, collating additional air photography, and obtaining plans from a French civilian source. Thereby the careful selection of crossing points meant that every tank bar one crossed this major obstacle successfully.[115]

Visualization, Feedback and Countermeasures

This exploration concludes with an examination of the various intelligence and reconnaissance products created and used by IOs and ROs in support of tank operations. Of course much of the pre-battle interaction between these officers and the tank crews was conducted in an impromptu, oral, and therefore ephemeral way. However, it has been possible to find some archival record of their activities and these can be categorized as follows: those products which assisted with 'visualization' of the ground and enemy positions; the filtering of the wider intelligence picture to provide feedback on tank operations; and a painstaking search for every scrap of information regarding German anti-tank activities.

From mid-1915 the standard trench maps used by the BEF were of 1:10,000 and 1:20,000 scale.[116] Tank units used these, sourced normally from local headquarters prior to operations.[117] From Arras onwards they also evolved a technique of 'layering' these standard issue maps by colouring them to emphasize their contours. It was

113 TNA, WO 95/99, BMS/106/29, 1st Brigade, 'Report on Operations, 21-25 August 1918', 29 August 1918. Emphasis added.
114 TNA, WO 95/10, 22nd Brigade, 'Report on Operations, 21 August to 3 September 1918', 10 September 1918, WO 95/101, Z7/22, 2nd Brigade, 'Report on Operations, 4 November 1918', 20 November 1918, WO 95/98, 4th Brigade, 'Report on Operations', October 1918, WO 95/112, 5th Brigade, 'Report on Operations by 2nd Tank Battalion with III, Australian and IX Corps, 18 September 1918', 'Report on Operations by 13th Tank Battalion with IX Corps, 24 September 1918' [September 1918].
115 TNA, WO 95/99, 1st Tank Brigade war diary, 21, 22 September 1918, WO 95/98, 1st Brigade, 'Report on Operations, 27-30 September 1918', 24 October 1918.
116 Chasseaud, *Astrologers*, pp. 31-32, 49, 72. For Third Ypres, HQ Tank Corps issued additional 'topographical maps'. TNA, WO 95/101, SZ187/54/22, 2nd Brigade, 'Report on Tank Operations, 31 July 1917', 21 August 1917.
117 TNA, WO 95/97, HQ Heavy Branch, 'Summary of Tank Operations, 1st Brigade, April-May 1917', 17 May 1917. At Third Ypres, and presumably symptomatic of the very extensive preparations for that battle, these maps were augmented by 1:5,000 scale 'battle charts' upon which information from air photography was transcribed. TNA, WO 95/97, BMS/282/77, 1st Brigade, 'Summary of Tank Operations, 31 July 1917', August 1917.

felt that the process of conducting this basic form of terrain analysis was 'the best method of learning the map'.[118] As one tank brigade put it: 'The value of a home-made layered map is much greater than that of a printed layered map, and it cannot be too strongly impressed on tank commanders that they must layer their own maps, however roughly, with the yellow and green crayons with which they are provided.'[119] However, this 'layering' was often done by company ROs or their assistants.[120] In the summer of 1917 the requirement for additional staff to conduct this sort of work had been realized. In order to relieve battalion ROs of compilation work and to free them to reconnoitre and liaise, a 'trained draughtsman' was used to 'plot all information' and act as a courier and general assistant.[121] By 1918 such men were also employed at company-level and the concentration of all of a battalion's ROs and draughtsmen in a single location was found to save 'much duplication of work and [ensured] proper distribution of information'.[122] Air photography augmented this visualization process, with tank commanders apparently favouring the use of oblique photographs, providing a sideways perspective upon the battlefield, to the more common vertical images.[123] Furthermore, in mid-1917, some use was made of plasticene models depicting the ground but their usage prompted mixed reviews.[124] More helpful was a very large

118 TNA, WO 95/101, SZ101/82, 2nd Brigade, 'Summary of Tank Operations, Battle of Messines', 22 June 1917, WO 95/104, 3rd Brigade, 'War Experiences', n.d. One RO claimed that the Germans copied the layering technique after capturing Tank Corps maps. Browne, *The Tank*, p. 53.
119 TNA, WO 95/102, 2nd Brigade, 'Report on Operations, 21 August to 3 September 1918', 10 September 1918.
120 TNA, WO 95/104, 3rd Brigade, 'War Experiences' n.d., WO 95/112, 13th Tank Battalion, 'War Experiences', n.d.
121 TNA, WO 95/101, No.6 Company, B Battalion, 'Report of Reconnaissance Officer', 10 June 1917, SZ101/82, 2nd Brigade, 'Summary of Tank Operations, Battle of Messines', 22 June 1917, SZ187/54/22, 2nd Brigade, 'Report on Tank Operations, 31 July 1917', 21 August 1917, WO 95/104, GS577, 3rd Brigade, 'Summary of Tank Operations, 31 July 1917' [August 1917].
122 TNA, WO 95/102, 2nd Brigade, 'Report on Operations, 21 August to 3 September 1918', 10 September 1918, WO 95/104, GS577, 3rd Brigade, 'Summary of Tank Operations, 31 July 1917' [August 1917].
123 TNA, WO 95/101, SZ101/82, 2nd Brigade, 'Summary of Tank Operations, Battle of Messines', 22 June 1917, WO 95/97, BMS/282/77, 1st Brigade, 'Summary of Tank Operations, 31 July 1917', August 1917, WO 95/104, GS No.1140, 3rd Brigade, 'Report on Operations with Third Army, 20-27 November 1917', 22 December 1917, WO 95/99, BMS/106/29, 1st Brigade, 'Report on Operations, 21-25 August 1918', 29 August 1918, WO 95/98, 1st Brigade, 'Report on Operations, 27-30 September 1918', 24 October 1918, WO 95/112, 5th Brigade, 'War Experiences', n.d.. For the wider use of air photography, see: Beach, *Haig's Intelligence*, pp. 146-154; Terrence Finnegan, *Shooting the Front: Allied Aerial Reconnaissance in the First World War* (Stroud, 2011).
124 TNA, WO 95/101, SZ101/82, 2nd Brigade, 'Summary of Tank Operations, Battle of Messines', 22 June 1917, WO 95/101, SZ187/54/22, 2nd Brigade, 'Report on Tank Operations, 31 July 1917', 21 August 1917.

model of the Ypres battlefield used by all arms for a general understanding of the ground. The tanks utilized it for the same purpose and as an aid to planning with the infantry.[125]

With regard to the effect of tank operations, when they were first used in September 1916, Fourth Army's intelligence staff reported that: 'Prisoners state that the tanks had a great moral effect. The Germans were apparently aware that some form of armoured car was to be used against them as their balloons saw some coming. The men were not informed as it was feared it would reduce their moral[e].'[126] Later feedback on tank operations can be seen very clearly in the Tank Corps intelligence summaries which survive from mid-September 1917 onwards.[127] These were standard textual products which, by this time, were normally issued daily by all BEF formations from division upwards.[128] They constituted a form of 'intelligence newspaper' which provided immediate updates and, using traditional cut and paste techniques, could be broken down into its constituent parts for filing information by subject. An August 1917 assessment of German attitudes towards tanks provides a useful datum for this reporting. Those soldiers that had 'only seen ditched or destroyed tanks' did not 'greatly fear' them, whereas for those who had experienced an attack the 'moral effect' had been 'very great'.[129] At Cambrai, prisoner testimony suggested immediately that the Germans were surprised by the employment of tanks even if they had been warned of a possible attack. Some prisoners also suggested that the tanks were a catalyst for surrender as 'resistance was useless' and that even their officers had told them not to bother firing at them. The Tank Corps assessment was that the use of tanks had 'surprised and demoralised' the enemy.[130] Reviewing the documentary evidence a few days later, they surmised that the Germans had 'failed to detect the approach or deployment of tanks' until the very last minute,[131] thereby vindicating the elaborate security measures already discussed.

---

125 C. & A. Williams-Ellis, *Tank Corps*, p. 134; James Edmonds, *Military Operations, France & Belgium, 1917*, Vol.2 (London, 1948), p. 147.
126 IWM, Fourth Army Papers, Vol.12, Fourth Army Intelligence, 15 September 1916. For the initial German intelligence response to the British tanks, see Trevor Pidgeon, *The Tanks at Flers* (Cobham, 1995), pp. 188-92.
127 Such specific feedback was not unusual as, for example, the GHQ intelligence summaries offered frequent mentions of the effect of gas upon the Germans. These seem to have been targeted at the Royal Engineers 'Special Brigades' responsible for its offensive usage. Beach, *Haig's Intelligence*, p. 40. For context, see: Donald Richter, *Chemical Soldiers: British Gas Warfare in World War I* (Lawrence, KS, 1992); and, Albert Palazzo, *Seeking Victory on the Western Front: The British Army and Chemical Warfare in World War I* (Lincoln, 2000).
128 Beach, *Haig's Intelligence*, pp. 183-5. We can also discern other forms of after-action work. For example, after the Battle of Arras, Hotblack examined the routes taken by the tanks. TNA, WO 95/91, HQ Tank Corps war diary, 17 May 1917.
129 TNA, WO 95/92, 'Prisoners' statements regarding Tanks' [August 1917].
130 TNA, WO 157/240, Tank Corps intelligence summaries, 20, 21, November 1917.
131 United States National Archives & Records Administration (hereafter, NARA), RG 120/161/6372, GHQ intelligence summary, 23 November 1917; TNA, WO 157/240,

During the initial British attacks in the summer of 1918 prisoner testimony continued to suggest that the 'moral effect [of tanks] was enormous'. Some German veterans felt that the latest tanks were a considerable improvement on their 1916 counterparts, and, as before, it was felt that the arrival of tanks 'rendered resistance useless'.[132] Documentary evidence from this period is intriguing with the German high command tacitly acknowledging problems by emphasizing individual acts of bravery when facing tanks.[133] Similarly, the Tank Corps cited a German high command document which noted that their troops 'lost their heads' when surprised by a massed tank attack.[134] At a lower level, they also quoted a German division which stated that their infantry was more than capable of 'repelling hostile infantry without assistance' but that a tank attack demanded 'stronger artillery defence'.[135] The overall assessment, signed off by Hotblack in mid-September, was that:

> The official German communiqués have frequently 'explained' their defeats by saying that the Allies used 'masses of tanks'. This is now having a considerable effect on the moral[e] of the German officers and men. They have in many cases come to consider the approach of tanks a sufficient 'explanation' for not fighting.[136]

By the end of September the judgement was that 'the German infantry still considers that as soon as tanks have broken through their line, further resistance is useless'.[137] Clearly there is a danger here of the Tank Corps discovering what it was hoping to find, but in the intelligence documentation at least the assessments are fairly restrained and rooted in the available evidence. But it is also interesting to note that some of this intelligence material was quoted, verbatim and at length, in Fuller's post-war book.[138]

Studying the 'enemy's anti-tank measures' became part of Hotblack's organizational remit in 1917.[139] Therefore the surviving Tank Corps intelligence summaries

---

    Tank Corps intelligence summary, 25 November 1917.
132 TNA, WO 157/243, Tank Corps intelligence summaries, 22, 31 July, 9 August 1918.
133 NARA, RG 120/161/6375-6376, GHQ intelligence summary, 30 August, 16 September 1918.
134 TNA, WO 157/243, *OHL* order, 11 August 1918, cited in Tank Corps intelligence summary, 10 September 1918.
135 NARA, RG 120/161/6376, Ia/54958, German 21st Division, 'Notes on Anti-Tank Defence', 15 August 1918, Annex to GHQ intelligence summary, 26 September 1918, TNA, WO 157/243, Annex to Tank Corps intelligence summary, 17 September 1918.
136 TNA, WO 157/243, Tank Corps intelligence summary, 20 September 1918.
137 TNA, WO 157/243, Tank Corps intelligence summary, 29 September 1918.
138 Fuller, *Tanks,* pp. 236-41.
139 Comparison of responsibilities listed in TNA, WO 95/91, 'Duties of General Staff, Heavy Branch' [April 1917], WO 95/91, HQ Tank Corps war diary, 13 February 1918 & Appendix 10, 'Duties of General Staff, Tank Corps'. For an early summation of German anti-tank activity, quoting some captured documents, see Browne, *The Tank*, pp. 289-300.

and other documents consistently report German anti-tank practices. In addition to general examinations of doctrine, this reporting included specific German countermeasures, both active and passive; armour-piercing ammunition, anti-tank rifles, grenades, mines, obstacles, and anti-tank guns.[140]

During November 1916 general information as to 'the enemy's methods or intentions for combating' tanks was sought from prisoners, but they were not very forthcoming beyond saying that they 'were not greatly feared' and the poor weather would severely restrict their cross-country movement.[141] In January 1917 came the first indication, from a deserter, that dummy tanks were now being used in training schools.[142] A clearer picture emerged in the spring, with a captured divisional order confirming earlier prisoner testimony that the infantry were being told not to retreat but to take cover from the tanks as 'the destruction of tanks is the task of the artillery'.[143] This doctrine was confirmed after Cambrai whereby the German infantry were told to 'allow undamaged tanks to pass through' their lines and focus upon fighting the British infantry. The document also stressed that 'anti-tank tactics must be discussed and practised' so that tanks would 'lose their terror'.[144] In early 1918 the Tank Corps noted a shift in practice, if not in official doctrine. Although some prisoners said that they had been told not to fire on tanks, it was noted that 'recently there has been a marked tendency in many units to encourage infantry, particularly machine gunners, to open fire on tanks and not to leave [their engagement] to the artillery'. It was thought that pamphlets suggesting the vulnerability of tanks to small arms fire had encouraged the German infantry to 'risk disclosing their positions'.[145] Evidence from late 1918 revealed the seriousness with which the Germans were taking the tank threat. One German corps exhorted their men to 'fight until the last tank has been put out of action. As soon as the tanks are destroyed, the whole attack has failed. This must be the common knowledge of the troops!'[146] There was also documentary evidence for the formation of 'anti-tank groups, under specially energetic leaders', the appointment of divisional anti-tank officers and, by late September, a new concept of

---

    What follows is, of course, a précis of what the British knew about German knowledge and intentions, rather than the reality revealed by hindsight.
140 After-action reporting from Ypres suggested an unsuccessful attempt to use aircraft in an anti-tank role. TNA, WO 95/101, SZ187/54/22, 2nd Brigade, 'Report on Tank Operations, 31 July 1917', 21 August 1917.
141 TNA, WO 157/15, GHQ intelligence summaries, 14, 21, 22 November 1916.
142 TNA, WO 157/17, GHQ intelligence summary, 1 January 1917, and see also, WO 157/241, Tank Corps intelligence summary, 3 March 1918.
143 TNA, WO 157/15, 19, GHQ intelligence summaries, 14 November 1916, 28 April 1917.
144 TNA, WO 157/240 Tank Corps intelligence summary, 2 December 1917, WO 157/26, GHQ intelligence summary, 3 December 1917.
145 TNA, WO 157/242, Tank Corps intelligence summary, 8 May 1918.
146 NARA, RG 120/161/6375, Ia/54450, 'Anti-Tank Defence', Annex to GHQ intelligence summary, 2 September 1918.

'tank forts' to be constructed behind the German main line.[147] At the same time the Tank Corps, citing a speech in the *Reichstag*, noted an official view that 'anti-tank defence is nowadays more a matter of nerves than material'.[148]

Moving from general doctrine to specific anti-tank weapons, the most basic defence came from infantry small arms and machine-gun fire. Initially, in 1916, prisoners suggested that they had been ordered to keep tanks 'under continuous fire so as to prevent the crew from emerging in case of a breakdown'.[149] In the spring of 1917 evidence emerged of armour-piercing (AP) ammunition being issued to the German infantry. This coincided with reporting that they were being trained to aim for the tank's 'vulnerable parts'.[150] This seems to have prompted Hotblack to inspect tanks that had been hit with these rounds and to conduct ballistic tests.[151] GHQ concluded that small quantities of this 'special ammunition' had been issued for anti-tank purposes.[152] The picture became clearer at Messines, with one RO reporting that some tanks were hit by AP rounds but they 'did not penetrate', and where a tank brigade noted very limited volumes of this ammunition and orders not to waste it on a tank's frontal armour.[153] Its ineffectiveness was confirmed at Ypres where some machine-guns were given only AP ammunition but caused 'very little damage except for splashes coming through the cracks in the [tanks'] sponsons'.[154] Despite this, after Cambrai, a captured order revealed that the German infantry had been told that: 'The most important means of engaging tanks is the armour-piercing bullet … It is feared by the tank crews, as it goes clean through [the armour], at the same time producing a long flame which frequently sets the petrol tank on fire.'[155] Similarly, in January 1918, a prisoner confirmed that AP ammunition was still being issued to machine-gunners and riflemen, and in July a corps order stressed that as a 'first duty' the machine-guns had to 'fight any tanks appearing within [their] zone of fire'.[156]

---

147 TNA, WO 157/243, Tank Corps intelligence summaries, 1 September and 8 October 1918; NARA, RG 120/161/6376, GHQ intelligence summaries, 16, 24 September and 7 October 1918.
148 TNA, WO 157/243, Tank Corps intelligence summary, 28 September 1918.
149 TNA, WO 157/15, GHQ intelligence summary, 19 November 1916.
150 TNA, WO 157/19, GHQ intelligence summaries, 18, 24 April 1917.
151 TNA, WO 95/91, HQ Tank Corps war diary, 2, 9 May 1917.
152 TNA, WO 157/20, GHQ intelligence summary, 8 May 1917.
153 TNA, WO 95/101, No.6 Company, B Battalion, 'Report of Reconnaissance Officer', 10 June 1917, SZ101/82, 2nd Brigade, 'Summary of Tank Operations, Battle of Messines', 22 June 1917.
154 TNA, WO 95/92, 'Prisoners' statements regarding Tanks' [August 1917], WO 95/101, SZ187/54/22, 2nd Brigade, 'Report on Tank Operations, 31 July 1917', 21 August 1917, WO 95/104, GS577, 3rd Brigade, 'Summary of Tank Operations, 31 July 1917' [August 1917].
155 TNA, WO 157/26, GHQ intelligence summary, 3 December 1917.
156 TNA, WO 157/241, Tank Corps intelligence summary, 29 January 1918; NARA, RG 120/161/6375, Ia/54450, 'Anti-Tank Defence', Annex to GHQ intelligence summary, 2 September 1918.

In July 1918 the British captured a large calibre rifle, designed specifically as an anti-tank weapon.[157] Heavy and clumsy, with an apparent range of 500 yards and a slow rate of fire, they judged it as not 'a formidable weapon'.[158] Subsequent examination of prisoners revealed that it was operated by two men who thought its recoil was 'excessive'.[159] Information from the French and further prisoners suggested that two were being issued to each regimental sector and that it had a reasonable AP capability.[160] They were encountered in tank operations on the Somme in August 1918 and captured instructions stated that the rifles should be used only by men who were 'powerful, resolute and cool'.[161] Other documents suggested that the Germans had placed them in their main line to compensate for their relatively short range.[162] However, after-action reporting suggested that although 'several of these weapons were found, but they did not appear to have been much used and did little damage'.[163] The reason for this limited impact would appear to lie in the difference between official German intent and frontline reality. As the Tank Corps explained:

> In most cases the rifles are being issued to German infantry soldiers immediately before they go into line in battle sectors. In most cases no time is available for training. There is a strong rumour among the German infantry that the kick of these rifles is terrible; in many cases, the infantry make up their minds that they will not use the rifle, and do not do so.[164]

The German infantry were also equipped with grenades but their effectiveness as anti-tank weapons was judged to be very limited. In October 1916 a prisoner suggested that the Germans intended to use 'bombs' against the tanks' tracks.[165] By the end of 1917 the Germans had standardized the use of bundles of seven stick grenades which, according to one document, were to be 'thrown under the tank'.

---

157 Later the British also learnt of a German intent to design an anti-tank machine gun on 'same lines as [their] anti-tank rifle'. NARA, RG 120/161/6377, GHQ intelligence summary, 23 October 1918.
158 TNA, WO 95/94, 'Summary of information', 7 July 1918; NARA, RG 120/161/6375, GHQ intelligence summary, 8 July 1918.
159 NARA, RG 120/161/6375, GHQ intelligence summary, 10 July 1918.
160 Later increased to three or four per sector. NARA, RG 120/161/6375, GHQ intelligence summaries, 17 July, 1, 21 August 1918; TNA, WO 157/243, Tank Corps intelligence summary, 2 August 1918.
161 NARA, RG 120/161/6375, GHQ intelligence summary, 12 August 1918; TNA, WO 157/243, Tank Corps intelligence summary, 14 August 1918.
162 NARA, RG 120/161/6375, GHQ intelligence summary, 1 September 1918; Ia/54450, 'Anti-Tank Defence', Annex to GHQ intelligence summary, 2 September 1918.
163 TNA, WO 95/112, 5th Brigade, 'Report on Operations with Australian Corps, 8-15 August 1918', 23 August 1918.
164 TNA, WO 157/243, Tank Corps intelligence summary, 2 September 1918.
165 TNA, WO 157/14, GHQ intelligence summary, 14 October 1916.

However it was conceded that this was 'not easy' and other reporting suggested it was an extemporised method which would, presumably, be displaced by better weapons.[166] The British conducted their own experiments on obsolete tanks which concluded that the bundle needed to be touching the armour when it detonated to have any effect.[167] Unsurprisingly, grenade bundles do not feature in the 1918 reporting on countermeasures.

Initially more threatening were German anti-tank mines. The British had first learnt of training exercises involving 'mined dug-outs' in April 1917 and by then knew of infantry units intending to use wooden boxes containing six kilograms of high explosive.[168] Reporting after Cambrai suggested that they could be detonated by contact with a tank's tracks.[169] There was then a hiatus until August when information from documents and prisoners confirmed the contact detonation, that they would be used in forward positions – mainly on likely routes such as roads – and that they had caused a number of accidents. At this stage, despite some losses, the Tank Corps assessed that they immobilized rather than destroyed the tank and so 'their effect has not been great'.[170] Intelligence from the later stages of the fighting provided additional details on their deployment, but did not alter these perceptions.[171]

The British believed that German policy regarding tank obstacles went through two distinct phases. First, in late 1916 there were attempts to systematically dig ditches or detonate craters on all roads.[172] But such reporting is then notable by its absence until December 1917 when a captured order noted than only 'trenches at least 13 to 16½ feet wide and 10 feet deep, and very deep mud' presented a barrier to tanks and, therefore, 'the construction of obstacles is not worth while; thorough offensive action is better'.[173] However, in the late summer of 1918 a second phase of obstacle construction was noted, with craters blown in roads and prisoners used to dig ditches across them. The Tank Corps concluded that recent Allied successes had prompted

---

166 TNA, WO 157/26, GHQ intelligence summaries, 3, 22 December 1917, WO 157/241, Tank Corps intelligence summary, 29 January 1918.
167 TNA, WO 95/93, 'Trials with German Stick Bombs on the Shell of an Old Mark I Tank' [February 1918].
168 TNA, WO 157/19, GHQ intelligence summary, 4 April 1917, WO 95/104, GS577, 3rd Brigade, 'Summary of Tank Operations, 31 July 1917' [August 1917].
169 TNA, WO 157/26, GHQ intelligence summary, 22 December 1917, WO 157/240, Tank Corps intelligence summary, 23 December 1917.
170 NARA, RG 120/161/6375, GHQ intelligence summaries, 11, 26 August 1918; Ia/53931, 'German Anti-Tank Mine', 15 August 1918; TNA, WO 95/112, 5th Brigade, 'Report on Operations with Australian Corps, 8-15 August 1918', 23 August 1918, WO 157/243, Tank Corps intelligence summary, 28 August 1918.
171 NARA, RG 120/161/6375, Ia/54450, 'Anti-Tank Defence', Annex to GHQ intelligence summary, 2 September 1918, RG 120/161/6377, GHQ intelligence summary, 1 November 1918; TNA, WO 157/243-244, Tank Corps intelligence summaries, 8, 29, 30 September, 7 November 1918, WO 95/95, Tank Corps Intelligence, 13 November 1918.
172 TNA, WO 157/14-15, GHQ intelligence summaries, 10, 30 October, 1 November 1916.
173 TNA, WO 157/26, GHQ intelligence summary, 3 December 1917.

this change of policy.[174] Later the British noted the used of large concrete blocks and, less effectively, improvised blockades, with one German army suggesting the use of agricultural machinery or heavy wagons pulled across roads.[175]

As indicated in the earlier discussion of doctrine, the British realized very quickly that the Germans gave prominence to the use of artillery. Therefore a considerable volume of reporting can be discerned regarding various calibres of weapon to be used in an anti-tank role. To begin with, in September 1916, an interrogation of artillery prisoners suggested accidental success as that they had simply engaged those tanks that 'happened to approach' their position.[176] In November came the first suggestion, from prisoners, that smaller calibre artillery pieces would be used against tanks 'at point blank range', a suggestion corroborated by reporting later that winter.[177] Just before the opening of the Arras offensive, GHQ confirmed the existence of field gun batteries 'reserved for anti-Tank defence', with one gun per kilometre of front.[178] Later evidence confirmed the use of 37 mm and 50 mm guns in camouflaged positions and, after Messines, it was noted that 76 and 77 mm pieces mounted on low wheels 'with the express purpose of repelling tanks' had been deployed and that AP shells had been issued.[179] However, after-action reporting noted that, despite the use of concrete emplacements for protection, 'nearly all the guns ... had been damaged by our artillery fire previous to the attack, and no tank appears to have been fired on my any of these guns'.[180] Ypres yielded no new information except for the use of an anti-tank gun mounted on a light railway train.[181] Cambrai gave some further insight, primarily from the capture of artillery prisoners. They revealed that, for a long period, new officers had been trained in firing over open sights at dummy tanks. More importantly, they noted a 77 mm field gun battery that had 'hauled their guns into the open and fired from there, [put] four tanks out of action' at short-range. However, a 'despondent' artillery officer prisoner thought that 'although one or two tanks could be put out of

---

174 TNA, WO 157/243, Tank Corps intelligence summaries, 24 August, 4 September 1918; NARA, RG 120/161/6375, GHQ intelligence summary, 1 September 1918.
175 TNA, WO 157/243, Tank Corps intelligence summaries, 8 September, 2 October 1918, WO 95/95, Tank Corps Intelligence, 13 November 1918; NARA, RG 120/161/6377, GHQ intelligence summary, 1 November 1918.
176 TNA, WO 157/13, GHQ intelligence summary, 24 September 1916.
177 TNA, WO 157/15 and 18, GHQ intelligence summaries, 19 November 1916, 15, 19, 25 March 1917; Service Historique de la Défense, Départment Terre, 17N 310, GHQ intelligence summary, 17 February 1917.
178 TNA, WO 157/19, GHQ intelligence summary, 7 April 1917.
179 AP shells were later confirmed. TNA, WO 157/19, 21, 25, GHQ intelligence summaries, 28 April, 9, 12 June, 24 October 1917.
180 TNA, WO 95/101, SZ101/82, 2nd Brigade, 'Summary of Tank Operations, Battle of Messines', 22 June 1917.
181 TNA, WO 95/97, Appendix H to BMS/282/77, 1st Brigade, 'Summary of Tank Operations, 31 July 1917', August 1917.

action [by a field gun] sooner or later the gun would be surrounded'.[182] Subsequent documentary evidence suggested that the Germans would site their anti-tank guns in 'the forward battle zone' because batteries 'kept in readiness well to the rear of the front line have no knowledge of what is going on and generally arrive too late'.[183]

But despite this evidence, in January the Tank Corps assessed that the Germans would continue to use mobile field guns rather than forward positioned specialist anti-tank guns.[184] Operations in the second half of 1918 undermined this assessment, with the Germans using well-camouflaged single field guns in forward positions to good effect. On the Somme in August there was also an improvement in the accuracy of fire which was attributed to 'a special anti-tank sight'.[185] However, German documents also revealed that when tanks broke through their lines: 'No defence could be made in time owing to the fact that batteries which had their guns dug in were insufficiently mobile and were only ready to open fire too late and to defend themselves against the Tanks, which attacked them from all sides.'[186] Adding to this fluctuating situation, the Germans also began to use anti-aircraft guns and guns mounted on lorries in a mobile anti-tank role.[187] The seriousness of the challenge facing the Germans was underlined by a captured divisional order which stated that 'the first duty of the field artillery is to keep off the enemy's tanks. All other duties must give way to this'.[188] Subsequent documents also revealed that the Germans sought to instil patience in their anti-tank gunners; ordering them to hold their fire until the last possible moment.[189] But this approach also had drawbacks. In October a tank brigade noted a German battery that: 'Remained silent and … withheld its fire until the tanks were close upon it when it opened fire point blank. [But] the infantry who had been behind the tank … surrounded and captured the battery and its personnel.'[190]

182 TNA, WO 157/240, Tank Corps intelligence summaries, 21, 28 November 1917.
183 TNA, WO 157/26, GHQ intelligence summary, 3 December 1917.
184 NARA, RG 120/161/6373, GHQ intelligence summary, 24 January 1918; TNA, WO 157/241, Annex to Tank Corps intelligence summary, 29 January 1918.
185 TNA, WO 95/112, 5th Brigade, 'Report on Operations with Australian Corps, 8-15 August 1918', 23 August 1918; NARA, RG 120/161/6375, Ia/54450, 'Anti-Tank Defence', Annex to GHQ intelligence summary, 2 September 1918.
186 TNA, WO 157/243, Tank Corps intelligence summary, 3 September 1918.
187 NARA, RG 120/161/6375, GHQ intelligence summary, 30 August 1918; TNA, WO 157/243, Tank Corps intelligence summary, 13 September 1918. Both of these reports might refer to lorry-mounted anti-aircraft guns.
188 NARA, RG 120/161/6376, GHQ intelligence summary, 16 September 1918.
189 TNA, WO 157/243, Annex to Tank Corps intelligence summaries, 17, 29 September 1918; NARA, RG 120/161/6376, Ia/54958, German 21st Division, 'Notes on Anti-Tank Defence', 15 August 1918, Annex to GHQ intelligence summary, 26 September 1918.
190 TNA, WO 95/98, 1st Brigade, 'Report on Operations, 27-30 September 1918', 24 October 1918.

Reflections

Overall, it is hoped that this chapter has reinforced Hammond's view that the Tank Corps' reconnaissance efforts 'provided crucial information that informed the logistical and practical arrangements [thus] helping to ensure operational success'.[191] From the evidence presented, it can be argued that Hotblack's men provided the organization with one of its bedrocks for success. At the most basic level, to enable their colleagues to use this new weapon system efficiently, they invested considerable effort in heightening the tank crews' awareness about the terrain over which they would be operating. Overlaying this they supplied information about the enemy's dispositions and, later on, insights into their anti-tank capabilities. Within the context of the BEF intelligence system, the Tank Corps was essentially parasitical. To deliver their unique capability, the tanks units turned up just before an operation and sought to exploit the available information resources in a short space of time. They put very little back in. At this point the local intelligence staffs would have been at their busiest and were unfamiliar with the tanks' needs; therefore the IOs and ROs acted an essential interface. Such a tailored service could not have been provided by the normal intelligence infrastructure.

In 1917 this 'reconnaissance imperative' acted as a brake on the Tank Corps' usage. Of course, there were also other limiting factors such as the transportation of tanks and the BEF's generally slow tempo of operations, but a *de facto* precondition of comprehensive information gathering was a key reason for not deploying tanks in haste. There was also an acceptance that the Germans were 'always forewarned when an attack on a large scale [was] pending'. Tanks had become a common feature of the larger operations and so were a major indicator of BEF offensive intent.[192] From Cambrai onwards the reconnaissance effort was deliberately sacrificed as the price to be paid for secrecy. Of course, by this stage the Tank Corps had, collectively, a depth of experience in carrying out their duties and so adequate information was a sufficient foundation. Although there was always a natural desire for tank commanders to have a preview of their battlefields,[193] there was also an embracing of the secrecy imperative. As one tank brigade put it:

> Given thorough secrecy and consequently a complete surprise, [a tank operation's] success is practically assured – even with the inevitable defects in organization and preparation that a high degree of secrecy necessarily entails. However, this drawback is recognized and must be accepted – for the most perfect and

---

191 Hammond, 'Theory and Practice', p. 397.
192 TNA, WO 95/92, GT3509, II Corps to Fifth Army, 15 August 1917.
193 TNA, WO 95/93, 3rd Tank Group, 'Tactical Experiences of all the past Tank Corps operations' [1918].

detailed arrangements are powerless to ensure success if the enemy should have discovered our intentions.[194]

In this regard, surveying across their operations, the Tank Corps' provides a useful example of intelligence as a force multiplier. In 1916 and early 1917 the work of an inexperienced corps was initially dependent upon, and later enhanced by good information provision. However, at Third Ypres the strength of such work could not compensate for basic operational difficulties. After Cambrai a more experienced and capable corps needed less multiplication to be effective. Indeed, during the 'Hundred Days' it seems to have scraped by with 'just enough' information.

Finally, credit must be given to the work of the IOs and ROs and the synergies between them. Theirs was an accidentally hybrid organization that, from the start, had to fuse intelligence and reconnaissance practices. They were fortunate that the BEF sent some of its most dynamic Intelligence Corps officers to provide leadership and an information management framework within which the battalion and company ROs could operate. Although they were the representatives of a wider system that was undergoing a wholesale doctrinal shift towards 'indoor' intelligence practice, it is interesting to observe that Hotblack, Nelson, and Williams-Ellis conformed to the 'outdoor' paradigm of 'manly' Edwardian reconnaissance work. They incurred personal risk to see the ground and situation for themselves and, in doing so, established credibility in the eyes of their contemporaries and set an example for their subordinates. Tank Corps reconnaissance and intelligence was therefore a curious mix of ancient and modern; a 'futuristic unit' employing cutting edge technology but encouraging old-fashioned behaviours in its information gatherers.

---

194 TNA, WO 95/99, 1st Brigade, 'Secrecy', 15 August 1918, Appendix B to BMS/106/29, 1st Brigade, 'Report on Operations, 21-25 August 1918', 29 August 1918.

6

The Development of Tank Communications in the British Expeditionary Force, 1916-1918

Brian N. Hall

In March 1917 the General Staff of the British Expeditionary Force (BEF) issued *SS. 148. Forward Inter-Communication in Battle*, the army's first authoritative training manual devoted entirely to the issue of communications. Encapsulating the lessons learnt from operations on the Somme the previous year, *SS. 148* devoted just two pages to the matter of tank communications, with the explanation that since tank development was 'still in an experimental stage… the best means of communication cannot be definitely laid down until further experience has been gained'. However, three months later the General Staff issued *SS. 167. Signal Organisation for Heavy Branch Machine Gun Corps*. Taking into account the experiences of the recent offensives at Arras and Messines Ridge, *SS. 167* stated unequivocally that 'a properly organised system of communications for Tanks is essential if full value is to be obtained from this arm'.[1] Thus, within nine months of the tank's debut, the British high command had come to realize that efficient communications were a prerequisite for the successful employment of tanks in battle.

However, despite this explicit acknowledgement of their importance, the issue of communications remains a practical aspect of British tank operations on the Western Front that, although frequently mentioned within the historiography, has not been

---

1   *SS. 148. Forward Inter-Communication in Battle* (March 1917), pp. 36-7; *SS. 167. Signal Organisation for Heavy Branch Machine Gun Corps* (June 1917), p. 3. The Heavy Branch was separated from the Machine Gun Corps in July 1917 and renamed the Tank Corps. For additional context on the BEF's training manuals, see Paddy Griffith, *Battle Tactics of the Western Front: The British Army's Art of Attack 1916-18* (New Haven, 1994), pp. 179-91; and, Jim Beach, 'Issued by the General Staff: Doctrine Writing at British GHQ, 1917-1918', *War in History*, 19 (2012), pp. 464-91.

considered by historians in any great detail.[2] Even the regimental histories of the Tank Corps and the Royal Engineers Signal Service pay little attention to the development of tank communications during the First World War.[3] This is a significant oversight because throughout the war tenuous communications had a profound impact on the tactical and operational effectiveness of tanks in action. This was due in part to the absence of efficient mobile, 'real-time' communications technology, which imposed profound restrictions on the ability of commanders of every arm, and in every army, to exercise command and control over their troops in the heat of battle, and also in part to the primitive nature of the tanks themselves. As one former British tank commander recalled after the war:

> To be in action inside a tank is to be like an ostrich with its head in the sand. Except for the officer, who must take risks if he wants to direct his tank efficiently, the crew get only fleeting glimpses of the outside world over their gun sights. This poor visibility, coupled with the thumping of the engine and the muffled roar of the guns, which is absolutely deafening, cuts the crew off almost completely from the hideous sights and sounds of the battlefield.[4]

Given, then, the failure by historians to consider in depth the role and significance of British tank communications during the war, the question needs to be asked: to what extent did the BEF achieve 'a properly organised system of communications for Tanks' by the end of the war? In seeking to answer this question, this chapter aims to fill a gap in the historiography by examining the developmental process by which the BEF's tank communications system evolved between 1916 and 1918. It adopts a chronological approach and argues that, although British commanders sought newer and better methods of conveying information in order to improve the BEF's tank communications system, by 1918 poor communications continued to hamper British tank operations on the Western Front. Such a conclusion lends further support to the

---

2   J.P. Harris, *Men, Ideas and Tanks: British Military Thought and Armoured Forces, 1903-1939* (Manchester, 1995), p. 91; David J. Childs, *A Peripheral Weapon? The Production and Employment of British Tanks in the First World War* (Westport, CT, 1999), pp. 128-9; Christopher Brynley Hammond, 'The Theory and Practice of Tank Co-operation with Other Arms on the Western Front During the First World War', PhD thesis, University of Birmingham, 2005, pp. 390-94.
3   Captain B.H. Liddell Hart, *The Tanks: The History of the Royal Tank Regiment and its Predecessors Heavy Branch Machine Gun Corps, Tank Corps and Royal Tank Corps, 1914-1945: Volume One: 1914-1939* (London, 1959), pp. 57, 62; R.E. Priestley, *Work of the Royal Engineers in the European War, 1914-19: The Signal Service (France)* (first published 1921; new ed., Uckfield, 2006), pp. 245-8.
4   F. Mitchell, *Tank Warfare: The Story of the Tanks in the Great War* (London, 1933), p. 153. The contribution of communications to British operations on the Western Front is examined in Brian N. Hall, 'The British Expeditionary Force and Communications on the Western Front, 1914-1918', PhD thesis, University of Salford, 2010.

argument made by some historians that, given the limitations of the technology at the time, the finite resources available and the circumstances in which tank crews operated, it is difficult to see how the BEF could have made greater and more successful use of tanks during the First World War.[5]

1916: Rudimentary and *ad hoc* Experiments

Since the onset of trench warfare in the winter of 1914/15, tenuous communications had imposed profound restrictions on the ability of British commanders to exercise efficient command and control over their troops during the heat of battle. This was one of the principal findings of 'The Committee on the Lessons of the Great War' in October 1932 when highlighting the inherent difficulty that the BEF had had in attempting to convert a *break-in* to an enemy position into a *breakthrough*. Telephone and telegraph lines were routinely cut by enemy artillery fire, wireless was both rudimentary and extremely fragile, whilst visual signalling and message carriers were slow, dangerous and unreliable means of conveying information. At Neuve Chapelle and at Loos in 1915, and on the Somme on 1 July 1916, 'once the battle was joined the higher command ceased to influence it'. In the absence of the smooth and rapid transfer of accurate information, vital decisions, such as committing reserves, were often made too late or not at all. Consequently, the momentum of the attack soon ground to a halt as opportunities to exploit any initial successes were lost and the Germans given ample time to call up their reserves and reinforce their defences.[6]

The introduction of tanks into the BEF's order of battle in September 1916, therefore, presented British commanders with a novel set of further communication dilemmas. Three channels of communication were necessary: first, tank-to-tank communication; second, communication between tanks and other arms with which

---

5   J.P. Harris, 'The Rise of Armour', in Paddy Griffith (ed.), *British Fighting Methods in the Great War* (London, 1996), pp. 113-37; J.P. Harris with Niall Barr, *Amiens to the Armistice: The BEF in the One Hundred Days' Campaign, 8 August-11 November 1918* (London, 1998), pp. 294-300; J.P. Harris, 'Haig and the Tank', in Brian Bond & Nigel Cave (eds.), *Haig: A Reappraisal 70 Years On* (Barnsley, 1999), pp. 145-54. For the argument that the BEF did not harness the full potential of tanks and other technologies during the war, see Tim Travers, *How the War Was Won: Command and Technology in the British Army on the Western Front, 1917-1918* (London, 1992), and, in particular, Tim Travers, 'Could the Tanks of 1918 have been War-Winners for the British Expeditionary Force?', *Journal of Contemporary History* 27 (1992), pp. 389-406.

6   The National Archives of the United Kingdom, Kew (hereafter, TNA), WO 32/3116, 'Report of the Committee on the Lessons of the Great War (The Kirke Report)', October 1932. For scholarly accounts of the battles in 1915, see Robin Prior & Trevor Wilson, *Command on the Western Front: The Military Career of Sir Henry Rawlinson, 1914-1918* (Oxford, 1992), pp. 17-134; and, Nick Lloyd, *Loos 1915* (Stroud, 2006). For 1916, see Tim Travers, *The Killing Ground: The British Army, the Western Front and the Emergence of Modern War 1900-1918* (London, 1987), pp. 127-99; Gary Sheffield, *The Somme* (London, 2003); and, Robin Prior & Trevor Wilson, *The Somme* (New Haven, 2005).

they were working, particularly the infantry; and, third, communication between tanks and formation headquarters in the rear. With regards to the first of these, it quickly became apparent to the first tank crews that coordinating their machines with each other whilst in action was going to prove highly problematic. The noise and poor lighting within the tank made it difficult for tank crews to communicate with each other, let alone with the outside world. As Lieutenant Frank Mitchell, 1st Battalion, Tank Corps, recalled after the war:

> One of the drawbacks of tanks in battle is the total lack of any means of communication with other tanks. When once inside, with doors bolted, flaps shut and loop holes closed, one can only make signs to a tank very near at hand by taking the great risk of opening the manhole in the roof and waving a handkerchief or a shovel.[7]

Experiments with electric signalling lamps were conducted in mid-1916 and, along with coloured flags, laid down as the primary method of inter-tank signals to be used during to the battle of Flers-Courcelette on 15 September.[8]

This reliance on simple visual signals to facilitate tank-to-tank communication was born out of necessity, since wireless sets in 1916 did not render reception inside tanks possible 'owing to noise and engine vibration'. With the transmission of human speech over radio waves (wireless telephony) at an early, experimental stage, the wireless sets employed by the BEF were 'almost exclusively Morse-operated with crystals or magnetized tape-detection for receivers and arc or spark-gap radiation for transmission'.[9] This meant that they were easily susceptible to damage, their operational range was limited and channel selectivity poor. Furthermore, very few sets could be employed on a given frontage without risk of mutual interference. Indeed, according to Major-General Sir Ernest Swinton, one of the tank's foremost pioneers, it was this latter drawback that forced the BEF's high command to abandon attempts to install and utilize wireless within tanks in 1916.[10]

In many respects, tank-to-tank communications during the latter stages of the Somme campaign were necessarily ad-hoc and experimental. Since a 'section commander's job was to be where he could be of most use to the infantry while still

---

7   Mitchell, *Tank Warfare*, p. 66.
8   Imperial War Museum, London (hereafter, IWM), Department of Documents, Fourth Army Records, Vol. 8 (Operation Orders and Instructions, 20 August-16 November 1916), 'Instructions for the Employment of "Tanks', 11 September 1916.
9   Liddell Hart, *The Tanks*, p. 62; Dean Juniper, 'The First World War and Radio Development', *Royal United Services Institute Journal* 148 (2003), p. 84.
10 Maj.-Gen. Sir Ernest D. Swinton, *Eyewitness* (London, 1932), pp. 250-51, 270-71. For additional context on the development of wireless within the British Army during the First World War, see Brian N. Hall, 'The British Army and Wireless Communication, 1896-1918', *War in History*, 19 (2012), pp. 290-321.

keeping control of his tanks', many found that they had no alternative but to lead their tanks into action on foot, or climb out of their tank in order to give verbal instructions to another tank's commander.[11] Such was the case on 18 November near Beaumont-Hamel, when the future Tank Corps' chief intelligence officer, Captain (later Major) Elliot Hotblack, won the Distinguished Service Order for personally guiding a stray tank towards a German strongpoint whilst under heavy fire.[12]

Arrangements for communications between tanks and other arms were, though, more clearly defined. In August, a General Headquarters (GHQ) memorandum, entitled 'Preliminary Notes on Tactical Employment of Tanks', stressed the particular necessity for infantry 'to cooperate closely with the tanks'. The specific details of this cooperation were worked out at a Fourth Army Conference on 10 September and issued as 'Instructions for the Employment of "Tanks"' the following day. The 'Instructions' stipulated that communication from tanks to infantry was to be facilitated chiefly by the use of coloured flags: a red flag would indicate that the tank was 'out of action', while a green flag would denote 'am on objective'.[13] Despite these provisions, however, time constraints and the inadequate number of tanks available meant that infantry-tank training prior to the battle of Flers-Courcelette was both haphazard and restricted, which partly explains why tank-infantry cooperation on the Somme was, on the whole, not a resounding success.[14]

Arrangements were also put into place to facilitate communication between tanks and aeroplanes. Following the first-ever instance of tank-aeroplane cooperation during the battle of Morval on 26 September, for instance, 2nd Division issued instructions in late October detailing the work to be carried out by assigned signallers, who would 'operate a lamp through the roof' of their respective tanks in order to send information regarding the infantry's advance to contact aeroplanes flying above.[15] However, the absence of clear visibility due to rain and low cloud during the closing weeks of the Somme campaign greatly hampered such work. Reflecting on the limited success

11 Captain D.E. Hickey, *Rolling into Action: Memoirs of a Tank Corps Section Commander* (Uckfield, 2007), p. 101.
12 Mitchell, *Tank Warfare*, p. 42; Harris, *Men, Ideas and Tanks*, p. 84; Jim Beach, 'British Intelligence and German Tanks, 1916-1918', *War in History* 14 (2007), pp. 454-75, here, 459-60.
13 TNA, WO 158/834, 'Preliminary Notes on Tactical Employment of Tanks', 16 August 1916; IWM, Fourth Army Records, Vol. 8, 'Instructions for the Employment of "Tanks"', 11 September 1916. See also TNA, WO 95/2632, 41 Division War Diary, '41st Division Operation Order No. 42', 13 September 1916.
14 Hammond, 'The Theory and Practice of Tank Co-operation', pp. 53-9; Trevor Pidgeon, *The Tanks at Flers: An Account of the First Use of Tanks in War at the Battle of Flers-Courcelette, The Somme, 15th September 1916* (Cobham, 1995).
15 Major A.F. Becke, comp., *History of the Great War: Order of Battle of Divisions Part 4, The Army Council, GHQs, Armies, and Corps 1914-1918* (Eastbourne, 2007), p. 272; TNA, WO 95/96, C Company Machine Gun Corps (Heavy Section) War Diary, '2nd Division Order No. 157', 22 October 1916.

of operations during this period, for example, General Sir Henry Rawlinson, GOC Fourth Army, noted in his diary that 'the absence of observation from the air has I think been enough to account for our failure'.[16]

With regards to communications between tanks and formation headquarters in the rear, it was decided that a proportion of fighting tanks were to be provided with two carrier pigeons to serve this purpose. The Carrier Pigeon Service had become an established branch of the BEF's Signal Service at the beginning of June 1915, following the successful employment of carrier pigeons during the Second Battle of Ypres, and grew rapidly in size to incorporate 20,000 pigeons and some 380 handlers by 1918.[17] Pigeons were much less susceptible to shell fire and the effects of poison gas than human despatch riders and runners, and in good weather could travel at speeds of 40-60 miles per hour.[18] However, the poisonous and sweltering interior conditions within First World War tanks could make the use of carrier pigeons problematic. As Lieutenant Frank Mitchell noted after the war:

> The poor pigeons were taken into action in a basket which, for lack of room, was often placed on top of the engine. In the heat and excitement of a battle they were sometimes overlooked, and when the basket was opened at last there emerged a decidedly overheated and semi-asphyxiated bird.[19]

Nevertheless, according to Colonel (later Brigadier-General) Christopher Baker-Carr, commanding 1st Tank Brigade (1917-18), the use of carrier pigeons at Flers-Courcelette was 'found to be the most rapid means of communication from the battle'. Much depended, though, on the value of the information contained within the message a pigeon was carrying. Baker-Carr recalled in his memoirs, for instance, an amusing incident during the closing stages of the Somme campaign in mid-November when a carrier pigeon flew into the loft at XIII Corps headquarters, whereupon the corps commander, Lieutenant-General Sir Walter Congreve, eagerly opened the message to read: 'I'm just about fed up with carrying this perishing bird… It can bleeding well go home. Signed John Brown, Pte.'.[20]

---

16   Churchill Archive Centre, Churchill College, Cambridge, General Lord Rawlinson Papers, RWLN 1/7, Diary, 12 October 1916.
17   Captain W.J. Gwilliam, R.E., 'Transmission of Messages by Carrier Pigeons', *The Post Office Electrical Engineers' Journal* 11 (1918-19), pp. 203-6; Lieutenant-Colonel A.H. Osman, *Pigeons in the Great War: A Complete History of the Carrier Pigeon Service During the Great War, 1914 to 1918* (London, 1928), p. 6.
18   National Archives and Records Administration, Washington D.C., Records of the American Expeditionary Force, RG120, Entry 404, NM-91, Box #2, 'Lecture No. 35. Military Use of Pigeons, Officers School – First Course, Monday, January 7th, 1918 to Saturday, February 2nd, 1918'.
19   Mitchell, *Tank Warfare*, p. 102.
20   Brig.-Gen. C.D. Baker-Carr, *From Chauffeur to Brigadier* (London, 1930), pp. 200-1.

Photo 7: Pigeon about to be released from tank sponson

It can be concluded, therefore, that the BEF's tank communications system in 1916 was both extemporary and rudimentary in nature. The provision and maintenance of communications for tanks added yet more pressure to an army already struggling to develop an efficient communications system capable of meeting the demands of a modern, industrialized conflict.[21] Moreover, the introduction of tanks into the BEF's order of battle also brought further disruption to the communication networks of other arms. As Sergeant J. Sawers, 2nd New Zealand Brigade Signal Section, recalled after the war, the tanks at Flers-Courcelette 'chewed up' infantry and artillery telephone lines during the course of the battle – 'a historic first for a subsequently far too frequent occurrence'.[22]

21 Hall, 'The British Expeditionary Force and Communications', pp. 175-219.
22 Royal Signals Museum Archive, Dorset, 914.2, Military Histories (General), 'Notes: Conversation with Sergeant J. Sawers', 14 July 1972.

1917: A Year of Steady Improvements

Taking into account the lessons learnt from the initial tank operations on the Somme, considerable ingenuity was applied in attempts to improve the BEF's tank communications system throughout 1917, though to varying degrees of success. These attempts mirrored those by the BEF as a whole, for although the offensives of 1917 failed to break the stalemate on the Western Front they did demonstrate the growing tactical and operational sophistication of British fighting methods.[23]

Of the three principal channels of communication required by tanks, tank-to-tank communications underwent the least dramatic improvement during 1917. This was due largely to the primitive nature of the communication technologies of the era and the difficulty, if not impossibility, of getting such devices to work successfully from within the confines of equally primitive armoured fighting vehicles. Indeed, following the battle of Arras in May 1917, it was noted that, 'owing to the extreme noise inside Tanks, Tank Commanders found the greatest difficulty in communicating instructions to their crews'. It was suggested, therefore, that 'some form of speaking tube' was required to rectify the problem.[24] However, it was remarked after the war that speaking tubes had been found 'quite useless, as they become red-hot, so that no one can touch them'. The majority of tank crews simply relied on shouting to each other whilst in action or using whistles to attract the driver's attention.[25] Prearranged hand signals amongst crew members also became common practice, especially when attempting to coordinate the rather complicated procedure of changing the direction the tank was moving in:

> First of all, the tank had to stop. A knock on the right side would attract the attention of the right gearsman. The driver would hold out a clenched fist, which was the signal to put the track into *neutral*. The gearsman would repeat the signal to show it was done. The officer, who controlled two brake levers, would pull on the right one, which held the right track. The driver would accelerate, and the tank would slew round slowly on the stationary right track while the left track

---

23 For scholarly accounts of the battles of 1917, see: Jonathan Walker, *The Blood Tub: General Gough and the Battle of Bullecourt 1917* (Staplehurst, 1998); Ian Passingham, *Pillars of Fire: The Battle of Messines Ridge June 1917* (Stroud, 1998); Peter H. Liddle (ed.), *Passchendaele in Perspective: The Third Battle of Ypres* (London, 1997); Robin Prior & Trevor Wilson, *Passchendaele: The Untold Story* (New Haven, 1996); and, Bryn Hammond, *Cambrai 1917: The Myth of the First Great Tank Battle* (London, 2008).
24 Liddell Hart Centre for Military Archives, King's College London (hereafter, LHCMA), Major-General J.F.C. Fuller Papers 1/4/1, 'Summary of Tank Operations 1st Brigade, Heavy Branch. 9th April-3rd May 1917', 17 May 1917.
25 TNA, WO 95/93, Tank Corps War Diary, 'Tactical Experiences of all Past Tank Corps Operations Collected and Issued by the 3rd Tank Group', n.d., but given that the 3rd Tank Group was not formed until 13 November 1918 the report must have been compiled post-war. See Becke, *Order of Battle of Divisions*, Appendix 5.

went into motion. As soon as the tank had turned sufficiently the procedure was reversed.[26]

Clearly the issue of internal tank communications was just as important as communication between tanks, since the smooth and efficient running of a tank relied a great deal on the close interaction and cooperation of the crew itself.[27]

Tank-to-tank communication in 1917 was accomplished chiefly by the medium of visual signalling. Each tank carried three coloured discs or lights – red, white and green – placed vertically on the side of the tank. Read from the top downwards, inter-tank signals would always begin by utilizing the white disc or light first, while tank-infantry signals would start with either the green or red disc. A single white disc, for example, conveyed the message 'forward, or come on', three white discs denoted 'concentrate on rallying point', while three red discs indicated the tank had broken down.[28] As crude as these coloured disc and light signals were, post-battle reports of the fighting at Arras confirmed that they had 'proved useful', with 'many messages [having been] sent from Tank to Tank'.[29] However, given the climatic and topographic conditions that generally prevailed on the Western Front, visual signalling was a precarious form of communication.[30] Fog, rain, dust and smoke, in particular, rendered the reading of simple coloured discs and lights on tanks extremely difficult. Therefore, just as on the Somme the previous year, many section commanders continued to deliver messages to each other personally and guide their tanks into action on foot. The most noteworthy example of the latter occurred on 4 October during the battle of Broodseinde at Ypres, when Captain Clement Robertson walked in front of his leading tanks, guiding them onto their objective whilst under heavy fire. Although he was killed in the process, he was awarded a Victoria Cross, the first for the Tank Corps during the war.[31]

Although the system of communication between tanks and other arms also did not undergo any radical transformation during the course of 1917, British commanders continued to stress the necessity for closer cooperation and improved methods of communication. As early as February, Major J.F.C. Fuller, chief staff officer of the Heavy Branch Machine Gun Corps, recognized that tanks had to 'work hand in glove with the other arms', and that successful cooperation could not be achieved without

---

26 Hickey, *Rolling into Action*, pp. 113-4.
27 Harris, 'The Rise of Armour', pp. 117-8.
28 *SS. 148. Forward Inter-Communication in Battle*, pp. 36-7, Appendix II; TNA, WO 95/91, Tank Corps War Diary, 'Preliminary Instructions No. 2', 19 March 1917.
29 TNA, WO 95/91, Tank Corps War Diary, 'Report on the Action of Tanks at the Battle of Arras. 9th to 13th April 1917', 27 April 1917, 'Summary of Tank Operations 1st Brigade, Heavy Branch. 9th April-3rd May 1917', 17 May 1917.
30 Hall, 'The British Expeditionary Force and Communications', pp. 104-5.
31 Hickey, *Rolling into Action*, pp. 63-4; Hammond, 'Theory and Practice of Tank Co-operation', p. 174.

a rapid and efficient communications system. This point was reiterated following the battle of Arras, as *SS. 164. Notes on the Use of Tanks* made clear: 'With Tanks, as with any other arm, satisfactory results can only be obtained by the close co-operation of all arms'.[32] This was particularly so with regards to tank-infantry cooperation. Summing up some of the chief lessons learnt as a result of the fighting at Arras, Messines and Third Ypres, a Tank Corps report in late October stressed that '[t]he closest possible liaison must exist between the Tank Units and the Infantry', and that '[t]his co-operation must be established right down to the Tank Commanders and the Infantry Battalions'.[33] This continuing emphasis on improved tank-infantry liaison was to pay-off at the battle of Cambrai the following month. As a 1st Tank Brigade report noted: 'The success of the early part of the Battle was largely due to the close co-operation with the Infantry'.[34] Improved means of tank-infantry communication were therefore imperative if better cooperation was to be achieved, and so existing methods were modified and new ideas tried and tested throughout the year.

Coloured disc or light signals, for instance, similar to those employed for tank-to-tank communication, were used to convey simple information from tanks to supporting infantry units, replacing the system of coloured flags used on the Somme.[35] According to *SS. 148*, all infantrymen had to know the following three general signals by heart: first, a single red disc or light, which meant 'danger, or wire uncut'; second, a single green disc or light, which denoted 'come on, or wire cut'; and, third, a red and green disc or light, which indicated 'wait'. The infantry were to acknowledge receipt of such tank signals by 'waving the rifle with bayonet fixed, from side to side above the head'. The fundamental method used by infantry to call for tank assistance, meanwhile, was made 'by placing the helmet on the end of the fixed bayonet and raising it straight above the head to the full extent of the Rifle'. Although dangerous, it was largely successful and so remained standard practice for the remainder of the war.[36]

If disc signals were not employed, or if they failed to attract the attention of the infantry, then the only other method for tanks to let the infantry know that they had achieved their objective and that it was safe for them to advance was by waving a

---

32 LHCMA, Fuller Papers I/TS1/1/6, 'Training Note No. 16', February 1917; *SS. 164. Notes on the Use of Tanks and on the General Principles of their Employment as an Adjunct to the Infantry Attack* (May 1917), p. 1.
33 TNA, WO 95/92, Tank Corps War Diary, 'Notes on Tank Operations, April-October 1917', 27 October 1917.
34 LHCMA, Fuller Papers 1/4/2, 'Summary of Operations. 20th November to 23rd November 1917. 1st Brigade Tank Corps', 9 December 1917.
35 LHCMA, Fuller Papers 1/4/1, 'Minutes of a Conference Held at Heavy Branch H.Q. on 26th of April 1917', 26 April 1917.
36 *SS. 148. Forward Inter-Communication in Battle*, p. 37; TNA, WO 95/93, Tank Corps War Diary, 'Tactical Experiences of all Past Tank Corps Operations Collected and Issued by the 3rd Tank Group', n.d. [late 1918].

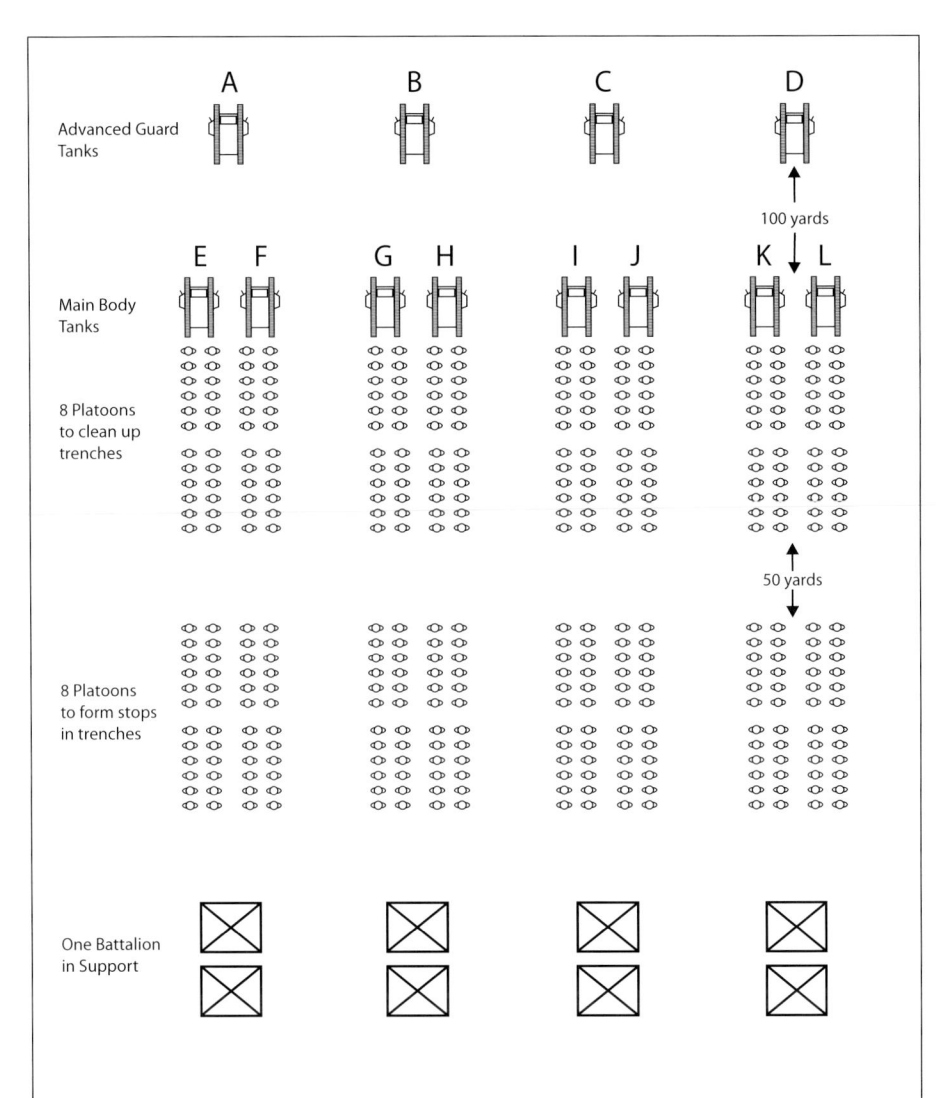

A, B, C and D are the Advanced Tanks, EF, GH, IJ and KL are the Main Body Tanks. According to 'TANK AND INFANTRY OPERATIONS WITHOUT METHODICAL ARTILLERY PREPARATION', "immediately behind these are placed 8 platoons each on a file frontage, that is two sections in single file side by side, and two in similar formation behind them, these 8 platoons form the Trench Cleaners. At 50 yards distance behind the Trench Cleaners come 8 more platoons in similar formation, these are the Trench Stops. Behind these, at whatever distance considered necessary, are drawn up the supports in two lines, consisting of 8 platoons each as shown ..."

Diagram 1: Tank Company and Infantry Battalion forming up for the attack

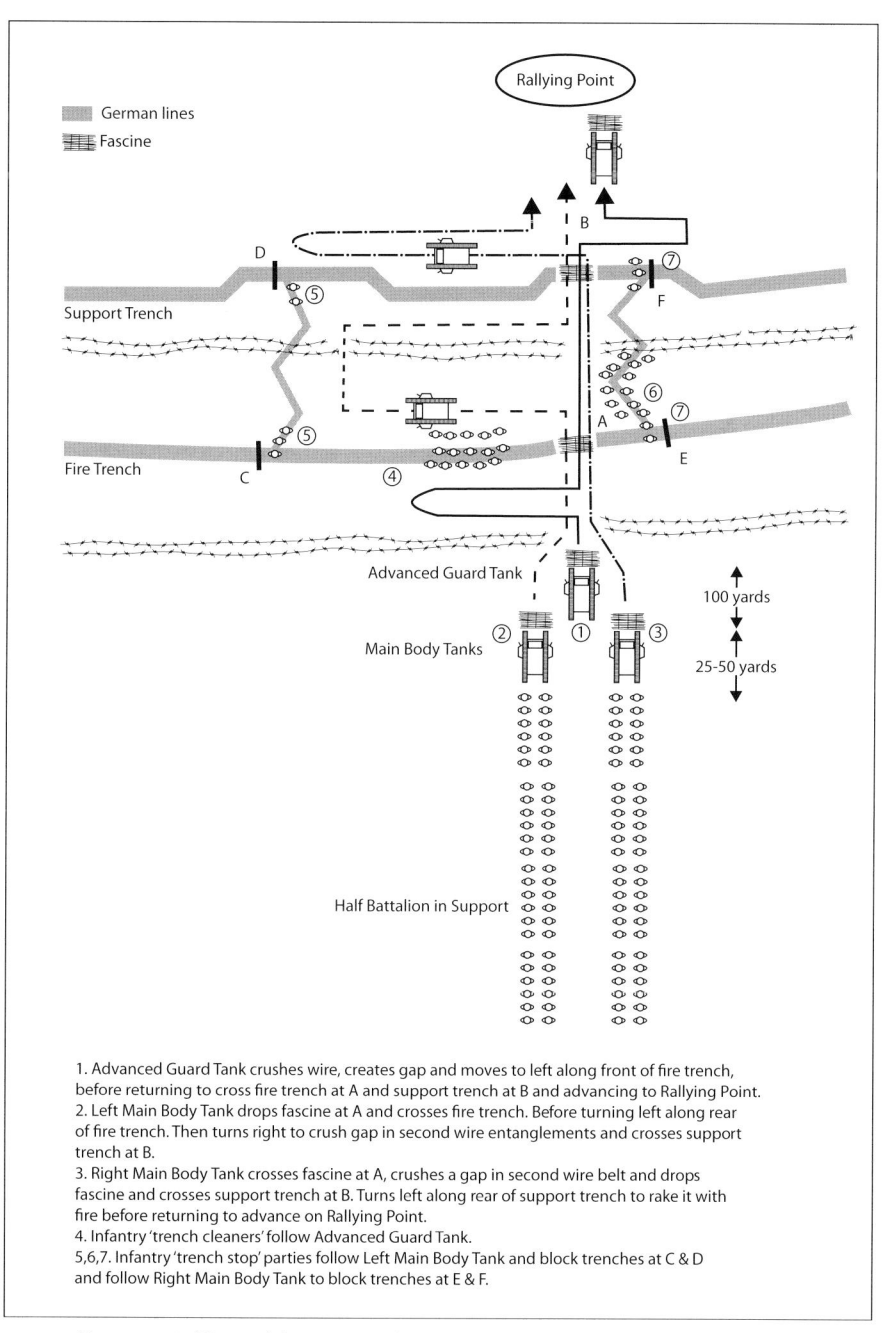

Development of Tank Communications in the British Expeditionary Force 147

1. Advanced Guard Tank crushes wire, creates gap and moves to left along front of fire trench, before returning to cross fire trench at A and support trench at B and advancing to Rallying Point.
2. Left Main Body Tank drops fascine at A and crosses fire trench. Before turning left along rear of fire trench. Then turns right to crush gap in second wire entanglements and crosses support trench at B.
3. Right Main Body Tank crosses fascine at A, crushes a gap in second wire belt and drops fascine and crosses support trench at B. Turns left along rear of support trench to rake it with fire before returning to advance on Rallying Point.
4. Infantry 'trench cleaners' follow Advanced Guard Tank.
5,6,7. Infantry 'trench stop' parties follow Left Main Body Tank and block trenches at C & D and follow Right Main Body Tank to block trenches at E & F.

Diagram 2: Tactical formation adopted by 6th, 20th and 12th Divisions for operations with tanks, 20 November 1917

shovel out of the manhole in the roof.[37] Although this worked reasonably well, there were many occasions when the infantry complained that they had had great difficulty in noticing such a signal.[38] Attempts to rectify this problem varied throughout the year. A report by XVIII Corps in August, for example, suggested that 'a more distinctive signal should be used in future', while Major-General George Harper, GOC 51st Division, stressed after the Battle of Cambrai in November that infantry 'must be within signalling distance' of the tanks they followed. The only other alternative was for a tank commander to leave his tank, or send one of his men, and deliver a message to the infantry in person, a hazardous and time-consuming endeavour.[39]

While tank-to-tank and tank-infantry communication remained somewhat crude, the system of communication between tanks and formation headquarters in the rear underwent a significant number of developments in 1917. At Arras the principal device employed for communication between tanks and rear headquarters was the Aldis Daylight Signalling Lamp. Introduced into the BEF in 1916, the Aldis Lamp was a powerful electric signalling apparatus requiring large accumulators. Although it was not portable enough for use within the infantry, it was ideally suited for tank and aeroplane communication.[40] Each pair of tanks carried an Aldis Lamp and a trained signaller to operate it. Upon reaching a rallying point, messages from tanks were sent using Morse code to a tank battalion transmitting station, located at a pre-determined position on the Black Line (first objective). The station consisted of an officer and a party of signallers and runners, and had to be within easy runner distance of company headquarters, yet also be in a suitable position to observe operations on the Blue Line (second objective).[41] Information received at the transmitting station was passed onto company headquarters, either by telephone or by runner, and then sent up the chain of command through divisional and corps telephone exchanges.[42] Liaison officers drawn from each battalion were also employed to work between Tank Brigade headquarters and divisional, corps and corps heavy artillery headquarters. These liaison officers were required to have 'a good knowledge of Tank Tactics and of the capabilities of

---

37   Capt. D.G. Browne, *The Tank in Action during the First World War* (first published 1920; new edn, Milton Keynes, 2009), p. 206.
38   LHCMA, Fuller Papers 1/4/2, 'Summary of Operations. 20th November to 23rd November 1917. 1st Brigade Tank Corps', 9 December 1917.
39   TNA, WO 95/92, Tank Corps War Diary, 'XVIII Corps. Report on Operations, August 19th, 1917, as the Result of Evidence Obtained from Officers Concerned', August 1917, WO 95/2846, 51 Division War Diary, '51st (HIGHLAND) Division. Instructions No. 1, Training Note. Tank and Infantry Operations Without Methodical Artillery Preparations', 7 November 1917; Mitchell, *Tank Warfare*, p. 108; Harris, *Men, Ideas and Tanks*, p. 91.
40   Priestley, *Work of the Royal Engineers*, p. 144.
41   TNA, WO 95/91, Tank Corps War Diary, 'Detailed Operation Order No. 11 Coy. by Lieut. Col. J. Hardress-Lloyd. D.S.O. Cmmdg. "D" Bn.', 8 April 1917; 'Preliminary Instructions No. 2', 19 March 1917.
42   TNA, WO 95/91, Tank Corps War Diary, '1st BRIGADE HEAVY BRANCH M.G.C. Operation Order No. 2', 31 March 1917.

Tanks, distances they can travel without re-filling... and intimate knowledge of the scheme of operations of the whole Brigade'.[43]

Post-battle reports concerning tank-to-rear headquarters communication at Arras were mostly positive, although four key issues were identified. Firstly, the Aldis Lamps proved their value on several occasions but 'require[d] a bracket outside the Tank to which they could be attached and worked from the inside'.[44] Of more pressing concern, however, were the difficulties caused by inadequate Aldis Lamp training in some battalions. According to the commander of 'C' Battalion, Heavy Branch Machine Gun Corps, Lieutenant-Colonel Sydney Charrington, officers and signallers 'require more training in wording their messages concisely, and intelligibly. Messages were received of a very vague character'.[45] This, however, was a problem that affected not just the Tank Corps but the BEF as a whole throughout the war.[46]

The second issue to emerge from the Battle of Arras concerned the means of communication available to tanks. The most efficient method of communication between tanks and rear headquarters appears to have been carrier pigeons. As supply was limited, two pigeons were allotted to each pair of tanks prior to the battle, though they were 'to be used at discretion' and only 'in cases of great emergency'.[47] However, not only were details of the infantry's advance 'in several cases first notified by means of Tank pigeons', and thereby proving they were 'the only reliable means of communication',[48] but according to a report by the 1st Tank Brigade, their efficiency 'would have been doubly more so if more pigeons had been made available'. The report suggested that if each tank carried four pigeons 'there should be no difficulty whatsoever in sending back quick and accurate information'.[49] Carrier pigeons subsequently formed the backbone of the system of information transfer between frontline tanks and formation headquarters for the remainder of the year.[50] At Cambrai, for instance, pigeons proved of considerable value to the 1st Tank Brigade, who sent and

43 TNA, WO 95/91, Tank Corps War Diary, 'Tanks in the Third Army Offensive', 3 March 1917; 'Preliminary Instructions No. 2', 19 March 1917.
44 LHCMA, Fuller Papers 1/4/1, 'Summary of Tank Operations 1st Brigade, Heavy Branch. 9th April-3rd May 1917', 17 May 1917.
45 TNA, WO 95/91, Tank Corps War Diary, 'Lessons Learnt During the Battle of ARRAS on 23rd April, 1917', 27 April 1917.
46 Hall, 'The British Expeditionary Force and Communications', pp. 335-41.
47 TNA, WO 95/91, Tank Corps War Diary, 'Detailed Operation Order No. 11 Coy. by Lieut. Col. J. Hardress-Lloyd. D.S.O. Cmmdg. "D" Bn.', 8 April 1917; '1st BRIGADE HEAVY BRANCH M.G.C. Operation Order No. 2', 31 March 1917.
48 TNA, WO 95/91, Tank Corps War Diary, 'Preliminary Summary of Tank Operations with the First, Third and Fifth Armies on 9th, 10th, 11th & 12th April 1917, n.d.; 'Preliminary Report on the Tank Operations at the Battle of Arras, 9th-13th April 1917', 2 May 1917.
49 LHCMA, Fuller Papers 1/4/1, 'Summary of Tank Operations 1st Brigade, Heavy Branch. 9th April-3rd May 1917', 17 May 1917.
50 TNA, WO 95/92, Tank Corps War Diary, 'Notes on Tank Operations, April-October 1917', 27 October 1917.

received over 38 messages on the first day of the battle alone. It was noted afterwards that '[a]lthough the weather conditions were very adverse, fairly good results were obtained on the first day... From the loft, messages were telephoned to the 1st Brigade Headquarters and a Despatch Rider brought in the originals every half hour'.[51]

The third issue to emerge from the Battle of Arras was the widespread call for 'Signal Tanks'. It was suggested that in future operations such tanks would act as mobile transmitting stations, equipped with an array of communication means, including pigeons, lamps and wireless, and consist of highly trained personnel. As Colonel Christopher Baker-Carr argued:

> The introduction of a Signal Tank will not only enable Tanks to communicate with their own H.Q. but with those of the Divisions and Corps and especially with the Artillery H.Q. Further, the introduction of such a Tank will form a mobile signal station for the infantry as well as for the Tanks themselves. Runners will be economized and the laying of cables and telephone lines reduced.[52]

Experiments with signal tanks were initiated shortly thereafter at the Central Workshops at Erin, using a number of Mark I and Mark II tanks, yielding 'most promising results'. According to *SS. 167*, '[t]he intention is to employ Wireless between the Signal Tanks at rallying points and fixed Wireless Stations erected at any suitable HQ such as an Infantry Brigade... It is expected that Signal Tanks will be able to accept messages, from Infantry and other units, for transmission to the rear by Wireless'.[53] Although British officers were clearly eager and enthusiastic, it must not be forgotten that wireless technology remained in its infancy. So, too, did the tanks themselves. Thus, in many respects the application of wireless to tanks during the First World War can aptly be described as 'an experiment inside an experiment', requiring constant modification and change, resulting in 'many initial failures'.[54]

Indeed, as a result of a conference held at the headquarters of the Heavy Branch Machine Gun Corps on 9 July, it was decided that nine signal tanks fitted with wireless would be made available for the upcoming Third Ypres campaign.[55] Of the nine tanks allotted, only four were actually employed on the opening day of the battle on

---

51 LHCMA, Fuller Papers 1/4/2, 'Report on Communications during Operations 20th November to 23rd November 1917', 9 December 1917. See also TNA, WO 158/383, 'IV Corps Report on Telephone and Telegraph Communications During Operations Commencing 20th November 1917', n.d.
52 LHCMA, Fuller Papers 1/4/1, 'Summary of Tank Operations 1st Brigade, Heavy Branch. 9th April-3rd May 1917', 17 May 1917. See also TNA, WO 95/91, Tank Corps War Diary, 'Preliminary Summary of Tank Operations with the First, Third and Fifth Armies on 9th, 10th, 11th & 12th April 1917, n.d.
53 *SS. 167. Signal Organisation for Heavy Branch*, p. 3; Bvt.-Col. J.F.C. Fuller, *Tanks in the Great War 1914-1918* (London, 1920), p. 180.
54 Priestley, *Work of the Royal Engineers*, p. 245.
55 TNA, WO 95/91, Tank Corps War Diary, 'S.G. 128/43', 11 July 1917.

31 July. Divided equally between 'C' Tank Battalion (15th Division) and 'F' Tank Battalion (55th Division), two wireless sets were used as forward transmitting stations and two as back receiving stations. Their purpose was twofold: first, to send back 'immediate tactical information… in regard to the progress of the battle'; and, second, 'to inform the [Royal] Flying Corps Headquarters of the number and location of hostile machines and of the progress of aerial fighting'. The results, however, were disappointing. The tank carrying the forward transmitting set in C Battalion suffered mechanical problems and had to be ditched, while the forward transmitting set in F Battalion was found to be faulty and so no messages were sent. Undeterred by these setbacks, signal tanks carrying wireless sets were utilized on several further occasions in August and September, with more favourable results. The converted Wilson spark transmitter and Mark III receivers employed gave 'strong signals over a distance of 15,000 yards'. In mid-August, it was noted that, as a result of wireless messages sent from signal tanks, 'very material benefit was obtained by the R.F.C. who were thus able to accelerate communication between their observers and Headquarters by about one hour'.[56]

These successes ensured that of the 476 tanks massed for the Cambrai offensive on 20 November, nine were fitted with wireless (one per tank battalion) and one carried telephone cable. The wireless tanks were made available for use by tank, infantry and artillery units, carrying sets which had to be offloaded and erected at preselected sites.[57] During the initial advance 'several messages containing valuable information' were received from these wireless tanks, such as that pertaining to the capture of Marcoing, sent only ten minutes after infantry from 6th Division had entered the village.[58] However, it was widely acknowledged by tank and infantry commanders after the battle that a far greater proportion of wireless messages could have been sent. A report by 1st Tank Brigade attributed this failure to two factors: first, to the wireless sets employed, which were described as 'only makeshift and exceedingly clumsy, especially in view of the fact that they were taken in Fighting Tanks'; and, second, to the arrangements under which the wireless equipment was transported. It cited one occasion when the wireless apparatus was divided between two tanks and one of the tanks broke down, rendering the set useless. In another incident, the equipment was

---

56   TNA, WO 95/92, Tank Corps War Diary, 'Report on the Use of Signal Tanks Since the Beginning of the Present Offensive – 31st July 1917', n.d., also WO 95/104, 3 Tank Brigade War Diary, '3rd Brigade Tank Corps. Summary of Tank Operations with XIX Corps – 31st July 1917', n.d.; and, Hall, 'The British Army and Wireless Communication', pp. 297-301.
57   TNA, WO 95/677, II Corps War Diary, 'III Corps Operations. Instruction No. 7. Communications', 14 November 1917; Capt. Wilfred Miles, *Military Operations: France and Belgium, 1917*, Vol. 3 (London, 1948), p. 28; Major-General R.F.H. Nalder, *The Royal Corps of Signals: A History of its Antecedents and Development, 1800-1955* (London, 1958), p. 138.
58   LHCMA, Fuller Papers 1/4/2, 'Report on Communications During Operations 20th November to 23rd November 1917', 9 December 1917; Mitchell, *Tank Warfare*, p. 150.

again divided between two tanks but before it could be utilized one of the tanks was 'knocked out' by enemy shellfire.[59] Thus, although some notable successes had been achieved with regards to the gradual employment of wireless in tanks during 1917, there were still a number of pressing issues that would need to be resolved if communication between tanks and rear headquarters was to become more rapid and efficient the following year.

The fourth, and final, issue to emerge from Arras was the provision and maintenance of communications between the various tank formation headquarters and the rest of the BEF. Since the concentration of tanks could not take place until it was known where and when an offensive would take place, and if, and how many, tanks were required, it was impossible to allocate a permanent system of telegraph and telephone lines to link tank formation headquarters. In late 1916 and early 1917 tank formation headquarters simply connected themselves to the lines already provided, operated and maintained by the infantry brigade, division and corps signal companies, and so tank units had only a very small number of linesmen to maintain and repair their own lines.[60] Consequently, faults on tank formation lines were commonplace and communication between headquarters severely impaired. As one tank brigade commander bemoaned after the Battle of Arras: 'The telephone system with which we worked can only be described as heart-breaking. Many times it was totally impossible to hear or to be heard when speaking to Corps H.Q. at a distance of 5 or 6 miles'.[61] Throughout 1917, then, signal companies were raised in order to provide, maintain and operate communications for and between Tank Corps headquarters and each tank brigade. Gradually, the system improved but it was still far from perfect at the end of the year. A post-battle report following the operations at Cambrai in December observed that more direct telephone lines to units of the Tank Corps should be made available, since 'Divisional and Infantry Brigade lines were very much congested and delay in getting through often occurred… It is therefore necessary that the greater part of the [Tank Corps telephone] system be built at very short notice by the Tank Brigade Signal Company'.[62]

The other chief problem experienced at Cambrai was the extensive damage to telephone and telegraph lines caused by tanks. Prior to the offensive, special crossing

---

59 TNA, WO 95/100, 1st Tank Brigade Signal Company War Diary, 'Report on Communications During Operations 20th November to 23rd November 1917', 9 December 1917. See also: TNA, WO 158/383, 'Cambrai-Havrincourt-Bourlon Wood Operations, IV Corps Report on Telephone and Telegraph Communications, 20th November-1st December 1917', n.d.; and, IWM, 83/23/1, Major E.F. Churchill Papers, 'Memories 1914-1919 by a Signal Officer', p. 36.
60 Priestley, *Work of the Royal Engineers*, pp. 245-6.
61 TNA, WO 95/91, Tank Corps War Diary, 'Summary of Tank Operations 1st Brigade, Heavy Branch. 9th April-3rd May 1917', 17 May 1917.
62 LHCMA, Fuller Papers 1/4/2, 'Report on Communications During Operations 20th November to 23rd November 1917', 9 December 1917.

places, where tank paths intersected cable routes, were constructed using poles to lift the lines 15 feet off the ground so that tanks could pass safely underneath them. Tanks fitted with fascines for clearing the wide trenches of the Hindenburg defences required a larger clearance of 20 feet. However, labour constraints meant that not enough of these crossings were built. Moreover, many tank units were simply not provided with enough information from the Signal Service pertaining to the exact location of these crossings. Once the battle began, tanks crushed and ripped apart these poled cable routes as well as those laid by the advancing infantry, impeding the rapid transmission of orders, reports and other vital information.[63] According to one account, 'the poles... chosen on account of lightness for easy transport, were very easily broken. They should... have been longer, to raise the cable high enough to clear the Tanks'.[64] Several suggestions as how best to overcome this problem in future operations were provided after the battle. For example, while Major-General Douglas Smith, GOC 20th Division, believed that 'routes for returning Tanks should be laid down and marked back to the original front line' in order to guide tank commanders away from vulnerable telephone lines, a Third Army report argued that 'special tanks, capable of carrying about 10 tons, and cutting a trench about 3 inches wide and 1 foot deep', should be provided for use by the Signal Service. Such tanks were to 'be fitted with a means of paying out multi-core cable from drums through a hawse pipe into the trench as it is cut', and 'all the apparatus for using the Tank as a Signal Office should also be provided'.[65] Thus, one of the principal lessons to emerge from the battles of 1917, particularly Cambrai, was the necessity for much closer liaison between the Tank Corps and the Signal Service. This had begun with the creation of signal companies for the Tank Corps and tank brigades, and was later cemented by the appointment of an Assistant-Director of Signals (AD Signals) for the Tank Corps, Lieutenant-Colonel J.D.N. Molesworth, whose task it was to supervise the tank signal companies and coordinate their efforts with the Signal Service, resulting in an improved system of communication for future Tank Corps operations.[66]

63 TNA, WO 95/3070, 62 Division War Diary, 'Notes on the Operations which Began on November 20th 1917 in Front of Cambrai', 7 December 1917; LHCMA, General Sir (Henry de) Beauvoir De Lisle Papers 3/2, 'My Narrative of the Great German War, Vol. 2', p. 55.
64 TNA, WO 158/383, 'IV Corps Report on Telephone and Telegraph Communications During Operations Commencing 20th November 1917', n.d.
65 TNA, WO 95/2097, 20 Division War Diary, 'Experiences Gained in the Recent Operations, 20th and 21st November, 1917', 10 December 1917, WO 158/316, Third Army Headquarters, Cambrai Lessons, 'Lessons Learnt from Recent Operations by the Third Army (November 20th to December 6th, 1917)', n.d.
66 Priestley, *Work of the Royal Engineers*, p. 246; Becke, *Order of Battle of Divisions*, p. 268; Fuller, *Tanks in the Great War*, p. 180. For additional information on the roles and responsibilities of senior Signal Service officers during the war, see Hall, 'The British Expeditionary Force and Communications', pp. 74-6.

1918: Innovations and the Challenges of Mobile Warfare

The war on the Western Front in 1918 fell into two main phases. The first phase, March to July, saw the German Army initiate a series of offensives against the BEF and its Allies, inflicting heavy losses and forcing them to retreat some 40 miles in the process, though ultimately failing to achieve a decisive victory. In the second phase, August to November, the BEF and its Allies mounted a series of offensives of their own, known collectively as the 'Hundred Days' campaign, the success of which eventually compelled the German Army to request an armistice.[67] The return of semi-mobile warfare to the Western Front after over three years of trench stalemate provided the BEF's Tank Corps with the ideal opportunity to build upon its successful performance at the Battle of Cambrai. However, as in 1916 and 1917, the ability of tanks to make a significant contribution to British operations in 1918 depended a great deal on the efficiency, integrity and speed of the communications system that supported them.

The methods employed to facilitate tank-to-tank communication in 1918 remained much as they had the previous year. Although use was made of coloured discs, flags and Aldis Lamps, it appears that many section commanders were often obliged to communicate with each other face-to-face, or to send a runner with a message, and to guide their tanks on foot, particularly during the 'Hundred Days'.[68] One tank commander recalled after the war his experience of trying to coordinate the movement of his section whilst supporting Australian infantry during a night attack at Amiens in August:

> Getting the tanks to go forward again was no easy job. I began with the rear tank, and had to batter on the front with my stick to attract the attention of the officer inside. It was like trying to turn a car in a narrow road, and there was a good deal of manoeuvring and reversing and shouting before the second and third tanks were finally turned… I felt rather like a wild animal tamer with huge beasts to control. In the dark the tank crews could not easily understand my directions nor hear my voice above the noise.[69]

Some company commanders were also urged to convey orders and other important information in-person, either on horseback or, during the last months of the war, in a Medium A (or 'Whippet') tank. As Brigadier-General John Hardress-Lloyd, GOC

---

67 For scholarly accounts of the fighting in 1918, see: Travers, *How the War Was Won*, pp. 32-182; Prior & Wilson, *Command on the Western Front*, pp. 289-391; Harris with Barr, *Amiens to the Armistice*; Martin Kitchen, *The German Offensives of 1918* (Stroud, 2001); and, Jonathan Boff, *Winning and Losing on the Western Front: The British Third Army and the Defeat of Germany in 1918* (Cambridge, 2012).
68 TNA, WO 95/93, Tank Corps War Diary, 'Tactical Experiences of all Past Tank Corps Operations Collected and Issued by the 3rd Tank Group', n.d. [late 1918].
69 Hickey, *Rolling into Action*, pp. 243, 246.

3rd Tank Brigade, reported in early September: 'It is clearly demonstrated that the Commander of a Whippet Company can best command his Unit by moving freely amongst the Whippets under his command. The Company Commander requires a mounted Orderly. He also requires a spare horse'.[70] Clearly the rudimentary nature of First World War British tanks, as well as the more fluid conditions that prevailed on the Western Front in the summer and autumn of 1918, militated against the successful application of more technologically sophisticated means of communication to convey important tactical information between tanks whilst in action.

Good communications between tanks and the other arms were deemed 'essential for success' in the more mobile operations that the BEF found itself fighting in 1918.[71] The signalling arrangements between tanks and infantry, for instance, were worked out at a conference held at Tank Corps headquarters on 5 June. Three flag signals were agreed: first, a tricolour flag (red, white and blue) would help infantry distinguish British tanks from German tanks, and would be flown when tanks were coming out of action or moving to the rear; second, a green and white flag, which indicated to the infantry 'come on'; and, third, a red and yellow flag, informing the infantry 'Tank broken down, go on'. The standard method used by infantry to attract the attention of tanks remained a helmet raised on a fixed bayonet.[72]

These means of tank-infantry communication persisted until the war's end. Although they proved generally successful, a number of problems were experienced. A post-war report by the 3rd Tank Group, for example, acknowledged that while 'the only method which has stood the test of time has been a few simple flag signals', adverse weather conditions, dust and smoke made it 'almost impossible' for infantry to read such signals. Likewise, many tank commanders found it difficult to detect infantry waving their rifles with helmets attached, 'as their attention is taken up by so many other details' during the course of a battle. It was suggested that 'when the helmets are put on rifles by the Infantry, they should if possible be hoisted two or three at a time'.[73]

A range of alternative tank-infantry signalling methods were also tried and tested, with mixed results. Smoke grenades fired by the infantry to point tanks in the direction of enemy strong points and machineguns that needed destroying were found to be 'unsatisfactory and confusing in the heat of battle'. The provision of bell pulls, first trialled at Ypres in July 1917 and reintroduced almost a year later at Hamel, met

---

70 TNA, WO 95/105, 3rd Tank Brigade War Diary, 'Report on Operations – 8th to 12th August 1918', 8 September 1918.
71 TNA, WO 95/94, Tank Corps War Diary, 'NOTES and Some Lessons Learned from the Experiences Gained During the Operations, August 8th to 12th, on the Somme', 15 August 1918.
72 TNA, WO 158/840, 'S.G. 175/12', 6 June 1918; *SS. 214. Tanks and their Employment in Co-operation with Other Arms* (August 1918), p. 18.
73 TNA, WO 95/93, Tank Corps War Diary, 'Tactical Experiences of all Past Tank Corps Operations Collected and Issued by the 3rd Tank Group', n.d. [late 1918].

'with fair success'.[74] Infantry would pull on a length of wire hanging out of the back of a tank which was connected to a bell inside the tank, attracting the crew's attention when rung. The positions of the bell and the bell pull, however, were found to be 'useless', since 'the former is too near the rear part of the Tank, and the latter is too near the exhaust'.[75] More successful than either smoke grenades or bell pulls was the provision of an infantryman (usually an NCO) to ride in the back of a tank and act as observer between his unit and the tank crew. According to the instructions of the Canadian Corps prior to the battle of Amiens, this man was to 'be responsible for watching the Infantry advance and the Infantry Signals and keeping the Tank Commander informed as to the Infantry progress and requirements'. It was also his responsibility to operate the signals from the tank to the infantry.[76]

Even more problematic than tank-infantry liaison was the coordination of tanks and aeroplanes. 'Notes on Co-operation between Tanks and Aeroplanes', issued on 30 June, highlighted 'the outstanding difficulty… of communication between Tanks and Aeroplanes' during active operations, recommending that '[a]ll methods [of communication] must be tried, and practice will show which are the most reliable'.[77] Although a variety of visual signals were tried and tested, including flares, smoke bombs, discs and Very lights, it was found that 'signals from Tanks to aeroplanes are considered to be of little practical value and are not advised'.[78] Direct voice communication between individual tanks and aeroplanes was simply not feasible given the inadequacies of the technology available. While the introduction of Continuous Wave (CW) wireless in 1917-18 provided the BEF with sets that were smaller, lighter and more powerful than their spark counterparts, not only were they in limited supply but they still could not function properly inside tanks due to excessive noise and engine vibration.[79] However, CW did provide the British and Allied forces with the opportunity to experiment with wireless telephony. At a conference held at RAF headquarters on 18 July, not

74 Ibid.
75 LHCMA, Fuller Papers 1/7, '4th Tank Brigade Report on Operations August 8th to 11th 1918', 24 August 1918; TNA, WO 95/94, Tank Corps War Diary, 'Minutes on Conference Held at Headquarters Tank Corps, July 10th 1918', 12 July 1918; Hammond, 'Theory and Practice of Tank Co-operation', pp. 392-3.
76 TNA, WO 95/1053, Canadian Corps War Diary, 'L.C. Instructions No. 2', 4 August 1918, and for more information on the role and duties of the signaller/observer, WO 158/803, 'The Distribution and Training of Tank Crews of Mark V & Converted Mark IV, Medium Marks A&B Tanks', 24 November 1917.
77 TNA, WO 95/94, Tank Corps War Diary, 'Notes on Co-operation between Tanks and Aeroplanes', 30 June 1918. For additional context on tank-aeroplane cooperation during the war, see David Jordan, 'The Army Co-operation Missions of the Royal Flying Corps/Royal Air Force, 1914-18', PhD thesis, University of Birmingham, 1997, pp. 285-9.
78 TNA, WO 95/93, Tank Corps War Diary, 'Tactical Experiences of all Past Tank Corps Operations Collected and Issued by the 3rd Tank Group', n.d. [late 1918].
79 Captain B.F.J. Schonland, 'W/T. R.E.: An Account of the Work and Development of Field Wireless Sets with the Armies in France', *The Wireless World*, VII (1919), p. 226.

only was the issue of wireless telephony between aeroplanes discussed but it was also recognized that there was 'a large field of usefulness for wireless telephones from air to ground principally in connection with reconnaissance, counter attack patrol work, and cooperation with Tanks'. Tests conducted throughout the summer revealed that 'it is quite practicable to speak from Tank to Tank or from aeroplane to Tank', but the operational range was limited to approximately 500 yards and further experiments were necessary 'to get the most efficient aerial to suit all requirements'.[80] Thus, tank-aeroplane and tank-to-tank communication by wireless telephony remained at a basic, experimental stage when the war ended.

Aeroplanes were of much greater value as a means of facilitating communication between tanks and rear headquarters. During the Third Ypres campaign in 1917, white 18-inch square boards placed on the roofs of tanks enabled aerial observers of the RFC to identify those tanks that had been ditched, knocked-out or broken down whilst in action. Post-battle reports, however, suggested that they were far from effective.[81] By early 1918, then, the decision had been made to paint a mark of three bars (white-red-white) on the top and sides of tanks, so as airmen could distinguish between British tanks and captured British tanks used by the Germans and, also, to enable aerial observers to report on the progress of tanks by dropping messages at rear headquarters.[82] This method had been introduced during the Battle of the Somme in 1916 to keep corps and divisional headquarters informed of the progress of the infantry. As Lieutenant-General Sir John Monash explained after the war:

> … the observer would mark down by conventional signs on a map the actual positions of our Infantry, of enemy Infantry or other facts of prime importance, and he often had time to scribble a few informative notes also. The "plane" then flew back at top speed to Corps H.Q., and the map, with or without an added report, was dropped in the middle of an adjacent field, wrapped in a weighted streamer of many colours. It was then brought by cyclist into the Staff Office.

According to the Australian Corps commander, this was 'a vastly superior method' of maintaining 'actual battle control', since '[t]he total time which elapsed between the

---

80 TNA, AIR 1/32/15/1/169, 'Minutes of a Meeting to Discuss the Tactical use of Wireless Telephony in the R.A.F., Held at H.Q., R.A.F.', 18 July 1918; WO 95/100, 1st Tank Brigade Signal Company War Diary, 'Experimental Work on Radio-Telephony', n.d. [summer 1918].
81 TNA, WO 95/92, Tank Corps War Diary, 'Notes on Tank Operations April-October 1917', 27 October 1917.
82 TNA, WO 95/105, 3rd Tank Brigade War Diary, 'Report on Operations – 8th to 12th August 1918', 8 September 1918; Hickey, *Rolling Into Action*, p. 199.

making of the observation at the front line and the arrival of the information in the hands of the Corps Staff was seldom more than ten minutes'.[83]

When applied to the Tank Corps in the summer and autumn of 1918, it proved just as successful. No. 8 Squadron, RAF, commanded by Major Trafford Leigh-Mallory, was detailed to undertake such work during the Battle of Amiens on 8 August, dropping news of progress at the advanced Tank Corps headquarters. Although headquarters were 'well posted with information' throughout the opening day of the battle, difficulties occurred during the subsequent days' fighting, as Leigh-Mallory recorded: 'It became practically impossible to communicate with the Tank Battalions, and very difficult to get in touch with the Brigades. Distances were great, the roads were bad, and blocked with traffic, and it was naturally impossible to communicate by phone'.[84] Undeterred, however, the method was revised and adopted with success by the 3rd Tank Brigade during its attacks on the Drocourt-Quéant Line on 2 September. As noted in an after-action report:

> An Aeroplane Dropping Ground was established at the Rallying Point… and with the exception of one message, which was considerably delayed by an Operator's error, the messages were received at the Brigade Signal Office at the very satisfactory average time of 20 minutes after being dropped.

During the battle of the St. Quentin Canal at the end of the month, the 3rd Tank Brigade improvised once more, this time using a wireless tank as an advanced dropping station for messages from cooperating aeroplanes. According to the Tank Corps chief of staff, J.F.C. Fuller, 'this proved a most useful innovation, for one aeroplane dropping its message at this station found, on its return home, that this message had been received by the headquarters to which it was directed within a few minutes of it having been dropped, in fact, far quicker than it would have been had the aeroplane dropped it at the headquarters itself'.[85]

While contact aeroplanes provided a steady flow of information from the battlefield to rear headquarters, the same cannot be said of carrier pigeons. Although they had formed the mainstay of the communication system between tanks and rear headquarters in 1916-17, pigeons were of limited value in the more mobile operations experienced by the BEF during the 'Hundred Days' because once pigeon lofts were moved forward in accordance with the general advance the birds had to be re-trained in order

---

83   Lt.-Gen. Sir John Monash, *The Australian Victories in France in 1918* (first published 1920; new edn, London, 1993), pp. 124-5.
84   TNA, AIR 1/1671/204/109/26, 'History of Tank and Aeroplane Cooperation', 31 January 1919; Fuller, *Tanks in the Great War*, pp. 245-7; Mitchell, *Tank Warfare*, p. 233.
85   TNA, WO 95/105, 3rd Tank Brigade War Diary, '3rd Tank Brigade. Report on Operations with Canadian Corps – 2nd September 1918', 18 September 1918, '3rd Tank Brigade Report on Operations with IX Corps on 29.9.18', 8 October 1918; Fuller, *Tanks in the Great War*, pp. 248-9.

Development of Tank Communications in the British Expeditionary Force   159

to get accustomed to their new route – a process that took a minimum of six weeks to accomplish.[86] Instead of having to repeatedly re-train carrier pigeons, however, many units chose to keep the lofts where they were. The downside to this, as noted by Lieutenant-General Sir Richard Butler, GOC III Corps, was that 'in the latter stages of the operations, when the lofts were a considerable distance from the line and the birds were taking anything from an hour to an hour and a half to fly from the frontline to the lofts', the messages 'proved absolutely valueless' as a result of the time delay.[87] Indeed, a report by the 4th Tank Brigade regarding communications during the battle of Amiens in August stated that the quickest time that a carrier pigeon message reached the brigade headquarters from a frontline tank was 49 minutes, while the longest time recorded was 3 hours and 52 minutes. Later that month, the 1st Tank Brigade also noted that pigeons were taking on average 55 minutes to reach their destination. Thus, as a report by the 2nd Tank Brigade summed up in November, owing to the rapidity of the British advance and the long time entailed in sending information by carrier pigeons, 'it will never be possible to count on this form of communication'.[88]

It was under these circumstances that wireless came to the fore as a prominent means of communication in the Tank Corps. As Major E.F. Churchill, a signal officer with the 1st Tank Brigade, noted after the war, 'communications [during the Hundred Days] were stretching a tremendous distance and if it had not been for wireless we could not have maintained them'.[89] CW wireless, in particular, proved an indispensable asset. During the Battle of Amiens, the 3rd Tank Brigade reported that 'in one case, a communication from Advanced H.Q. Tank Corps, sent by Wireless, Wire, and by D[espatch].R[ider]. arrived – by Wireless 1 hour before the Wire, and 1¼ hours before the D.R.', while in late August the 1st Tank Brigade observed that messages were sent by wireless tanks and received at control stations over a distance of 13.5 miles, giving 'excellent results'. As a post-war report by the 3rd Tank Group testified: 'If a good [wireless] tank is well forward where information can easily reach it, and is well and bravely handled, there is no question that the information sent back is of the greatest value, and much in advance of any other method yet tried in the Tank Corps'.[90]

---

86 *SS. 123. Notes on the Use of Carrier Pigeons* (August 1916), p. 4.
87 IWM, 69/10/1, Lieutenant-General Sir Richard Butler Papers, 'Report on Operations of III Corps from July 1918 to October 1st, 1918', 11 November 1918.
88 LHCMA, Fuller Papers 1/7, '4th Tank Brigade Report on Operations August 8th to 11th 1918', 24 August 1918; TNA, WO 95/100, 1st Tank Brigade Signal Company War Diary, 'Report on Operations 21st-25th August 1918', n.d.; IWM, Fourth Army Records, Vol. 65 (Canadian, Cavalry, II American, Machine Gun and Tank Corps Narratives, August-November 1918), '2nd Tank Brigade. Report on Operations: 4th November, 1918', 20 November 1918.
89 IWM, 83/23/1, Churchill Papers, 'Memories 1914-1919 by a Signal Officer', p. 36.
90 TNA, WO 95/105, 3rd Tank Brigade War Diary, 'Report on Operations – 8th to 12th August 1918', 8 September 1918, WO 95/100, 1st Tank Brigade Signal Company War

In spite of these successes, however, the Tank Corps' use of wireless in the summer and autumn of 1918 was still not problem-free. For instance, although Mark V and Mark IV 'Baggage' tanks were found to be the most suitable tanks for carrying wireless equipment, the former tended to damage the sets they carried, on account of the set being transported in the rear of the tank with the aerial run out behind, while the latter tank was too slow to keep up with the speed of the attack. A report by the 4th Tank Brigade following the Battle of Amiens, for example, stated that three out of the four wireless tanks allotted to the brigade 'had engine trouble at some point during the operations… [and] were not fast enough for the pace of the advance'. Despite acknowledging that wireless communication itself 'proved very satisfactory', the report concluded that by the end of the first day 'the distance over which they were working was too great, and the directing stations were moved forward… and an additional station was erected'.[91] Poor weather conditions also hampered the Tank Corps' efforts to make the most of wireless communication. During the Battle of the St. Quentin Canal on 29 September, for example, the 3rd Tank Brigade reported that although its wireless tank produced 'very satisfactory results, dense mist reacted against the efficient working of the system'.[92]

It was also often the case that when telephonic communication between the various report centres and connecting headquarters remained unbroken wireless was not used as much. Standard practice during the 'Hundred Days' was to establish a forward central telephone exchange at an advanced tank brigade command post. Cable tanks would then connect this command post to the main divisional cable-head, thus enabling direct telephonic communication between the command post, tank battalions and Tank Brigade headquarters.[93] By the end of September, tank battalion and company commanders usually attached themselves respectively to the headquarters of the infantry brigades and battalions they were supporting, 'where they were better able to keep in touch with events, and where they could easily be found'.[94] Thus, although British commanders in 1918 were clearly receptive to new methods of communication,

    Diary, 'Report on Operations 21st-25th August 1918', n.d., WO 95/93, Tank Corps War Diary, 'Tactical Experiences of all Past Tank Corps Operations Collected and Issued by the 3rd Tank Group', n.d. [late 1918].
91 LHCMA, Fuller Papers 1/7, '4th Tank Brigade Report on Operations August 8th to 11th 1918', 24 August 1918.
92 TNA, WO 95/105, 3rd Tank Brigade War Diary, '3rd Tank Brigade Report on Operations with IX Corps on 29.9.18', 8 October 1918.
93 TNA, WO 95/95, Tank Corps War Diary, 'Report on Communications during Operations with the IX Corps on 29th/30th September', 8 October 1918, WO 95/93, Tank Corps War Diary, 'Tactical Experiences of all Past Tank Corps Operations Collected and Issued by the 3rd Tank Group', n.d. [late 1918].
94 Browne, *The Tank in Action*, p. 458. See also LHCMA, Fuller Papers 1/7, 'Report on Operations. 4th Tank Brigade September 27th to October 17th 1918', 27 October 1918.

they still found it difficult to completely let go of their trench-bound communication habits.[95]

Conclusion

What, then, does this survey of the development of British tank communications during the First World War tell us about its relative importance in the success of tank operations? How successful were the British in achieving 'a properly organised system of communications for Tanks' by the end of the war? There can certainly be no doubting the significance of communications for tanks. In his account of tanks in the war, Fuller wrote:

> The importance of signaling in a formation such as the Tank Corps cannot be over-estimated, and this importance will increase as more rapid-moving machines are introduced, for, unless messages can be transmitted backwards and forwards without delay, many favorable opportunities for action, especially the action of reserves, will be lost. Making the most of time is the basis of all success, and this cannot be accomplished unless the commander is in the closest touch with his fighting and administrative troops and departments.[96]

Fuller's sentiments were echoed several years later by General Heinz Guderian, one of the chief pioneers in the development of German armoured warfare doctrine during the interwar period. According to Guderian, himself a signal officer in the German Army during the First World War: 'In the World War the shortcomings of the signals and communications systems greatly impeded the command of tank forces, and their cooperation with other arms… Here is the origin of the accusation that tanks are "deaf"'.[97] Although both Fuller's and Guderian's observations must be treated with a degree of skepticism given their unwavering faith in the significance of tanks and mechanization, their conclusions are nonetheless correct.

In examining the development of the BEF's tank communications system during the First World War, this chapter has shown that although the BEF did achieve a properly organized system of communications for tanks by the end of the war, the limitations of the communications technology at the time, combined with the inadequacies of the tanks themselves, continued to impose profound restrictions on the tactical and operational effectiveness of tanks in battle. Thus, the argument made by some historians that, 'if properly used, and available in sufficient numbers, tanks could have played a more decisive role in 1918', is not supported by the weight of evidence on

---

95 Hall, 'The British Army and Wireless Communication', pp. 310-11.
96 Fuller, *Tanks in the Great War*, p. 183.
97 Heinz Guderian, *Achtung-Panzer! The Development of Tank Warfare* (first published 1937; new edn, London, 1999), p. 197.

the early attempts to build and improve communications in the British Army's Tank Corps.[98]

However, although tenuous communications hampered British tank operations throughout the second half of the war, the BEF's tank communications system in the summer and autumn of 1918 was certainly much more flexible, robust and sophisticated than it had been in 1916. From the initial use of tanks at the Battle of Flers-Courcelette until the end of the war, the Tank Corps continuously strove to improve the speed, integrity and capacity of its communications system, exhibiting a keen interest in adaptation, experimentation and innovation. The development and employment of wireless, particularly CW wireless, for communication between tanks and rear headquarters, as well as the experiments conducted in wireless telephony for tank-aeroplane communication, provides further evidence to support the argument of some historians that British commanders did exploit the newest, state-of-the-art technologies available to them within the limits of their potential.[99] Moreover, British innovations in tank communication pointed the way to the possibilities of armoured warfare in the future. Indeed, the dramatic successes achieved by generals such as Heinz Guderian between 1939 and 1941 would not have been possible without the type of signals system which the British first pioneered during the First World War.[100]

---

98 Travers, 'Could the Tanks of 1918 Have Been War-Winners', p. 389.
99 Harris with Barr, *Amiens to the Armistice*, pp. 294-300; Albert Palazzo, *Seeking Victory on the Western Front: The British Army and Chemical Warfare in World War One* (Lincoln, 2000); Gary Sheffield, *Forgotten Victory: The First World War – Myths and Realities* (London, 2001), pp. 140-6; Gary Sheffield & David Jordan, 'Douglas Haig and Airpower', in Peter W. Gray & Sebastian Cox (eds.), *Air Power Leadership: Theory and Practice* (London, 2002), pp. 264-82; and, Hall, 'The British Army and Wireless Communication', pp. 319-21.
100 On the importance of communications to German armoured warfare during the Second World War, see Robert Citino, 'Beyond Fire and Movement: Command, Control and Information in the German *Blitzkrieg*', *Journal of Strategic Studies*, 27 (2004), pp. 324-44.

7

Beyond the Western Front: Tanks in Palestine and Russia, 1916-1921

Steven J. Main & Alaric Searle

While the image of the tank in the First World War held by many has been conditioned by photographs of machines lumbering across muddy battlefields marked by shell holes and criss-crossed with barbed-wire, tanks were used in theatres other than the Western Front. Very little is known about the dispatch of a handful of tanks to Palestine in 1916, even if slightly more has been written about the training of Russian White forces in the use of British Mark V tanks in order that they could be sent into combat against the Red Army.[1] This is frustrating because there are many unanswered questions as a result of these gaps in our knowledge. Were there parallels in tactical experiences to those on the Western Front? How did Russian soldiers, for example, react during their first encounters with tanks? In order to throw some new light on a series of intriguing issues, this chapter will consider four related subjects: first, the employment of tanks in Palestine in 1917; second, the supply of British Mark V and Whippet tanks to the White Russian forces; third, the Red Army's employment of captured tanks and their manufacture of a copy of the Renault FT-17 tank; and fourth, the impact of tanks on the Civil War in the realm of propaganda, but also as a catalyst for the decision of the 'Soviet Republic' to build its own machines.

---

1   The little knowledge we have can be found in B.H. Liddell Hart, *The Tanks: A History of the Royal Tank Regiment and Its Predecessors, Vol. One: 1914-1939* (London, 1959), for Egypt, pp. 125-7, for Russia, 211-3. In terms of English-language material on the Russian Civil War, three works provide some background information: David Bullock, *Armoured Units of the Russian Civil War: White and Allied* (Oxford, 2003); John Milson, *Russian Tanks, 1900-1970* (London, 1970); and, Patrick Wright, *Tank* (London, 2001), pp. 139-42.

British Tanks in Palestine, 1916-18

All that was really known for many years about the British use of tanks in Palestine was located in a short section in Basil Liddell Hart's history of the Royal Tank Regiment.[2] In brief, in December 1916 a tank detachment of eight machines was sent to Palestine together with E Company, which consisted of twenty-two officers and 226 other ranks. On 26 March 1917, they were deployed to be used in an attack but never saw action, although on 17 April the tanks were split up, so that individual machines took part in different, individual attacks. These machines had in actual fact been demonstration tanks, so they were among the earliest models. Towards the end of 1917, however, the detachment was 'reinforced' with three Mark IV tanks. Six machines of the eight then took part in the offensive in Gaza on 2 November 1917; although five were disabled later, they played a significant part in the break-in operation. There was a plan to obtain new Whippet tanks, but this was abandoned after the start of the German March offensive in 1918. This is, in essence, what Basil Liddell Hart provided to readers of his history of Britain's armoured force.[3] On the basis of official records, it is now possible to add more detail to this thumbnail sketch of an obscure and largely forgotten episode in the Great War.

This chapter in the early history of the tank began on 30 October 1916, just a month and a half after the first offensive action by British tanks on the Western Front. Brigadier-General W.D. Bird, Director of Staff Duties at the War Office, wrote to GHQ in France that: 'A detachment, strength half a company, of the Heavy Branch, Machine Gun Corps ("Tanks") is to be sent to Egypt during the next month.' The minute included the question as to whether a Major and a Captain with experience in France could be found to accompany the tanks. This minute was forwarded to HQ 'Tanks', which received it on 6 November.[4] On 20 November 1916, the commander of the Heavy Branch, Machine-Gun Corps, Hugh Elles, wrote to the Egyptian Expeditionary Force, including notes on the employment of tanks. His letter highlighted bluntly the limitations of the machines. He wrote: 'Egypt must adapt our experiments to their conditions which I imagine are quite different both as regards ground and opposition.' He also warned that 'these Tanks can't do half the things the "Daily Mail" says they can', adding also that 'machinery won't do more than a very definite amount – and it cannot make an extra effort as a man can'.[5]

---

2   At the same time, we should not forget the useful information offered in Maj. Clough Williams-Ellis & A. Williams-Ellis, *The Tank Corps* (London, 1919), pp. 145-52.
3   Liddell Hart, *The Tanks. Vol. One*, pp. 125-7.
4   The National Archives of the United Kingdom, Kew (hereafter, TNA), WO 158/844, SECRET, Brig.-Gen. W.D. Bird to GHQ, France, 30 October 1916. It was suggested after the war that the intention had been to test the tank's capabilities in another theatre. C. & A. Williams-Ellis, *The Tank Corps*, p. 145.
5   TNA, WO 95/4366, fol. 57, SECRET, Hugh Elles (HQ, Heavy Branch) to GOC, Egyptian Expeditionary Force, 20 November 1916.

Photo 8: Derelict Mark I, Gaza, 1917

On 15 December 1916, the Chief of the General Staff of the Egyptian Expeditionary Force (EEF) communicated to the General Officer Commanding, Eastern Force, that a tank unit was due to arrive on 19 December. He enclosed Elles' letter, together with the notes produced by the latter, which were 'a summary of various papers on the subject which have been issued'. Particularly revealing was the request to the commander of the Eastern Force, 'will you please say what you wish done with them on arrival'.[6] The consternation as to the purpose of these new weapons of war was understandable.

In the notes which Elles had sent, which represented a summary of the first experiences in the employment of tanks, it was emphasized that all means had to be used in the approach march before tanks advanced towards enemy trenches. If a tank attack was to be launched after dawn, the machines had to be placed in concealed pits, but the 'concealment of these pits presents considerable difficulties'. When moving uphill,

---

6 TNA, WO 95/4366, fol. 56, SECRET. G.S. 397, Chief of the General Staff (EEF) to Gen. Commanding Officer, Eastern Force, 15 December 1916, fol. 57, Elles to GOC, EEF, 20 November 1916.

or over difficult ground, tanks had proved slower than the infantry. A key part of the document was the statement that: 'In the present stage of their development Tanks must be regarded as entirely accessory to the ordinary methods of attack, i.e. to the advance of Infantry in close co-operation with Artillery.' It was also noted that the ideal outcome which the document outlined – essentially that the tanks reached the enemy trench-system just ahead of the infantry – was 'undoubtedly difficult to attain'. It was mentioned, in addition, that 'Tanks experience considerable difficulty in surmounting obstacles by night', and that the failure in the attempt by the Fourth Army to leave lanes for tanks during artillery barrages had resulted in the breakdown of several machines.[7] This was not a great deal for the Egyptian Expeditionary Force to go on, especially considering that there was little time to prepare before the first tank action took place in April 1917.

The War Diary of the Tank Detachment shows that the men disembarked at Alexandria on 9 January 1917 (fifteen officers and 123 other ranks); all the tanks were inspected by the Commander-in-Chief on 15 January at 14.45. The tanks were first loaded onto railway trucks on 24 January, ready to proceed to Gilban. On 27 February the unit was inspected again by the Commander-in-Chief, who paid them a further visit on 25 March during which 'tactical operations' were carried out. On 27 March the tanks and baggage were prepared for departure for Khan Yunus.[8] While the precise details are not absolutely clear, tanks did go into action during the course of the Second Battle of Gaza which ran from late 16 April to 20 April 1917.[9]

The preparations for the use of tanks indicate the way in which ideas were being developed. On 10 April a brief two-page document of instructions was issued. This made very obvious use of the set of notes provided in late 1916 by Elles; in some paragraphs, the wording is identical. Where some adaptation had taken place was in the plan that tanks would operate in pairs, a sensible measure given that only eight machines had been shipped to the EEF. Six tanks were to be allotted to the right attack, two to the left. In the section on the capacity of tanks to crush barbed-wire, the only addition to Elles' document was the comment: 'They may also be useful in clearing lanes through cactus hedges.'[10] In an instruction to the 52nd (Lowland) Division the following day, this final comment was modified slightly, providing detail which suggests that perhaps some tactical experimentation had taken place: 'They can

---

7   TNA, WO 95/4366, fol. 58-60, SECRET, 3 pages of untitled notes, n.d. [20 November 1916]
8   TNA, WO 95/4407, EEF, War Diary, Heavy Branch, Machine Gun Corps, January – April 1917.
9   On the Second Battle of Gaza: David R. Woodward, *Hell in the Holy Land: World War One in the Middle East* (Lexington, KY, 2006), pp. 56-80; Jake D. Grainger, *The Battle for Palestine 1917* (Woodbridge, 2006); and George MacMunn & Cyril Falls, *History of the Great War: Military Operations, Egypt and Palestine*, vol. I (London, 1928), pp. 326-67.
10 TNA, WO 95/4450, Eastern Force, April 1917, Appendix 1, SECRET, Special Instructions – Tanks, 10 April 1917.

Tanks in Palestine and Russia, 1916-1921   167

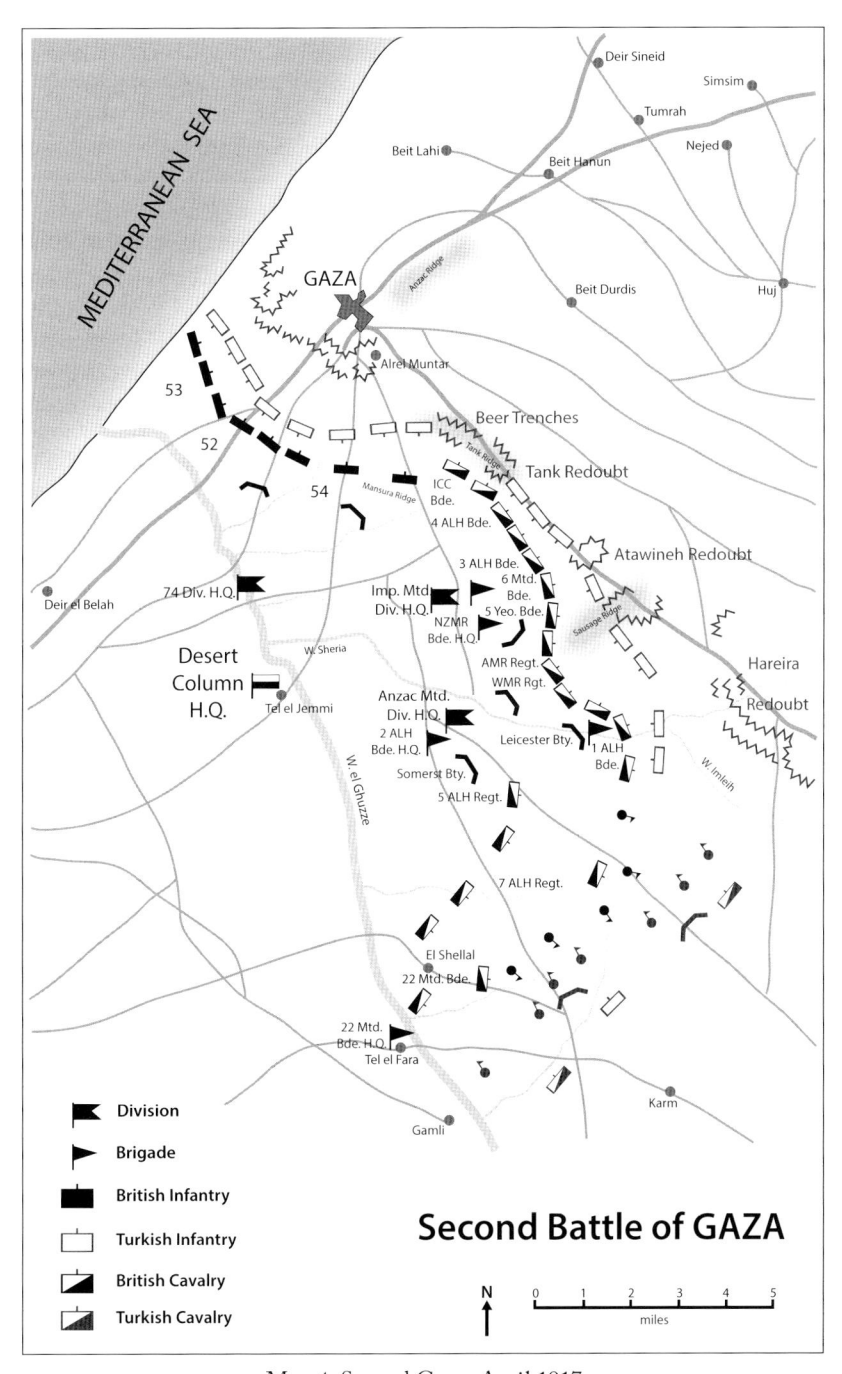

Map 4: Second Gaza, April 1917

clear lanes through cactus hedges, flattening to some extent the mud banks in which the cactus hedge is planted.'[11]

In the initial plan of attack, two tanks were allotted to the 54th Division, while four tanks were assigned to the 52nd (Lowland) Division and were to move up Wadi Nukhabir to the Mendur-Gaza road crossing, from where they would await orders from the commander of the 157th Infantry Brigade. The remaining two tanks were to remain in reserve at the disposal of the commander of the 52nd.[12] As the offensive developed, fresh orders were issued on 18 April that the four tanks assigned to the 52nd should move across from Wadi Nukhabir to the Happy Valley to a position about Kurd Hill. On arrival they were to report to the commander of the 155th Infantry Brigade. After the capture of Green Hill, the commander of the 155th Brigade was to send forward two tanks to support the 156th Infantry Brigade. Following the capture of the enemy's position on Ali Muntar, two tanks were to proceed to assist the advance of the 157th Infantry Brigade and 54th Division on Anzac Ridge.[13] As we know, the attack on 19/20 April failed during its decisive phase.

The fate of the tanks (a mixture of Mark I and IIs) was, at least in part, intertwined with the failure of the operation itself. On 17 April, one of the tanks assigned to the 54th Division received a direct hit and was put out of action; but the other inflicted heavy casualties on the Turks. On the night of 18/19 April, four tanks moved from Wadi Nukhabir to take up a position near Kurd Hill. At 7.30 on the morning of 19 April, the tank 'Otazel' became ditched on a Wadi and had to be dug out. At the same time, the tank 'War Baby' moved towards Green Hill in advance of the infantry, but as 'Otazel' was out-of-action it moved towards Outpost Hill, which was taken and further casualties inflicted upon the enemy. But while moving towards enemy machine-gun positions, the track broke and the tank was hit by a shell, although the crew were all able to escape. At 11.30 the tank 'Kiaora' moved towards Outpost Hill to assist the infantry, but when it arrived at the position it was discovered there was no infantry and the position could not be held. It opened fired on enemy machine-gunners, but owing to mechanical difficulties needed to return to its start line. At 14.00, the tank 'Puncher', which had been held in reserve up to this point, was ordered up to move forward to attack, although at 17.50 the decision to attack was reversed. At 1.30 on 19 April the tank 'Tiger' went into action. After repairing a shed track, the tank recaptured El Arash Redoubt and held it for twenty minutes. Due to intense shell fire, and the fact all the gunners had been wounded, and the commander and driver slightly wounded, the tank was forced to retire.[14]

11   TNA, WO 95/4597, 52nd Division (G.S.) Circular Memorandum No. 9, [sgd.] Lt.-Col., G.S., 52nd Division, 11 April 1917.
12   TNA, WO 95/4597, 52nd Division Order No. 56, 16 April 1917.
13   TNA, WO 95/4597, 52nd Division Order No. 57, 18 April 1917.
14   TNA, WO 95/4407, report of 19 April 1917, in EEF, War Diary, Heavy Branch, Machine Gun Corps, April 1917; C. & A. Williams-Ellis, *The Tank Corps*, pp. 147-9.

In an after-action report on the operations, the commander of the 52nd Division, Major-General W.E.B. Smith, took care to describe the role of the tanks 'War Baby' and 'Kiaora'. In conclusion, he explained that the failure of the 155th Infantry Brigade to achieve its objectives was not the result of lack of determination: they had suffered 30% casualties. The reason was that, 'owing to the intense concentration of the enemy's artillery and machine gun fire and the extremely difficult nature of the ground, affording, as it does, concealed protection and immunity from shell fire to innumerable riflemen and machine guns, a further advance was practically impossible.'[15] The total casualties for the tank detachment were one officer who died later and seven men taken prisoner, nine men killed in action, and three officers and nine men wounded. On 23 April the remaining tanks were withdrawn from the divisions to which they had been assigned.[16] But tanks were also to play a part in the much more successful Third Battle of Gaza.[17]

After the failure of the Second Battle of Gaza, the tank detachment had been placed in a base towards the rear. There they languished until September, when three inspections by the GOC took place, on 4, 9 and 18 September, with a practice carried out on the first and third visits, suggesting that an attack was being prepared. Before the Third Battle of Gaza unfolded, the detachment was reinforced with three Mark IV tanks. Prior to this battle, the tank commanders had the opportunity to conduct more thorough reconnaissance than had been possible before the previous offensive. Two tanks were held in reserve, while the other six were given no less than twenty-nine objectives to attack. In the early morning of 2 November, all tanks had arrived at their start positions. The two machines which had been ordered to attack the El Arish redoubt drove the enemy out, but while moving through a complex trench system, which included cactus hedges, one received a direct hit, while the other became stuck and had to be abandoned. The sixth tank captured its objective, and then cleared enemy trenches and attacked three strong points. At the end of what was a decisive battle, only one tank had failed to reach its first objective, four had reached their second, third and fourth, while one tank had achieved its fifth objective. Five machines had been damaged, yet were subsequently salvaged.[18]

---

15 TNA, WO 95/4597, Maj.-Gen. W.E.B. Smith, Report of Operations 16th-20th April, 1917, 6 May 1917.
16 TNA, WO 95/4407, EEF, War Diary, Heavy Section, Machine Gun Corps, April 1917.
17 On this battle, see: Lt.-Gen. Archibald P. Wavell, *The Palestine Campaigns* (London, 3rd edn, 1931), pp. 95-141; Woodward, *Hell in the Holy Land*, pp. 104-37; George MacMunn & Cyril Falls, *History of the Great War: Military Operations, Egypt and Palestine*, vol. II/Part I (London, 1930), passim; Matthew Hughes, *Allenby and British Strategy in the Middle East* (London, 2005), pp. 43-59.
18 TNA, WO 95/4407, EEF, War Diary, Detachment, Tank Corps, Sept. – Nov. 1917, and, Appendix to War Diary of Nov. 1917, No. 2; C. & A. Williams-Ellis, *The Tank Corps*, pp. 149-52.

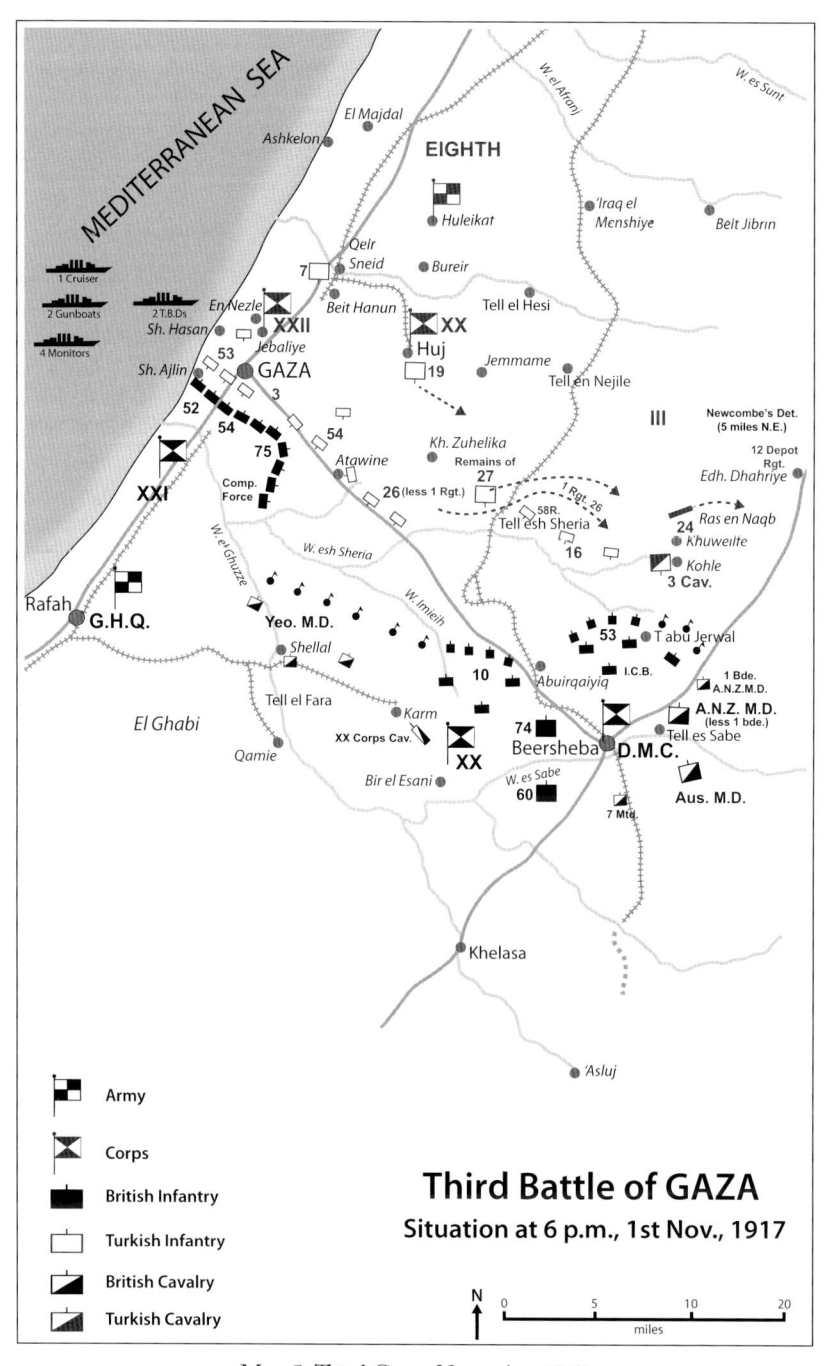

Map 5: Third Gaza, November 1917

By 18 November, the final tank of the eight which had participated in the Third Battle of Gaza had been successfully salvaged. Casualties had been light: according to the War Diary, one man had been killed and one wounded. For reasons lost to history, the tank detachment was never used again in combat, even though there was interest in using Whippet tanks. But the mission sent to France to request them arrived on 21 March 1918, just as the German Spring offensive was unleashed. The final entry in the War Diary on 30 April 1918 gives no indication as to when the detachment returned to England, although it was probably shortly afterwards. Still, it had been demonstrated that, with minor technical adjustments, tanks could operate in the desert. At the same time, the quality of the machines sent, and the low numbers, meant that few meaningful lessons could be drawn from this most curious of episodes in the history of British tanks during the Great War.[19] Much more, extensive, however, was the deployment of British tanks to the White Russian forces in 1919 while the Russian Civil War was raging.

The Supply of Tanks to the White Russians, 1919-20

It seems, in fact, that the first case of the employment of tanks in Russia occurred on 7 February 1919 in the Odessa area of the Ukrainian Front when French Renault FT 17 tanks were used in the capture of Tiraspol. A tank detachment of five machines, and three mechanics, under the command of a French lieutenant, and one lorry carrying 500 gallons of petrol, had entrained at the Odessa goods station the day before. Early on the morning of 7 February, three tanks advanced ahead of the infantry into the town as part of a joint Polish-French attack. Soon after, at the station at Tiraspol, two tanks, which had been posted there as a reserve, helped break up a counter-attack by about 300 Red Army soldiers by a flanking manoeuvre. The three other tanks played a significant part in the clearing of the town. The French suffered no casualties during the action, although Polish forces lost three dead and ten wounded. The tanks suffered no mechanical problems and fired ninety-seven 37 mm shells and five strips of machine-gun bullets.[20]

But what of the British tanks sent to Russia? Liddell Hart recounts briefly in his history of the Royal Tank Regiment that in 1919 three small tank detachments were dispatched to assist the White Russian forces. British officers to man and maintain the machines were only permitted if they were volunteers. In March 1919, six Mark Vs and six Whippets were sent to General Anton Denikin's forces in south Russia. In July 1919 more tanks were sent from Britain, thus bringing the total to fifty-seven

---

19   TNA, WO 95/4407, EEF, War Diary, Detachment, Tank Corps, November 1917 and April 1918; C. & A. Williams-Ellis, *The Tank Corps*, pp. 151-2.
20   University Archive & Special Collections, Rutgers University (hereafter, UA&SC Rutgers), Major-General J.F.C. Fuller Papers, box 16, S.D.7, Weekly Tanks Notes No. 53, 'French Tanks in Russia', 16 August 1919.

172 Genesis, Employment, Aftermath

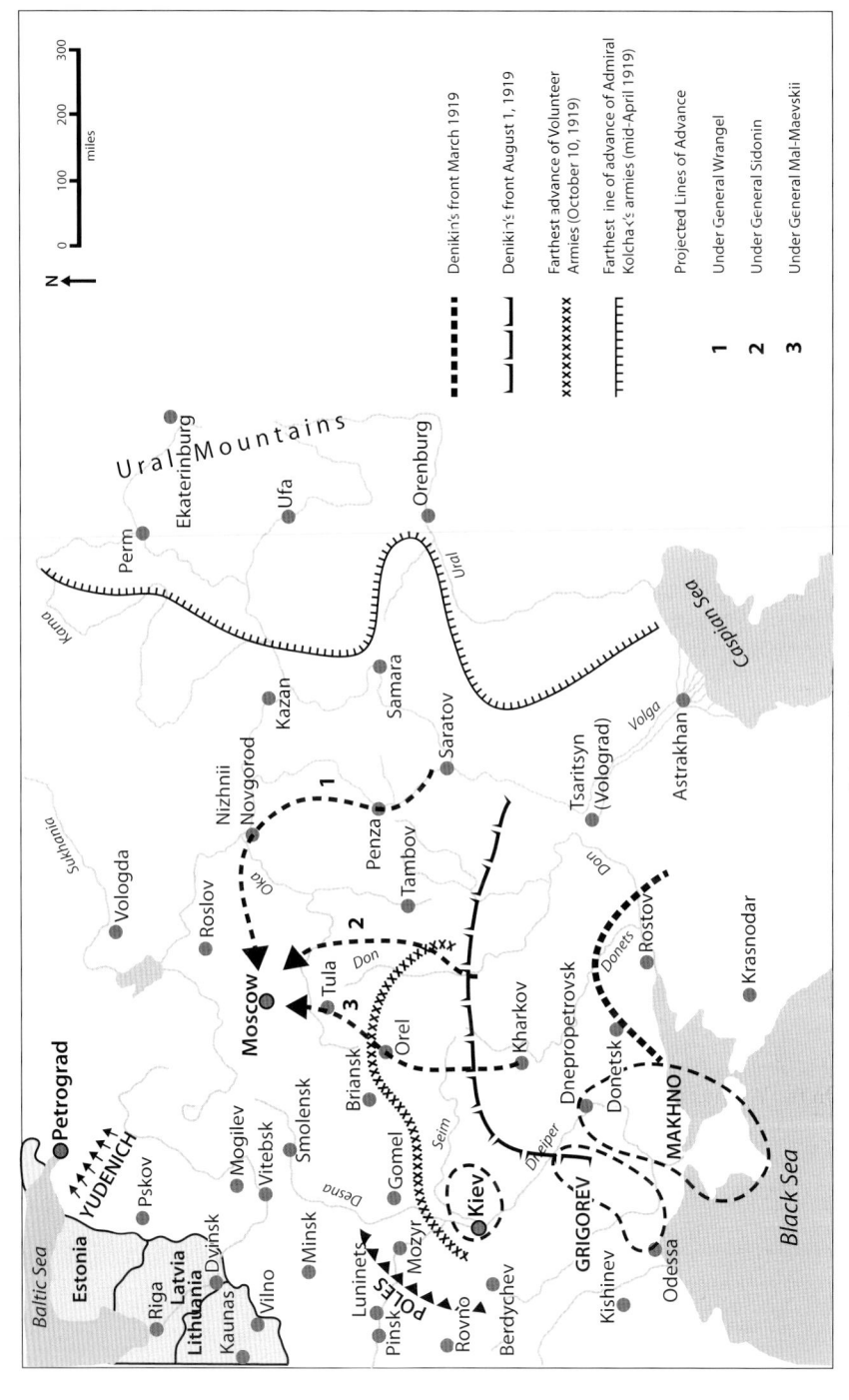

Map 6: Russia, 1919

Mark Vs and seventeen Whippet machines. Despite a spectacular success at Tsaritsin, and valuable rear-guard fighting, it was a case of too little too late, not to mention the problems created by poor Russian maintenance. The South Russian Tank Detachment was then transferred with the remnants of Denikin's forces to the Crimea. In July 1919, a second tank detachment had been assembled to aid General Nikolai Yudenich's force in north-west Russia, which disembarked on 5 August at Reval. A third detachment was sent to northern Russia in August 1919 with the purpose of covering the withdrawal of British forces from Archangel.[21] It is possible, though, by using a variety of sources to put together a more detailed picture of what actually occurred.

The most effective detachment appeared to be the one sent to Denikin's army in south Russia, the first group of White forces to receive a consignment of tanks.[22] Although it is impossible to establish precise details, a group of White officers were trained at Bovington Camp in the use of tanks and in their maintenance in early 1919, so clearly it was these men who were later sent to south Russia.[23] In addition to the reinforcements dispatched in July 1919, this tank unit possessed the advantage of a secure base at the Baltic Works in Taganrog, at which shells had been produced during the war. This doubled up as 'Central Workshops' and a Tank School. The British Detachment instructed the Russians in maintenance, driving, Hotchkiss and 6-pounder gunnery, while twenty *versts* from Taganrog a target range had been established. A British officer who visited Taganrog from July-September 1919 judged the course of instruction to be a great success. As proof of the quality of the maintenance, he pointed out that, since the first combat action in May, of the first twelve machines to be delivered, all of these tanks were 'still fighting-fit in the forward area' at the end of September, with the exception one machine which was under repair having been hit by five shells.[24]

The establishment of the tank force sent to southern Russia makes clear that it represented the main pillar of the British attempt to support the White forces. In terms of personnel, it consisted of thirteen officers, one warrant officer, three staff sergeants, sixteen sergeants, thirty-three corporals and 105 other ranks. Its transport was also sizeable, consisting of: one motor car, one Box Car, twenty 3-ton lorries, two water lorries, two tank workshop lorries, three other lorries and several motor-cycles.

21 Liddell Hart, *The Tanks. Vol. One*, pp. 211-3.
22 On the Volunteer Army in the south, see: George A. Brinkley, *The Volunteer Army and Allied Intervention in South Russia, 1917-1921* (Notre Dame, IN, 1966), esp. for the course of the fighting, pp. 185-274; and, John Bradley, *Allied Intervention in Russia* (London, 1968), pp. 132-83.
23 Imperial War Museum, London, Dept. of Sound Records, Acc. No. 870/09, transcript of interview with Maj.-Gen. H.L. Birks, n.d. [1977], pp. 42-3, who describes the Russians as 'Kerensky people'. He recalled they spent 'about six weeks' at the camp. Photographs also exist of the group sent to Bovington, although it has not been possible to establish precise dates for their stay.
24 Anon., 'A Visit to the South Russian Tank Corps: July to October, 1919', *Tank Corps Journal*, 1 (1919-1920), pp. 219-22, here 220.

Spare parts for tanks, tools, ammunition and other equipment had all been included with great precision in the planning.[25] Officially, the Russians were supposed to crew the tanks, while the British officers attached to Denikin were there to offer advice, assist in training and organize maintenance and repair.[26] At the end of July 1919, sixteen additional Mark V tanks arrived at Novorossisk to swell the numbers of Whippets and Mark Vs which were already being employed as part of Denikin's force. On 6 October, another ship arrived with eleven Whippets and eighteen Mark Vs on board.[27]

It appears that the first action of tanks supplied to Denikin's Volunteer Army took place on 8 May 1919 in the Voskreseensky Shiroky area, during which three Mark Vs and two Whippets took part. The Red forces began with heavy rifle and machine-gun fire, but could not penetrate the tanks' armour; the Whippets took part in the pursuit, although the Mark Vs could not keep up. The following day, the tanks required technical repairs and the crews needed rest. But, on 10 May, tanks saw action again in the advance on Khanyenkovo on the Khartsissk sector, causing the Reds to abandon their positions and leave equipment behind. On this occasion, the Reds had used artillery fire to try and combat the machines. A report by the Chief of Staff of the 2nd Army Corps of 12 May 1919 noted that there had been some tactical errors committed due to insufficient training, while better cooperation between Whippets and the Mark Vs would be desirable in the future. A letter from an officer from the Tank Detachment recorded another example of the employment of tanks which began on the night of 20 May, involving three Whippets and two Mark Vs, which succeeded in driving Bolshevik forces from their positions.[28]

Another successful action took place on 17 August 1919 when two Mark V machines supported an attack by the 2nd Kornilov Regiment which ejected Red forces from the village of Nagolnoe. On 20 August both machines returned from repairs, together with a Whippet, and were used to re-take the village after it had had to be abandoned. The attack was then pressed home, so that by 9 am Pseletskoe had also been captured, followed by Obayan in the afternoon, driving the Red forces northwards in the direction of Kursk.[29] But tanks were not always successful. In operations on the Don Front from 15-20 August 1919, an initial tactical success near the Kardail station

---

25 Tank Museum Archive & Reference Library, Bovington Camp, Dorset, box MH.4 355.48.4, Armoured Cars and Tanks, E2007.26, Establishment of the Tank Force, Southern Russia, 35pp, n.d. [1919].
26 J.F.C. Fuller, *Memoirs of an Unconventional Soldier* (London, 1936), p. 374.
27 TNA, WO 95/4959, South Russia Detachment, Tank Corps, War Diary, Aug. 1919, and, entry, 6 Oct. 1919.
28 UA&SC Rutgers, Fuller Papers, box 14, Weekly Tank Notes Nos. 48 and 47, 12 and 5 July 1919.
29 UA&SC Rutgers, Fuller Papers, box 16, Weekly Tank Notes No. 76, 31 Jan. 1920, Operations Report from 2nd Section 1st Russian Tank Div., Capt. Borschov, Kharkov Station, 2 Sept. 1919.

on 19 August was interrupted after a Whippet developed engine trouble, while the following day it suffered a defect in the oil pump, bringing any further tank action to a premature end.[30] A rather more proficient attack involved the employment of three tanks (a fourth was unfit due to magnetic trouble) at Tsaritsin by General Pyotr N. Wrangel on 8 September. During this action, a Red Army attack was repulsed, ten guns and 2,000 prisoners were captured and the 28th Soviet Regiment lost its colours.[31]

The end of the British involvement in southern Russia came in part as a result of reverses at the front. By early December the Don Front was starting to retreat rapidly. There was friction between the White command and the British forces, with the complaint being made that tanks from No. 4 section had been used for patrol work, which increased the wear and tear on the machines for little return. On 22 December, two Whippets at Liski had to be blown up before the Red Army reached the station there. On 24 December 1919, orders were given to the staff and the tank school to evacuate Taganrog due to the advance of the Bolshevik forces. By 29 December all tanks from Central Workshops were ready to move off, although the evacuation did not take place until 1 January 1920.[32] However, no transportation was provided by Denikin, so that about twenty-five tanks, 50 tons of stores and fifteen lorries had to be abandoned; the tanks were rendered unserviceable. This left forty-nine tanks remaining in the detachment serving with Denikin's army, with British officers drawing up plans to establish tank workshops at Sevastopol in the Crimea.[33]

In comparison, the tank detachment sent to aid General Yudenich's forces in North-West Russia was a modest affair, more on the scale of the detachment sent to Palestine.[34] This never had more than six tanks available to it; when the initial detachment landed at Reval on the night of 5/6 August 1919 it only had four Mark Vs, together with the commander Lieutenant-Colonel E. Hope-Carson, six captains, fifteen lieutenants, two NCOs, three artificers and twenty-nine servants. The remaining two tanks arrived at Narva in the first week of September. When the White troops first saw the tanks, they were deeply impressed. In successive actions, tanks from the detachment acquitted themselves well. In an attack on the town of Yamburg, it was found that the Reds had dug a crude form of anti-tank ditch, nine-feet broad, in anticipation of tank support for the attack. In fact, so positive was the effect of the tanks in several battles that the White commanders became increasingly persistent in their demands, showing little understanding of the actual endurance of

---

30   UA&SC Rutgers, Fuller Papers, box 16, Weekly Tank Notes No. 75, 24 Jan. 1920.
31   TNA, WO 95/4958, Report of Operations of Tanks of 1 Division of R.T.C. [Russian Tank Corps] at Tsaritsin, [sgd.] Col. Teminkoff, Taganrog, 13 Sept. 1919.
32   TNA, WO 95/4959, South Russia Detachment, Tank Corps, War Diary, Oct. 1919-Jan. 1920.
33   UA&SC Rutgers, Fuller Papers, box 16, S.D.7, Weekly Tank Notes No. 78, 14 Feb. 1920.
34   On the Civil War and the Allied intervention in North-West Russia, see John Bradley, *Civil War in Russia, 1917-1920* (London, 1975), pp. 143-61.

a machine, or of the needs which crew and machine had in terms of rest and maintenance. The Russian crews suffered, as had British crews during the Great War, from poisoning from the engine fumes, although they would continue to man the machines. But despite the detachment's best efforts, as the British commander noted ruefully, the Allies had failed to make an accurate estimation of the actual position of the outnumbered North-West Army.[35]

Towards the end of November 1919, the British personnel of the detachment were withdrawn, with the exception of three officers, who presumably remained because it had not been decided how to dispose of the six Mark V tanks left at Reval. Reports received in the War Office highlighted the problems in dealing with Russian commanders, the mechanical trouble which had started to plague the six tanks because they had been involved in more or less continuous fighting for over two months, but that the six-pounder guns had been very effective in supporting the infantry. Curiously, the decision to withdraw personnel was made after the dispatch of a further Mark V and two Medium B tanks, which were then loaned to the Letts 'as a temporary measure'.[36]

Even more modest in scale was the tank detachment sent to Archangel to support the evacuation of British forces.[37] Only four tanks were sent; these even arrived after the men of the tank detachment itself, which first departed by ship for north Russia on 19 August 1919. The purpose of these machines was simply to cover the retirement of British troops, which had been there since 1918, and bolster the morale of the civilian population. The country around Archangel was, in fact, poor for tanks, since it contained swamps, rivers and impassable forests. But it seems to have been the case that the arrival of the few tanks did stiffen the morale of British troops, since many sent to Archangel had never seen a tank before because, either Russia was their first theatre of operations, or they had been wounded early on in the Great War. The obvious psychological impact of the machines led members of the Tank Corps to reflect that had they appeared earlier they might have degraded the morale of the Red Army in the region.[38]

---

[35] Lt.-Col. E. Hope-Carson, 'British Tanks in North-West Russia', *Royal Tank Corps Journal*, 8 (1926-27), pp. 36-9, 72-4, 168-71, 201-3, 275-7, 321-3, 433-6; 9 (1927-28), pp. 7-9, 42-4, 123-4, 179-80; UA&SC Rutgers, Fuller Papers, box 16, S.D.7, Weekly Tank Notes No. 57, 13 September 1919.

[36] UA&SC Rutgers, Fuller Papers, box 16, S.D.7, Weekly Tank Notes Nos. 66 (15 November 1919), 68 (29 November 1919), 70 (13 December 1919).

[37] On the Allied forces at Archangel: John Swettenham, *Allied Intervention in Russia 1918-1919* (London, 1967), pp. 187-231; Clifford Kinvig, *Churchill's Crusade: The British Invasion of Russia, 1918-1920* (London, 2006), pp. 33-49, 167-205, 237-69.

[38] Maj. J.N.L. Bryan, 'With the Tanks in North Russia', *Tank Corps Journal*, 1 (1919-20), 194-6, 234-6, 247-50, 274-7, 302-5, 332-5; 2 (1920-21), 8-9, 44-5; Edmund Ironside, *Archangel 1918/19* (London, 1953), esp. Ch. 12, 'The Successful Evacuation', pp. 169-87, which does not, though, mention the tank detachment.

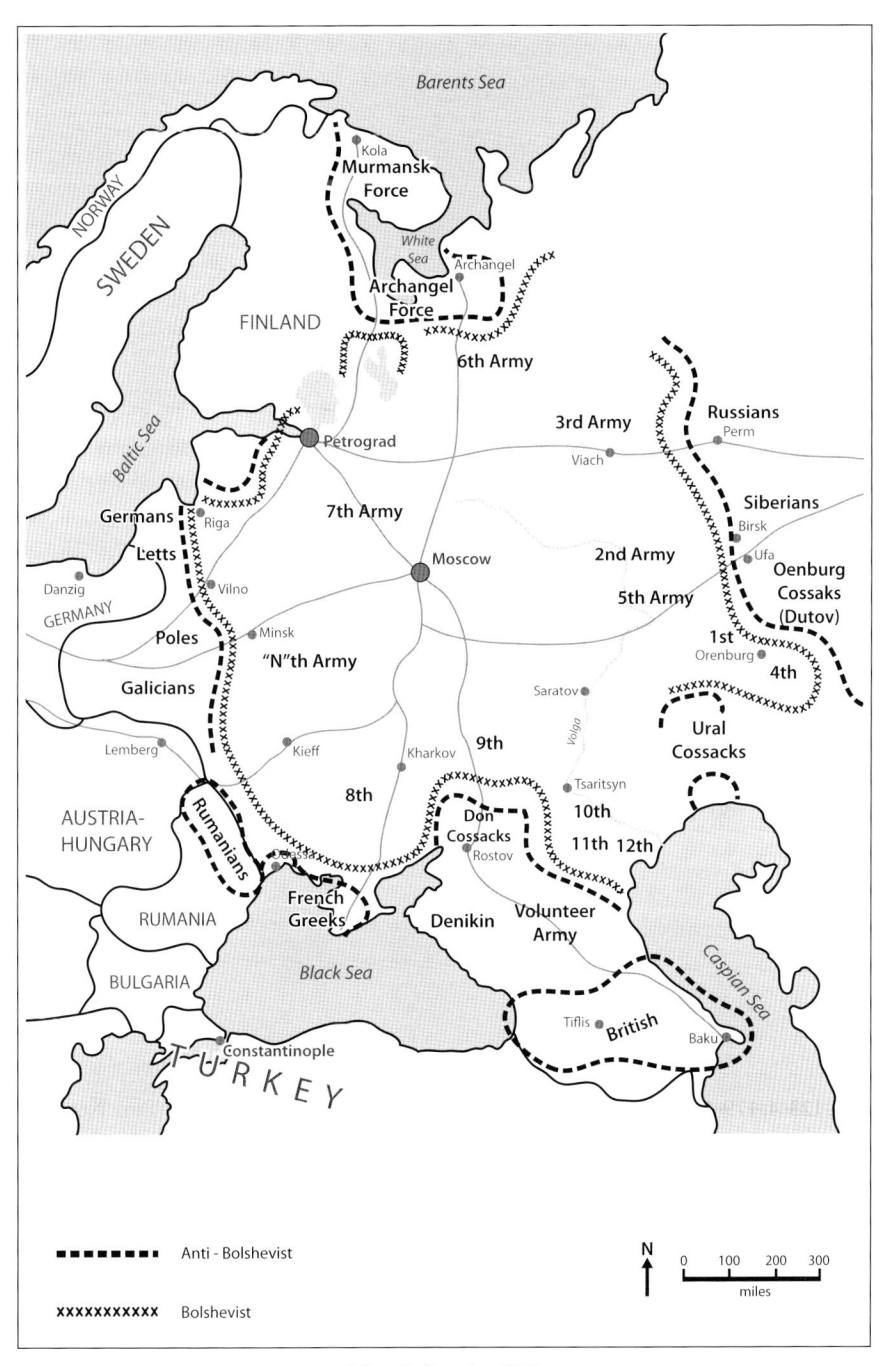

Map 7: Russia, 1919

However, the most curious aspect of this affair was the decision to leave two tanks behind with the White forces, which led to the foundation of a Tank School for the Russians at Archangel. To this end, ten Russian officers and twenty-four other ranks were selected. The commander of the new 'North Russian Tank Corps' was a Colonel Kenotkenich, who spoke English, was an admirer of Britain and had visited England earlier in the war to purchase automobiles for the Russian Government. He had, in fact, been invited to Bovington Camp to watch a display of tanks, which had made a deep impression on him. All those selected as gunners had already used Vickers and Lewis guns, but they took very quickly to the Hotchkiss .303. Only the officers were used as drivers, due to question marks about the loyalty of the lower ranks. The point which the Russian crews found hardest to accept was that speed was not always good for their tanks. On 24 September, just before the evacuation, one Mark V and one Medium B were handed over to the Russians. Shortly before the evacuation the two tanks went into action; later a cable was received that they had captured five fortified points and Plesetskaia Station. The ultimate fate of these White Russians is not known.[39]

The successes of tank units employed as part of the operations conducted by the White forces is actually confirmed, albeit rather grudgingly, by later Soviet writers. According to one, writing in the early 1930s:

> The slow British (heavy) tanks and the French (light) tanks of the World War, acquired by the White troops from the interventionists, were not able to play a prominent role in the Civil War. During the imperialist war, tanks were never used on the Russian Front. That is why their appearance on the fronts of the Civil War was completely unexpected even for those Red Army soldiers who had previously fought [in the Great War]. The partial tactical successes of the Whites, when using the tanks were, on the whole, explained by their newness and the unexpectedness of the appearance of the weapon.[40]

While there is an obvious uneasiness on the part of the author to admit the success of tanks against Red Army troops, there is the admission of 'partial tactical successes' nonetheless.

Red Army Employment of Tanks in the Russian Civil War

In later accounts of the Russian Civil War published in the Soviet Union, it was noted that no tank units existed at the start of the fighting. Moreover, it was also admitted: 'The Red Army's first tanks were trophy tanks, captured from the French, when the

---

39   Bryan, 'Tanks in North Russia', 2 (1920-21), pp. 74-5, 96-8.
40   Tau, *Motorizatsiya i mekhanizatsiya armiy i voina* (Moscow, 1933), p. 46.

latter quit Odessa, or from the British during their expulsion from Archangel.'[41] For a number of reasons, the Tsarist government had not seen the need to construct and develop the tank and, despite a number of designs and models being tested pre-1917, none made series production.[42] In other words, had it not been for the captured British and French tanks, there would have been few if any tanks in the Red Army until well after the end of the Civil War. Indeed, the Renault FT-17, Mark V and Whippet tanks sent to Russia continued to be employed by the Red Army after they had been captured.

According to one Soviet encyclopaedia, the White forces received 130 tanks from their Western Allies during the war, of which eighty-three were later captured and employed by the Red Army.[43] Further information is provided by V.D. Mostovenko, writing in the mid-1950s, who notes that some French 'Reno' tanks were captured at Odessa in March 1919. He also claims that in the Ukraine, in the spring of 1919, Red troops destroyed a group of large British Mark V ('Ricardo') tanks. He continues: 'One of these tanks was sent to Moscow, as a present to V.I. Lenin, from [the] Ukrainian Soviet Army'. Apparently, in the autumn of 1919 approximately twenty British tanks (probably Mark Vs) were captured from Denikin's troops which were operating in the south. Further tanks (the implication is both British Mark Vs and Whippets) were captured in the defeat of Yudenich and in the liquidation of the 'White Guardists' in northern Russia. In December 1919 and January 1920, soldiers of the Southern Front captured further tanks during the liberation of Rostov-on-Don. In the course of 1920, further tanks were seized from General Wrangel and the 'White Poles'. Finally, as Mostovenko concludes: 'The presence of several tens of tanks, seized, repaired and restored led to the creation in the Soviet Army of motor-tank units in January, 1920.' According to Mostovenko, the motor-tank unit consisted of three tanks, two to three light vehicles, three to four trucks and two to three motor cycles.[44]

A more recent and detailed description of the auto-tank units notes how, as the demands of the front changed, so too did their structure. As more and more 'trophy tanks' fell into the hands of the Red Army, the fire-power of the Red Army's motor-tank units increased. These consisted of a command and staff HQ, a tank detachment (from August 1920 two detachments), from July 1920, a protection squad, control and communication teams, technical and budgetary squads, and a train squad. In battle, these units formed a combat element which was made up of a tank detachment (from May 1920 three different types of tank), or two tank detachments (from August 1920

---

41 S. Derevtsov & A. Pushkin, *Spravochnik po bronevomu delu dlya komandnogo sostava RKKA vsekh rodov voisk* (Moscow-Leningrad, 1927), p. 20. At least one photograph has been identified which appears to show one of these captured machines in Red Army service in Kharkov in 1919. See Steven J. Zaloga, *The Renault FT Light Tank* (London, 1988), p. 14.
42 'Tank', *Bols'shaya Sovetskaya Entsiklopediya*, t.53 (Moscow, 1946), pp. 552-560, here 552.
43 S.S. Khromov (ed.-in-chief), *Grazhdanskaia voina i voennaya intervenstiya. Entsiklopedia* (Moscow, 1st edn, 1983), p. 577.
44 V.D. Mostovenko, *Tanki* (Moscow, 1955), pp. 68-9.

four tanks of the same type, two each per detachment), tank protection teams (thirty rifles, two machine guns), a combat-reserve HQ, control and communications, three to four light and three to four heavy vehicles. Between May 1920 and the end of the Civil War, eleven motor-tanks units were formed, each consisting of 81-113 men, three to four tanks, one or two guns and twelve to twenty-eight machine guns.[45] This source continues:

> The first time they were used in battle was in July 1920, in the attempt of 33rd Rifle Division on the Western Front to break through the position defence of the 17th Rifle Division of the Poles in the area 40 km west of Polotsk [Ziyabki]. Subsequently, motor-tank units were successfully used in October 1920 in the region of the station at Urul'ga, disbanding the White Guardist bands of Ataman Semyonov and in February 1921 in the liberation of Tiflis. In May 1921, they were re-named tank detachments.[46]

In essence, Red Army tank units played a part in the Civil War up to its final conclusion, employing captured French and British machines. It is worth considering what Soviet sources have to say about the three main battles in which these machines were used.[47]

Although the majority of Russian-language works consider the first Red Army tank action to have taken place at the battle at Ziyabki (Vitebsk *oblast'*, Republic of Belarus') in July 1920, it has been suggested recently that the first action may have taken place the previous year. According to the reminiscences of A.I. Selyavkin, on 26 June 1919 the Reds used tanks in the defence of Novomoskovsk against Denikin's troops: 'In this battle, for the first time in the history of the Soviet Army French trophy "Renault" tanks were used. With their appearance and their firepower they helped [our] success.' It is claimed that for his role in the battle, Selyavkin was awarded the Order of the Red Banner.[48] Given both Selyavkin's position at the time of the events he described – he was both commander and commissar of the armoured special unit attached to People's Commissariat of Military Affairs of Ukraine, and his subsequent post-Civil War career, including a spell with the Cheka – it is difficult to see how he would have got these facts so badly wrong, mistaking time, event and place, not least because, as a result of his actions in one engagement, he received one of his two Orders

---

45 S.S. Khromov (ed.-in-chief), *Grazhdanskaia voina i voennaia interventsiya v SSSR* (Moscow, 2nd edn, 1987), p. 23.
46 Ibid., p. 23.
47 Before Stalin's death, official explanations for the general causes of victory were highly ideological, such as in the Commission of the C.C. of the C.P.S.U.(B) (ed.), *History of the Communist Party of the Soviet Union (Bolsheviks). Short Course* (Moscow, 1939), pp. 236-47.
48 *Ziyabki – perviy boy sovetskikh tankistov* (Iul', 1920) <http://www.kharkovforum.com/showthread.php?p=10243118>

of the Red Banner.[49] One recent English-language study provides further information on Selyavkin's role at this time, apparently confirming his reminiscences of these events.[50]

Despite this correction to the received historical wisdom, the Ziyabki battle has long been held as the birth of Red Army tank troops in battle and the first significant use of Red Army tanks in the Russian Civil War. It has been described in some detail by V.D. Mostovenko, who identifies the units involved as the 2nd Tank Detachment, Armoured Train No. 8 and Armoured Automobile Detachment No. 14. On 4 July 1920, it was decided to break through a reinforced enemy position, between the lakes of Sviada [Sviatioe] and Dolgoe, which consisted of barbed-wire and three trenches, strengthened by support points. On the night of 1-2 July, the tank detachment commander with his tank commanders conducted reconnaissance of the area up to the first line of trenches to establish the accessibility of the small river which flowed up to the forward defence area of the enemy for the tanks. Conditions for the operation of the tanks were difficult as they had to advance forward to the enemy's trenches in the open. In order to distract the enemy, the armoured train was called into service. Before the attack of the tanks, artillery opened fire. Within two hours after the opening of the battle, the tanks had breached the enemy's defences. The tanks were supported by cavalry, infantry and the armoured car detachment. The enemy fled in panic. As a result of the battle, many prisoners were taken, as well as eight guns, about twenty machine guns and other trophies.[51]

The significance of this battle for the Red Army is demonstrated by the place it found in one of the 'classics' of Soviet military thought of the 1920s. In A. Verkhovskiy's *General Tactics* [*Obshchaia taktika*], which by 1927 had already entered its third edition, it was pointed out how, even with a relatively weak armoured force, important results could still be obtained on the battlefield. The Polish position was very well reinforced, it possessed a depth of 1 km, and it was protected by a river. The tank and armoured train units operated under one command and according to one plan were assigned specific tasks. Verkhovskiy concluded that 'the armoured cars entered the fray at the decisive moment and aided the strength of the blow… the reconnaissance carried out by the armoured units before the battle had begun was most exact and the blow ended in complete success.'[52] Ziyabki was thus important because it was the first battle in which the Red Army made a *planned* use of tanks, and it was the first instance of a combined force of armour, involving tanks, an armoured train, armoured cars, and non-armoured units (cavalry and infantry) taking part in a joint operation to dislodge an enemy from a well-defended position.

49 Khromov (ed.-in-chief), *Grazhdanskaia voina* (1st edn), pp. 540-1.
50 David Bullock, *Armored Units of the Russian Civil War: Red Army* (Oxford, 2006), p. 36.
51 Mostovenko, *Tanki*, pp. 69-70.
52 A. Verkhovskiy, *Obshchaia taktika* (Moscow, 3rd edn, 1927), p. 302.

It is also noteworthy that involved in the planning of the battle, and at the same time the commander of the armoured train, was none other than K.B. Kalinovskiy, one of the later creators of the Red Army's theory of deep battle.[53] Moreover, one of the particularly noteworthy features of the battle, the use of a brief artillery barrage rather than a long one, a significant feature of some of the battles of the British Tank Corps on the Western Front, appeared later in textbooks and became a key aspect of Red Army teaching on the employment of armoured forces.[54]

The second important engagement in which tanks of Great War vintage were employed was the battle of the Kakhovka bridgehead in October 1920, but this time the Reds were attempting to destroy tanks belonging to the White forces. The Red Army had created the 42nd Heavy Armoured Auto-Detachment from existing units in August 1920. The decisive battle at Kakhovka lasted three days, with the Red forces occupying a carefully prepared system of defensive positions, consisting of trenches, barbed-wire and anti-tank ditches. The White forces attacked frontally in dispersed formation, but were outnumbered and were gradually worn down.[55] What made this engagement truly significant was that it was the first systematic anti-tank defensive battle fought by the Red Army. According to a book on tactics published in the USSR in the 1920s: 'In the history of the Civil War, we find examples when, due to high morale, the infantry were able to independently fight against a small number of tanks. This was the case in relation to Detskiy Sel in October 1919 and in August 1920 around Kakhovka.'[56]

Retrospectively, this battle was viewed as particularly significant by the Red Army. In an invaluable three-volume collection of essays on the Russian Civil War, published towards the end of the 1920s, there is a whole chapter devoted to the battle at Kakhovka. Written by two men who played important roles in the fighting, not only was the immediate strategic background outlined – an important landmark in the eventual and final expulsion of the Whites from the south of the Soviet Republic – but the ebb and flow of the battle itself and the role played by the armoured element on both sides were described. Throughout the chapter, there are a number of references to 'armoured cavalry', 'armoured cars', 'armoured units', but it is only towards the end of the piece that the word 'tank' is used, despite the fact the chapter also carries a photograph of a trophy Mark V British tank.[57]

---

53 'Brigada Kalinovskogo' <http://www.osnova-nf.ru/index.php?a=62>and, Mostovenko, *Tanki*, p. 70.
54 Mary R. Harbeck, *Storm of Steel: The Development of Armor Doctrine in Germany and the Soviet Union, 1919-1939* (Ithaca & London, 2003), p. 14.
55 Bullock, *Armoured Units... Red Army*, p. 35.
56 P. Gladkov, *Taktika bronevykh chastey* (Moscow-Leningrad, 3rd edn, 1927), p. iii.
57 K. Stutska & S. Belitskiy, 'Kakhovka', in *Grazhdanskaia voina, 1918-1921. Tom perviy. Boevaya zhizn' Krasnoi Armii* (Moscow, 1928), pp. 312-32. It is also worth noting that the Commander of the 51st Division at Kakhovka was no less than the future Marshal of

With reference to the events in October, it was noted that in mid-October 1920 an attack had been launched on Red Army positions using 'a large number of tanks'; '[h]owever, our infantry calmly let the tanks pass through their ranks and then turned on the enemy infantry. Without protection, the tanks became easy prey for our artillery.'[58] Both here and in another account of the battle at Kakhovka, there is confirmation that the Red Army's soldiers had overcome their initial fear of tanks on the battlefield and had already developed a series of anti-tank measures, including the creation of anti-tank pits which not only would appear to have worked quite effectively, but also proved that against a small number of tanks the natural fear of the men could be assuaged and that they could engage in combating the armoured menace.[59] In fact, the Civil War was later acknowledged by military authors in the USSR as significant for the development of anti-armour tactics: 'in the struggle against tanks, the Red Army learnt how to apply both artillery and [various] obstacles which, combined with the manoeuvre, on a number of occasions led to complete success'.[60]

Other than Ziyabki, the only other significant operation involving the Red Army's use of tanks in the Civil War was in the capture of Tiflis (Tbilisi) in 1921.[61] Mostovenko's book provides details of the actual operation. In a number of respects, the use of Red armour in the capture of Tiflis mirrored for the Bolsheviks what had occurred earlier at Ziyabki:

> Tanks were used by the Soviet Army in the liberation of the Georgian capital, Tbilisi on 25 February 1921. Here the battle was characterized by the good cooperation of tanks with infantry and armoured trains. The latter, similar to the battle near the station at Ziyabki, attracted the artillery fire [of the enemy], making it easier for the tanks to carry out their combat tasks.[62]

A more recent account of the operation shows that a significant armoured force was at the disposal of the Red Army's 11th Army (commanded by A.I. Gekker), including seven armoured trains, and eight tanks and armoured cars. For their part, the opponents of the Bolsheviks in the area also possessed a not inconsiderable armoured force: four armoured trains, and sixteen tanks and armoured cars.[63]

It is worth noting that British 'trophy tanks' were used in the final conquest of Georgia during February 1921. After the Soviet 11th Army's first attack on Tiflis had

---

the USSR, V.K. Bliukher. *V K Bliukher v Kitaye. 1924-1927 gg. Novye dokumenty glavnogo voennogo sovetnika* (Moscow, 2003), p. 12.
58 Stutska & Belitskiy, 'Kakhovka', p. 331.
59 Ibid., p. 326; B. Tyncherov, *Britanskiye tanki pod Kakhovkoi* <http://bulattyncherov.io.ua/s286126/britanskie_tanki_pod_kakhorkovy_1920>
60 Tau, *Motorizatsiya i mekhanizatsiya*, p. 47.
61 Derevtsov & Pushkin, *Spravochnik po bronevomu*, p. 20.
62 Mostovenko, *Tanki*, p. 70.
63 Khromov, *Grazhdanskaia voina* (2nd edn), p. 593.

stalled on 16 February, the 2nd Tank Detachment (which consisted of four Mark Vs) joined five armoured trains, the 55th Armoured Car Detachment (four machines), and supporting infantry and cavalry, in a renewed offensive on 24 February. While suppressing fire was provided by the armoured trains, the tanks and infantry penetrated enemy positions on the Kodzhorsk heights which caused the Georgian army to withdraw. Six crewmen from the 2nd Tank Detachment received the Order of the Red Banner for their bravery. Two Mark Vs were discovered inside Tiflis in a poor state of repair.[64] The use of tanks in the liberation of Tiflis was important because it reinforced previous lessons, especially the use of armoured trains to attract the fire of the opponent's artillery, so allowing the tanks greater freedom of manoeuvre, in addition to the significance of the cooperation between tanks and infantry.[65]

The Impact of Tanks during the Russian Civil War

Despite the Soviet-era judgement that the number of tanks which were employed during the Civil War meant that they had no decisive impact upon the outcome of the conflict, the impact of the new weapons of war extended far beyond the individual battles and tactical actions in which they were involved: they had an effect on propaganda in the Civil War, they acted as a catalyst for later Soviet indigenous tank production and for Red Army tank doctrine, as well as the impact they exerted on Soviet commemoration and memory of a war which secured the immediate future of the new 'Soviet Republic'. Ultimately, they exerted a very specific effect upon the 'Soviet psyche' and the attitudes which developed towards the 'interventionists', as they were often referred to.

When it came to propaganda, the Russian Civil War was marked by claims and counter-claims in relation to the employment, destruction and capture of British and French tanks. In the early stages of the war, it appeared as if some official communiqués issued by the Soviet Republic sought to use White tank actions as a way of explaining reverses on the battlefield. In two wireless statements on 27 and 29 May 1919, it was noted during the admission of 'two considerable withdrawals on Denikin's front' that tanks had been used against them in both cases.[66] Similarly, in the fighting around Archangel, the presence of tanks served as an explanation for reverses. A military report issued by the Soviet Republic on 5 October stated: 'Area of the Archangel

---

64 Bullock, *Armoured Units… Red Army*, p. 41.
65 An interesting comment made by one writer is that, despite their successes on the battlefield, virtually next to nothing is known about the tank crews of these early Red Army tank units: 'as regards the armoured technology which was used by the Red Army, it is a matter of great regret that, about the crews of [both] the tanks and the armoured cars, ensuring not only victory at Kakhovka, but also the successful breakthrough in the Crimea, we know so little (approximately as much as we know about the captured enemy tanks'. Tyncherov, *Britanskiye tanki pod Kakhovkoi*, no pagination.
66 UA&SC Rutgers, Fuller Papers, box 14, Weekly Tank Notes No. 43, 7 June 1919.

railway. The enemy supported by intensive artillery fire, and under cover of Tanks, launched an offensive and slightly pressed us back.'[67]

The reverse side of the coin was, naturally, that the capture or damage of a British tank became an important news item of much propaganda value. In one communiqué in early June 1919, dealing with the reverses the Red Army had suffered against Denikin, it was stated that 'after fierce fighting we slightly damaged a hostile Tank'.[68] On 4 October 1919, the Soviet Republic issued a statement which claimed that their forces had captured a 'number of British tanks'. Three weeks later, on 25 October, the British officially refuted these claims. On 1 November 1919, a further statement was issued in which it was claimed that in fighting at the station at Liski on Denikin's front, the Red Army had captured a tank.[69] Around the same time, there were a number of announcements made by the Soviet Republic that they had used tanks of Russian manufacture on the Petrograd front. The British countered this by stating that these were armoured cars fitted with tracks, but which did not enable them to cross trenches.[70]

Denikin, himself, realized the propaganda value of the British tanks: when the first twelve machines arrived in May 1919, he organized a demonstration for the press which led to the desired newspaper coverage in his area.[71] On 1 October 1919, the battle practice range near Taganrog was closed, but during the final day's practice a propaganda film was made, presumably to stiffen the morale of civilians and White troops.[72] Among the Western Allies, tanks were also viewed as possessing propaganda value, so that reports that Red Army troops had fled on seeing tanks, leaving behind rifles and equipment, were regarded as newsworthy. A special correspondent of the *Times* in southern Russia wrote of 'the great moral stimulus given to the Volunteer Army by British support, of which the Tanks are the most vivid evidence'.[73]

Although there are no sources, other than the internal War Office publication, 'Weekly Tank Notes', from which any conclusions might be inferred, it does seem that the British had recognized the importance of the tanks sent to the White forces in stiffening the morale of the civilian population as well as the White troops. Thus, in a report on the tank detachment posted to the British Military Mission attached to the North-West Russian Army, it was noted that the arrival on 6 August of a tank at Narva, on the border between Russia and Estonia, had 'created much interest among the local inhabitants'. When General Nikolai Yudenich appeared the following day

---

67 UA&SC Rutgers, Fuller Papers, box 16, Weekly Tank Notes No. 61, n.d. [Oct. 1919].
68 UA&SC Rutgers, Fuller Papers, box 14, Weekly Tank Notes No. 44, 14 June 1919.
69 UA&SC Rutgers, Fuller Papers, box 16, Weekly Tank Notes No. 65, 8 November 1919.
70 UA&SC Rutgers, Fuller Papers, box 16, Weekly Tank Notes No. 66, 15 November 1919.
71 UA&SC Rutgers, Fuller Papers, box 14, Weekly Tank Notes No. 48, 12 July 1919.
72 TNA, WO 95/4959, South Russia Detachment, Tank Corps, War Diary, entry, 1 Oct. 1919.
73 UA&SC Rutgers, Fuller Papers, box 14, Weekly Tank Notes Nos. 45 and 46, 21 and 28 June 1919.

to inspect the machine, 'a large crowd assembled in the station yard to watch the ceremony'. On 22 August, a demonstration of tanks crossing obstacles was given, attended by Yudenich, his staff and members of the British Military Mission. The same report in 'Weekly Tank Notes' observed that, referring also to southern Russia, 'there is no doubt that Tanks achieved considerable moral effect even before they were used in action.'[74]

The special place of tanks in the propaganda battle during the Civil War may have exerted some impact upon the Soviet decision to attempt to create early on indigenous tank production facilities, which was no doubt also influenced by the realization that the Tsarist Army had been amongst those armies in the Great War which had failed to produce a single functioning machine. In a work published in the late 1920s, it was noted that 'not wishing to be limited [in operations] by the number of captured tanks, but wishing to firm up their production within the country, our government decided to attempt to create tanks in our own factories and this attempt was crowned with success.'[75] Thus, on 31 August 1920, the first Soviet tank – christened 'Freedom Fighter V.I. Lenin' – drove out of the factory gates of *Krasnoye Sormovo*, no mean feat considering the lack of technical inheritance in this particular area left by the Tsarist government. It may have been a glorified French Renault, but it was a start, nevertheless, and showed that, even under such difficult economic and military conditions, the Bolshevik government was determined to build its own native tank industry and not rely on captured 'imports'.[76]

The construction of the first Russian light tank, the Reno M-17, commenced at the end of 1919. The production base involved three separate factories: the AMO factory in Moscow, which reworked an Italian Fiat engine; the Izhorsk factory in Petrograd, which handled the armour, and the Sormovo factory near Nizhniy Novgorod, where the final assembly of the machines took place. For a country suffering under the deprivations of a civil war, the eight months required for production was something of an achievement. The first series totalled fifteen tanks, some of which carried machine guns only, while others mounted a 37mm Hotchkiss gun. The speed of the tank was 9 km per hour. By the end of 1920, the first 'Russian Reno' had participated in battles on the Polish, Southern and Caucasus fronts.[77] Thus, it was later argued that despite the limited resources to hand not only was the 'Russian Renault' as good as its Western counterparts of the period but, more importantly, it displayed a number of features

---

74 UA&SC Rutgers, Fuller Papers, box 16, Weekly Tank Notes No. 57, 13 September 1919.
75 Tau, *Motorizatsiya i mekhanizatsiya*, p. 40.
76 See here Mostovenko, *Tanki*, p. 73. In another publication, Mostovenko refers to a decision taken by the Council of Military Industry in September 1919, chaired by P.A. Bogdanov, which passed a resolution calling for the production of '15 combat [capable] machines at the Sormovo factory'. Col. V. Mostovenko, 'Pervye tanki nashey strany', *Krasnaya Zvezda*, 8 August 1967.
77 'Tank', *Bol'shaia Sovetskaia Entsiklopedia*, t.53 (Moscow, 1946), p. 559.

which were an advance on anything which the West then possessed in its armoured forces: a light tank with both cannon and a machine-gun.[78]

The function of French and British tanks during the Civil War as a catalyst was also felt in the field of armour doctrine. In the month immediately following the appearance of the first Soviet tank, the first Red Army tank manual was published, entitled the *Instructions Concerning the Use of Tanks in the Red Army*, and dated September 1920.[79] Specifically, the *Instructions* examined the role of tanks in breaching the reinforced defensive positions of the enemy, the overcoming of barbed wire and other obstacles, the fire support of the troops, seizing and holding reinforced points until the arrival of friendly troops. The role of tanks in attack was viewed as a means of supporting the artillery. Tanks were not seen as being technically capable of acting independently of the infantry or cavalry for any significant periods of time. They were largely viewed as infantry support weapons. The role of tanks in defence was also examined, as well as in a counter-attack. However, 'the inadequacies of tanks of the period, especially as a result of their low speed, insufficient fuel reserve capability, excluded the possibility of using them to develop success on the battle front.'[80]

Nonetheless, the Red Army's armoured forces appeared by the end of 1920 to have established themselves: there were fifty-five armoured car and ten motor-tank units. Among the latter units were a number of British Mark Vs, French Renault FT-17s and various armoured cars. In May 1921, by order of the Revolutionary Military Council of the Republic, the Administration of the Armoured Forces of the Red Army was created.[81] The combat strength of the country's armoured forces at this time was 103 armoured trains, fifty-one armoured car and eleven motor-tank detachments, sixteen motorized infantry units attached to the armoured trains.[82] According to one source, the number of personnel in the armoured forces was about 29,000.[83] This was a not inconsiderable military unit, given that, when the Bolsheviks had seized power a mere three years earlier, few Russians had ever seen a tank.

Conclusion

In summary, the case of the eight tanks sent to Palestine in 1916, the machines sent to the White forces in southern Russia, to Archangel and to north-west Russia, not to mention the employment of tanks captured by the Bolshevik forces, highlight

---

78 Mostovenko, *Tanki*, p. 74. The French Renault could only mount either a 37mm gun or a machine-gun in its turret. Zaloga, *Renault FT Light Tank*, passim, esp. pp. 3, 24.
79 Mostovenko, *Tanki*, p. 69.
80 Ibid.
81 Khromov, *Grazhdanskaia voina* (2nd edn.), pp. 74-75; and, I. Drogovoz, *Zhelezniy kulak RKKA. Tankovye i mekhanizirovannye korpusa Krasnoi Armii 1932-1941 gg* <http://commi.narod.ru/txt/kulak/index.htm>
82 Khromov, *Grazhdanskaia voina* (2nd edn), p. 74.
83 Drogovoz, *Zhelezniy kulak RKKA*, no pagination.

many interesting aspects which recur later in the history of tank warfare. The Russian case does demonstrate that the significance of First World War tanks extended well beyond the armistice in the West on 11 November 1918. As regards the machines sent to Palestine, the actual motivation was to test tanks in a desert environment, even if the experience did not appear to have led to any solutions in the immediate post-war world.[84] In contrast, the motivation during the Russian intervention was to compensate for lack of troops, but there must have been some expectation that tanks would be able to cope with the demands of the extremes of Russian terrain. There are, however, two dimensions to the employment of tanks in Palestine and Russia which both cases have in common: the psychological impact of tanks; and the potential for success in adverse circumstances.

Considering the psychological effect of tanks, the case of Palestine presents no immediate evidence, other than the rather limited tactical effect during the Second and Third Gaza battles. There is no indication, either, of any attempt to impress the local population by parading tanks. Nonetheless, there is at least anecdotal evidence that some thought was given to the potential psychological impact of the tank upon Turkish troops. While ideas of painting all manner of images on the side of the tank largely ignored the high levels of discipline and combat performance of the Ottoman Army, such thoughts showed that the moral effect of tanks had suggested itself to British officers.[85] But during the Russian intervention, the potential impact upon a civilian population unsure of which side it should support was obvious at Archangel, in northwest Russia and in the south. The shows of strength, newspaper and film reports, and public displays of tanks, echoed the later employment of much more advanced machines for very similar purposes. At Archangel, in particular, tanks were viewed as especially important in preventing further mutinies of Russian troops.[86]

---

84   In a paper produced for the Secretary of State for War in January 1922, the Chief of the General Staff, Field Marshal Henry Wilson, noted that 'we do not at the present time possess any tanks that are suitable for operations in a hot climate'. TNA, CAB 24/132, fol. 89-93, Secret. CP 3619, The Interim Report of the Committee on National Expenditure, Henry Wilson to Sir Laming Worthington-Evans, 10 January 1922, quote, fol. 92, para. 12. 'Tanks'.
85   Major-General Ernest Swinton had made certain suggestions to the War Office in 1917, although he was later hesitant to say exactly what he had had in mind, merely quoting from a German article which claimed he had proposed to inscribe verses from the Koran and paint 'frightful faces' on the tanks present in Palestine. Ernest D. Swinton, *Eyewitness* (London, 1932), pp. 305-8. For an assessment of Turkish military performance and casualty rates, see Edward J. Erickson, *Ordered to Die: A History of the Ottoman Army in the First World War* (Westport, Conn. & London, 2001), pp. 207-16, 237-43.
86   It is interesting to note in the case of the tanks sent to Archangel, one tank, destined for Bakeritsa, was 'to be used as a moral decisive factor to hearts that wavered', while another was sent to the settlement of Ekonomika where the surviving Russian mutineers from 'Dyer's Battalion' were incarcerated. Bryan, 'With the Tanks in North Russia', 1 (1919-20), pp. 303, 333-4. For an account of the mutiny on 7 July 1919 and its aftermath, Kinvig, *Churchill's Crusade*, pp. 197-205.

In the various combat actions in which tanks took part in both Palestine and Russia, two common lessons emerge in relation to the overall performance of the tanks. On the one hand, the tanks employed stood up remarkably well to the conditions which faced them. In the desert, this was sand and heat, which required a few minor modifications to the machines, whereas in Russia it was cold and a range of different types of terrain, not to mention the long marches to which they were subjected. But wherever British maintenance teams were involved, the tanks were able to perform just as well as they did on the Western Front. On the other hand, the observation which can be made on the tactical impact of tanks in both theatres is that their success or failure was closely linked to the overall operational circumstances which faced the units to which they were attached. Hence, at Second Gaza, where the plan of attack was flawed in a number of respects, the tank forces, although performing well in a difficult situation, took heavier casualties than during the much more successful Third Battle of Gaza. In south Russia, where the overall situation was promising for Denikin, tanks were able to achieve a lot more than when he was pushed onto the defensive.

The significance of the tanks in Palestine and Russia went, though, beyond psychological intimidation and tactical success in battle. When it came to accounts of the campaigns, war reporting and commemoration, there is no doubt that the presence of tanks in both Palestine and Russia left its mark. In the case of the British tanks sent to Palestine, they were reported on with enthusiasm in the 'instant histories' which were published during and immediately after the Great War.[87] In one illustrated account, there were several photographs of tanks going into action at the Second Battle of Gaza. One photograph, showing a tank, driving along a road flanked with palm trees, seems to project a sense of military superiority, the machine representing British industrial might. Although the number of tanks in Palestine at any one time never reached double figures, the photographs do communicate their inherent 'newsworthiness'. In the case of the Russian Civil War, as we have seen, tanks became a vital part of the propaganda battle between the Allies and the Bolsheviks, on some days bolstering the Allied cause, on others providing a reason for Red Army reverses, later reinforcing Red successes through the capture of Allied machines.

Finally, the wider psychological and symbolic impact of the presence of Allied, but mainly British, tanks in the Russian Civil War was of immense significance. The effect on the Bolshevik political leadership was to make plain the backward nature of Russia in terms of industry and production capacity. Their sense of vulnerability, of being surrounded and under siege was increased, as demonstrated by speeches made

---

87 H.W. Wilson & J.A. Hammerton, *The Great War*, x (London, 1918), p. 69, photograph with caption 'Debut of the "Tank" in the Holy Land', xi (London, 1918), p. 25, two photographs, one captioned 'On Tank Redoubt at Gaza', the other 'Aid for a Tank', showing a tank being dug out, xii (London, 1919), p. 355, untitled photograph showing a tank driving past palm trees.

during the Civil War.[88] The capture of the tanks sent by the 'interventionists' came to symbolize victory itself, perhaps in part because some Russians will already have associated tanks with the Western powers before the Revolution.[89] Hence, in several cities across the Soviet Union, British tanks were placed on plinths as war memorials, several of which still exist today, notably in Archangel.[90] They seemed to represent the triumph of the simple Russian peasants and workers over machines built by imperialists.

Yet, there was another element to the message: the appearance of British tanks had made plain the need for a Russian tank industry and more modern weapons. In the Soviet narrative of history, the appearance after the Second World War of T-34 tanks on plinths, acting as war memorials, established a clear link between victory over Nazi Germany and the earlier victory over the 'interventionists' in the Civil War.[91] The message was powerful and long-lasting: after the defeat of the interventionists' machines in 1919 and 1920, the USSR had marched on successfully to develop its own war-winning tanks which had defeated Nazi Germany in 1945.

---

88 As one example, Grigory Zinoviev stated before a military audience in Petrograd in October 1919 that the White commanders Yudenich and Kolchak had boasted that they were receiving tanks from Britain. G. Sinowjew, *Die Sowjetmacht und der Offiziersstand (Rede in einer Versammlung von 3000 Militärfachleuten Petrograds und des Petrograder Bezirks im Uriziki-Palast (Oktober 1919)* (Berlin, 1919), pp. 56-7.

89 A poster for a film entitled 'Battle for the Freedom of Nations (Steel Wonders)', probably for an imported Western film, shows what appears to be a British Mark IV tank, and can probably be dated to the first half of 1917. Hence, many Russians will have known what a tank looked like, even before the appearance of tanks in the Civil War. See here Hubertus F. Jahn, *Patriotic Culture in Russia during World War I* (Ithaca & London, 1995), pp. 73, and, for a reproduction of the poster, 76.

90 A book has been published recently, dedicated entirely to the Mark V monument at Archangel! See I.M. Gostev, *Tank Mark V: tanki v Grazhdanskoi voine na Severe i pamiatnik v Arkhangel'ske* (Archangel, 2011).

91 Among the numerous examples which could be given are the T-34 memorial at Tiraspol, placed next to an orthodox church, which commemorates the dead of the Great Patriotic War, the war in Afghanistan and the Transdniestrian War of 1990-92, and the Franz Grinkevich Memorial in Donetsk, Ukraine, commemorating the commander of the 32nd Guards Tank Brigade, one of the units which liberated the city during the Great Patriotic War. Photos of these memorials can be viewed at <http://mamayevkurgan.wordpress.com>.

8

'A Charming Toy': The Surprisingly Long Life of the Renault Light Tank, 1917-1940

Tim Gale

What follows is the extraordinary story of the Renault light tank (popularly known as the Renault FT-17), a tank that was very nearly not manufactured at all but which became the tank with the longest service history of any armoured vehicle, a record now very unlikely to be broken.[1] Examples of the Renault light tank fought across the globe, from Morocco to Estonia, from France to China, until well into the Second World War. Indeed, four Renaults were captured by US and Allied troops in Afghanistan in 2003.[2] It is thus surprising that the Renault light tank design was very nearly not adopted into service and, perhaps more surprisingly, it was the French civilian authorities that produced the most obstacles to its manufacture. However, there were also many military officers who had their doubts about the Renault light tank, one describing it as 'a charming toy'.[3] The subsequent history of the Renault light tank was to prove these officers' judgement in this case to be very poor.

---

1 In official French Army documents of the Great War, Renault tanks are referred to as light tanks (*chars légers*) or Renault tanks (*chars Renault*). Although the majority of light tanks were manufactured at the Renault factory, a number of other manufacturers were later brought in to boost production, as will be discussed. However, all French light tanks in this chapter will be referred to as Renaults, as the design remained the same, regardless of the manufacturer. FT was a Renault production designation and 17 referred to the year it was to come into service, although, in the event, the tank did not see service until 1918. See Jean Perré, 'Naissance et évolution de la conception du char de combat en France durant la guerre 1914-1918', *La Revue d'infanterie,* January 1935, pp. 13-30, here 24.
2 See <http://the.shadock.free.fr/Surviving_Panzers.html>.
3 *Sous-lieutenant* Hubert of the tank consultative committee. See note 9 below.

Organizational Context

To understand the difficulties that occurred over the development of the Renault tank between General Jean Baptiste Estienne (commander of the French tank force, the *Artillerie Spéciale – Special Artillery,* hereafter *AS*) and the civilian authorities, it is important to understand that the administration of the French military effort during the war was organized in two distinct parts: the *zone des armées*, under the control of the military, and the *Interior*, where various civilian ministries exercised their responsibilities. Thus, in the French tank programme, control and responsibilities were split between the army and the government, which resulted in Estienne and the *AS* being caught up in a complicated web of bureaucracy. The *AS* was originally attached to the *Sous-secrétariat de l'Artillerie* (Under-secretariat for Artillery), within the *ministère de la Guerre* (Ministry of War). Albert Thomas was in charge of this department and when he became *ministre de l'Armement* (Armaments Minister), in November 1916, the artillery and *AS* were moved with him. His ministry also controlled the *Direction Service Automobile* (hereafter, *DSA*), the organization responsible for all motor transport in the French Army. Estienne was instructed to report to both Albert Thomas and the chief of the *DSA*.[4] In addition, the *DSA* ran the *AS* camps outside of the *zone des armées* and was responsible for initial training of *AS* personnel.[5] Two other parts of the ministry were closely involved with the tank programme: the *Sous-secrétariat d'Etat des Inventions* (Under-secretary for Inventions) was responsible for military inventions, the *Sous-secrétariat d'Etat des Fabrications de guerre* (Under-secretary for War Manufacture) being responsible for military manufacturing. As the department with ultimate responsibility for the Army, the *ministère de la Guerre* was also involved. Thus Estienne was required, to some degree or another, to negotiate with two ministers, the *DSA*, two under-secretaries and, of course, the French Army's commander-in-chief at GQG (French General Headquarters) over all tank matters.

In particular, the relationship of the *AS* with the *ministère de l'Armement* and the *DSA* was problematic from the start of the tank programme. There had been many arguments over the medium tanks (the Schneider and the St Chamond) between the ministry, the *DSA* and Estienne. Léon Dutil, an *AS* staff officer during the war, compared the situation to a customer and his supplier, the *AS* being the client, who wanted specific equipment, and the ministry being the supplier. However, in the case of the *AS,* the customer was under the orders of the supplier. This 'bizarre situation,'

---

4   See Albert Thomas, Le sous-Secrètaire d'etat de l'artillerie et des munitions à Monsieur le général en chef (1 Bureau), 30 September 1916. This is in a carton at the French military archives at Vincennes (Service Historique de la Défense – SHD). SHD Cartons are numbered in series, all referred to in this chapter are from series 16N (part of the Great War series). This document is from carton 16N2121.
5   Ibid.

as Dutil characterized it, resulted in much friction between the *AS* and the ministry.[6] There were two major areas of concern; the difficulties that the *AS* had getting modifications made to the existing tank designs and the considerable problems with deliveries of both new tanks and the spare parts needed to keep them in operation. In addition, the ministry constantly interfered in organizational matters, particularly in relation to the training camps, as well as, surprisingly, questions of tactics.

Despite Estienne warning Joseph Joffre (then Commander-in-Chief) in 1915 that the tank project could only be done quickly if no supervising committee was put in place, French bureaucracy required such a committee be formed and it duly was. This committee was tasked with advising Thomas on all issues concerning the tanks, except tactical and operational matters and was called the *Comité consultatif de l'artillerie d'assaut* (hereafter referred to as the *Comité*). Its *Président* (Chairman) was Jules-Louis Breton, leader of the *Sous-secrétariat d'Etat des Inventions*.[7] The other *Comité* members were Estienne and his technical adviser for the *AS*, General Mourret and Lieutenant-colonel Picoche for the *DSA*, Lieutenant-colonel Deslandres and Commandant Ferrus from the artillery, Commandant Boissin, from the technical section of the engineers, Mario Roques and Captain Leisse from the *ministère de l'Armement*, with *sous-lieutenant* Hubert as secretary to the committee and two captains and another *sous-lieutenant* in support.[8] There were also three representatives from the St Chamond factory and one each from the Schneider and Renault factories. This resulted in a somewhat unwieldy body, as there were often over twenty representatives, with very different agendas, attending meetings. It has already been noted that Mourret from the *DSA* was not enthusiastic about the tank project in general and this attitude was shared by other members of the *Comité*.[9] The continual problems connected with the development and production of the new tank, the Renault light tank, were, with hindsight, the most egregious, as this was to prove the most successful tank design.

---

6   Léon Dutil, *Les Chars d'Assaut. Leur Création et leur Rôle pendant la Guerre (1915-1918)* (Paris, 1919), p. 108.
7   SHD 16N2129, Ministère de l'Armement, Service Automobile, Comité consultatif de l'artillerie d'assaut, procès-verbal 1ère réunion, 17 décembre 1916, 21 December 1916. The representatives changed over time but the organisations sending delegates to the *Comité* were fairly constant.
8   Ibid.
9   In particular, Hubert had a low opinion of Estienne and closely allied himself with Roques and the *ministère de l'Armement*. See here Gilbert Hatry, *Renault, Usine de Guerre 1914-1918* (Paris, 1978), p. 190, note 184. He unhelpfully described the Renault tank in a letter to the *ministère de l'Armement* as a 'charmant joujou' (a charming toy), quoted in Hatry, *Usine de Guerre*, p. 60. However, it is worth noting that this was somewhat balanced by the fact that Ferrus was a friend and long-term associate of both Estienne and Louis Renault.

Designing the Light Tank

The idea of a light tank appears to have germinated in Estienne's mind when he visited the British tank factory at Lincoln in June 1916, where he saw that the British tanks were going to be considerably heavier than the French designs.[10] As an artilleryman, he was used to the concept of different classes of artillery and realized that the combination of the heavy British tanks and the French mediums would potentially give a tank force more flexibility in combat.[11] Further consideration of this idea led him to see that a light tank for reconnaissance, direct support of the infantry and as a commander's tank would be extremely useful. Estienne had a fortuitous meeting the following month with Louis Renault at Claridges' Hotel in Paris where the idea of a light tank, armed with a machine gun, was discussed. Although Renault had declined to participate in the initial tank programme due to pressure of other war-work, he had since become interested in armoured vehicles and had made some preliminary tank studies with the naval builders *Société des Forges et Chantiers de la Méditerranée*.[12] Estienne clearly caught Renault's imagination as it was late in the evening when they finished their discussions, the outcome of which was that Renault agreed to make a preliminary study of the tank, producing a wooden mock-up by October 1916. Estienne's initial specifications were for a tank weighing no more than four tonnes, with a machine gun in a turret and a two-man crew, capable of up to twelve kilometres per hour.[13] Estienne approached Mourret at the *DSA* in order to formalize the arrangement with Renault but Mourret refused to do so, saying that the *DSA* would not be ordering any further combat tanks.

Estienne was forced to bypass Mourret and the *DSA* to keep the light tank project alive and he wrote directly to Joffre in November 1916. Estienne said that he believed that a two-man light tank could be produced and that this type of tank could be useful for both the *AS* and as special support-units for infantry divisions engaged in offensives.[14] He pointed out that production of light tanks would be easier for French industry than any of the proposed heavy tanks and that production could be implemented quickly, suggesting that one thousand should be ordered subject to a successful prototype.[15] Joffre wrote to Albert Thomas asking for an order to be made for one thousand light tanks, stating that the Renault factory had made considerable progress on a prototype but Thomas refused to make the order until a working prototype was

---

10 SHD 16N2121, Estienne, 3 Corps d'armée, Artillerie, Compte-rendu d'une mission en Angleterre les 25 et 26 juin 1916, 26 June 1916.
11 Ibid.
12 Hatry, *Usine de Guerre*, pp. 58-9. This company eventually went on to manufacture the 2C heavy tank.
13 SHD 16N2121, Estienne, Le Général commandant l'AS à Monsieur le général commandant en chef, 27 November 1916.
14 Ibid.
15 Ibid.

demonstrated satisfactorily.[16] A prototype tank was shown to the *Comité* at the Renault factory at Billancourt on 30 December 1916.[17]

The prototype was subject to a heated debate within the *Comité* about its merits and there were numerous objections from members in relation to its small size. Mourret started the discussion by stating that the Renault was too small to be militarily useful, although he rather disingenuously stated he had no objection in principle to it.[18] Estienne responded that the light tank could be a decisive method of bringing machine guns to the front line and he sharply reminded the *Comité* that the decision to develop a light tank had already been made by the Commander-in-Chief. Louis Renault pointed out that the tank was small so that they could manufacture a great number in a short time, certainly compared with the very slow manufacture of the medium tanks. He had also designed the tank around an existing and well-proved car engine, with ease of manufacturing thus built in. As the Renault tank was to have the same thickness armour as the medium St Chamond, arguments about its armour quickly petered out. Many remained unconvinced and three members (out of ten) of the *Comité* voted against an initial order of 100-200 tanks from Renault.

During January and February 1917, Albert Thomas and his ministry continued to strenuously oppose the Renault being manufactured, as it was believed that it would interfere with the ongoing manufacture of the Schneiders and the St Chamonds. Although this appeared unfathomable to the *AS* officers, as completely different factories were being used, the ministry's concern was in fact related to the availability of raw materials, particularly steel plate. The project was further delayed by the new Commander-in-Chief Nivelle deciding to prioritise artillery tractors, a position that Thomas was delighted to support.[19] This is a good example of where genuinely difficult questions about resources for the French Army were complicated by prejudice within the civilian bureaucracy.

However, as the light tank studies developed, the argument turned quickly in its favour. In particular, it was soon apparent that the Renaults would have a clear operational advantage over the existing medium tanks. Unlike the latter, the Renaults could be transported on lorries or light trailers, as well as by train.[20] By moving on the road network, the light tanks could be rapidly transported and concentrated on any part of the front for both offensives and counter-attacks, without tying up valuable space on the rail network. On a tactical level, the light tanks' battlefield mobility, being able

---

16   Ministère de la Guerre, Le sous-Secrétaire d'etat de l'artillerie et des munitions à Monsieur le général commandant en chef, 13 December 1916.
17   SHD 16N2129, Ministère de l'Armement, Service Automobile, Comité consultatif de l'artillerie d'assaut, procès-verbal 2ème réunion, 30 décembre 1916.
18   Ibid.
19   SHD 16N2121, Ministère de l'Armement, Service Automobile, Monsieur le ministre de l'armement et des fabrications de guerre au général commandant en chef, 5 February 1917.
20   The Renaults needed ten-tonne wagons for rail transportation and seven-tonne trailers, pulled by tractors or lorries, for the roads.

to go where the French medium and British heavy tanks could not, was yet another advantage. It also appeared that the light tank would be more difficult for German artillery to hit than the much larger French medium tanks.[21] In order to get a move on, Estienne had the Renault prototype taken to the main *AS* base at Champlieu for tests. Although Renault and his tank were only there for a day, Thomas was furious and accused Estienne of both over-stepping his authority and colluding with Louis Renault.[22] Estienne responded that he had informed both Breton and the *DSA* before the test and the test itself had been very useful on a technical level.[23] After further tests on the Renault before the *Comité* at Champlieu April, Nivelle was persuaded to reverse his earlier decision and give priority to tank production, in particular recommending concentrating resources on the machine-gun armed light tanks.[24]

The next problem was caused from within the *AS*. Further tests took place at Marly on 22-23 April, under the supervision of Commandant d'Alincourt, the *AS* base's commander (although a *DSA* officer), and Commandant Ferrus from the *Comité*. Although the latter's report was in favour of the light tank, d'Alincourt's was not. D'Alincourt declared that effective machine-gun fire from the light tank was impossible and, in any case, the gunner would suffocate in the turret from engine fumes whenever the tank was stationary. In addition, the turret gunner would be isolated 'both materially and morally,' creating 'irredeemable problems.'[25] He made recommendations about radical changes to the turret in order to incorporate two crew members, which would essentially have required a complete re-design of the tank. Thomas seized upon the report as an excuse to suspend production and he wrote to Pétain, now Commander-in-Chief, on 1 May 1917 demanding further feasibility studies, clearly threatening to delay the project further.[26] By the time Pétain received this, Thomas was already on his way to Russia to see the Kerensky government. There was thus no-one in the ministry with the authority to change his decision and the long journey to Russia via Scotland and Norway made communication difficult.

---

21 A point made by Captain Chanoine in his report on the fighting on 16 April 1917. SHD 16N2161, Le capitaine Chanoine à M. le Général commandant l'AS, 17 April 1917.
22 SHD 16N2121, Ministère de l'Armement, Service Automobile, Monsieur le ministre de l'armement et des fabrications de guerre au général commandant l'AS, 17 March 1917. A copy of this letter was sent to Nivelle.
23 SHD 16N2121, Le Général commandant l'AS à Monsieur le ministre de l'armement et des fabrications de guerre, 21 March 1917. This was sent via Nivelle.
24 SHD 16N2120, Le Général commandant en chef à Monsieur le ministre de l'armement et des fabrications de guerre, 13 April 1917.
25 SHD 16N2120, Rapport du commandant d'Alincourt, Généralities sur le rôle des servants et conclusion à en tirer pour les dimensions du réduit, 23 April 1917.
26 SHD 16N2121, Le Ministre de l'armement et des fabrications de guerre au général commandant en chef, 1 May 1917.

Thomas' unilateral action in halting production caused predictable outrage within the *Comité*.[27] Thomas and his ministry's opposition were then undermined by one of the light tanks' most vocal critics, General Mourret. He had commissioned a series of tests, during which a Renault had driven continuously for seven hours, only stopping when its drive-sprocket broke.[28] He reported to the *Comité* that the tank was ready and was 'very superior' to the existing medium tanks.[29] Mourret's known initial antipathy to the light tanks gave his positive report considerable weight within the *Comité* and gave Estienne further ammunition to press for immediate manufacture. He wrote to GQG the following day.[30] It was a matter of 'great astonishment that the minister has so abruptly suspended production,' wrote Estienne.[31] After representations from the *Comité* and Pétain, it was agreed that a Renault tank would be sent for tests at Champlieu.

For these tests, which took place over three days, members of the *Comité* were joined by seven *AS* officers, all tank-combat veterans from the Nivelle Offensive. The tests were a triumph and it was unanimously agreed that the Renault was significantly better than the medium tank designs and that it should be the subject of 'intensive construction.'[32] These results were discussed at the *Comité* meeting of 10 May. D'Alincourt continued to argue for a two-man turret but he was over-ruled by the *Comité*, which recommended ordering 1,150 Renaults.[33] Pétain's accession to commander-in-chief fortuitously coincided with this test and he immediately wrote to the ministry asking for two thousand Renaults to be ordered, although the ministry only agreed to increase the order to 1,000 light tanks.[34] Estienne continued to press for more light tanks to be ordered at every opportunity and, in September, Pétain placed an order for a further 2,500 Renaults, to be delivered by the spring of 1918.[35]

27 SHD 16N2129, Comité consultatif de l'artillerie d'assaut, Réunion de 4 mai 1917, 9ème Séance.
28 SHD 16N2121, Le Colonel Directeur de la section technique du service automobile à M. le Général Mourret, Directeur des services des inventions, études et des expériences techniques automobiles, no. 2.824, n.d.
29 Ibid.
30 SHD 16N2121, Estienne, Le Général commandant en chef les armées du Nord et du Nord-est, (1 Bureau), 6 May 1917.
31 Ibid.
32 SHD 16N2120, Rapport, Commission d'officiers de l'artillerie d'assaut, 10 May 1917.
33 SHD 16N2129, Comité consultatif de l'artillerie d'assaut, Réunion de 10 mai 1917, 10ᵉ Séance.
34 SHD 16N2120, GQG, Le Général commandant en chef à Monsieur le ministre de l'armement et des fabrications de guerre, Bureau de matériel, no. 9.418, 10 May 1917. This was in addition to the 150 Renaults initially ordered.
35 See, for example, SHD 16N2120, Le Général commandant l'AS à Monsieur le général commandant en chef du Nord et du Nord-est, 12 June 1917, where Estienne asks for 3,000 light tanks. See also SHD 16N2120, GQG, 1 Bureau, Le Général commandant en chef à Monsieur le ministre de l'armement et des fabrications de guerre, 18 September 1917.

Production Challenges

The size of these orders presented the ministry with a new and difficult manufacturing problem, as it was already struggling to deliver the ordered medium tanks. Although Albert Thomas had originally promised to deliver the entire order of 400 Schneiders before the end of 1916, in the event, the majority of the Schneiders were delivered during 1917, with the final deliveries only taking place in 1918.[36] With the St Chamonds there were even greater delays and the initial order for 400 tanks was never completed.

The light tanks would not be made at the same factories as the medium tanks but the large number ordered would still require a considerable amount of steel plate that had to come from the UK or the US, as this was in short supply in France.[37] Steel was in particularly short supply throughout 1917, putting much pressure on the ministry in relation to priorities. In addition, it quickly became clear that the Renault factory would not be able to deal with the size of the order, Estienne suggesting as early as July 1917 that the US should be asked to manufacture light tanks to alleviate the burden on French industry, a good example of his foresight.[38] Other French manufacturers, Berliet, SOMUA and Delaunay-Belleville, were brought in to help with manufacture but this did not speed up deliveries significantly. By October 1917, only 114 light tanks had been manufactured and the majority of these were not delivered to the army until the following year; in December 1917 the army had thirty-one un-armoured Renaults available, suitable for training only.[39]

In one of the many changes of French government during the war, Albert Thomas was replaced as *ministre de l'Armement* by Louis Loucheur.[40] Unfortunately, Loucheur was to prove just as resistant to prioritising light tank manufacture as his predecessor had been. For example, Loucheur considered that the heavy CAR3 tank design should take priority over the light tanks, despite continual pressure from Pétain and Estienne to prioritise the latter. Loucheur told Pétain in late October that the extra Renaults

---

36 Le sous-secrétaire d'état de la guerre (Artillerie) à M. le général en chef, 27 February 1916. Document in the French official history; AFGG 4/2, annexes 1, 1, Ministère de la Guerre, *Les Armées françaises dans la grande guerre*, 105 volumes, published in Paris from 1923. The tome covering September 1915 to April 1916 is Tome 4, which is split into three volumes of text, with appendix volumes. Thus the first text volume would be abbreviated as AFGG 4/1. A document in an annexe volume would be AFGG 4/1, annexes 1, 2, 3 etc, followed by the number of the document.
37 See Stephen D. Carls, *Louis Loucheur and the Shaping of Modern France 1916-1931* (Baton Rouge, 1993), pp. 33-5.
38 SHD 16N2121, Estienne, Le Général commandant l'AS à Monsieur le général commandant en chef les armées du Nord et du Nord-est, 1 Bureau, 22 July 1917.
39 Ibid, Estienne, Artillerie d'assaut, Le Général commandant l'AS à Monsieur le général commandant en chef les armées du Nord et du Nord-est, 1 December 1917.
40 The Painlevé government took office on 12 September 1917. For a modern examination of Loucheur's work, see Carls, *Loucheur*.

Photo 9: Renault tanks, 1918

ordered in September 1917 (bringing the total order to 3,650 light tanks) could not be delivered, saying that 1,000 Renaults might be available by March 1918.[41] Pétain responded that manufacturing should be concentrated on the Renaults.[42] In response, Loucheur expressed 'surprise' at the contents of Pétain's letter and complained about the considerable amount of time and money spent on the CAR3.[43] Why, he asked, had not Estienne and Pétain decided to cancel the CAR3 previously, conveniently ignoring the fact that Estienne had written to him previously calling for the CAR3 project to be suspended.[44] Loucheur also cast doubts on the light tank, saying that it would not be available in time anyway. He ended by telling Pétain that he would refuse to carry on down this route, leading as it would to 'disorder.'[45] Pétain responded by saying that the *Comité*, which had many representatives from the ministry within

---

41 Ministère de l'Armement, Service Automobile, Le ministre de l'armement et des fabrications de guerre à M. le général commandant les armées du Nord et du Nord-est (État-major général et 1 Bureau), 28 October 1917, AFGG 5/2, annexes, 1284.
42 GAN, 1 Bureau, no. 36825, Le Général commandant en chef à M. le ministre de l'Armament (Cabinet), à Paris, 29 October 1917, AFGG V/2, annexes, 1291. See also Estienne's document, SHD 16N2120, GQG, Artillerie d'Assaut, Le Général commandant l'AS à M. le général commandant en chef les armées du Nord et du Nord Est, (1 & 2 Bureaux), 29 October 1917.
43 SHD 16N2120, Ministre de l'Armement, Le ministre de l'armement et des fabrications de guerre à M. le général commandant en chef, 2 November 1917.
44 Estienne's primary objection was to the low-powered engine (only 76 HP for a tank larger than the St Chamond) that was proposed for the tank.
45 Ministre de l'Armement, Le ministre de l'armement et des fabrications de guerre à M. le général commandant en chef, 2 November 1917.

it, had advised that the light tank would be more 'appropriate to the [current] necessities of the battle.'[46] Even after this exchange, there were further arguments. Pétain wrote a sharp letter to Loucheur in December insisting that a 'great effort' be made over the winter to manufacture the light tanks and, once again, received promises that were simply not kept.[47] The ministry continued to deliver tanks that were completely unfit for purpose; by 21 March 1918, the army only had one Renault in 'a state to go into combat.'[48] A further 234 light tanks were manufactured in March but only 225 of these were delivered.[49] However, these all needed 'complete revision' by workers from the factories before they could be used, due to their poor manufacture.[50] The feeling within the *AS* was that the main aim of the ministry from this point was to deliver the greatest number of tanks, regardless of their serviceability.[51] There continued to be disputes about responsibility, Loucheur told Poincaré, on 1 April, that the light tanks were ready but that Estienne and the other *AS* officers were 'hesitant' to use them, 'under a variety of pretexts.'[52] Only by July 1918 were there over a thousand light tanks in service with combat units. Nonetheless, Loucheur did ensure that production of the light tank increased considerably during the latter part of the war, albeit not at the speed wished by the *AS*. It is also worth noting that the agreement with Britain and the US over the supply of steel had not produced the amount for France that had been expected and thus Loucheur was under as much pressure in relation to steel resources as Thomas had been.[53]

Despite improvements in the production figures, the Renault tank continued to have problems with its engine and Colonel Mercier, in charge of *AS* material, wrote to Estienne on 10 June 1918 that two particular faults with the Renaults' motors were causing considerable concern to the Renault crews due to these occurring with worrying frequency. The regulations had been loosened in respect of revving the engine to try and gain more speed. The Renault factory mechanics had asserted that the engine could support this rpm but it appeared that they were wrong; Mercier was asked to carry out tests to see if this was true and that the pump and the fan belt

---

46 SHD 16N2120, GQG, 1 Bureau, no. 5962, Le Général commandant en chef à Monsieur le ministre de l'armement et des fabrications de guerre (Cabinet), 6 November 1917.
47 Quoted in AFGG 6/1, p. 177.
48 GQG, 3 Bureau, Le général commandant en chef, à Monsieur le président du conseil, ministre de la guerre, sous-direction de l'artillerie d'assaut, 24 April 1918, AFGG 6/2, annexes 2, no. 58.
49 État-major Général de l'Armée, 1 Bureau, Bordereau d'envoi à M. le général commandant en chef les armées alliées du front franco-britannique, 22 April 1918, AFGG 6/1, annexes 3, 1862.
50 SHD 16N2120, GAN, 3 Bureau, Note sur la sortie des chars légers, 22 April 1918. Defects ranged from motor problems, in particular with the fan belts, to badly fitting turrets.
51 Dutil, *Les Chars*, p. 113.
52 Poincaré, *Au service de la France, Neuf années de souvenirs*, Vol. X, p. 104.
53 Carls, *Loucheur*, p. 76.

were failing because of excessive rpm.[54] Technical difficulties continued until the end of the war; for example, there were 225 light tanks at Cercottes waiting for replacement drive-sprockets on 5 October 1918.[55] There was also a continuing problem with spares; as late as 5 November, Aubertin was complaining that there were insufficient spare parts available for AS370 and three other Renault companies had no rail disembarking ramps.[56] In addition, the other factories brought in to manufacture the light tanks had their own difficulties. For example, even the official *AS* technical bulletin conceded that the Berliet-manufactured light tanks had 'numerous defects', although many of these were serious.[57]

One aspect of the Renault design that was revolutionary, but that there was not time to properly develop during the war, was its adaptability. The original intention was for Renault sections to have one tank fitted with a 75 mm howitzer in its turret, for the demolition of fixed defences that the 37 mm gun-armed Renaults could not deal with. This model did not see action during the war, although a number were used in the inter-war period. There were a number of other projects started that would have given the Renault units a very wide range of capabilities. In the archives at Vincennes, there are Renault blueprints that show what might have been developed; these include a bridge-laying light tank, that would have enabled the tanks to cross a four-metre wide trench, and what appears to be an anti-aircraft tank.[58] In the event, these proposals were dropped when the war ended, but the Polish army went on to develop a smoke-generating version of the Renault, illustrating how versatile the Renault design had been.

Planning for Combat

Integrating the new light tanks into the French Army was not difficult as the army had already developed a sound doctrine for armoured warfare, compiled in the *Instruction Provisoire sur l'emploi des chars d'assaut* of 29 December 1917. This was based on the experience gained in the Nivelle Offensive and the Battle of Malmaison.[59] It was followed by the first light tank regulations, *Reglement Provisoire de manœuvre des unités de chars légers* of 10 April 1918,[60] which became in turn, with minor modifica-

---

54   SHD 16N2133, Artillerie d'Assaut, Inspection Générale du Matériel, Le Colonel Mercier inspecteur général du matériel de l'AS à Monsieur le général commandant l'AS, 10 June 1918.
55   SHD 16N2120, Sous-direction d'artillerie d'assaut, Le Président du conseil à M. le ministre de l'armement et des fabrications de guerre, 9 October 1918.
56   SHD 16N2150, Aubertin, Le Président du conseil à M. le Lt-Colonel Commandant le CAMA, 5 November 1918.
57   *Bulletin Technique de l'artillerie d'assaut*, no 2, October 1918, p. 8.
58   These are in SHD 16N2133.
59   SHD 16N2142, GQG, *Instruction Provisoire sur L'Emploi des Chars d'Assaut*, 29 December 1917.
60   Ibid.

tions, the *Instruction Provisoire de manœuvre des unités de chars légers* of 24 June 1918.[61] The *Reglement Provisoire* was very similar to the *Instruction* of December 1917, with variations to take into account the differences in combat, organization and maintenance between the Renaults and the medium tanks. In particular, the light tanks would be acting more closely with the infantry than the medium tanks had and the former were organized along infantry lines, in battalions and companies, unlike the latter which was organized like the French artillery, in *groupements* and *groupes*.

The primary unit for the Renault tanks was the company, composed of three identical combat sections, a resupply/repair unit and a *TSF* tank. The effectives of the company were 115 men, including five officers, fifteen *sous-officiers* and eighteen *brigadiers* (cavalry NCOs). (A further three *sous-officiers* and six men were to be added for the 75 mm gun tanks.)[62] Sections had five tanks and were commanded by an officer in a gun tank, with two *demi-sections* (half-sections) of two tanks, each *demi-section* having a gun tank and a machine-gun tank. Three companies were in each battalion (*Bataillon de chars légers* – BCL) and by mid-1918 tank regiments were being formed with three battalions each.[63]

In June 1918, Pétain issued a note for the infantry officers on the employment of the light tanks which summarised the relevant parts of the *Reglement*.[64] The light tanks were to fight in the ranks of the infantry and it was expected that the tanks would give the infantry a tool for clearing strong points, such as machine-gun nests, as well as fighting off counter-attacks. For this reason, it was emphasized that the infantry should not modify its tactics because tanks were attached. Infantry battalion commanders were not to split their tank sections or use them on a front wider than 600 metres.[65] Pétain ordered that the section of light tanks was never to be used alone; it was only there to support the infantry. As per the tank regulations, the light tank section was normally to be with the advance elements of the infantry, only advancing beyond them when attacking a strong point or stopping counter-attacks. There were no arrangements for efficiently signalling between the tanks and the infantry, the only method mentioned in Pétain's note was for the infantry to fire in the general direction of points of resistance, which the tanks would take as a signal to attack. The tanks would often be able to push forward of the infantry but 'their actions are in vain if not supported properly by the infantry.'[66] The tank section commander was also responsible for making sure the infantry occupied any ground the tanks had taken. There was an important prescription attached to the end of the note. It said that the light tanks were only to be used *en masse* (that is one battalion per infantry division) in

---

61 Ibid.
62 Ibid., p. 1.
63 1 BCL's companies were designated as *AS301, AS302* and *AS303*, 2 BCL's companies *AS304, AS305* etc.
64 SHD 16N2142, Pétain, Note sur l'emploi des chars légers, 9 June 1918.
65 Ibid.
66 Ibid.

properly organized offensives and that any derogation from this rule must be immediately reported to Pétain.[67]

The Renault crews were given further instructions emphasizing what were seen as the points of 'extreme importance' from the regulations; in particular, both section and tank commanders were reminded never to *cavalier seul* (go into action by themselves).[68] The section commander was reminded never to split up his section, to remain behind the infantry until resistance was encountered and then engage this without waiting for orders. They were never to fire on the move; 'efficient fire [i.e. stationary], [is] the quickest means of advancing.'[69]

The Renault in Action on the Western Front

It had been the intention of GQG to initiate the light tanks only as part of a large-scale offensive but the Renault tank was forced by necessity to debut during the desperate defensive battles against the German spring offensives. On 31 May 1918, the Renaults entered combat for the first time as part of a counter-attack against the German VII Army, which was making alarming progress south-west of Soissons and thus in the general direction of Paris. GQG had ordered that all combat troops were to be thrown into the battle to stop the Germans entering the forest of Villers-Cotterets (south-west of Soissons), 'whatever the cost.'[70] 2 BCL was given to French 1st Corps, which was making a two-division local counter-attack.

What became known later as the 'Charge at Chaudun' was a mixed success as an operation but was a great success for the Renault light tank. This was despite the fact that their first engagement had been in 'the most unfavourable conditions,' particularly in relation to the state of their infantry support.[71] The engagement was a considerable boost for morale in the *AS*; it had left the light tank crews 'full of confidence and joy' about their success.[72] The tank attack had been beaten off, eventually, by the Germans but the offensive capacity of two German divisions had been 'crippled.'[73] It seems that the first appearance of the light tanks caused 'a real panic' in the German ranks.[74] The Renault design had proved to be even more effective than anticipated; Colonel Velpry, commander of 501 RAS, reported that 'the material worked well' and he commended

---

67　SHD 16N2142, Pétain, Note sur l'emploi des chars légers, 9 June 1918.
68　SHD 16N2148, GQG, Artillerie d'Assaut, Ordre Général No 48, 3 May 1918.
69　Ibid.
70　Captain Delacommune and Captain Cornic, 'Le premier engagement des chars Renault en 1918,' *La Revue d'infanterie*, August 1932, pp. 215-23, 223.
71　SHD 16N2165, 2 BCL, Note transmissive du rapport de commandant du 2 bataillon de chars légers à la suite de l'engagement du 31 Mai 1918, 3 June 1918.
72　Ibid.
73　Heinz Guderian, *Achtung Panzer*, English trans. by Christopher Duffy (London, 1992), p. 94.
74　SHD 16N2150, GQG, Artillerie d'assaut, Historique des opérations des unités de chars légers du 501 RAS du 30 Mai au 18 Juin, 30 June 1918, p. 2.

the tanks' speed on the battlefield.[75] Only five tanks had been permanently lost out of the thirty-one that had gone into action.[76]

An even more startling illustration of the effectiveness of the Renaults occurred on 3 June 1918, again in the Chaudun area. An hour after a two-regiment German attack, the French launched an improvised counter-attack, with the Renaults from 3 BCL.[77] Lieutenant Boudon was leading a section of five Renaults.[78] His section's advance was initially 'as though on exercises,' with 60 metres between tanks, despite the 'truly terrifying' German fire that was directed on the tanks.[79] His tanks broke through the first German battalion they encountered, but Boudon became separated from his tank section and the infantry.[80] The tank accompanying him broke down and was left for later recovery. As he moved forward he was joined by a Renault that had been separated from another section.[81] While Boudon was lost, the tanks from his section continued their advance and drove back an adjoining German battalion.[82] They then fought off a two-battalion German attack but eventually succumbed to an attack by a total of five German battalions, which forced the survivors of the tank section to retreat.[83] In the interim, Boudon had received a serious eye injury when his tank was attacked by a German plane.[84] His driver had been blinded earlier by splinters and was relying on Boudon's instructions to steer the tank. With the latter's sight now similarly impaired, the tank became immobilized after driving into some treetrunks.[85] Boudon continued firing until he ran out of ammunition and then decided to evacuate the tank. While Boudon and his driver were getting out of their tank, they were attacked by furious German infantry determined to lynch the two Frenchmen. A German officer fortuitously then appeared and rescued them.[86] Boudon was taken to a First Aid Post where he counted 300 German casualties, all the result of tank fire, he was told.[87] One of the German regiments lost 500 officers and men that day

---

75 SHD 16N2159, 501 RAS, 2 BCL, Rapport 31 Mai 1918, 1 June 1918.
76 SHD 16N2159, 501 RAS, Compte-Rendu Sommaire du 31 Mai, 1 June 1918.
77 RAS 501, *JMO*, 29 May 1918 and 3 June 1918.
78 SHD 16N2165, 3 BCL, AS 309, 1 Section, Compte-Rendu de l'engagement du 3 Juin 1918, SHD 16N2165. In addition, Lieutenant Boudon wrote an account of this action for the Service Historique in 1930, in SHD 16N2165.
79 SHD 16N2165, Boudon's account, p. 2.
80 Ibid.
81 The difficulty of identifying which tank unit an individual tank belonged to in combat was addressed by the Renaults painting on playing card markings, each section being represented by a different ace, a practice that the medium tanks already adhered to. SHD 16N2159, AS GQG, 275/PC, Note au sujet de l'engagement du Btn. Wattel (à lire dans toutes les unités), 2 June 1918.
82 SHD 16N2165, 3 BCL, AS 309, Compte-Rendu de l'engagement du 3 Juin 1918.
83 Guderian, *Achtung Panzer*, p. 94; and, AS 309, *Compte-rendu*.
84 SHD 16N2165, Boudon's account, p. 3.
85 Ibid.
86 Ibid.
87 Ibid., p. 4.

and the German 28th Division took two days to restore to combat readiness.[88] Thus five light tanks had reduced a German division to complete disorder in less than three hours. The French losses were four missing (including Boudon and his driver), two killed and two wounded, with two tanks left in German hands.[89] Of course, this was an unusual incident, but we might wonder what impact there would have been on the war if the French had been in possession of the 1,000 Renaults that were supposed to be available by this date.

Renaults were to fight in all the major battles of the French Army after June 1918, including the important battles of Soissons, Montdidier and Champagne, in July, August and September respectively. Although the Renault was theoretically weaker than the French medium tanks, the Germans never really came up with a successful tactic to deal with them and the light tank became an essential component of the late-war French Army combined-arms offensives. By September 1918, many of the medium tank battalions were composed largely of Renaults due to the attrition of the medium tanks. A total of 440 Renaults were destroyed in action during the war, including twelve by mines.[90]

The Post-war History of the Renault Light Tank

Despite wartime losses, the French had well over 2,000 Renault tanks left at the end of the war but little fighting to do, so thoughts turned to potential civilian uses for them. The *ministère des Travaux Publics* experimented with unarmed Renault light tanks in late 1918. The French public services were faced with considerable difficulties as the war was ending; the newly liberated regions needed supplying but the road and rail networks were already very stretched. In addition, a very large number of horses had been killed in the war, meaning that as the canal networks got back into action, there were few means to haul the barges. Tests on the Renault were made with extemporised brackets to hold cables and with the turret removed.[91] As the Renault had not been designed with this use in mind, it is perhaps not surprising that the light tanks never became a major feature of the French canals. Despite not being found suitable for civilian use, the Renault light tank still had plenty of military utility and was in action again very shortly after the Armistice.

AS303 (from 1 BCL) was engaged during February and March 1919 in the region of Odessa on the Black Sea, fighting with French, Polish and Greek troops alongside

---

88 Jean Perré, Commandant Aussenac & Capitaine Suire, *Batailles et Combats des Chars français. La Bataille défensive, Avril-Juillet 1918* (Paris: Lavauzelle, 1940), p. 200. One of the other German regiments had lost over 600 men in this fight. Guderian, *Achtung Panzer*, p. 94.
89 501 RAS *JMO*, 3 June 1918.
90 SHD 16N2120, Tableau Rectifie des pertes des chars et personnel, par engagement, au cours de la campagne, AFE, 9 September 1919.
91 'Chars d'assaut et péniches [barges],' *La Nature*, no 2336-2361, 1918-9, pp. 225-7.

the White Russians against the Bolsheviks. The Allied troops were fairly unenthusiastic about their deployment to Russia and most engagements were light. However, on 19 March, while supporting Greek troops, section 4 of *AS303* ran into serious trouble when it found itself fighting an armoured train and the crews abandoned their tanks, an official comment on this being that it was a 'regrettable incident'.[92] This gift of five Renault tanks was gratefully accepted by the Bolsheviks and these tanks in due course became the basis of the Soviet armoured corps. As the Soviet Union was one of the few countries that France would not sell Renaults to, the Soviets in essence reverse-engineered the captured Renaults to produce their own copy, the Reno light tank.

Both the French and the Spanish were to deploy Renault light tanks in their long mutual struggle against the Rif Republic, led by the outstanding military leader Abd-el Krim. The first time that the light tanks were used in battle by the Spanish Army (a battery of Schneider tanks had been engaged the previous week) was in March 1922 at Amber and it was not a successful experience.[93] The Spanish Renault tank crews had several months training but were highly inexperienced in both tank operations and tank maintenance. They were also asked to fight in terrain that would have alarmed their French tank contemporaries, involving an advance into a ravine, and they were fighting with troops with no training in infantry-tank co-ordination. The latter factor was somewhat mitigated by the fact that the infantry were well-trained and motivated troops from the Spanish Foreign Legion.

On 18 March 1922, twelve Renaults (eleven machine-gun armed and one radio tank) advanced, supported by two *Banderas* of the Spanish Foreign Legion, against Beni Said and Beni Ulixech tribesmen, the Spanish intention being to take Ambar (south-west of Melilla). Initially the tribesmen were forced to retreat by the legionaries, the latter well covered by machine-gun fire from the Renaults, but the tanks were soon separated from the Spanish infantry. Once this occurred, the Rif troops exhibited their customary bravery and attempted to engage the tanks in close combat, using mainly rocks. Without infantry support and probably without knowledge of the drills the French had developed to fight off close-quarter attacks on their tanks, the Spanish tanks were in trouble anyway, but their situation got worse as their machine-guns began to malfunction and they were soon all without any working armament. As they retired, most of the tanks ran out of petrol and one by one they were abandoned, the crews making their way back to the Spanish lines as best they could.[94] Although this was not an auspicious start for the Renaults' career in the Spanish Army, Francisco Franco came away from this battle, in which he had participated, believing that the tanks had made a bad showing largely due to the poor training of the crews. The problems with the machine-guns were down to the crews not being

---

92   SHD 16N2120, Table of *AS* engagements & losses, n.d.
93   José E. Alvarez, *The Betrothed of Death – The Spanish Foreign Legion during the Rif Rebellion 1920-1927* (London, 2001), p. 78.
94   Ibid.

skilful enough in their maintenance and this also accounted for the tanks running out of petrol. He saw that the limited weapons available to their opponents meant that the tanks were almost invulnerable and thus could add considerable fire-power to the Spanish infantry.[95] Interestingly enough, although the Rif troops had been forced to attack the Renaults at Ambar with rocks and knives, they quickly adapted their tactics. By 1924, their skill was such that the Spanish were very careful when exposing their tanks to combat, often being withheld where there was risk of Riffian traps and ambushes.[96]

In July 1936, the Spanish Army had two tank battalions, one in Madrid and the other in Zaragoza. Both were equipped with Renualt light tanks, theoretically organized in companies of three sections with five tanks each, three gun and two machine-gun. However, there were less than twenty tanks in a combat-ready condition.[97] With deliveries from the Soviet Union of T-26 light tanks in 1936 and, subsequently, the BT-5 fast medium tank, the Renault was completely outclassed in government service and they were gradually replaced by the more modern tanks.

Some countries adopted the Renault as the main component of their new armoured force, in particular Poland and Finland. In April 1919, a Polish Army was being formed in France and the equipment and some personnel from RAS 505 was transformed into the Polish 1st Tank Regiment.[98] This had 120 Renaults and was, unsurprisingly, organized along French army lines. By 11 June 1919, the final portion of the Polish regiment had left Martigny for Poland.[99] This was just as well as by August 1919, the Polish Renaults were in action against the Soviets in the Russo-Polish war. These tanks fought in numerous battles, including the Battle of Warsaw in August 1920, and by the end of the war eight had been destroyed, with another twelve badly damaged but to a degree which allowed them to be repaired.[100] The Renaults remained in Polish service until the Second World War, when they were relegated to a minor role befitting their now primitive design, although a number saw good service as a component of armoured trains.[101]

---

95   Francisco Franco Bahamonde, *Francisco Franco's Moroccan War Diary 1920-1922*, trans., with notes, by Paul Southern (Bromley, 2007), pp. 130-1.
96   Alvarez, *The Betrothed of Death*, p. 144, note 20. There are fascinating pictures of his uncle's service with Renaults in the Rif War on the website of Jesus Dapena, http://home.comcast.net/~dapena/tanks/cipri.htm.
97   F.C. Albert, *Carros de Combate y Vehiculos Blindados de la Guerra 1936-1939* (Barcelona, 1980), p. 11.
98   SHD 16N2150, Pétain to Estienne, Constitution d'EM de Régiment et de Bataillon de chars blindés pour l'Armeé Polonais, 21 May 1919.
99   SHD 16N2150, Commandant Troupes Polonaise to GQG, Compte rendu du départ de Martigny les Bainsle 11 juin du dernier train du transport des éléments du 1er Régiment de chars d'assaut polonais, 11 June 1919.
100 See http://derela.republika.pl/en/ft17.htm.
101 Ibid.

The fledgling Finnish Army bought thirty-two Renaults (fourteen gun and eighteen machine-gun) from France in 1919 and these were to remain the main component of the Finnish armoured force until well into the Second World War. As there was no experience in Finland of armoured operations, a small French advisory team was sent to supervise training.[102] The French leant on the Finnish government to lend three Renaults to the White Army of General N.N. Yudenich, which was advancing from Estonia towards Petrograd. These tanks, crewed by Russians, saw action in October 1919, but were returned to Finland as Yudenich's army retreated back into Estonia.[103] The Finns did little to modify the Renaults over the next twenty years, other than to replace the Great War vintage Hotchkiss machine-gun with a more modern Finnish model and to try to address the fan-belt problem. Perhaps unsurprisingly considering French war-time experience, the Finns had considerable problems with the Renault's fan-belts and were forced to design a replacement in 1926; despite this, the fan-belt remained the most fragile component of the tank.[104]

Although the Finnish Army had recognized that the Renaults were outdated by the early 1930s, by the beginning of the war with the Soviet Union these still comprised the majority of its tank force. The Finns prudently did not attempt to use the Renaults in an offensive role and the light tanks were used for training and also as recovery vehicles for captured Soviet tanks. As the Finnish situation deteriorated during the Winter War, the Renaults were pressed into service as improvised bunkers, being dug-in, leaving only the turrets exposed. These rarely saw action and the light tank force was further depleted when the Soviets captured nearly half a Renault company waiting to entrain. By the end of the war, there were only four surviving Renaults and three of these were scrapped, the remaining one being given to the armour museum at Parola, where it resides to this day.[105]

The Renault design was not only sold abroad, it was also widely copied. During the Great War, the French had agreed internally in November 1917 that the US would be asked to construct 1,200 light tanks, this subsequently being agreed by the US government.[106] However, the US light tank programme was a disaster; despite the French shipping to the US two Renaults in February and March 1918, the first two American-manufactured Renaults arrived in France nine days after the armistice.[107]

---

102 For more on the Finnish Renault programme, see Urho Myllyniemi, *Suomen Puolustus-Voimat* (Helsinki, 1994), with interesting photographs of Finnish infantry with Renault tanks on p. 55.
103 D. Bullock & A. Deryabin, *Armoured Units of the Russian Civil War – White and Allied* (Oxford, 2003), p. 16.
104 <http://www.jaegerplatoon.net/TANKS1.htm>.
105 Ibid.
106 SHD 16N2120, GAN, Le Général commandant les armées du Nord et du Nord-est à Ministre armement – cabinet (Réponse à télégramme 55 361 I/SA du 24 novembre), 26 November 1917.
107 Dale E. Wilson, *Treat' Em Rough: The Birth of American Armor, 1917-20* (Novato, CA, 1990), p. 86.

The US eventually got a light tank manufacturing programme into action and, by 1921, there were over 1,000 examples of the US version of the Renault (the Six-Ton tank) with the US Army.[108] The Italians also decided to in effect copy the Renault design for their Fiat 3000 light tank.

Epilogue

By the Second World War, the Renault was clearly outclassed by just about every contemporary tank and yet the light tank's combat life was by no means over. There were still well over 1,000 Renaults in French service when the Germans invaded in 1940 and the Germans captured the majority of these, most being pressed into German service. The German Army and Air Force called the captured Renaults the PzKpfw 18R 730(f) and they were used extensively for both airfield security and internal security operations in occupied France until the liberation. Captured Renaults were also deployed in anti-partisan duties in Yugoslavia and one even ended up in Norway as a coastal defence position.[109]

As a result of the brilliant design work by the Renault factory, its light tank was sold or copied across the world, meaning that examples are still being found to this day. This is in itself extraordinary for a Great War tank design as, for instance, there is only one example left in the world of each French medium tank design, both now kept at the French tank museum at Saumur, along with a Renault light tank. There are over fifty known Renaults still in existence and this number does not include the surviving US 6-ton tanks.[110] Renault light tanks can be seen today in Australia, Belgium, Brazil (six examples are on public display), the Netherlands, Poland, Romania, Russia, Serbia, United States and, perhaps most surprisingly, there is one still to be found in Mali. Thus this clever design, opposed so strongly by many of the French military and civilian authorities in 1916-17, proved to be much more than a 'charming toy', and many of the tanks themselves have managed to outlive their opponents.

---

108 David E. Johnson, *Fast Tanks and Heavy Bombers: Innovation in the US Army 1917-1945* (Ithaca, 1998), p. 73.
109 <http://the.shadock.free.fr/Surviving_Panzers.html>.
110 Complete pdf list can be found at http://the.shadock.free.fr/Surviving_Panzers.html.

9

The Battle of Cambrai: Reactions, Commemoration and Symbolism, 1917-1942

Alaric Searle

In March 1962, the curator at the Royal Armoured Corps Museum at Bovington received a note from a retired officer about a letter written by Lieutenant-Colonel R.W. Dundas, MC, to his wife on 20 November 1917, at the end of the first day of the Battle of Cambrai. The family had specified that the letter could be used for display in the museum.[1] The letter conveys some sense of the excitement within the Tank Corps after the opening of the battle:

> This has been "Der Tag" for the Tank Corps. We have been asking and praying for it all this year and at last it came at 26 days' notice. You can imagine we have worked night and day for those 3 ½ weeks, and I think it is safe to say that the Boche has had the worst surprise of his life. It has been a tank battle primarily…
>
> The final scene when the battle started – there had been complete silence till the whistle blew, not a shot fired: the secrecy and surprise was a complete success – , was beyond all description.
>
> By tomorrow it will be in your papers, I suppose.
>
> It has been a truly great day. Unless some mischance occurs this afternoon the Tank has finally established itself as a weapon of warfare. G.H.Q. are simply tumbling over us![2]

---

1 Tank Museum Archive & Reference Library, Bovington Camp, Dorset (hereafter, TMARL), M.H.3. 355.48.3, Cambrai 20.11.1917, box 1, Lt.-Col. R.N. Wilson to Brig. A.W. Brown, 8 March 1962.
2 TMARL, Cambrai box 1, copy of letter, Lt.-Col. R.W. Dundas to his wife, 20 November 1917.

The interest with which the letter was met at the museum of the then Royal Armoured Corps also provides an indication of the significance of the battle for the identity and traditions of the British Army's armoured force.

Much has been written about the Battle of Cambrai, the early spectacular successes, the ingenious tactic of the fascines dropped into the wide German trenches to create a bridge to allow the tanks to cross, followed by the dramatic German counter-attack which drove the British back in some places to beyond their start lines. Given the scrutiny which the offensive has been put under, it is unlikely that any new facts could be uncovered or new perspectives offered on the planning, decision-making or the actions of individual tanks, units or divisions.[3] But this is not the intention here. The question which has received less attention is what reactions the battle provoked, in the press, among politicians and soldiers. Few battles in history have come to symbolise a new form of warfare in the way in which Cambrai did. But was this reaction restricted to the British Army, or even simply the Tank Corps?

After GHQ issued its first statement on the battle on 21 November, it was reported in an article in the *Times* the following day that the Third Army, under the command of General Sir Julian Byng, had launched a number of attacks between St. Quentin and the River Scarpe, which had been carried out without any artillery preparation. The enemy had been surprised, there had been an advance of four to five miles on a wide front and several thousand prisoners had been taken. The attack on the main front had been led by 'a large number of Tanks', which had moved in advance of the infantry, breaking through successive belts of German barbed-wire. More interesting was the final part of the article, subtitled, 'Joy-Bells – The Popular Instinct'. It was reported that a representative of the newspaper had spoken to the Bishop of London, the Lord Mayor, the Secretary for War and officials at the War Office, all of whom thought that 'some popular demonstration' of joy ought to be made as soon as more definite information was received. In an obvious attempt to encourage the idea, the *Times* remarked: 'Doubtless as news of the project as proposed spreads throughout the country other cities and smaller towns will also ring their bells.'[4]

On 24 November, the *Times* carried several articles reporting on the scenes of celebration across the country, the fact that victory peals had been rung at St. Paul's, as well as the continuing development of the battle.[5] On the same day, the *Daily*

---

3   On Cambrai, see: B.H. Liddell Hart, *The Tanks. Volume One: 1914-1939* (London, 1959), pp. 128-53; Bryan Cooper, *The Ironclads of Cambrai* (London, 1967); Tim Travers, *How the War Was Won: Command and Technology in the British Army on the Western Front, 1917-1918* (London, 1992), pp. 11-31; William Moore, *A Wood Called Bourlon: The Cover-up after Cambrai* (London, 1998); and, Bryn Hammond, *Cambrai 1917: The Myth of the First Great Tank Battle* (London, 2008).
4   'Great British Victory. Byng Strikes on the Right. Five Mile Advance. Hindenburg Line Broken. A Battle of Tanks. 8,000 Prisoners', *The Times*, 22 November 1917, p. 7.
5   'Battle for Cambrai', 'Victory Peals at St. Paul's: Scenes of Enthusiasm', 'German Comment: "A Local Success"', 'Opening of New Attack. The Great Work of Ulstermen.

Mirror carried a front-page photograph of the Tank Corps commander, Hugh Elles, with the caption, 'Brigadier Hugh Jameson Elles DSO, the "admiral" of the tanks in the great push', as well as photographs of a tank and General Sir John Capper.[6] On 28 November, the satirical magazine *Punch* published a full-page cartoon, depicting Sir Douglas Haig sitting on the roof of a British tank, dressed as a Roman centurion, holding a shield with a St. George's Cross painted on it, aiming his spear at a reptile-like creature, which is already becoming crushed under the tracks of the tank. Needless to say, the half-crocodile, half-dragon like creature is wearing a German *Pickelhaube*. The cartoon carried the subtitle, 'With Mr. Punch's jubilant compliments to Sir Douglas HAIG and his Tanks'.[7]

The reaction of the public to the success at Cambrai was striking; and, it suggests immediately that the debate which the battle produced went well beyond the confines of the British Army. The emotions involved were not restricted to wartime as the battle became the central point of commemoration for the Tank Corps, the very key to its identity, not least of all because later historical interpretations varied greatly, both in the writing of the history of the Great War and in military debates. Ironically, in the study which has done most to promote interest in the visual connotations of the tank, there is no mention of the symbolism with which the Battle of Cambrai was invested.[8] Hence, our purpose here is to consider wartime reactions to the battle, its later commemoration and the historical and military debate over its significance. What follows is, in essence, a study of the symbolic quality of a battle which was to become such a central part of the debate on the tank after the Great War.[9]

The First Controversy: The Enquiry into the German Counter-Attack

On 29 November, the *Daily Graphic* published four separate photographs of tanks which covered the whole of its front page. The captions communicate something of the insatiable desire of the public for images of the new weapon of war: 'Well over uneven ground'; 'Going into action in line ahead of formation'; 'Taking a rise without difficulty'; and, 'Occupying the whole street in a battered village'. In the brief text at the foot of the page it was noted that tanks had come into their own at Cambrai and,

---

    Gallantry of Tank Officers', *The Times*, 24 November 1917, p. 7.
6   'The Admiral of the Tanks', *Daily Mirror*, 24 November 1917, p. 1.
7   'St. George Out-Dragons the Dragon', *Punch*, 153 (28 November 1917), p. 367.
8   Patrick Wright, *Tank: The Progress of a Monstrous War Machine* (London, 2000), pp. 77-80, 105-6, 109, 120-2, 152, 176, for the references to Cambrai, which are largely based on well-known sources.
9   There is perhaps only one enduring visual symbol of the Battle of Cambrai: photographs of Mark IV tanks fitted with fascines on rail-carriages prior to the battle, such as one in J.F.C. Fuller, *Memoirs of an Unconventional Soldier* (London, 1936), plate facing p. 226. However, although visual symbolism is part of the story of reactions to Cambrai, the main symbolism lay in its military significance as a turning point in warfare.

Photo 10: 'With Mr Punch's jubilant compliments to Sir Douglas HAIG and his Tanks'

214   Genesis, Employment, Aftermath

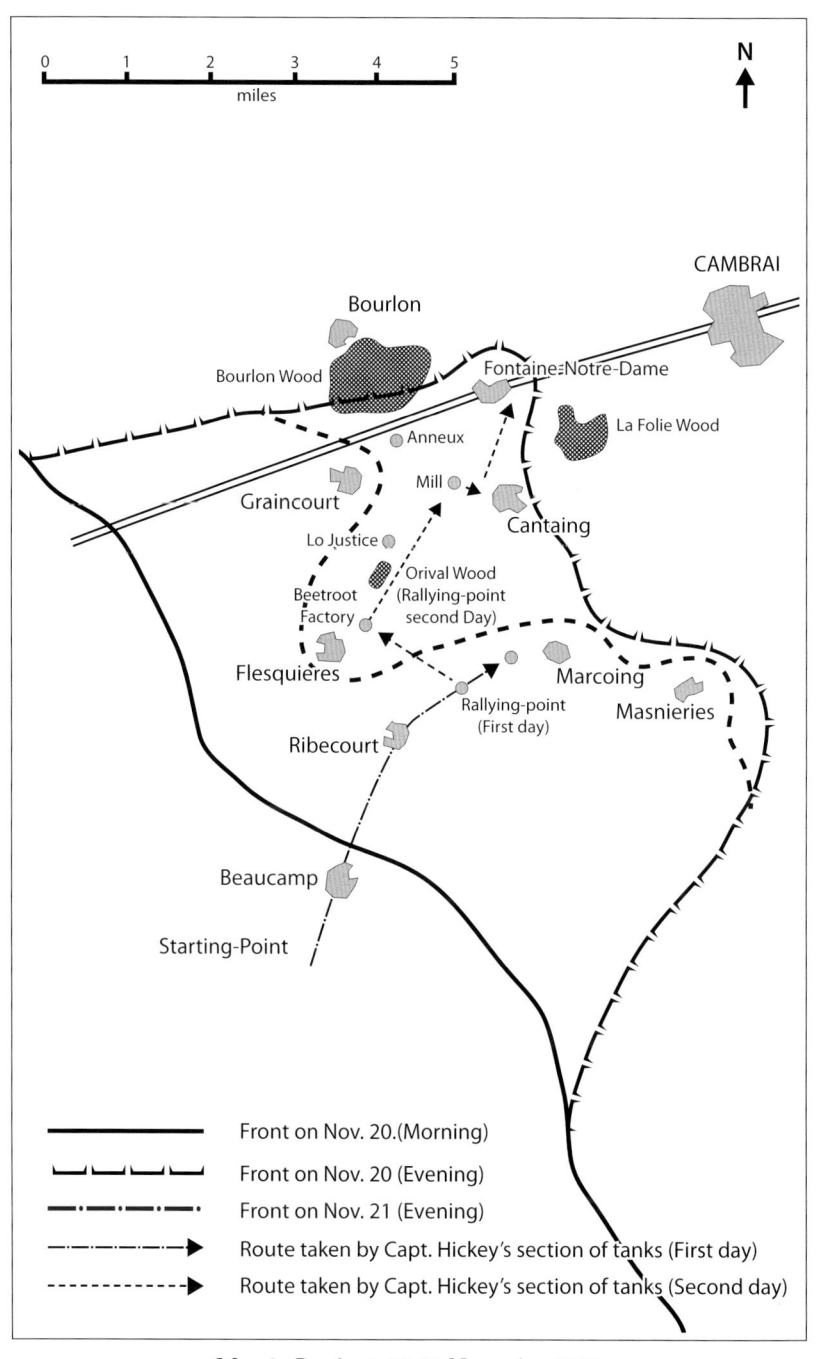

Map 8: Cambrai, 20-21 November 1917

as a result, had 'introduced a novelty into warfare' which had had a staggering effect on the enemy. It was claimed that German resistance had been light: 'They beheld, with utter stupefaction, the "tanks" looming out of the grey mist, and as amazed and bewildered a garrison as ever confessed defeat, came up from its impregnable dug-outs to surrender without firing.'[10]

On the following day, however, 30 November, the Germans launched a counter-offensive which caught the British off-guard. When the fighting finally petered out on the evening of 7 December, the German divisions involved had successfully reconquered most of the gains in ground made by the British. In terms of the conduct of the war at the highest military and political levels, the reverse at Cambrai appeared to be a serious defeat. It seemed to confirm that the British Army could not defeat the Germans, nor could it carry on losing men at the rate of 50,000 a month as it had been since September 1916.[11] Some newspaper reports on the German counter-attack appeared to try and mask the actual gravity of the new developments, such as articles which were published in the *Daily Mail* and *Daily Chronicle*.[12]

On 6 December, negative press coverage was brought to the attention of the War Cabinet. In particular, a dispatch from the Special Correspondent of the *Daily Telegraph*, which had appeared on 3 December, led to a discussion as to why the War Cabinet had not been informed of the complete surprise achieved by the Germans. The apparent disparity between official information and the scale of the surprise led to the suggestion that a 'full enquiry ought to be made'. While the enquiry was to be left up to Sir Douglas Haig, the Secretary of State for War was given the task of ensuring that Haig's reports would give the 'fullest detail possible'.[13] The first response from Haig, on the number of divisions on the Cambrai front on 30 November, was forwarded to the War Cabinet on 9 December.[14]

According to Lord Beaverbrook, in the mind of the Prime Minister, David Lloyd George, 'Haig had muddled the battle of Cambrai.' The press was allegedly only informed 'slowly and reluctantly' of the failure by GHQ. From the point of view of a leading politician the worst possible accusation which could be made towards a general was uttered: 'The public had been swindled by means of suppression and deception.'[15] The level of the initial euphoria had led to calls for an enquiry as to what

---

10 'The "Tanks" in their Greatest Victory', *Daily Graphic*, 29 November 1917, p. 1.
11 Brock Millman, *Pessimism and British War Policy 1916-1918* (London, 2001), pp. 106-8.
12 Martin J. Farrar, *News from the Front: War Correspondents on the Western Front 1914-18* (Stroud, 1998), pp. 180-88.
13 The National Archives of the United Kingdom, Kew (hereafter, TNA), CAB 21/22, fol.224, War Cabinet No. 292, 6 December 1917.
14 TNA, CAB 21/22, fol.217, Col. W. Kirke (War Office) to Secretary, War Cabinet, 9 December 1917.
15 Lord Beaverbrook, *Men and Power 1917-1918* (London, 1956), pp. 186-7.

had gone wrong.[16] The Secretary of State for War, Lord Derby, wrote to Haig on 12 December 1917 that he did not share 'the great feeling in this country' that someone had been to blame, as war would always involve ups-and-downs. At the same time, 'the public will not be satisfied if the whole affair is passed over without a full explanation'. Thus, Derby requested Haig to find out who had let him down, then to send him home.[17] The political arguments over what had gone wrong did seem to demonstrate one thing: the politicians sensed the anger of the public mood after the psychological release which the initial gains had brought following the debacle of the Third Ypres offensive.

Given the political pressure for answers, Haig sent a detailed memorandum to the War Cabinet on 24 December, which was followed on 3 January by two briefer memoranda, one from General Jan Smuts, the other from the Chief of the Imperial General Staff, Sir William Robertson.[18] A Court of Enquiry then convened at Hesdin in northern France on 21 January 1918 with the declared aim of reporting on the sequence of events and the causes of the German success. But if the politicians in London had hoped to find scapegoats through the enquiry, it seems that GHQ had little intention of adopting such an approach. In an instruction issued by Lieutenant-General Alexander Hamilton-Gordon, it was stated:

> It is… proposed to afford any person summoned as a witness an opportunity of perusing, before he gives evidence, such portions of the evidence already given as may affect him detrimentally, and a further opportunity of perusing any subsequent evidence which, in the opinion of the Court, may similarly affect him.[19]

After the evidence was gathered, the Court identified nine major factors which were seen as providing an explanation for the German success, including some fairly obvious points, such as the surprise in the outpost lines and lack of a defence in depth. In particular, it was noted that the moral effect of German low-level aircraft attacks had been considerable and out of all proportion to the actual impact of the fire delivered, while a lack of defensive doctrine was identified as an important cause of the

---

16   For the overall strategic and political background, which conditioned the way in which the recriminations unfolded in Whitehall, see David French, *The Strategy of Lloyd George's Coalition, 1916-1918* (Oxford, 1995), pp. 148-70.
17   Derby to Haig (Strictly Personal and Confidential), 12 December 1917, cited in Beaverbrook, *Men and Power*, p. 372.
18   TNA, CAB 21/22, fol. 158-76, memorandum, Sir D. Haig to CIGS, 24 December 1917, fol. 152-7, memorandum by CIGS, 3 January 1918, fol. 148-51, SECRET, War Cabinet, Cambrai Inquiry, memorandum by General Smuts (circulated with ref. to War Cab 309 Minute 8), 3 January 1918.
19   TNA, WO 158/53, fol. 14, Lt.-Gen. A. Hamilton-Gordon, GHQ, 1st Echelon, 21 January, 1918.

disaster.[20] When the report was forwarded to the Chief of the General Staff at the beginning of February, it was noted that there was little likelihood of disciplinary action arising, 'owing to the number and the nature of the causes to which the Court attributes the German success'.[21]

But the perceived slowness of the proceedings, and the failure to make public the results of the internal enquiry, led to a series of questions in the House of Commons in January and February 1918. On 15 January 1918, in responding to a question on the results of the enquiry, Bonar Law stated that the report had been examined by the Committee of Imperial Defence and a committee of the War Cabinet. It had been concluded that the High Command had not been surprised on 30 November. It was considered that an open discussion of the issue would be 'highly detrimental to the public interest'.[22] The issue was raised again in the Commons on 21 January, when a question was posed as to whether the findings had been reported to the War Cabinet or had been subject to revision by the Army Council or the Secretary of State for War. The retort by Bonar Law on behalf of the Government, that he had nothing to add to his statement of 15 January, caused one MP to ask whether the honourable gentleman was 'aware that a very great deal of dissatisfaction is being expressed outside this House as to the withholding of the result of this inquiry from the public?'[23]

Two days later Walter Roch enquired whether the Prime Minister could, bearing in mind the public interest, say who had constituted the Court of Inquiry. The response was that Sir Douglas Haig had submitted the evidence to the War Office.[24] The scale of discontent over the refusal of the Government to come clean over the enquiry was shown again a week later when another MP, Mr. Lynch, asked whether a secret sitting of the House could be organized, 'so that the truth of the Cambrai affair may be told?' The negative response by Bonar Law on behalf of the Government provoked the retort from Lynch: 'Will the right hon. Gentleman give an assurance that at least the Western Front will be as stubbornly defended as the reputations of those unsuccessful generals?'[25] The refusal of the government to be drawn received its final punctuation mark on 26 February when Colonel Sir Frederick Hall asked the Under-Secretary of State for War whether the failure to press home the advantage at Cambrai had been due to a lack of sufficient reserves and whether any request for additional men had

20 TNA, WO 158/53, fol. 3-12, Proceedings of the Court of Enquiry on the Action Fought South of Cambrai on November 30th, 1917, [sgd.] Lt.-Gen. A. Hamilton-Gordon, Cmdg IX Army Corps, n.d.
21 TNA, WO 158/53, fol. 17-18, SECRET, Adjutant-General GHQ to CGS, 2 February 1918.
22 Hansard, HC Debates, 15 January 1918, vol. 101, cc144-5.
23 Hansard, HC Debates, 21 January 1918, vol. 101, cc666-7.
24 Hansard, HC Debates, 23 January 1918, vol. 101, c977.
25 Hansard, HC Debates, 30 January 1918, vol. 101, cc1556-7.

been made to the home authorities. The reply remained the same – in other words, that nothing would be added to previous statements.[26]

The official version of the enquiry, signed by Sir Douglas Haig, was finally published on 1 March 1918. It did not go into detail on the causes of the success of the German counter-attack, which would have hardly made sense from a security point of view, but it did give due credit to the performance of the tanks on 20 November as the report began with the opening of the British offensive, which was described as a 'remarkable success'. But Haig also stated that '[m]any of the hits upon our tanks at Flesquières were obtained by a German artillery officer who, remaining at his battery, served a field-gun single-handed until killed at this gun.' When it came to the search for commanders who might have been at fault for the later reverse, Haig was in no mood to apportion blame, with General Byng praised for his 'skill and resource… throughout the Cambrai operations'. In his final comments, he sought to deflect attention from the reverse by highlighting the way in which the initial breakthrough had 'had a most inspiring moral effect on the Armies I command'.[27] But this was not very convincing. In an appendix to the proceedings of the enquiry, Lieutenant-General Ivor Maxse observed that 'the Battle of Cambrai has by now come to be regarded as a German success instead of a British victory', the cause of which had been the inadequate methods of the military in their communication of information to the public at home.[28] In fact, the public, political and internal military pressure did lead to prominent departures from GHQ: Lieutenant-General Sir Ronald Maxwell, Brigadier-General John Charteris (Haig's head of intelligence) and Lieutenant-General Sir Lancelot Kiggell. The Cambrai failure was not the sole cause of the dismissals; it had simply brought existing discontent to a head.[29]

Yet, despite the reverses caused by the German counter-attack, the initial psychological release provided by the Battle of Cambrai was not completely eradicated by the political and military repercussions. The tank had already penetrated deeply into the consciousness of the British public by this stage, as shown by the numerous visual references to the machine which had appeared in newspapers and satirical weeklies,

---

26 Hansard, HC Debates, 26 February 1918, vol. 103, c1231.
27 TNA, CAB 21/22, fol.58ff, Supplement to *The London Gazette*, dated 4 March 1918 (published 1 March 1918), Despatch from Sir Douglas Haig, GHQ, France, 20 February 1918.
28 TNA, WO 158/53, fol. 15-16, Proceedings of the Court of Inquiry, Appendix L: Comments and suggestions concerning RUMOURS by a member of the Court, [initialled] IM, n.d. Maxse proved himself as an able divisional and corps commander during the war. For his career: John Baynes, *Far From a Donkey: The Life of General Sir Ivor Maxse* (London, 1995); and, C. Barnett, rev. R.T. Stearn, 'Sir (Frederick) Ivor Maxse (1862-1958)', *Oxford Dictionary of National Biography* (online edn 2008), www.oxforddnb.com/view/article/34955.
29 Important background on this can be found in: J.P. Harris, *Douglas Haig and the First World War* (Cambridge, 2008), pp. 409-27; and, Jim Beach, *Haig's Intelligence: GHQ and the German Army, 1916-1918* (Cambridge, 2013), pp. 262-72.

such as *Punch*.³⁰ The hope which the tank seemed to offer, namely, that the British would win through against all the odds, was expressed in an interesting fashion in the *Daily Graphic* on 21 December 1917. In a cartoon, a pacifist is depicted in the foreground, looking at five black mountains; each is labelled, from left to right, 'Air Raids', 'Man Power', 'Food Problem', 'Russia's Failure' and 'U Boat Menace'. On top of the 'Man Power' mountain there is a signpost, containing the words, 'To Victory'. A tank is already climbing the mountain labelled 'U Boat Menace', on the right of the picture, at a steep angle, with a determined human face visible. The words 'British Tenacity' are painted on its side.³¹

Military Reactions during the War

In the wake of the first news of the success of 20 November, a mood of self-congratulation could be found even inside the army. On 27 November, Sir Julian Byng, writing from Third Army Headquarters to Hugh Elles stated that, for the Tank Corps, the operations of the Third Army had now come to an end. In offering his profuse thanks, he noted that the attack at Cambrai would have been impossible without tanks: 'No one could have been so well supported, so greatly helped and so consistently strengthened in the plan as I have been by you and your Staff. And no Army has ever been so splendidly led and so fully assisted as mine was by your Corps.'³² On 28 November, Major-General J.E. Capper, the Director General of the Tank Corps, issued Special Order No.7 for distribution to all ranks of the Tank Corps. It read:

> As representing the Tank Corps as a whole I desire in the name of the Corps to congratulate you and the Officers and men under your command on the great success attained by the Corps during the recent operations.
>
> The hard and constant work cheerfully endured during training and preparations, combined with the stout heart, courage and skill shewn by all ranks in action have resulted in one of the most important successes of the British Army in this Campaign.
>
> The conduct of yourself, your Staff, and all those under you have brought great honour to the Corps.

---

30 See the following cartoons: 'Tank on the Brain: Exciting Dream of Breadwinner Jones', *Punch*, 151 (18 October 1916), p. 280; 'At the Front', *Punch*, 152, 'Punch's Almanack for 1917', no pagination; cartoon, with woman telling small boy, 'Oh, you awful boy – you've left the tacks in the road, and now the tank will get a puncture', *Punch*, 153 (10 October 1917), p. 262. See also the cartoon in the *Daily Mirror*, 4 December 1917.
31 Untitled cartoon, *Daily Graphic*, 21 December 1917.
32 TMARL, Sir Hugh Elles Papers, box 1, Byng (HQ, Third Army, BEF) to Elles, 27 November 1917.

> To me personally it is a source of great pride to be the representative of such a Corps.[33]

As we know, it was a note of celebration which was premature.

Within the army, there was obvious disillusionment produced by the turnaround in the fortunes of the attack. In his regular summary of recent military operations, Colonel W.P. Blood wrote in January 1918 that the Germans had 'had no suspicion of the novel form [the attack] would take'. While the ground over which the tanks had advanced had been 'exceptionally favourable', the offensive had created a large salient, eight miles in breadth and five deep. However, the dramatic success of the first day had given rise 'to some ill-timed jubilation; and the disappointment was all the keener when the later course of the battle failed to realise the exaggerated hopes which had been entertained at the outset.' The final judgement was that the attack had been undertaken with insufficient force, probably because of the dispatch of troops to Italy, while it had prevented corresponding German troop transfers to Italy, which might have heightened the crisis there.[34] Less circumspect in his comments was an anonymous officer writing to a military newspaper, who suggested that the government had protected those who were to blame, namely, the divisional and brigade commanders on the section of the front where the Germans had attacked. He even made the accusations that these commanders were probably not regulars, but those who owed their promotion to political influence.[35]

In contrast to the disappointment on the home front caused by the German counter-attack, at Tank Corps Headquarters Cambrai became the perfect 'case study' to quote in documents. In a series of notes produced by J.F.C. Fuller on Tank Corps organization, probably just a few weeks after the battle, he collected his thoughts under the heading, 'The Utility of Tanks in the Third Army Operations'. The most important points were: there had been no preparatory bombardment, which allowed surprise; the front line had been penetrated to a depth of 10,000 yards from a base of the same distance in 24 hours; four defence lines were penetrated within 12 hours; there had been no infantry casualties prior to zero hour; there had been 'abnormally low' infantry casualties during the attack; 8,000 prisoners had been taken, together with 100 guns; and, the infantry had succeeded wherever the tanks had. The ultimate message which Fuller sought to create from the success of the first day at Cambrai was that tanks could economize manpower: personnel used in battle amounted to 690 officers and 3,500 others ranks, while at the Third Ypres battle the total number of artillery personnel had been 121,000.[36]

---

33 TMARL, Elles Papers, box 1, Special Order No. 7, 28 November 1917.
34 W.P. Blood, 'Art. 15: The Course of the War', *Quarterly Review*, 229 (January 1918), pp. 269-92, esp. 271-5.
35 'The Set-Back at Cambrai' ('Lieutenant-Colonel' to the Editor, 29 January 1918), *The Army & Navy Gazette*, 59 (2 February 1918), p. 79.
36 TMARL, Major-General J.F.C. Fuller papers, Acc. No. 1880, Private Journal of Lt.-Colonel J.F.C. Fuller, December 1917 to July 26, 1918, A1, The Utility of Tanks in the Third Army Operations, n.d. [Dec. 1917].

These basic thoughts were refined in subsequent documents in which the message was stated more explicitly. The facts were expanded to include various examples where tanks had saved the lives of infantry; and these facts were prefaced by a series of bold statements. The tank saved men and time, it had ushered in a new epoch in warfare, which represented as great a change as gunpowder or steam had in their day. One tank army, 'if skilfully directed', could defeat an entire group of armies without tanks. For a short time, the British Army would possess a weapon which could not be countered.[37] In a series of notes compiled by Fuller for a GHQ Conference on 2 March 1918, he made the point that tanks were weapons of mobility and surprise and, clearly drawing on the experience of Cambrai, argued that an essential principle for any operation was that a reserve force of tanks be kept in hand; if there was an infantry reserve, there had to be a tank reserve as well. These notes included as an appendix a reworked version of his original observations on the utility of tanks on 20 November 1917.[38] In what represented an early version of what was later to become 'Plan 1919', which called for an increase in tank production and preparations for a decisive battle, material from earlier documents was combined; it was taken to GHQ by Elles on 19 March 1918. The memorandum referred again to the lessons of Cambrai, called for wider attack frontages and included a lengthy appendix on the battle.[39]

What is also of interest is that Fuller's attention was drawn to German press comment on Cambrai. On 1 April 1918, he noted that he had read an interesting piece by a German civilian who had observed that the main lesson of Cambrai was 'surprise in all forms', but, Fuller added, 'We with our wooden headed C in C go on ignoring it.' According to the German article, 'The case of Cambrai is epoch-making. The surprise is the tactics of the future.' It was argued that the battle on a broad front, with massive artillery support, now belonged to the past. The lesson of the Battle of Cambrai was that '[s]urprise and swift movement are essential to success.'[40] However, despite all Fuller's pessimism about the abilities of the Commander-in-Chief, he did make an extract from a report by the Chief of the Imperial General Staff which had been submitted to the War Cabinet. This drew a comparison between the battles of Messines and Cambrai, coming to the conclusion that the saving in infantry casualties was quite significant when the two were compared. In essence, the CIGS had taken Fuller's arguments and made them his own. Since an independent study had

---

37 TMARL, Fuller Papers, Private Journal, A2, Tanks as Time and Man Savers, 12 December 1917.
38 TMARL, Fuller Papers, Private Journal, A15, Notes for GHQ Conference, March 2nd, 1918, n.d., with appendix, 'The utility of Tanks in the Battle of Cambrai 1917'.
39 TMARL, Fuller Papers, Private Journal, A21, SECRET, Tank Programme 1919, n.d., esp. pp. 11-12, Appendix B, Tank operations Battle of Cambrai, and Fuller diary entry, 19 March 1918.
40 TMARL, Fuller Papers, Fuller diary entry, 1 April 1918, and B14, trans. of article, Von Salaman, 'Criticism of Operations', *Vossische Zeitung*, 13 March 1918, extracted from 'Daily Review of the Foreign Press', 25 March 1918.

reached the conclusion that the savings in an infantry assault during a tank attack was 30% compared to an assault by infantry following up an artillery bombardment, he concluded that the study undertaken was 'so favourable to the tank attack that it appears to me to warrant a trial on a much larger scale.'[41]

In the wake of Cambrai, the Tank Corps gained some powerful advocates, such as Winston Churchill and Sir Tennyson D'Eyncourt, who were prepared to argue for increased tank production. Haig was much more circumspect; his worry was a looming manpower crisis and a need for infantry weapons. Although the Tank Corps won another advocate when Sir Henry Wilson became Chief of the Imperial General Staff in February 1918, some of the more ambitious schemes were washed away by the German March offensive. Still, the later successes with tanks in August 1918 owed much to ideas which emerged during Cambrai.[42]

Commemoration, Memory and History

The commemoration of the Battle of Cambrai arguably began on the day of its first anniversary. On 20 November 1918, Major-General Sir Hugh Elles, at that time still the commander of the Tank Corps in the field, issued a special order to all those under his command, the first part of which ran as follows:

1   Today is the anniversary of the CAMBRAI Battle.
2   During the memorable twelve months just elapsed, the Tank Corps, whilst undergoing laborious measures of expansion and reorganisation, has taken an honourable part in the great defensive and offensive battles of the year.
3   At CAMBRAI which marked the beginning of a definite era in method of attack and again in the defensive actions of the Spring Campaign the Tank Corps was fought practically to a standstill.
    The first counter offensive on the Western Front was led by our units on July 4th, and since that date we have had the privilege of fighting at the head of the Armies in eleven pitched battles and 26 lesser engagements.

Elles thanked all those who had fought under him, as well as the devotion of the essential engineer, training and administrative units; he concluded by looking to the future, which he thought would be met with the same spirit of patience and steadfastness.[43]

---

41 TMARL, Fuller papers, Fuller War Diary entry, 27 April 1918, B42, Extract from Report of CIGS, n.d.
42 For a survey of thinking on tanks in the British Army between Cambrai and the German spring offensive, see J.P. Harris, *Men, Ideas and Tanks: British Military Thought and Armoured Forces, 1903-1939* (Manchester, 1995), pp. 126-53.
43 TMARL, Elles papers, box 1, Special Order No. 19, by Maj.-Gen. H.J. Elles, CB, DSO, Commanding TANK CORPS in the Field, 20 November 1918.

From this moment on, the Battle of Cambrai became an event which was to be commemorated annually, not least of all because Tank Corps officers considered that it had ushered in a new era of warfare. Hence, on 20 November 1919 the first Cambrai dinner was held. The following year it was decided to formalize this through the founding of a 'Tank Corps Dinner Club', along the lines of earlier regimental dining clubs. The Chairman of the Committee was Brigadier-General Sir Hugh Elles, with the annual subscription set at 25 shillings. A general call was put out to communicate the name and address of any former member of the Corps who would be interested in joining.[44] It was laid down in the club rule book that the President of the Club was to be the Commander of the Tank Corps, the dinner would be held every year on 20 November to celebrate the anniversary of the battle, and the club would be open to 'every officer who served in the Tank Corps or its precursor organisations or who were attached to the Corps'.[45] At the second dinner, held on 20 November 1921, Winston Churchill was the guest of honour.[46]

At the Cambrai dinner on 20 November 1925, General Sir John Capper presided, while Basil Liddell Hart was invited by the Inspector-General of the Tank Corps, Colonel George M. Lindsay, on account of a positive article he had published in the *Daily Telegraph* entitled 'Fresh Light on the Battle of Cambrai' which had appeared that morning.[47] Liddell Hart was invited again the following year and took his seat at the top table next to Sir Hugh Elles; he was complimented by both Sir Ernest Swinton and Lindsay for his 'propaganda' on behalf of the tank.[48] The commemoration of Cambrai was clearly still important to him years later. Writing about the offensive into Cyrenaica in North Africa on 20 November 1941, he was quick to note the 'significant coincidence' that this had been made known to the public on 'Cambrai Day'.[49] Even for those who had not been present at the battle, its commemorative meaning remained in the mind after the outbreak of the Second World War.

Leading members of the Tank Corps played a significant role in the shaping of the historical memory of the battle, first Major Clough Williams-Ellis, in his history of the Tank Corps in 1919, then Fuller in his 'rival history'. Williams-Ellis sought to portray it as a battle apart; but one reason for this was that in the modern battle the general commanded from the rear, however at Cambrai Elles had led the tanks into action. The new tactics used, the employment of fascines to allow tanks to cross

---

44 Caird Library, National Maritime Museum, London (hereafter, NMM), Sir Eustace Tennyson D'Encourt papers, DEY/60, circular letter to Tank Corps personnel, [sgd.] Lt.-Col. F.H. Fernie, London, 1 September 1920.
45 NMM, D'Eyncourt papers, DEY/60, TANK CORPS DINNER CLUB: Rules, 1 September 1920.
46 'Tank Corps Dinner', *Daily Telegraph*, 21 Nov. 1921.
47 Liddell Hart Centre for Military Archives, King's College London (hereafter, LHCMA), Sir Basil Liddell Hart Papers, LH 11/1925/1, note on Tank Corps dinner [1925].
48 LHCMA, Liddell Hart Papers, LH 11/1926/1, diary entry, 19 November 1926.
49 B.H. Liddell Hart, *This Expanding War* (London, 1942), pp. 127-8.

wide trenches, the use of aircraft to drown out the noise of tanks moving up before the attack, all these innovations were highlighted. In addition, the action of the 'lone German gunner', who had allegedly knocked out sixteen tanks at Flesquières, was described. Of significance, too, was the employment of tanks to deal with the German counter-attack which came on 30 November, which showed that tanks were not just of use in a 'full-dress attack'.[50] Fuller repeated many of the same points in his account published the following year, concluding: 'When on November 21 the bells of London pealed forth in celebration of the victory… to their listeners they tolled out an old tactics and rang in a new – Cambrai had become the Valmy of a new epoch in war, the epoch of the mechanical engineer.'[51] Albert Stern and Ernest Swinton made many similar points, while they portrayed the War Office as the enemy of the tanks, always ready to interfere and prevent the successful employment of the new weapons. For them, Cambrai was the vindication of the claims of the pioneers. The squandering of the success was due to the myopia of others.[52]

If we consider Winston Churchill's *The World Crisis*, we find the very specific accusation that the British High Command ignored the possibilities of tank warfare up until Cambrai. Since Churchill considered that the Tank Corps had been 'mishandled' up to that moment, he let his imagination run away with him, claiming that something comparable to Cambrai could have been conducted a year earlier. This argument flew in the face of what was possible, the training and tactics required, not to mention the machines which would have been needed. Yet, his real argument was directed against the conception of the Third Ypres offensive, since Cambrai provided the signpost that alternatives could have been pursued.[53] The arguments could have been Fuller's. Yet, in *Memoirs of an Unconventional Soldier*, published in 1936, the chapter on Cambrai is remarkably restrained, despite the fact that the book itself contains several attacks on Sir Douglas Haig. The main intention appears to be the justification of the tactics used, although he does criticize the attitude of GHQ very briefly, as well as the stubbornness of the commander of the 51st Highland Division, General George M. Harper.[54]

In the battle over the history of the war, there is little doubt that Lloyd George's war memoirs occupy a special place.[55] Needless to say, he had some forthright opinions to offer on Cambrai. Certainly these remarks need to be seen within the wider

---

50 C. & A. Williams-Ellis, *The Tank Corps* (London, 1919), pp. 100-20.
51 J.F.C. Fuller, *Tanks in the Great War 1914-1918* (London, 1920), pp. 140-53, quote, 153.
52 Albert Stern, *Tanks, 1914-1918: Log-Book of a Pioneer* (London, 1919), pp. 190-6; Maj.-Gen. E.D. Swinton, 'Tanks', in *The Encyclopaedia Britannica: The New Volumes*, iii (London & New York, 12th edn, 1922), pp. 677-98, here 686.
53 Winston S. Churchill, *The World Crisis 1911-1918* (London, 1931), pp. 718-21.
54 Fuller, *Memoirs of an Unconventional Soldier*, pp. 192-219.
55 George Egerton, 'The Lloyd George War Memoirs: A Study in the Politics of Memory', *Journal of Modern History*, 60 (March 1988), pp. 54-94; and, Andrew Suttie, *Rewriting the First World War: Lloyd George, Politics and Strategy 1914-1918* (Basingstoke, 2005).

context of his interpretation of the Great War, especially in relation to his critique of the conduct of the Third Ypres offensive. Still, he follows the account offered by Fuller quite closely, with the first day characterized as 'a brilliant success'. But Lloyd George is absolutely clear that the blame for the lack of reserves at Cambrai was to be laid at the door of GHQ, although he asserts that '[i]t is generally acknowledged now that the advance was badly muddled by General Byng and that he could, even with the resources at his command, have made a much better job of it.' He is also caustic about the 'staff who were responsible for the joy-bells [who then] were ashamed to publish news of the reverse'. He was particularly angered at the way in which the War Cabinet had not been informed. For Lloyd George, the manipulations of the news by GHQ represented a last straw which had finally broken the patience of public opinion. And, he lashed out at the Court of Enquiry which had exonerated the High Command from any blame, even though they had 'prepared the plans, knowing that they had not sufficient troops, guns and aeroplanes to carry them out'. For Lloyd George, Cambrai was the final chapter in the sorry tale of the Third Ypres offensive.[56]

It is interesting to note that Lloyd George's opinions, as expressed in his memoirs, aroused anger in certain quarters of the British Army. Particularly revealing in this respect is an editorial comment published in the *Army Quarterly* in January 1937, which commented on the sixth and final volume. The editor complained that Lloyd George, who is referred to as an 'amateur strategist', had not sent any of the volumes of his memoirs to the journal for review, 'presumably because it is a military journal and therefore considered by the distinguished author to be incapable of giving an intelligent opinion upon military matters'.[57] This virulent attack provides an indication that the military establishment could still react in a cantankerous fashion to criticisms of the British High Command, even in the late 1930s. And, there can be no doubt that the events at Cambrai were an essential part of the debate over the alleged culpability of the High Command in the blood-letting on the Western Front.

The memoirs of some of the leading soldiers and politicians were, however, by no means a reflection of the general historical wisdom on the battle which emerged in the immediate post-war period. Of course, it needs to be borne in mind that the history of the war started to be written before the conflict was over. One of the several 'instant histories' to discuss Cambrai was Wilson and Hammerton's *The Great War*. In a volume published in 1918, the battle was portrayed as the brilliant conception of the Commander-in-Chief. Despite the 'later local British reverse', this could not alter 'the main result that the strategic genius of Sir Douglas Haig and the executive ability of Sir Julian Byng' had produced, which had had a significant impact on the Italian front. The lack of a decisive victory, it was asserted, 'in no way reflected upon British leadership and soldiership'. Nevertheless, the myth of the lone German gunner

---

56 David Lloyd George, *War Memoirs*, ii (London, 2 vol. edn, n.d.), Ch. 64, 'The Battle of Cambrai', pp. 2252-63, quote, 2254.
57 Editorial, 'Lloyd George's War Memoirs', *Army Quarterly*, 33 (January 1937), pp. 199-202.

was repeated; this tale was used to explain the failure of the 51st Highland Division to advance quickly enough. The successful German resistance was ascribed to bad luck with the weather and an 'abundance' of reserves arriving from Russia, while the counter-attack was played down.[58]

In one of the first, post-war, 'foundational histories' produced by John Buchan, we find a broadly accurate but largely uncritical version of events. Again, much of the credit for the plan was given to Haig: 'The mind of Haig, like that of Ludendorff, was working towards the discovery of new tactics.'[59] The battle was interpreted as an isolated test of new tactics, with their origin attributed to Sir Julian Byng working in concert with Hugh Elles. The initial success was praised, while the Germans were credited with the subsequent tactical surprise. Buchan's final verdict was that Cambrai had had no impact on the course if the war, since casualties were about even on both sides and German morale did not suffer due to their quick recovery. But, for Buchan, 'it was a brilliant feat of arms, which reflected great credit on the British troops and their commanders'.[60] As has been cogently argued, it would be unfair to accuse Buchan of writing propaganda, although what he did produce was history for the political and military establishment which was full of praise for the leadership at GHQ and designed to reassure the nation as to the sacrifices made during the war.[61]

Needless to say, the general tone of the historical writing in Britain in the first half of the 1930s was different to that of the first half of the 1920s, as illustrated by the writing of Basil Liddell Hart and C.R.M.F. Cruttwell.[62] In Liddell Hart's *The Real War*, published in 1930, his account of Cambrai differed fundamentally from that of Buchan. It was much more analytical and unsparing in criticism. The reverse of 30 November 1917 was not only highlighted, but the real complaint was the recasting of Fuller's original proposal for a 'theatrical blow' into something much bigger by Byng, yet one constructed without the necessary reserves. Furthermore, 'against expert advice', tanks attacked across the whole frontage with no tank reserves in hand. By the time of Liddell Hart's account, the historical mist surrounding the battle had started to clear as the action of the reputed lone German gunner who had knocked out sixteen tanks was dismissed as a legend. Most significant is his reference to the official

---

58   Edward Wright, 'The Cambrai Battle of Surprises', in H.W. Wilson & J.A. Hammerton (eds.), *The Great War: The Standard History of the World-Wide Conflict*, xi (London, 1918), pp. 223-60, esp. 225.
59   John Buchan, *A History of the Great War*, iv (London, 1922), p. 87.
60   Ibid., pp. 87-104, quote, 102.
61   Keith Grieves, 'Early Historical Responses to the Great War: Fortescue, Conan Doyle, and Buchan', in Brian Bond (ed.), *The First World War and British Military History* (Oxford, 1991), pp. 15-39, here, 29-37.
62   This was obviously not only due to the publication of new histories, but also to a changing social and cultural environment, as noted in Dan Todman, *The Great War: Myth and Memory* (London, 2005), pp. 17-28.

enquiry into the reverse, complaining that the troops at the front-line were blamed, rather than the commanders responsible.[63]

Cruttwell, like Liddell Hart, saw Cambrai as worthy of a short chapter in its own right in his history of the war; and, just as Liddell Hart had done, he too saw its significance in the correct tactical employment of tanks, which was then repeated successfully the following year in July and August, and the rediscovery of the lost art of surprise. He was also critical of the refusal of the commander of the 51st Highland Division to make use of proper tank-infantry cooperation and to use his local reserve on the first day. He was even critical of Haig for continuing the battle for a week without reserves. Although Cuttwell's critique could be found more between the lines of his prose than in the case of Liddell Hart, it was nonetheless still quite obvious, not least of all as he dismissed the claim that the battle had diverted reinforcements from the Italian front as unfounded.[64] As Hew Strachan has pointed out, both Liddell Hart and Cruttwell were coloured by their own experience of the war, yet they still managed to achieve a degree of objectivity.[65] Their work marked essentially the end of the dominance of uncritical, patriotic history.

Cambrai as a Factor in Military Debates

If we consider the place of Cambrai in military discussions in Britain during the interwar period, it is clear that the main route through which the battle permeated military education was through the introduction of the principles of war into the doctrine of the British Army via new provisional *Field Service Regulations* in 1920.[66] Cambrai was often used to make points about future warfare, especially the value of tanks in battle, but its most common usage was as an example to illustrate the principle of surprise. This can be seen in a lecture by an officer to the Cambridge University Officer Training Corps in the early 1920s. It was asserted that among the lessons of Cambrai was that surprise was still possible under the conditions of

---

63   B.H. Liddell Hart, *The Real War 1914-1918* (London, 1930), pp. 369-80. A subsequent newspaper account of the battle by Liddell Hart delivered the same critical message in more dramatic language. See his article, 'Sixteen Years Ago To-morrow the Tanks Broke Through', *Sunday Express*, 19 November 1933.

64   C.R.M.F. Cruttwell, *A History of the Great War 1914-1918* (Oxford, 2nd edn, 1936), pp. 467-77. On the issue of General Harper's behaviour at Cambrai, it is interesting to note that after the war he noted in a letter to Liddell Hart that the 'slow moving tank gets knocked out, and what are the infantry to do then?' Liddell Hart had underlined this sentence and added, 'Has at last learned his error at Cambrai!' LHCMA, Liddell Hart Papers, LH 7/1919/7, Harper to Liddell Hart, 6 September 1919.

65   Hew Strachan, '"The Real War": Liddell Hart, Cruttwell, and Falls', in Bond (ed.), *British Military History*, pp. 41-67.

66   On this subject, see Alaric Searle, 'Inter-service Debate and the Origins of Strategic Culture: The "Principles of War" in the British Armed Forces, 1919-1939', *War in History*, 21 (January 2014), pp. 4-32.

trench warfare; moreover, the battle had also shown the importance of cooperation between tanks, infantry and cavalry. At the same time, the battle had demonstrated that combined-arms action had not yet been mastered given the success of German artillery employed against tanks. Nonetheless, the British had understood the lessons of Cambrai better than the Germans.[67]

Cambrai as a case study in surprise during the Great War worked its way very quickly into instructional literature, with the battle considered to be 'the great strategic surprise of positional warfare' which had demonstrated the true potential of tanks when properly employed.[68] The issue of the finalized *Field Service Regulations* in 1924 led to the publication of instructional material to assist officers in preparing for examinations where reference to Cambrai could also be found. In its consideration of the principles of war, one such work cited Cambrai as an example of surprise by tactical method. The battle was the first time when tanks had been used en masse, the attacking troops were brought up by rail at the last moment and there was no preliminary bombardment. Not only was the attack a huge success, but for 'all the future battles of the war, these ideas… were the basic principles of the attacks made by both the Allies and the Germans.'[69] The early successes at Cambrai were put down, in part, to the use of smoke-shells which covered the advance of the tanks. The battle was used to illustrate the issue of the depth of objectives in an operation (the plan for Cambrai had not taken account of the enemy's reserves), as an example of the danger of flanking counter-attacks in the wake of an offensive, and as a good example of the conduct of a deliberate attack which had had only limited success due to lack of reserves and because the infantry reserves were held too far back.[70]

The battle was mentioned by Major-General W.E. Ironside during a lecture at the Royal Artillery Institution on 18 November 1923 on the subject of the development of modern weapons. In considering tanks, aircraft and transport, Ironside took a positive view of the future of tanks, although he did balance this by arguing that static anti-tank defences would still be important. Unusually for a supporter of the tank, he cited Cambrai as an example of 'sudden short range fire against tanks'.[71] Cambrai was also referred to in discussions of the future of armoured warfare. For instance, in a debate following another lecture at the Royal Artillery Institution in October 1928, Major-General H. de Pree questioned Colonel C.F.N. Broad on his views that the tank-infantry cooperation as practised during the Great War would have to be abandoned

---

67 Manuscripts Division, National Library of Scotland, Edinburgh, Acc. 8681, Further Papers of Major-General D.N. Wimberley, Item 47, Thornton, Surprise in War, lecture 1, Cambridge University OTC, n.d. [1924?]
68 Bt. Lt.-Col. Philip Neame, *German Strategy in the Great War* (London, 1923), p. 100.
69 Maj. H.G. Eady, *Historical Illustrations to the Field Service Regulations Vol. II* (London, 1926), pp. 29-30.
70 Ibid., pp. 70, 159, 167, 179-80, 199-200.
71 Maj.-Gen. Sir W.E. Ironside, 'The Development of Modern Weapons', *Journal of the Royal Artillery*, 50 (January 1924), pp. 347-57, esp. 351.

in certain circumstances. De Pree argued that if tanks became separated from the infantry, then enemy forces would wait until the tanks had passed, then would emerge to prevent the advance of the infantry, and that this had 'frequently happened at the first battle of Cambrai'.[72]

However, in addition to discussions over the lessons of the battle, Cambrai could be re-interpreted according to the opinions of a writer on the general subject of the future of the tank. This is illustrated nowhere better than in a book designed to attack the arguments of the advocates of the tank, published in 1927 under the title of *The "Mechanization" of War*.[73] Victor Germains sought to downplay the role of the tank in the Great War by arguing, first, that the Germans had launched their March 1918 offensive without tanks and had achieved success. Moreover, before this offensive, General Georg von der Marwitz had launched a 'terrific counter-stroke at Cambrai – November 30th, 1917'. He questioned whether Cambrai was the beginning of a new epoch in war, the epoch of the mechanical engineer, because other weapons, even the rifle magazine, could be considered as 'mechanisms'. He emphasized, in addition, the scale of tank casualties by the second day. Finally, he sought to attack the pro-tank school through his emphasis of the argument that the Germans had surprised the British at Cambrai without tanks.[74] What is perhaps most noteworthy is that Germains felt the need to begin his attack on the 'Fuller school' by questioning their claims about the significance of the Battle of Cambrai.

It seems difficult to reach any conclusion other than that here was a concerted attempt by a group of senior officers to attack the theories of Fuller and his supporters on the future of the tank and the need for a science of war. The key figure in this campaign was Major-General Frederick Barton Maurice, who was tasked with offering an official interpretation of the revised list of seven principles of war which the army issued as part of new field service regulations in 1929. In the chapter on the principle of surprise in his work *British Strategy*, Maurice notes that even at Cambrai, where surprise was achieved by the mass use of tanks and the lack of preliminary artillery bombardment, 'only a moderate degree of success was obtained'. That the novelty of the battle was downplayed, with its main significance identified as its part in a process of experimentation which led to the success of 8 August 1918, was in keeping

---

72 Col. C.F.N. Broad, 'Tactics of Armoured Fighting Vehicles: A Lecture delivered at the Royal Artillery Institution, on Tuesday, 23 October 1928', *Journal of the Royal Artillery Institution*, 55 (January 1929), pp. 415-37, esp. 433-5.
73 Victor Wallace Germains, *The "Mechanization" of War* (London, 1927). The work even received a form of semi-official blessing through a foreword provided by Major-General Sir Frederick Maurice, who praised Germains' 'honest discussion of problems', and took the opportunity to undermine the claims made by 'the tank experts' on what the new weapon had actually contributed to the outcome of the war. Ibid., pp. vii-xiv.
74 Ibid., pp. 1-13.

with the purpose of the book.[75] Fuller had perturbed the army by publicly making it known in print that the original eight principles of war had been his; furthermore, he had changed his mind and revised them; and, this was obviously the reason why the army sought to regain control of the principles by revising them again.[76] Maurice also dealt with the new seven principles in a series of lectures delivered at the Staff College, Camberley, in January 1930. Still, in his lecture on the principal of security, Cambrai was given as an example of boldness of action as a means of obtaining security. Likewise, in his lecture on the principle of mobility he argued that this principle was one means of achieving manoeuvre and surprise, since surprise could not be obtained solely by the use of materiel, with Cambrai given as one of the examples.[77]

Thus, even in the case of Maurice, it can be seen that Cambrai could not be ignored in any serious consideration of either the principles of war, or the changes which had occurred in warfare as a result of the tactical and technological developments in the Great War. For officers who continued to serve after the war in the armed forces, Cambrai held an enduring value whenever the question of combined arms cooperation was debated; likewise, the German counter-attack held many lessons, not least of all the use made by the Germans of close-air-support.[78] This existed completely independently of its commemorative and symbolic value for members of the Royal Tank Corps, not least of all as the use of Cambrai as a perfect example of surprise continued until the end of the interwar period.[79]

Needless to say, an investigation of the actual events of the battle proved extremely important for the 'corporate identity' of the Royal Tank Corps. The memory of Cambrai was kept alive through an annual 'staff ride' to the battlefield, the surviving notes for which provide an indication of the way in which historical investigation and the identity of the Royal Tank Corps had become closely linked. According to the notes of F.E. Hotblack,[80] the Tank Corps had stood up well to the test of the battle

---

75 Maj.-Gen. Sir F. Maurice, *British Strategy: A Study of the Application of the Principles of War* (London, 1929), p. 207.
76 Searle, 'Inter-service Debate', pp. 16-19.
77 NMM, Vice-Admiral Thomas Hope Troubridge Papers, TRO/401/21, Item 3, Maj.-Gen. Sir Frederick Maurice Barton, Senior and Junior Divisions, Principles of War III, The Principle of Security, lecture script, Staff College, Camberley, January 1930, Item 5, Maj.-Gen. F.B. Maurice, Senior and Junior Division, Principles of War V, Principle of Mobility, lecture script, n.d. [1930].
78 Maj.-Gen. H. de Pree, 'The Cooperation of Tanks with Other Arms at the Battle of Cambrai, November, 1917', *Army Quarterly*, Part I, 29 (October 1934), pp. 18-29, Part II, 29 (January 1935), pp. 219-31; and, Maj. Oliver Stuart, 'Air Forces in the Great War: Some Strategical Lessons', *RUSI Journal*, 79 (May 1934), pp. 289-93, here, 290.
79 Maj.-Gen. H. Rowan-Robinson, *Imperial Defence: A Problem in Four Dimensions* (London, 1938), pp. 17, 74, 77.
80 Frederick Elliot Hotblack (1887-1979) transferred to the Heavy Branch, Machine-Gun Corps in 1916, winning the DSO in November of that year. He was a key figure in the intelligence and reconnaissance work carried out in the British Tank Corps. He later

and emerged strengthened from it. One of the main effects of the battle had been that the infantry became convinced of the value of tanks; previously, many had seen abandoned tanks which could not be salvaged, so they held negative associations when they saw them. It was noted that prisoners had talked before the offensive opened, which had allowed the local German commander to take precautionary measures, although the opening day of the battle was extremely successful. Fuller is credited with having had the vision necessary for the development of many of the ideas upon which the plan for Cambrai was based. The message which was communicated on the staff rides was of the significance of the battle as a symbol of Tank Corps qualities; while future conditions would be very different, the qualities present at Cambrai – vision, resource, fitness, courage and an unselfish team spirit – would solve future problems.[81] What is particularly striking about the documents for the staff ride was the extensive use made of the German official histories, which provided valuable information as the British account of Cambrai was not to be completed until 1949.[82]

It is interesting to note from the information drawn up for the staff ride that further elements which made up the ethos of the Tank Corps were linked to Cambrai. High morale at the battle, despite some terrible set-backs during 1917, was attributed to the system of individual training which had expanded during the war in the British Expeditionary Force. At the same time, Fuller had quickly introduced the philosophy of Sir John Moore into the Tank Corps whereby the men were treated as well as possible under the circumstances. Between December 1916 and June 1917, the Corps had also been able to train for an uninterrupted period. On the other hand, as a new corps, Cambrai 'had the effect of weeding out the less desirable elements that were still left among regimental officers and men'. Cambrai was seen as the final stage in a process which saw an essentially civilian body of volunteer soldiers turned into a new corps. Finally, the battle was interpreted in another interesting fashion: 'Each Tank played a lone hand and fought an individual action, and yet if one crew failed to play its part it might spell disaster to everyone concerned.'[83] The feeling of individual battles being fought as part of a larger whole was integral to the investment of Cambrai with the values of the new tank force.

    served as military attaché in Berlin (1935-7) and became Deputy Director of Staff Duties at the War Office in 1937. He was invalided out of the army in 1941.
81 TMARL, MH.3. 355.48.3, Cambrai 20.11.1917, box 2, War Office (RTC) Cambrai Battlefield Tour, compiled by F.E. Hotblack, 25-29 March 1935, pp. 2-3, 10-11, 23, 30.
82 Capt. Wilfred Miles, *Official History of the Great War. Military Operations: France and Belgium 1917. Volume III: The Battle of Cambrai* (London: HMSO, 1949).
83 TMARL, Cambrai, box 2, War Office (RTC) Cambrai Battlefield Tour, pp. 38-43, quote, 43.

The German View of Cambrai

Of course, it cannot be forgotten that reactions in Britain to the Battle of Cambrai, as well as its historical treatment, memory and discussion in military debates, played its part in influencing German reflections on the battle. However, initially, the account provided by Erich Ludendorff in his memoirs exerted a negative effect. The few brief remarks offered centred on the difficulties he had faced in moving reserves to counter the breach in the German lines. At the same time, he heightened the sense of drama through his assertion that the British military leaders had failed to exploit their huge early success. Essential in the containment of the break-in was the presence of the 107th Infantry Division which had just arrived from Russia. The counter-attack he considered a remarkable success because it had been undertaken with troops who had been engaged in heavy fighting beforehand; but the scale of the success was reduced by a division which failed to advance because it had started to plunder an enemy supply depot.[84]

What is noteworthy here is that Ludendorff's account appeared to influence the way in which German military debates in the 1920s largely ignored the spectre of the Battle of Cambrai. While Ludendorff had an interest in playing up the difficulties he had faced in order to heighten the sense of German achievement in mastering another crisis, the attack presented a significant challenge to explanations as to why they had lost the war, since it raised questions about why Germany had failed to prioritise tank design in 1917. Discussion of such issues might also have challenged Ludendorff's 'stab-in-the-back' thesis.[85] Perhaps for this reason, early German debates on the employment of tanks avoided not only mention of Cambrai but also the overall significance of tanks in the war.[86] This can be seen in some of the early studies of tank warfare to be published in Germany by the first authority on the subject, Ernst Volckheim. His first book, and also his early journal articles, concentrated on tactics, technology, organization and training, yet without making any explicit reference to the employment of tanks in the Great War.[87]

---

84 Erich Ludendorff, *Meine Kriegserinnerungen 1914-1918* (Berlin, 1919), pp. 394-7.
85 Useful for general context here is Roger Chickering, 'Sore Loser: Ludendorff's Total War', in Roger Chickering & Stig Förster (eds.), *The Shadows of Total War: Europe, East Asia, and the United States, 1919-1939* (Cambridge, 2003), pp. 151-78.
86 For historical context and background on early German armour developments, see James S. Corum, *The Roots of Blitzkrieg: Hans von Seeckt and German Military Reform* (Lawrence, KS, 1992).
87 Ernst Volckheim, *Der Kampfwagen in der heutigen Kriegführung. Organisation, Verwendung und Bekämpfung* (Berlin, 1924); idem, 'Betrachtungen über Kampfwagen-Organisation und -Verwendung', *Wissen und Wehr*, 5 (May 1924), pp. 359-73; and, idem, 'Kampfwagen und Abwehr dagegen', *Wissen und Wehr*, 6 (May 1925), pp. 309-20. Articles by other authors which considered tanks in a future war also avoided mentioning any employment of tanks in the war. See, for example: 'Zukunftskrieg und Motorisierung', *Wissen und Wehr*, 7 (May 1926), pp. 294-308; and, Oberstleutnant a.D. v. Seißer, 'Einfluß der Motorisierung

Part of the reserve towards the Battle of Cambrai was broken when volume 31 of the series 'Battles of the World War' was published in 1929 with the title, 'The Tank Battle at Cambrai, 20-29 November 1917'. In order to understand why this volume was less interested in the details of the German counter-attack, it is necessary to make a brief excursion into the thinking behind this particular series.[88] While the control of the German official history of the war had been subject to constant bureaucratic and political battles, the traditional General Staff approach remained largely undisputed and meant that few veterans would be likely to read it. So, it was decided that a series of much shorter and more readable individual volumes would be published which would reflect the experience of the men at the front rather than simply an overview of grand strategy. The series ran to 36 volumes, although publication ceased in 1931. While the intention was clearly to give expression to the heroism of the frontline soldier, the chief architect of the series, George Soldan, argued that lost battles should also be included because the reader had the right to discover the causes of the German defeat and to draw lessons for the future.[89]

In the volume on Cambrai an impressive narrative of the battle was offered, based on extremely detailed research in German Army war diaries, which offered detail down to regimental level, including the names of commanders and individual officers, as well as the casualties sustained by individual units. The British plans were described, based on post-war publications by Fuller and others, while the German counter-attack and its preparations were sketched out. The historical significance of the battle was seen in the fact that it was a 'tank battle', even if this battle had no immediate strategic impact on the course of the war. Yet there was significance for the further war effort, given the unique offensive achievements of the British tanks on the first day. Finally, it was suggested between the lines that because the counter-attack had succeeded in preventing a serious disaster, the true threat of tanks in the following year of the war had been underestimated.[90] The implications of the battle as explained by the author were obviously understood by one reviewer of the book writing in a German military journal. He agreed that the British High Command had committed serious errors,

---

der Kampftruppen auf die Operationen und die Kampfführung', *Wissen und Wehr*, 8 (July 1927), pp. 385-403.

88 Hauptmann a.D. Georg Strutz, *Die Tankschlacht bei Cambrai 20.-29. November 1917* (Oldenburg / Berlin, 1929), Schlachten des Weltkrieges Band 31.

89 Markus Pöhlmann, *Kriegsgeschichte und Geschichtspolitik: Der Erste Weltkrieg. Die amtliche deutsche Militärgeschichtsschreibung 1914-1956* (Paderborn, 2002), pp. 194-202.

90 Strutz, *Tankschlacht bei Cambrai*, passim, but esp. pp. 178-83. It is interesting to note that Strutz had written to the Historical Section of the Committee of Imperial Defence, asking for the name of the German officer who had reputedly destroyed 16 tanks at Flesquières, but was told he had not been identified. Ibid., p. 48. This passage was noted by Hotblack in his notes for the Cambrai staff ride. TMARL, Cambrai, box 2, War Office (RTC), Cambrai Battlefield Tour, p. 18.

but argued that if these were not repeated it was obvious that the tank would play a major role in future warfare.[91]

The volume on Cambrai seemed to break what had been a form of self-imposed censorship, so that in the 1930s the battle was referred to in the wider debate on tank warfare. Significant was the treatment in a book by the Austrian officer Ludwig Ritter von Eimannsberger, *Der Kampfwagenkrieg*, published in 1934, which paid close attention to the historical experience of the Great War. His account of Cambrai was detailed and perceptive. He described the British preparations and attack in detail and noted that the British Tank Corps knew the battle would decide their future. While he was clear in his mind that the breakthrough on the morning of 20 November was an outstanding success, he asked why the British High Command had given the attack such ambitious goals. He argued that while the British had been able to break through the German line they had not been able to turn an initial success into a victory.[92] But the rather sceptical tone of Eimannsberger was to be replaced by more positive interpretations two years later: Heinz Guderian noted that Cambrai was viewed by Germany's opponents as 'the birth of a new weapon', while Walther Nehring suggested that the development of armoured ships might be mirrored in the development of the tank, with Cambrai 1917 as the starting point.[93]

In the wake of these varying assessments, an article in the General Staff journal *Militärwissenschaftliche Rundschau* published in mid-1939 confirmed that German military thought had now come to see Cambrai as possessing considerable lessons for the future. The author characterized Cambrai as an attack which employed surprise in three ways: tanks were used *en masse* for the first time, there was no heavy artillery preparation before the attack, with the infantry following behind the tanks, while the attack was to be launched on a quiet area of the front with weak defensive forces. It was concluded on the basis of the details of the battle that one of the lessons was that, in the future, it would not be advisable to mass tanks so close to the battlefront and within range of enemy artillery: this had been necessary at Cambrai due to the slow speed of the Mark IV tank. One of the causes of success had been, however, the excellent reconnaissance of the ground; at the same time, the failure to reconnoitre the position of German batteries at Flesquières had led to considerable tank losses. It was highlighted that tanks could not achieve victories without support from other arms, although it was argued that it was exclusively the result of the employment of tanks that such remarkable successes had been achieved within a few hours on 20 November 1917, even if warnings were sounded about the limitations of tanks in villages and

---

91 "S.", 'Die Tankschlacht von Cambrai', *Deutsche Wehr*, No. 37 (2 October 1929), pp. 812-3.
92 Gen.d.Art. i.R. Ludwig Ritter von Eimannsberger, *Der Kampfwagenkrieg* (Munich, 1934), pp. 7-24.
93 Oberst [Heinz] Guderian, 'Kraftfahrkampftruppen', *Militärwissenschaftliche Rundschau*, 1, Heft 1 (1936), pp. 52-77, here 59-61; Oberstleutnant [Walther] Nehring, 'Panzerabwehr', *Militärwissenschaftliche Rundschau*, 1, Heft 2 (1936), pp. 182-203, here 202.

towns in which anti-tank weapons had much greater opportunities to make use of camouflage.[94]

The article contains some other, quite remarkable, judgements on the significance of the battle, not least of all the fact that Cambrai was the first mass employment of tanks in history. The fact that no previous experience could be called on explained the rather schematic tactics used, but also the limited goals of the attack. That the success of the tanks was not exploited to the full extent was the fault of the higher command, not the tanks. The question was posed whether a repeat success would be possible today. Here the opportunity was taken to dispense with the common argument against the tank in the interwar period – in effect that the increase in the power of anti-tank weapons had made the tank more vulnerable – by noting that the capabilities of tanks had likewise increased. It was concluded that it would be a mistake to interpret the battle at Cambrai purely as a German defensive success because this might lead to incorrect lessons. The tanks had reached their offensive goals and, in some cases, exceeded them.[95] This detailed consideration of Cambrai was, in many ways, not surprising given that it complemented the increased interest in surprise which had emerged in German military literature in the 1930s.[96]

In fact, by the outbreak of the Second World War, German military thought had ceased to play down of the Battle of Cambrai because the tank had in great measure been acknowledged as a weapon of decision in future conflict. In a survey of the development of tank warfare, published in 1939, Major Ernst Volckheim noted that, at the time of the Cambrai attack the Germans did not have any organized anti-tank defence, but afterwards Crown Prince Rupprecht had issued a series of instructions as to how future tank assaults could be combatted. Furthermore, even if the first attack by British tanks in September 1916 had come as a complete surprise, it had been the Battle of Cambrai which had provided the evidence that Germany needed its own tanks. He even suggested that had tanks been available in greater numbers, they might have turned the tide of the war in the Germans' favour.[97]

---

94 Maj. Eduard Müller, 'Der englische Panzerangriff bei Cambrai am 20.11.1917 und seine Lehren für die Gegenwart', *Militärwissenschaftliche Rundschau*, 4, Heft 3 (1939), pp. 389-409.
95 Ibid.
96 See, for instance, Gen.d.Inf. a.D. [Georg] Wetzell, 'Operative und taktische Überraschungen', *Militär-Wochenblatt*, No.6 (1937), col. 313-7, and Generalleutnant Waldemar Erfurth, *Die Überraschung im Kriege* (Berlin, 1938), both of which do not give the Battle of Cambrai as an example of surprise.
97 Maj. Ernst Volckheim, 'Die deutsche Panzerwaffe', in Gen.d.Inf. a.D. [Georg] Wetzell (ed.), *Die deutsche Wehrmacht 1914-1939: Rückblick und Ausblick* (Berlin, 1939), pp. 293-338, esp. 294-5, 314-6.

Conclusion

To sum up, we have seen that the immediate reactions to the Battle of Cambrai, and the subsequent debate over its historical and military significance, tell us much about the history of the tank in Britain during and after the Great War. The euphoria with which the initial success was greeted, with the ringing of church bells, was at one level certainly – as later asserted by Ernest Swinton in his memoirs – a form of emotional release from the disasters of 1917.[98] The sorry tale of the enquiry into the German counter-attack was not, however, the end of the story. The tank had so gripped the imagination of the British public that it is hard to conceive that a battlefield success without tanks would have unleashed such enthusiasm. The tank continued to symbolize for many on the home front British inventiveness, unorthodoxy and stoicism, which would ultimately defeat the militarily better drilled German Army.

For members of the Tank Corps, the Cambrai battle quickly established itself as the perfect piece of 'evidence' which could be used to argue for the effectiveness of the tank, its potential, its war-winning capacities and the need for it to be employed correctly. The use of Cambrai as a symbol was carried on into the Second World War by former Tank Corps members. For J.F.C. Fuller, writing in November 1941, on 20 November 1917, 'it was not numbers of men which won us a startling success; instead, it was a novel tactical idea'. To win this war, it would be once again not numbers, but a new idea which would have to be used.[99] In his 1942 Lees Knowles Lectures at Trinity College, Cambridge, Major-General George M. Lindsay commented that Cambrai 1917 had been a success of the unorthodox over the orthodox mind. It had marked a new epoch in the history of warfare. It was the moment of birth for *Blitzkrieg* – 'Twenty-one years later it had reached manhood.'[100]

In the public battle over the history of the Great War, the events at Cambrai represented for Lloyd George further proof of his contentions about the incompetence of Haig and the higher British commanders at Third Ypres. The close connection between Cambrai and Third Ypres continued after 1945 in the controversy over the official history. It was perhaps fitting that the study of Cambrai followed closely on the heels of the 'Passchendaele' volume, which had quickly generated controversy in the reviews. So much so, that the editors of the *Listener*, in which Basil Liddell Hart had published a cutting review of the book, felt it politic to publish his review of the Cambrai volume anonymously. Liddell Hart approved of the message of the work, namely, that the 'real importance of the Cambrai offensive lay, not in what it achieved but in what it foreshadowed, by demonstrating how surprise could be reintroduced

---

98 Maj.-Gen. Sir Ernest D. Swinton, *Eyewitness* (London, 1932), p. 313.
99 J.F.C. Fuller, *Machine Warfare* (London, n.d. [1942]), p. 17.
100 Maj.-Gen. George M. Lindsay, *The War on the Civil and Military Fronts* (London, 1942), p. 16.

into warfare'. He attempted to defend Sir Julian Byng, in particular he thought he deserved credit for understanding the potential of the new style of attack, as he had been criticized strongly by Sir James Edmonds in his preface. For Liddell Hart, this was because there was still a tendency among certain individuals to try and defend Sir Douglas Haig.[101]

The appearance of Captain Wilfred Miles' volume on Cambrai did, arguably, usher in a new phase in the treatment of the battle. With the appearance of the first reviews, the battle had now *finally* become history – and the object of *historical* controversy and debate. The memories and symbolism of the battle developed by its architects and witnesses were now fading as it slipped from the view of the professional soldier and more into the field of vision of the historian. Yet, the interest in a letter from the first day of the battle which could be created, even in March 1962, shows that the memory, commemoration and symbolism of the Battle of Cambrai always lay very close together throughout the twentieth century.

---

101 LHCMA, Liddell Hart Papers, 10/1949/4-5, which includes both reviews, with the review of the Miles' volume in *The Listener*, 25 August 1949, pp. 325-6, but also Liddell Hart's original manuscript which identifies him as the review's author.

Select Bibliography

Beach, Jim, 'British Intelligence and German Tanks, 1916-1918', *War in History*, 14 (2007), pp. 454-75.
Browne, D.G., *The Tank in Action* (London: Wm. Blackwood, 1920).
Bullock, David, *Armoured Units of the Russian Civil War: Red Army* (Oxford: Osprey, 2006).
Chamberlain, Peter & Chris Ellis, *Making Tracks: British Carrier Story 1914 to 1972* (Windsor, Berks.: Profile Publications, 1973).
Childs, David, *A Peripheral Weapon? The Production and Employment of British Tanks in the First World War* (Westport, Conn., & London: Greenwood, 1999).
Cooper, Bryan, *The Ironclads of Cambrai* (London: Souvenir Press, 1967).
Dutil, Léon, *Les Chars d'Assaut. Leur Création et leur Rôle pendant la Guerre* (Paris: Berger-Levrault, 1919).
Fletcher, D.J., 'The Origins of Armour', in J.P. Harris & F.N. Toase (eds.), *Armoured Warfare* (London: Batsford, 1990), pp. 5-26.
Fletcher, David, *Landships: British Tanks in the First World War* (London: HMSO, 1984).
Fletcher, David, *British Mark I Tank 1916* (Oxford: Osprey, 2004).
Fletcher, David, *Mark V Tank* (Oxford: Osprey, 2011).
Fletcher, David, *British Mark IV Tank* (Oxford: Osprey, 2012).
Fox, Paul, '"A New and Commanding Breed": German Warriors, Tanks and the Will to Battle', *War & Society*, 30 (March 2011), pp. 1-23.
Fuller, J.F.C., *Tanks in the Great War 1914-1918* (London: John Murray, 1920).
Fuller, J.F.C., *Memoirs of an Unconventional Soldier* (London: Ivor Nicolson & Watson, 1936).
Gale, Tim, *The French Army's Tank Force and Armoured Warfare in the Great War: The Artillerie Spéciale* (Farnham: Ashgate, 2013).
Gudmundsson, Bruce I., *On Armour* (Westport, Conn., & London: Praeger, 2004).
Greenhalgh, Elizabeth, 'Technology Development in Coalition: The Case of the First World War Tank', *International History Review*, 22 (December 2000), pp. 806-836.
Harris, J.P., *Men, Ideas and Tanks: British Military Thought and Armoured Forces, 1903-1939* (Manchester: Manchester UP, 1995).

Harris, J.P., 'Haig and the Tank', in Brian Bond & Nigel Cave (eds.), *Haig: A Reappraisal 70 Years On* (Barnsley: Pen & Sword, 1999), pp. 145-54.

Liddell Hart, B.H., *The Tanks: The History of the Royal Tank Regiment and its predecessors, Heavy Branch Machine-Gun Corps, Tank Corps and Royal Tank Corps. Volume One: 1914-1939* (London: Cassell, 1959).

Martel, Giffard le Q., *In the Wake of the Tank: The First Fifteen Years of Mechanization in the British Army* (London: Sifton Praed, 1931).

Miles, Capt. Wilfred, *History of the Great War. Military Operations, France and Belgium, 1917: The Battle of Cambrai* (London: HMSO, 1948).

Milsom, John F., *Russian Tanks, 1900-1970* (London: Arms and Armour, 1970).

Pidgeon, Trevor, *The Tanks at Flers: An Account of the First Use of Tanks in War at the Battle of Flers-Courcelette, the Somme, 15th September 1916* (Cobham: Fairmile, 1995).

Ramspacher, E.-G., *Le general Estienne 'père de chars'* (Paris: Charles-Lavauzelle, 1983).

Stern, Albert, *Tanks 1914-1918: Log-Book of a Pioneer* (London: Hodder & Stoughton, 1919).

Swinton, Ernest D., *Eyewitness: Being the Personal Reminiscences of Certain Phases of the Great War, Including the Genesis of the Tank* (London: Hodder & Stoughton, 1932).

Swinton, Ernest D., 'Tanks', in *The Encyclopaedia Britannica: The New Volumes*, vol. iii (London & New York: Encyclopaedia Britannica, 12th edn, 1922), pp. 677-98.

Travers, Tim, 'Could the Tanks of 1918 Have Been War-Winners for the British Expeditionary Force?' *Journal of Contemporary History*, 27 (1992), pp. 389-405.

Travers, Tim, *How the War Was Won: Command and Technology in the British Army, 1917-1918* (London: Routledge, 1992).

Volckheim, Lt. [Ernst], *Der Kampfwagen in der heutigen Kriegführung: Organisation, Verwendung und Bekämpfung. Ein Handbuch für alle Waffen* (Berlin: E.S. Mittler, 1924).

Volckheim, Maj. Ernst, 'Die deutsche Panzerwaffe', in Gen.d.Inf. a.D. Georg Wetzell (ed.), *Die Deutsche Wehrmacht 1914-1939. Rückblick und Ausblick* (Berlin: E.S. Mittler, 1939), pp. 293-338.

Wells, H.G., 'The Land Ironclads', *Strand Magazine*, December 1903, pp. 751-64.

Wells, H.G., *War and the Future: Italy, France and Britain at War* (London: Cassell, 1917).

Williams-Ellis, Major Clough & A[mabel]. Williams-Ellis, *The Tank Corps* (London: Country Life, 1919).

Wilson, Dale E., *Treat 'Em Rough! The Birth of American Armour, 1917-1920* (Novato, CA: Presidio, 1990).

Windrow, Martin & Gerry Embleton, *Tank and AFV Crew Uniforms since 1916* (Cambridge: Patrick Stephens, 1979).

Wright, Patrick, *Tank: The Progress of a Monstrous War Machine* (London: Faber & Faber, 2000).

Zaloga, S.J., *The Renault FT Light Tank* (London: Osprey, 1988).

Zaloga, S.J., *German Panzers 1914-18* (Oxford: Osprey, 2006).

Index

Administration of the Armoured Forces of the Red Army, establishment of 187
Aberlard (philosopher) 50, 113
Allied Tank Factory, see Neuvy Pailloux
Aisne, Battle of (Sept. 1914) 34
Amiens, Battle of (Aug. 1918) 51-2, 122-4, 154, 156, 158, 160
Anti-tank, mines 131
Anti-tank, defence 130-3
Archangel (N Russia) 176, 178, 184-5, 187-8, 190
Armoured car, Austro-Daimler 25
Arras, Battle of (Apr.-May 1917) 41, 119, 124, 136, 143, 145, 148-50, 152
Artillerie Spéciale 61-2, 73-5, 192
Artois Offensive (Sept.-Nov. 1915) 58
Asquith, Herbert 6
Assault Artillery 61, 78-9

Baden-Powell, Robert 114
Baker-Carr, Col. Christopher 43, 141
Balkan War (1912-13) 59
Bauer, Col. Max 83
Beaverbrook, Lord 215
Benz, Karl 16
Berry-au-Bac, Battle of (Apr.-May 1917) 67, 74
Beutepanzer, see Tanks, captured machines
Bird, Brig.-Gen. W.D. 164
Blood, Col. W.P. 220
Boissin, Commandant 193
Bonar Law, Andrew 217
Bossut, Major Louis-Marie 73
Boucher, Arthur 24
Boudon, Lt. 204-5
Bovington Camp, Dorset 173
Bremer, Hugo 85
Breton, Jules-Louis 63, 193
Brillié, Eugène 60
Broad, Col. C.F.N. 228

Brown, Pte. John 141
Browne, Douglas 117
Buchan, John 116, 226
Burstyn, Gunther 3, 28
Butler, Lt.-Gen. Sir Richard 159
Byng, Gen. Sir Julian 48, 211, 219, 225-6, 237

Cambrai, Battle of (Nov.-Dec. 1917) 6, 50, 121-2, 126, 128, 131-2, 135, 145, 147-54, 210-237
Capper, Gen. Sir John E. 212, 219, 223
Castelnau, Gen. Noël Édouard de 60
Champagne, Battle of (Sept. 1918) 205
Champagne Offensive (Sept.-Nov. 1915) 58
Chanoine, Capt. 196
Charrington, Lt.-Col. Sydney 149
Charteris, Brig.-Gen. John 112, 115, 218
Chaubès, Major Louis 72
Churchill, Maj. E.F. 159
Churchill, Winston S. 4, 6, 222-4
Clemenceau, Georges 74, 79
Communication, tank-to-tank 139-40, 143-4, 154-5
Communication, tanks and other arms 140-1, 145, 148, 155-8
Communication, tanks and HQ 141, 148-52, 159-61
Congreve, Lt.-Gen. Sir Walter 141
Cruttwell, C.R.M.F. 226-7

Daimler, Gottlieb 16
Denikin, Gen. Anton 171, 173-5, 180, 184-5
Derby, Lord 216
D'Alincourt, Commandant 196-7
D'Eyncourt, Sir Tennyson 222
Diesel, Rudolf 16
Doumenc, Col. Joseph-Aimé 62

Drocourt-Quéant Line, attack on (Sept. 1918) 52, 158
Dundas, Lt.-Col. R.W. 210
Dutil, Léon 192-3

Edmonds, Brig.-Gen. Sir James 237
Egyptian Expeditionary Force (EEF) 164-6
Eimannsberger, Ludwig Ritter von 234
Elles, Brig.-Gen. Sir Hugh 4, 40, 55, 164-5, 212, 219, 222-3, 226
Erhardt anti-balloon-gun 25
Erin, Central Workshops (France) 150
Estienne, Gen. J.E.B. 5, 57, 59-64, 69-71, 74, 78-79, 193-4, 196-200

Ferrus, Maj. 60, 193, 196
Ferry, Abel 79
Field Service Regulations (1909), British Army 32
Field Service Regulations (1920), British Army 227
Field Service Regulations (1924), British Army 228
Field Service Regulations (1929), British Army 229
Flers-Courcelette, Battle of (Sept. 1916) 47, 139-40, 142, 162
Fouché, Second-Lt. Charles 65
Franco, Francisco 206
Franco-Prussian War (1870-71) 29
French Campaign (1940) 11, 209
Fuller, Col. (later, Maj.-Gen.) J.F.C. 3, 6-8, 22, 37-8, 49-50, 108, 110, 121, 127, 144-5, 158, 161, 220-1, 224-6, 229, 233, 236

Gaza, Second Battle of (Apr. 1917) 164, 166-9, 188-9
Gaza, Third Battle of (Nov. 1917) 164, 169-71, 188-9
Gekker, A.I. 183
Germains, Victor 229
Glasgow, tanks for crowd control in 10
Goebel, Friedrich 27
Guderian, Col.-Gen. Heinz 161-2, 234

Haig, Field-Marshal Sir Douglas 3, 48, 212, 215-8, 224-6, 236
Hall, Col. Sir Frederick 217
Hamel, Battle of (July 1918) 155
Hamilton-Gordon, Lt.-Gen. Alexander 216

Hardress-Lloyd, Brig.-Gen. John 154-5
Harper, Maj.-Gen. George M. 148, 224, 227
Heavy Branch Machine-Gun Corps (British Army) 108, 149, 164
Hindenburg Line, attack on (Sept. 1918) 52
Hindenburg, Paul von 14, 91
Hofmann, Prof. 86
Hohenborn, Adolf Wild von 84
Hope-Carson, Lt.-Col. E. 175
Hoppenstedt, Julius 24
Horch, *Direktor* 86
Hotblack, Capt. F.E. 50, 111-3, 116-7, 127, 129, 135, 140, 230-1, 233
Hubert, *sous-lieutenant* 193
'Hundred Days Campaign' (8 Aug.-11 Nov. 1918) 7, 53-54, 135, 154, 158-60

Inter-Allied Tank Committee 5
Intelligence, Tank Corps, British Army 109-11, 114-8, 124-35
Ironside, Maj.-Gen. W.E. 228

Janin, Gen. Maurice 60
Joffre, Gen. (later Marshal) Joseph 60, 62, 65, 68, 193-4
Junck, *Kommerzienrat* 86

Kabisch, Gen. Ernst 14
Kakhovka, Battle of (Oct. 1920) 182-3
Kalinovskiy, K.B. 182
Kenotkenich, Col. 178
Kerensky Government 173, 196
Kiggell, Lt.-Gen. Lancelot 48, 218
Kolchak, Admiral Alexander V. 190
Kriegstechnische Zeitschrift (military journal) 27
Krim, Abd-el 206
Kuhl, Lt.-Gen. Hermann von 14

Lefebvre, Maj. Hubert 72
Leigh-Mallory, Maj. Trafford 158
Leisse, Capt. 193
Lenin, V.I. 179
Liddell Hart, Capt. B.H. 164, 171, 223, 226-7, 236-7
Lincoln tank factory 194
Lindsay, Maj.-Gen. George M. 223, 236
Link, *Oberingenieur* 86
Lloyd George, David 41, 215, 224-5, 236
Loos, Battle of (Sept.-Oct. 1915) 138

Loucheur, Luois 198-200
Ludendorff, Gen. Erich 14, 91, 96, 226, 232
Lynch, A.A. (MP) 217

Malmaison, Battle of (Oct. 1917) 75, 201
Mandelberg, Sir Charles 10
Marly-le-Roi, training centre 62
March offensive (Mar. 1918) 164, 222
Marwitz, Gen. Georg von der 229
Matz, Battle of (June 1918) 76
Maurice, Maj.-Gen. F.B. 229-30
Maxse, Lt.-Gen. Sir Ivor 218
Maxwell, Lt.-Gen. Sir Ronald 218
Mercier, Col. 200
Messines, Battle of (June 1917) 120, 135, 145
Miles, Capt. Wilfred 237
Military innovation 16-22
Militär-Wochenblatt (military journal) 19, 26
Mitchell, Lt. Frank 139
Mole, L.E. de 3
Molesworth, Lt.-Col. J.D.N. 153
Monash, Lt.-Gen. Sir John 157-8
Monhoven, Col. Jean 62, 75
Montdidier, Battle of (Aug. 1918) 205
Moore, Sir John 231
Moreuil, Battle of (July 1918) 5
Morval, Battle of (Sept. 1916) 140
Moscow
Motor-Tank Units, Red Army 179-80, 187
Moulin de Laffaux, Battle of (May 1917) 74
Mourret, Gen. Léon 65, 193-6

Narva 175
National War Savings Committee 9
Nehring, Walther 14-15, 234
Nelson, Thomas 116, 135, 234
Neuve Chapelle, Battle of (Mar. 1915) 138
Neuvy Pailloux, Allied Tank Factory at 5
Ney, Marshal Michel 50, 113
Nivelle Offensive (Apr.-May 1917) 71, 197, 201
Nivelle, Robert 71, 79, 195-6

Odessa 171, 179
Opel, *Geheimrat* von 86

Painlevé, Paul 58
Pershing, Gen. John J. 77
Pétain, Gen. Philippe 60, 64, 73, 196-200, 202-3

Picoche, Lt.-Col. 193
'Plan 1919' 37, 221
Poincaré, Raymond 65, 74, 200
Pree, Maj.-Gen. H. de 228-9
Prototypes and designs (Germany):
 Bremerwagen 85-86, 91
 Dürwagen 85
 Erhardtwagen 26, 29
 Fahrpanzer 13, 25, 29
 K-Wagen 92-4, 96, 104
 Krupp-Protze 103-4
 Landpanzerkreuzer 85
 Leichter-Kampfwagen 95, 103-4
 Marienwagen 86, 104
 Meteor 25
 Motorgeschütz 27-9
 Oberschlesienwagen 104
 Orion-Wagen 85, 87, 94
 Steil-Wagen 85
 Treffas-Wagen 85, 94
 Überlandwagen 85
 Zechlin-Wagen 85
Punch (satirical weekly) 8, 212-3, 218-9

Rawlinson, Gen. Sir Henry 48, 141
Renault, Louis 60, 193-4
Reval (NW Russia) 173, 176
Rif Rebellion (1922-26) 206-7
Rimailho, Col. Emile 68
River Selle, crossing of (Oct. 1918) 52
Robertson, Capt. Clement 144
Robertson, Gen. Sir William 216
Roch, Walter (MP) 217
Rohr, Willy 96
Roques, Mario 193
Rostov-on-Don, capture of (Jan. 1920) 179
Royal Air Force (RAF) 36, 156-7
Royal Armoured Corps (RAC) 210-11
Royal Flying Corps (RFC) 36, 110, 151
Royal Naval Air Service (RNAS) 4
Royal Tank Corps (RTC) 230
Royal Tank Regiment (RTR) 171
Rupprecht of Bavaria, Crown Prince 235
Russian Civil War (1919-21) 180, 190, 205-6
Russo-Polish War (1919-20) 207
Russo-Japanese War (1904-5) 14, 18, 29

Salford, presentation tank '214' 9-10
Sawers, Sgt. J. 142
Schlieffen, Field-Marshal Alfred von 23

Schumann, Maximilian 25
Searle, Lt.-Col. Frank 53
Selyavkin, A.I. 180-1
Smith, Maj.-Gen. W. Douglas 153
Smith, Maj.-Gen. W.E.B. 169
Smuts, Gen. Jan 216
Soissons, Battle of (July 1918) 205
Soldan, George 233
Somme, Battle of (July-Nov. 1916) 3, 5, 138
South African/Boer War (1899-1902) 18, 25, 113
South Russian Tank Detachment, British Army 173
Soviet-Finnish War (1939-40) 11, 208
Soviet Union, invasion of (1941) 12
Spanish Civil War (1936-39) 11, 207
Spartacus Uprising (1919) 10
Stern, Albert 224
Storey, Second Lt. C.E. 42
St. Quentin Canal, Battle of (Sept.-Oct. 1918) 158, 160
Sturm-Panzerkraftwagen-Abteilungen 86, 97
Swinton, Maj.-Gen. Ernest D. 3, 5, 28, 34, 139, 188, 223-4, 236

Taganrog, Central Workshops (Russia) 173
Tank, definition of 57
Tank, invention of 3
Tank, tactics 146-7
Tank Corps, British Army 1, 4, 44, 105, 109, 110
Tank Corps, United States Army 7
Tanks, American:
    Renault FT-17 5, 11, 62, 208-9
    Mark VIII 'Liberty' 5
Tanks, British:
    Mark I 3, 39-40, 42, 150, 168
    Mark II 39, 150, 168
    Mark III 39
    Mark IV 7, 39-41, 43, 98, 100, 160, 164, 190, 212, 234
    Mark V 5, 11, 41, 43-45, 160, 163, 171, 174-6, 179, 182, 184, 187, 190
    Mark V* 43-44, 50
        Medium A (Whippet) 11, 37, 41, 43, 101, 103, 154-5, 163-4, 171, 173-5, 179
        Medium B 176
        Medium C 37
        Medium D 37
Tanks, French:
    Renault FT-17 7, 8, 67, 163, 171, 179, 187, 191-209
    Schneider C.A.1 4, 8, 57, 62, 65-67, 70-71, 76-78, 192, 195, 198, 206
    St Chamond 4, 8, 57, 62, 68-71, 76-78, 102, 192, 195, 198
Tanks, German:
    A7V 4, 7, 87-90, 92-98, 100-104
    Pzkpfw 18R 730(f) 11-12, 209
Tanks, Italian:
    Fiat 3000 (copy of Renault FT-17) 209
Tanks, Russian:
    Reno M-17 179, 186-7, 206
    T-34 190
Tanks, Prototypes and Designs
    See Prototypes and designs
Tanks, captured machines 12
Tanks, employment of 48-50
Tanks, employment in anti-partisan duties 209
Tanks, internal security role 11-12, 209
Tanks, occupation duties 11-12
Tanks, presentation machines 8-9
Tanks, symbolism of 12, 79, 184-5, 188-90, 212, 218-9, 230-1, 236-7
Tanks, use as war memorials 12, 190
Thomas, Albert 63, 65, 68, 78, 194-8
Tiflis, capture of (Feb. 1921) 180, 183
Tiraspol 171, 190
Tucker, Corporal W.S. 35
Tucker microphone 35

Velpry, Col. 203
Verkhovskiy, A.I. 181
Villers-Bretonneux, Battle of (Apr. 1918) 7, 99-100
Volckheim, Maj. Ernst 232, 235
Vollard-Bockelberg, Maj. Alfred von 83
Vollmer (German engineer) 92, 94

Warsaw, Battle of (Aug. 1920) 207
Wells, H.G. 24, 28
West, Lt.-Col. R.A. 44
Williams-Ellis, Maj. Clough 29, 116-9, 135, 223
Wilson, Field-Marshal Sir Henry 188, 222
Wilson, Maj. Walter G. 4
Winkler, *Direktor* 86
Winter War, see Soviet-Finnish War
Wrangel, Gen. Pyotr N. 175, 179

Yudenich, Gen. Nikolai 173, 175, 179, 185-6, 190, 208
Yugoslavia, German invasion of (1941) 11, 209
Ypres, Second Battle of (Apr.-May 1915) 141
Ypres, Third Battle of (July-Nov.1917) 120-2, 135, 145, 150-1, 155, 157

Zinoviev, Grigory 190
Ziyabki, Battle of (July 1920) 180-1, 183